Mao Cult

Rhetoric and Ritual in China's Cultural Revolution

Mao Zedong's political and cultural legacy remains potent even in today's China. Many books have explored his posthumous legacy, but none has scrutinized the cult of Mao and the massive worship that was fostered around him at the height of his powers during the Cultural Revolution. This riveting book is the first to do so. By analyzing previously secret archival documents, obscure objects, and political pamphlets, Daniel Leese traces the tumultuous history of the cult within the Communist Party and at the grassroots level. The party leadership's original intention was to develop a prominent brand symbol that would compete with the Nationalists' elevation of Chiang Kai-shek. They did not, however, anticipate that Mao would use this symbolic power to mobilize Chinese youth to rebel against the party bureaucracy itself. The result was anarchy, and when the army was called in, it relied on mandatory rituals of worship, such as daily reading of the Little Red Book or performances of the "loyalty dance" to restore order. Such fascinating detail sheds light not only on the personality cult of Mao, but also on hero worship in other traditions.

Daniel Leese is Assistant Professor at the Institute of Chinese Studies at Ludwig-Maximilians-University in Munich. He is the editor of *Brill's Encyclopedia of China* (2009).

Mao Cult

Rhetoric and Ritual in China's Cultural Revolution

DANIEL LEESE
Ludwig-Maximilians-University

CAMBRIDGE
UNIVERSITY PRESS

CAMBRIDGE UNIVERSITY PRESS
Cambridge, New York, Melbourne, Madrid, Cape Town,
Singapore, São Paulo, Delhi, Mexico City

Cambridge University Press
The Edinburgh Building, Cambridge CB2 8RU, UK

Published in the United States of America by Cambridge University Press, New York

www.cambridge.org
Information on this title: www.cambridge.org/9780521152228

© Daniel Leese 2011

First published 2011
First paperback edition 2013

A catalogue record for this publication is available from the British Library

Library of Congress Cataloguing in Publication Data
Leese, Daniel.
Mao cult : rhetoric and ritual in China's Cultural Revolution / Daniel Leese.
p.   cm.
Includes bibliographical references and index.
ISBN 978-0-521-19367-2 (hardback)
1. China – History – Cultural Revolution, 1966–1976 – Sources.
2. China – Politics and government – 1949–1976 – Sources.
3. China – History – 20th century – Sources.   I. Title.
DS778.7.L44   2011
951.05′06–dc22   2010054238

ISBN 978-0-521-15222-8 Paperback

For Lia Cara, Amelie, and Justus

This land so rich in beauty
Has made countless heroes bow in homage
But alas! Qin Shihuang and Han Wudi
Were lacking in literary grace,
And Tang Taizong and Song Taizu
Had little poetry in their souls;
And Genghis Khan,
Proud Son of Heaven for a day,
Knew only shooting eagles, bow outstretched.
All are past and gone!
For truly great men
Look to this age alone.

"Snow," Mao Zedong

Contents

Illustrations, Figures, Maps, and Table

Illustrations

Figures

Maps

Table

Preface

In 1921, the Chinese Republic was shaken by a seemingly obscure scandal, the so-called Eight-Thousand Hemp Sacks Incident (*baqian madai shijian*). The Historical Museum, an institution entrusted with archival duties after the fall of the Qing dynasty, had upon instruction of the Ministry of Education sold some 75,000 kilograms of archival materials to a wastepaper trader. The revenue of four thousand silver dollars was to help ameliorate the ministry's dire financial situation and simultaneously relieve the staff of the burden of classifying and arranging the huge amount of material. The documents had in 1909 already been singled out for destruction, but upon intervention of an upright official, Luo Zhenyu, had been retained and stored in thousands of hemp sacks. In 1921, it was again Luo Zhenyu who discovered parts of these materials on markets in Beijing and decided to buy and preserve the documents. The scandal drew wider circles and nationalist sentiments ran high when Luo a few years later had to sell part of the stacks to other collectors, including a former Japanese official in China. The famous writer Lu Xun, who in the early Republican era had worked in the Ministry of Education and was well informed about the extent of private appropriation of archival documents through the ministry's staff, remarked sarcastically that "archaeological endeavors" among the stacks had become a favorite pastime among officials.[1] The stacks that had finally been sold as wastepaper, in Lu's opinion, therefore had found an adequate destiny.

Today, scholars trying to write a social or cultural history of the 1950s and 1960s sometimes cannot help but feel reminded of the hemp sacks

---

[1] See Lu Xun, "Tan suowei 'Danei dang'an'" [Discussing the So-Called "Palace Archives"], in *Yusi* 4.7 (28 January 1928), 5. For a detailed discussion of archival politics and practice in Republican China, see Vivian Wagner, *Erinnerungsverwaltung in China. Staatsarchive und Politik in der Volksrepublik* [Administrating Memory in China: State Archives and Politics in the People's Republic], Cologne: Böhlau, 2006, Part I.

incident when searching for sources. Although the possibility of archival access has greatly improved during the past decade, the documents allowed for public perusal have usually, but not always, been carefully sorted and arranged to suit the Chinese Communist Party's (CCP) official interpretation of events. Local archives or *danwei* offices, however, faced financial pressures that resulted in the vending of stacks of documents to wastepaper traders or collectors. Thus over the years, flea markets and secondhand bookshops have occasionally become a welcome treasure trove of local-level documents that allow for a partial reconstruction of everyday life and administration otherwise nonexistent in official archival memory.

During an occasional visit to the flea markets while studying in China, I bought a stack of obscure documents related to the veneration of a certain Comrade Men He, who, I later learned, was one of the Cultural Revolution's foremost model heroes in 1968. Because I was unclear about what to make of the documents, which mainly consisted of congratulatory statements and "lively applications" of Mao Zedong Thought, they gathered dust on my bookshelves for several years. When searching for a suitable topic for a doctoral dissertation, I reconsidered the stacks again, and after an exchange of ideas with the doyen of Chinese "garbology" (*lajixue*), Swedish historian Michael Schoenhals, I decided to pursue the topic of the Maoist personality cult further. As no predefined body of texts existed or, to put it differently, not even the type of sources from which to draw evidence on the cult could be clarified in the first place, the initial research consisted of literally digging through stacks of old documents, mimeographed pamphlets, and obscure objects from flea markets, private collections, and finally archives.

Many people have contributed to this work by sharing their ideas, comments, and criticism, though not of all them can be mentioned here. I explicitly thank my former dissertation committee members Johannes Paulmann, Nicola Spakowski, and Jürgen Osterhammel for making the endeavor possible; their work continues to be a major source of inspiration. I would further like to thank the people at the Universities Service Centre in Hong Kong, which hosted me for several months, and Roderick MacFarquhar and the participants of the Sixth Annual Conference on International History at Harvard in 2006. Barbara Mittler, Jan Plamper, Rudolf Wagner, and Vivian Wagner offered very helpful comments during different stages of the project. The History Department and International Relations Department at Beijing University, especially professors Niu Dayong and Yin Hongbiao, provided me with valuable support, without which archival access would not have been possible. The same holds true for Tang Shaojie at Qinghua University. Thanks also to Li Zhensheng and Contact Press Images, who allowed me to reproduce some of Li's most fascinating images from his *Red Color News Soldier*. Furthermore, I would like to thank the staff at the National Library of China in Beijing, the Hebei Provincial Archives, the Bavarian State Library, and all other institutions and individuals who helped to accommodate my obscure research interests.

My colleagues at the University of Munich, especially Hans van Ess, enabled me to finish the dissertation and turn it into a book while taking on the duties as an assistant professor. Oliver Heitmann, Ingna Marquard, Bernhard Gissibl, Anna-Maria Pedron, Sophie Gerlach, Laura Petican, Philippa Söldenwagner, Sonja Kienzler, and Sebastian and Gabi Stamminger provided excellent companionship in Bremen and made the stay at International University Bremen worthwhile. In the archives, Jeremy Brown turned out to be a like-minded *ziliaomi*. Michael Schoenhals incessantly encouraged the ongoing work through generously sharing his unparalleled knowledge of the period. I further owe a great deal to Marigold Acland, Joy Mizan, and Andy Saff at Cambridge University Press, who guided me with great enthusiasm, efficiency, and professionalism through the production of this book. It has become much better due to their efforts. All remaining errors fall within my own responsibility. Financial support was granted continuously by the German National Academic Foundation (Studienstiftung des Deutschen Volkes) and International University Bremen. The largest debt, however, I owe to my family, which supported me throughout the whole process of research and writing. This book is dedicated to them.

Munich, 20 February 2011

Chronology of Major Events

1893 Mao Zedong is born in Shaoshan, Hunan province

1921 CCP is officially founded in Shanghai; Mao is among the
founding members

1927 United Front between CCP and Nationalists is
terminated; Mao withdraws with followers to Jinggang
Mountains, later to Jiangxi province, to organize rural
soviets

1935 Mao is elevated to Central Secretariat membership at the
Zunyi Conference

1936 Long March ends in northern Shaanxi; Yan'an becomes
the new communist capital; Mao is interviewed by Edgar
Snow, resulting in *Red Star over China* (1937)

1937–42 Mao strengthens his position as political leader and
foremost theoretician within the CCP, aided by
ghostwriters, including Chen Boda; the first visual
instances of the leader cult appear in party newspapers

1942–3 Rectification campaign firmly establishes Mao-centered
narrative as standard party history; Mao Zedong
Thought becomes the guiding ideology; Mao Zedong is
elevated to Chairman of Central Secretariat

1943 Chiang Kai-shek's book *China's Destiny* is published;
the Mao cult is elevated to counter Nationalist claims for
legitimacy to rule China

1945 Seventh Party Congress formally elects Mao Zedong as
Central Committee chairman

1949 Communists claim victory and the Nationalists
withdraw to Taiwan

1953   Stalin dies
1956   Khrushchev criticizes Stalin's cult of personality at the
              Twentieth CPSU Congress; Mao calls for the Hundred
              Flowers campaign; there is a short-term liberalization of
              the directed public sphere; criticism of leader cults is
              voiced
1957   Hundred Flowers campaign is terminated and critics of
              CCP politics are persecuted as Rightists
1958   Mao distinguishes between two types of cults at the
              Chengdu Conference; the correct cult is to serve in the
              destruction of superstition in the Soviet development
              model
1958–61   Great Leap Forward, an attempt of utopian social
              engineering, leads to the largest famine in world history,
              with tens of millions starving to death
1959   Lin Biao is elevated to minister of defense after the
              Lushan Plenum
1960–1   Group study of Mao writings and emotional bonding
              through various rituals are employed in the PLA to
              counter the disruptive influence of the Great Leap
1964   First internal version of the Little Red Book is compiled
              within the PLA; a national campaign is forged to "Learn
              from the PLA"
1966   Cultural Revolution unfolds; eight mass receptions take
              place at Tiananmen Square and other venues; the "four
              olds" (old ideas, old culture, old customs, and old habits)
              face destruction and the great "exchange of experiences/
              link-up" (*chuanlian*) begins
1967   **May:** First Mao statue is unveiled at Qinghua University
              September: Mao's Great Strategic Plan is published to hand
              over leadership to revolutionary committees
              November: Report of unit 8341 from the Beijing General
              Knitting Mill spreads the example of ritual Mao worship
1968   Ritual Mao worship reaches high tide; Three Loyalties
              campaign takes place
1969   **April:** Ninth Party Congress is held in Beijing; the victory
              of the Cultural Revolution is officially declared; Lin

Biao's position as heir apparent is written into the party statutes

June: CCP Circular banishes ritual expressions of the Mao cult

1970	Second Lushan Plenum entails criticism of the "genius" cult
1971	Lin Biao Incident occurs; Lin Biao and family die in plane crash in Mongolia
1974	"Criticize Lin Biao and Confucius" campaign takes place; public criticism of cult rituals is expressed through Li-Yi-Zhe posters
1976	Mao Zedong dies
1981	Resolution on party history casts verdict on Mao's culpability for the Cultural Revolution while retaining his historical merits

Abbreviations

CCP	Chinese Communist Party
CCRG	Central Cultural Revolution Group
CPSU	Communist Party of the Soviet Union
CRDB	Chinese Cultural Revolution Database
DXG	Dang de xuanchuan gongzuo wenjian xuanbian (Selection of Documents on Party Propaganda Work)
HPA	Hebei Provincial Archives
NRGM	New Red Guard Materials (Song Yongyi, ed., 40 vols.)
PLA	People's Liberation Army
PRC	People's Republic of China
RGM	Red Guard Materials (Zhou Yuan, ed., 20 vols.)
YLF	Yi Lin futongshuai wei guanghui bangyang wuxian zhongyu weida lingxiu Mao zhuxi (With Vice-Commander Lin as Glorious Example Boundlessly Loyal toward the Great Leader Chairman Mao)
ZGXG	Zhongguo gongchandang xuanchuan gongzuo wenxian xuanbian (Selection of Documents on CCP Propaganda Work)

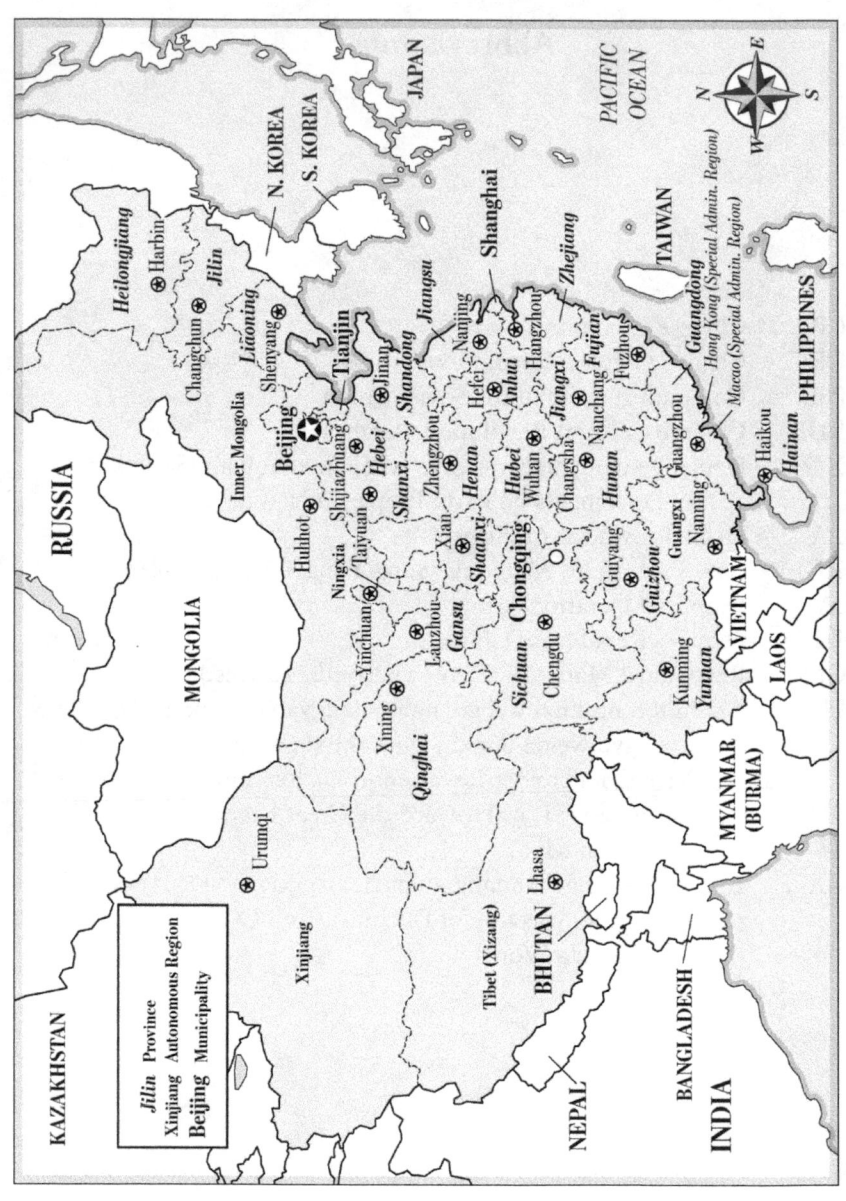

MAP 1. Administrative divisions of China

Introduction

At the turn of the twentieth century, the Confucian reformer Kang Youwei set out to describe an ideal future world order in his *Book of Great Equality*. Kang envisioned a society in which emotional bonds had been reduced to a minimum. The creation of a global state was to be realized by overcoming the boundaries of nation, class, or gender, even the distinction between man and animal. Marriage was to be replaced by short-term contracts and care for infants and elderly persons was to fall under the duty of specific state institutions. The assignment of work should follow a standard pattern according to age, covering all types of labor within a lifetime. In the age of great equality, there would be no personal property or family structures. The differences between the races would have vanished over time through constant crossbreeding, the white and yellow race having proven their superiority. By eliminating all racial, social, and national segregation, Kang hoped to circumvent the dangers of emotion and irrational behavior, which so far had prevented the rule of peace and harmony in the world.

Among the few things Kang Youwei feared to have a disruptive impact on the state of perfect harmony were both continuing competitiveness among citizens and overt laziness given the privileges of the ideal society. Yet what he feared most was the rise of "exclusive worship" (*du zun*), the building of a cult around a religious or secular leader. This kind of worship would threaten the very foundations of the global state by arousing the passions that the new order had tried to overcome. The worship of powerful leaders bore the danger of throwing the world back into the previous turmoil and was to be prevented at all costs:

> [I]f some leaders are idolized, inequalities will gradually return, they will gradually develop into autocratic institutions and slowly lead to strife and murder, until the world relapses into the state of disorder. For that reason, everyone who leads large masses of people and is excessively idolized by

them must be vigorously opposed, however enlightened or holy he might be, irrespective of his office or profession, and even if it is the leader of a party. For if someone wishes to become emperor, king, prince, or leader in such a time, he sins against the principle of equality and becomes guilty of the most serious breach of morals. For these worst of all crimes, the public council should incarcerate him.[1]

Roughly six decades after Kang Youwei wrote his tractate on the ideal world order, the People's Republic of China was to be found amid the struggles of the Great Proletarian Cultural Revolution. In the name of cherishing CCP Chairman Mao Zedong, countless factions carried out warfare against each other, sometimes with stones and clubs, sometimes with heavy artillery stolen from army units. Ritual modes of worshipping the "great helmsman" of the Chinese Revolution had come to dominate everyday life. These included the "daily reading" (*tiantian du*) of the Little Red Book (termed the "Mao Bible" in the West); confessions of possible thought crimes in front of Mao's portrait; and even physical performances such as the "loyalty dance" (*zhongzi wu*). Without doubt, Kang Youwei's worst fears had come true and China had relapsed into a passionate state of utter disorder and idol worship.

Explanations of the Cultural Revolutionary Mao cult, in China and the West alike, usually refer back to two conversations of Mao Zedong with journalist Edgar Snow that took place shortly before and after the Cultural Revolution's most violent phases. Snow had first visited the communist areas in northern Shaanxi in 1936 and conducted a series of interviews with Mao Zedong that, through their publication in Snow's world famous *Red Star over China*, exerted a tremendous impact on Mao's image in China and the West.[2] Snow presented a highly favorable picture of Mao: "[W]hile everyone knows and respects him, there is – as yet, at least – no ritual of hero-worship built up around him. I never met a Chinese Red who drivelled 'our-great-leader' phrases."[3]

Upon his return to China thirty years later in 1965, Snow witnessed a completely changed situation. He explicitly commented on Mao's

---

[1] Quoted from Wolfgang Bauer, *China and the Search for Happiness: Recurring Themes in Four Thousand Years of Chinese Cultural History*, translated by Michael Shaw, New York: Seabury Press, 1976, 323.

[2] See Ding Xiaoping, "Fulu: 'Mao Zedong yinxiang' jiuban tushu kaozheng suoyin" [Appendix: Verified Index to Old Editions of the "Accounts of Mao Zedong"], in Ding Xiaoping and Fang Jiankang (eds.), *Mao Zedong yinxiang* [Accounts of Mao Zedong], Beijing: Zhongyang wenxian chubanshe, 2003, 299.

[3] Edgar Snow, *Red Star over China*, London: Victor Gollancz, 1937, 83.

"immoderate glorification" after having been witness to the staging of the revolutionary epic *The East Is Red* (*Dongfang hong*) in Beijing:

> Giant portraits of him now hung in the streets, busts were in every chamber, his books and photographs were everywhere on display to the exclusion of others. In the four-hour revolutionary pageant of dance and song, *The East Is Red*, Mao was the only hero. As a climax of that performance ... I saw a portrait copied from a photograph taken by myself in 1936, blown up to about thirty feet high.[4]

While attending the Labor Day parade, Snow discussed the subject of the cult again with his Chinese hosts, vice-ministers of foreign affairs Gong Peng and Qiao Guanhua. Their explanations highlighted the popular origins of and demand for the cult. Three thousand years of emperor worship could not be wiped out in an instant because peasant mentalities still lingered behind: "It takes time to make people understand that Chairman Mao is not an emperor or a god but a man who wants the peasants to stand up like men."[5] Snow's hosts told him about special guards who had been employed in the early 1950s to prevent peasants from prostrating themselves before Mao's image at Tiananmen Square, where it had been on display twice a year, on National Day and Labor Day. The level of worship permitted by the authorities should thus be considered negligible given what it might have looked like, if it had not been restrained.

In 1970, Edgar Snow returned one last time to China just as the most chaotic period of the Cultural Revolution had passed. In their discussions, Mao explicitly commented on the publication of Snow's impressions during the prior visit that had included the portrayal of his burgeoning cult:

> [You] say, I am [fostering] a personality cult. Well, you Americans really are [cultivating] a personality cult! Your capital is called Washington. The district in which Washington is located is called Columbia. ... Disgusting! ... There will always be people worshipping! If there is no one to worship you, Snow, are you happy then? ... There will always be some worship of the individual, you have it as well.[6]

---

[4] Edgar Snow, *The Long Revolution*, New York: Random House, 1972, 68f.

[5] Ibid., 69.

[6] Mao Zedong, "Huijian Sinuo de tanhua jiyao" [Summary of Mao's Conversations with Snow], 18 December 1970, in Song Yongyi (ed.), *Chinese Cultural Revolution Database* (CD-ROM), Hong Kong: Chinese University Press/Universities Service Centre, 2006.

Mao in retrospect justified the need for a personality cult at the outset of the Cultural Revolution by claiming that he had been unable to control the party machinery:

> At that time I said I did not care about personality cults, yet there even was a necessity for a bit of personality cult. The situation now is not the same anymore; the worship has become excessive, resulting in much formalism. Like those "four greats," "Great Teacher, Great Leader, Great Supreme [sic] Commander, Great Helmsman" [English in original], annoying! One day these will all be deleted, only keeping the "teacher."[7]

Mao divided the motifs of the cult supporters into three categories: true believers, opportunists, and fake supporters. He admitted that during the period of anarchy between 1967 and 1968, the distinctions had become hard to discern. While a CCP decision of March 1949 was still being followed, forbidding the naming of cities, streets, and places after political leaders, the Red Guards had invented new forms of worship such as signboards, portraits, and statues, which, according to Mao's description, resisted state control: "This has developed during the past few years, as soon as the Red Guards stirred up trouble and attacked. It was impossible not to conform to it! Otherwise they would say you are against Mao, 'anti-Mao'!"[8] In his account of the conversation, Snow concluded his observations by underlining the crucial importance of the cult and its manipulation for understanding the Cultural Revolution: "In one sense the whole struggle was over control of the cult and by whom and above all 'for whom' the cult was to be utilized."[9]

MODERN PERSONALITY CULTS

The worship of religious or secular leaders in China has not been limited to the twentieth century. The emperor had been worshipped as the Son of Heaven, but besides rituals and ceremonies conducted at the imperial court, the ordinary populace came into little contact with the cult. The emperor did not have temples erected in his name or cities named after him. His legitimacy as a ruler was deeply intertwined with the concept of the Mandate of Heaven, the worship of ancestors, and ritual offerings to various deities that restricted the glorification of the emperor himself. Besides certain taboo words and prostration rules, the cult was confined to a small circle of people in the emperor's immediate surroundings. Yet leader cults in traditional China had not been confined to the court. Within

---

[7] Ibid.
[8] Ibid.
[9] Snow, *Long Revolution*, 66.

the Chinese popular tradition, there are numerous examples of local leaders cultivating excessive personality cults, the most prominent example being the messianic cult of Taiping Heavenly King Hong Xiuquan, who considered himself the incarnation of Jesus's younger brother. Hong was worshipped as the "sun" during the Taiping Rebellion (1853–64) and would inspire later political leaders such as the young Sun Yat-sen.[10]

The main difference between modern and traditional leader cults is not to be observed with regard to the worship of political leaders but rather rests with the cult's legitimacy, intensity, and reach. Unlike the worship of the emperor that was grounded in his capacity as Son of Heaven, the modern personality cults lacked an external or even transcendental source of legitimacy. Modern political leaders had to establish their preeminent status by claiming to represent popular movements or "the people" in general. The advent of mass society with the institutions of the modern state such as schooling, military, and infrastructure exerted a much more profound influence on the life of every citizen, not least by means of mass media. Modern personality cults have therefore been defined as "godlike glorification of a modern political leader with mass media techniques,"[11] and often came to be accompanied by excessive demonstrations of public worship and the emergence of mass-manufactured, standardized cult products. The rise of the competing nationalist and communist movements in China was highly intertwined with state building, literacy campaigns, and the construction of media networks providing the possibilities of centralized communication and the distribution of national symbols. How far these symbols could be disseminated within the public media depended critically on the level of political control, and thus truly national leader cults in China developed only after the Guomindang and the Communists, respectively, consolidated their rule.

The first modern personality cult in China was the cult fostered around Sun Yat-sen as the founding father of New China. Sun during his lifetime already consciously employed his media image to strengthen the claim of representing the Chinese Revolution.[12] The creation of his heroic image

---

[10] Harold Z. Schiffrin, *Sun Yat-sen and the Origins of the Chinese Revolution*, Berkeley: University of California Press, 1968, 23.

[11] Jan Plamper, "Introduction. Modern Personality Cults," in Klaus Heller and Jan Plamper (eds.), *Personality Cults in Stalinism – Personenkulte im Stalinismus*, Göttingen: V&R unipress, 2005, 33.

[12] For a recent Chinese account of the Sun Yat-sen cult, see Chen Yunqian, *Chongbai yu jiyi. Sun Zhongshan zhuhao de jiangou yu chuanbo* [Worship and Memory: The Construction and Propagation of the Political Symbol Sun Zhongshan], Nanjing: Nanjing daxue chubanshe, 2009.

started in 1896 when members of the Chinese legation in London captured
Sun. Sun managed to alert his friends secretly about his imprisonment and
imminent execution. The dramatic circumstances drew the attention of the
British press and soon of media worldwide.[13] By the time Sun Yat-sen was
released from prison, he had risen to celebrity status and quickly sought to
draw political gains from the media attention. In a short booklet entitled
Kidnapped in London that was published in January 1897,[14] his unique
capabilities were extolled by friends. Flattering articles entwined his personal qualities with the fate of the Chinese nation: "Dr. Sun was the only
man who combined a complete grasp of the situation with a reckless
bravery of a kind which alone can make a national regeneration. ...
Beneath his calm exterior is hidden a personality that cannot but be a
great influence for good in China sooner or later."[15]

Sun's meteoric rise to political stardom had been owed to both personal
charisma and contingent environmental factors. Sun held a strong belief
in his personal mission to lead the Chinese Revolution, bordering
on self-conceit in his later years, and obviously displayed a personal
"magnetism"[16] that allowed him to build up a circle of Chinese and
Western supporters who were willing to further his cause. Without early
Western mentors such as Sir James Cantlie or fervent admirers during his
later life, most notably Paul "Judge" Linebarger and his son,[17] Sun would
not have been able to catch similar media attention that turned out to be
crucial for fostering his public image and likewise to raise funds for his
revolutionary activities. The early Sun Yat-sen cult thus was a hybrid
product, a blend of Western projections and the Chinese revolutionary
mission, but did not automatically translate into political power. Sun's
attempts to topple the Qing government produced a series of failures and

---

[13] See the incredibly meticulous study by John Y. Wong, *The Origins of an Heroic Image: Sun Yat-sen in London, 1896–1897*, Hong Kong: Oxford University Press, 1986. See further Marie-Claire Bergère, *Sun Yat-sen*, translated by Janet Lloyd, Stanford: Stanford University Press, 1998 [1994], 69ff.

[14] Sun Yat-sen, *Kidnapped in London. Being the Story of my Capture by, Detention at, and Release from the Chinese Legation, London*, Bristol: Arrowsmith, 1897.

[15] Ibid., 115.

[16] C. Martin Wilbur, "Environment, Character, Chance, and Choice: Their Interplay in Making a Revolutionary," in Eto Shinkichi and Harold Z. Schiffrin (eds.), *China's Republican Revolution*, Tokyo: University of Tokyo Press, 1994, 119.

[17] The best-known examples are Paul Myron Wentworth Linebarger, *Sun Yat-sen and the Chinese Republic*, New York: AMS Press, 1969 [1925], and Paul Myron Anthony Linebarger, *Gospel of Sun Chung Shan, According to Paul Linebarger*, Paris: Editions-Mid-Nations, 1932.

his role during the revolution of 1911 was marginal at best.[18] His image was transformed into a truly national symbol only after his death in March 1925.[19]

Although China remained fragmented by the time of Sun's death in March 1925, his physical remains and image as "father of the nation" (*guofu*), a title formally decreed by the Guomindang in April 1940 only, came to serve as symbols for a new and united China and formed the nucleus of the Guomindang's claim for power. Sun's mausoleum on Purple Mountain in Nanjing, to which his body had been transferred in 1929 after having been temporarily placed to rest in the Temple of Azure Clouds in Beijing's Western Hills, sought proximity to the tomb of Ming dynasty founding emperor Zhu Yuanzhang and resembled the traditional architectural style of the emperors' mausoleums.[20] The forms of honoring the deceased Sun bore both foreign and distinctively Chinese characteristics. Besides massive media campaigns eulogizing the importance of his teaching, there were broadcasts of Sun's speeches in public parks and obligatory weekly remembrance meetings in schools, factories, and Guomindang offices. Sun's portrait was even displayed above the former emperor's throne in the newly established Palace Museum on the first anniversary of his death[21] and he continued to be honored during the following decades. Both Chiang Kai-shek and Mao Zedong were to rely on the Sun cult to legitimate their own positions as heirs of the Chinese Revolution.

The history of the early Mao cult has been researched in great detail and can be traced back to the late 1930s, when after the disastrous Long March Mao had slowly gained supremacy within the CCP. Despite his being among the party's founding members, Mao did not hold truly important posts within the party hierarchy until the Long March. At the Zunyi Conference in January 1935, Mao became a member of the Politburo Secretariat and the Military Council, but his ascent to power was by no means inevitable. There are only sporadic instances that hint at a public

[18] Joseph Esherick, "Founding a Republic, Electing a President: How Sun Yat-sen Became Guofu," in Shinkichi and Schiffrin (eds.), *China's Republican Revolution*, 129–52.

[19] On this point, see especially Henrietta Harrison, *The Making of the Republican Citizen: Political Ceremonies and Symbols in China 1911–1929*, Oxford: Oxford University Press, 2000, 207–39.

[20] For a recent Chinese account of the mausoleum as political symbol, see Li Gongzhong, *Zhongshan ling. Yi ge xiandai zhengzhi zhuhao de dansheng* [The Sun Yat-sen Mausoleum: The Making of a Political Symbol in Modern China], Beijing: Shehui kexue wenxian chubanshe, 2009.

[21] Lyon Sharman, *Sun Yat-sen: His Life and Its Meaning*, Stanford: Stanford University Press, 1968 [1934], 316.

display of a leader cult before 1942. During Mao's struggle with his Soviet-trained and -supported rival Wang Ming in mid-1937, a woodcut of Mao Zedong was published in the Communist Party newspaper *Liberation Weekly* (*Jiefang zhoukan*) that, as Raymond Wylie observed, already embodied motifs of the later cult: moving masses, flags, and sunrays, as opposed to the static portrayal of other CCP leaders such as military leader Zhu De (see Illustrations 1 and 2).[22] Mao's image closely resembled the photograph taken by Snow the previous year and is a first proof of the interrelation between the national and international dimensions of the cult.

The cult as a combination of rhetorical flattery and omnipresent imagery rose to full prominence during the so-called Rectification campaign of 1942–3 that witnessed the unyielding acceptance of Mao's status as leader and theoretician of the Chinese Revolution. The campaign consisted of a series of consecutive study and (self)-criticism sessions during which the participants were supplied with a common perception of the present development and revolutionary goals, as well as with the suitable terminology to describe it. David Apter and Tony Saich, in their highly influential work on the campaign, have coined the term "exegetical bonding"[23] for the creation of an integrated vision of the revolutionary process. The result of the campaign was the "Sinification" of Marxism-Leninism, to be officially termed "Mao Zedong Thought" after 1942.

While Mao's writings clearly dominated the study schedule and Mao's trusted party members organized festivities in his honor such as the "Zedong Day" on 8 February 1942,[24] the Rectification campaign was not the only factor contributing to the rapid rise of the cult. As the Allied victory over Germany and especially Japan had become only a matter of time, the enmity between the Guomindang and the CCP, which under external pressure had formed the Second United Front against the Japanese invasion in 1937, broke forth again with a vengeance. Both sides intensified their efforts to construct a vision for China's future that was at once "distinctly Chinese and undeniably modern."[25] Simultaneously

---

[22] See Raymond F. Wylie, *The Emergence of Maoism: Mao Tse-tung, Ch'en Po-ta, and the Search for Chinese Theory 1935–1945*, Stanford: Stanford University Press, 1980, 41.

[23] David E. Apter and Tony Saich, *Revolutionary Discourse in Mao's Republic*, Cambridge: Harvard University Press, 1994, 263ff.

[24] Gao Hua, *Hong taiyang shi zenyang sheng qilai de. Yan'an zhengfeng yundong de lailong qumai* [How the Red Sun Rose: A History of the Yan'an Rectification Movement], Hong Kong: Chinese University Press, 2000, 606.

[25] Wylie, *Emergence of Maoism*, 199.

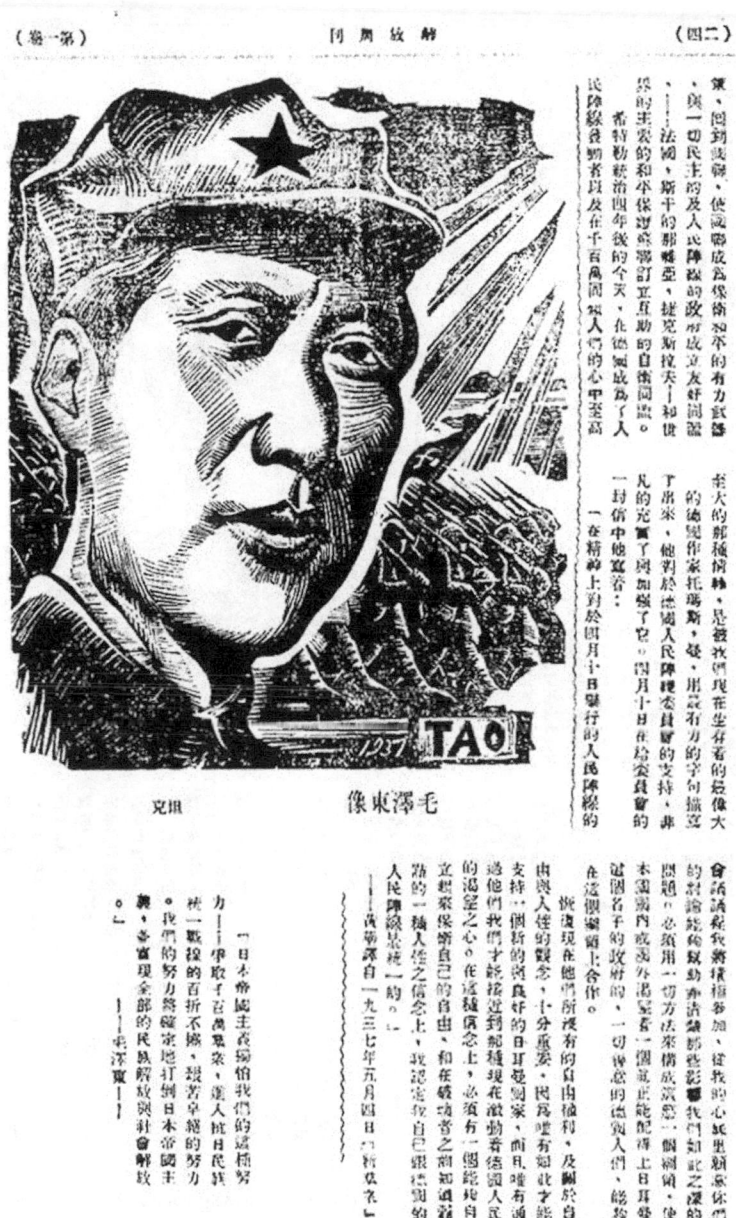

ILLUSTRATION 1. Mao woodcut in the party newspaper *Liberation Weekly*,
22 June 1937. (Author's personal copy.)

ILLUSTRATION 2. Zhu De woodcut in the party newspaper *Liberation Weekly*, 14 June 1937. (Author's personal copy.)

both political parties championed their respective leaders and the deceased Sun Yat-sen with all media means available.[26]

In March 1943, the Guomindang published Chiang Kai-shek's book *China's Destiny*, promoting it with a massive media campaign in which the "Generalissimus" was portrayed as the only person capable of rescuing China from the ruins of factional warfare and foreign aggression.[27] The CCP leadership, which had closely monitored the development of staging Chiang as unquestioned "national leader"[28] since the late 1920s,[29] reacted by boosting the image of Mao Zedong as supreme party leader and eminent Marxist-Leninist theoretician. The elevation of Mao was to provide the CCP with a powerful symbol to rally around during the campaign and to send a signal beyond the confines of the Soviet base areas to attract new followers among China's mostly illiterate populace.

The cult, however, could not have been propagated nationwide without sufficient backing from within the CCP leadership. The change in rhetorical style from treating Mao as first among equals toward advocating a full-blown leader cult is best seen in a number of speeches and editorials published in the name of high-ranking political and military leaders in the party newspaper *Liberation Weekly* in early July 1943. Liu Shaoqi, the CCP's main organizer of resistance against the Guomindang in the Nationalist-dominated "white areas," set the tone by declaring that the party had finally found its own leader in Mao Zedong, who possessed "boundless loyalty to the Chinese working class."[30] In his article, Liu consciously took up the term "Mao Zedong Thought" and provided it with authoritative backing. All high-ranking members of the CCP and the army, including Zhu De, Zhou Enlai, Zhang Wentian, and Deng Xiaoping, followed with similar tributes during the next days and proved both their acceptance of the designations and their loyalty to Mao Zedong.[31] Liu Shaoqi's motives for praising Mao's

---

[26] On the propagation of the Chiang cult, see Jeremy E. Taylor, "The Production of the Chiang Kai-shek Personality Cult, 1929–1975," in *China Quarterly* 185 (2006), 96–110.

[27] Chiang Kai-shek, *China's Destiny*, New York: Macmillan, 1947.

[28] Mao Zedong, "The Situation after the Repulse of the Second Anti-Communist Onslaught," 18 March 1941, in *Selected Works of Mao Tse-tung*, vol. 2, Beijing: Foreign Languages Press, 1967, 459–62.

[29] Early examples include Chen Tsung-Hsi, Wang An-Tsiang, and Wang I-Ting, *General Chiang Kai-Shek: Builder of New China*, Shanghai: Commercial Press, 1929, and especially F. T. Ishimaru's biography of Chiang first published in Japanese in 1937 and shortly after in Chinese and various European languages as well; see, for example, F. T. Ishimaru, *Chiang Kaishek ist Gross* [Chiang Kaishek Is Great], Hankow: Chengchung Verlag, 1938.

[30] Wylie, *Emergence of Maoism*, 206.

[31] Gao, *Hong taiyang*, 608–14.

genius have been subject to much speculation. He immediately afterward assumed the second position within the party hierarchy, but it seems plausible that along with other Politburo members he perceived the necessity of fabricating the Mao cult in order to counter Guomindang claims that Chiang represented the sole legitimate heir to rule China. That the image of Mao, which Liu Shaoqi helped to create, would be instrumental in securing his own downfall two decades later is an irony of history .

The political expediency of countering Chiang Kai-shek's claims to national leadership as well as toppling inner-party rivals by establishing a larger-than-life image of Mao Zedong from the outset played a crucial role, as Mao conceded himself in his talk with Edgar Snow: "It has been [a measure] to oppose Liu Shaoqi. In the past it has been [instrumental] to oppose Jiang Jieshi [Chiang Kai- shek], afterwards to oppose Liu Shaoqi. They established Jiang Jieshi. Therefore we had to establish someone as well."[32] The example set by Liu Shaoqi inspired the rise of enormous activities of praise and the composition of panegyrics and hymns.

By the time the CCP celebrated its Seventh Congress in 1945, the dual glorification of Mao Zedong and his thought had been well established. Mao's portrait assumed center stage in the meeting hall and the frequent references in the delegates' speeches to his invincible thought demonstrated the outstanding position Mao had acquired as CCP leader and theoretician. Mao's image was to find further nourishment after the successful defeat of the Guomindang forces and the proclamation of the founding of the People's Republic on 1 October 1949. The birth of the New China had thus become inextricably linked with the image of Mao Zedong and the corresponding narratives of national salvation.[33]

INTERPRETING MODERN PERSONALITY CULTS

In recent years, the study of leader cults has received renewed attention. In particular, the improvement of archival research opportunities in the former Soviet Union has prompted a substantial number of works dealing with Eastern European leader cults.[34] The heavily debated paradigms of totalitarianism, political religion, and charismatic rule have continued to

---

[32] Mao, "Huijian Sinuo."

[33] See, as well, Daniel Leese, "Mao the Man and Mao the Icon," in Timothy Cheek (ed.), *A Critical Introduction to Mao*, Cambridge: Cambridge University Press, 2010, 219–40.

[34] See, for example, Balázs Apor, Jan C. Behrends, Polly Jones, and E. A. Rees (eds.), *The Leader Cult in Communist Dictatorships: Stalin and the Eastern Bloc*, Houndmills: Palgrave Macmillan, 2004.

provide frameworks of interpretation, but the specter has been widened by employing interdisciplinary methodology. Jan Plamper distinguishes three dominant trends among scholarly explanations of personality cults: first, universal approaches, mainly employed by sociologists and anthropologists relying on the works of Max Weber, Edward Shils, and Clifford Geertz; second, sociohistorical explanations focusing on the functional aspects of the cult as a means of integration; and third, the reappraisal of the notion of political religion and sacralization, especially in the works of Emilio Gentile.[35] One might furthermore add an increased scholarly interest in artistic representations of leader cults, yet such interest is mostly found in the form of anthologies and without further aims of comprehensive explanation.

The study of the Cultural Revolutionary Mao cult, which by its sheer extent surpassed every other twentieth-century leader cult, has been affected only marginally by these general debates. With the exception of a few dissertations by political scientists written in the late 1960s[36] and a brief but insightful study by German sinologist Helmut Martin, originally published in 1978, on the canonization of Mao's works that touches on the issue of the cult,[37] there is no Western monograph on this subject. The Mao cult has therefore remained a phenomenon "to be explained more than something useful for explaining further effects."[38] However, the topic has frequently been discussed within the larger framework of the Cultural Revolution. Explanations might heuristically be divided into structural approaches, focusing on long-term determinants, and actor-based approaches that highlight the functionalist and utilitarian aspects of the

---

[35] See Plamper, "Introduction," 33–41.

[36] Robert W. Rinden, *The Cult of Mao Tse-Tung*, Ph.D. dissertation: University of Colorado, 1969, and James T. Myers, *The Apotheosis of Chairman Mao: Dynamics of the Hero Cult in the Chinese System 1949–1967*, Ph.D. dissertation: George Washington University, 1969. See further Mildred Lina Wagemann, *The Changing Image of Mao Tse-Tung: Leadership Image and Social Structure*, Ph.D. dissertation: Cornell University, 1974.

[37] Martin explicitly states that the political importance and editing of Mao's works are of primary interest to him and not the multifarious expressions of the cult. Nevertheless, he briefly hints at differing motivations for fostering the cult, including party unity, revolutionary immortality, and immediate political expediency within inner-party "line struggles." See Helmut Martin, *Kult und Kanon. Entstehung und Entwicklung des Staatsmaoismus 1935–1978*, Hamburg: Institut für Asienkunde, 1978, 12. An expanded version of the book, covering the events until the proclamation of the *Resolution on Party History in 1981*, was published in English shortly after; see Helmut Martin, *Cult and Canon: The Origins and Development of State Maoism*, Armonk, NY: M. E. Sharpe, 1982.

[38] Lynn T. White III, *Policies of Chaos: The Organizational Causes of Violence in China's Cultural Revolution*, Princeton, NJ: Princeton University Press, 1989, 31.

cult. Structural explanations usually refer back to the influence of traditional modes of religious or emperor worship in China, although few have
ventured so far as to claim the identity of modern and traditional leader
cults.[39] Maurice Meisner, in a most revealing essay, distinguished between
the Cultural Revolutionary cult, which he described as "patently manufactured product, deliberately contrived from immediate political ends,"[40]
and the social origins and functions of the cult. Mao, unlike Stalin, had
been the hero of a national liberation movement and thus commanded
enormous popularity, especially among the peasants. The cult, according
to Meisner, was thus irreducible to political instrumentalization, since its
origins and forms were strongly linked to the Chinese peasants. Yet
Meisner concedes that during the later stages of the Cultural Revolution
political instrumentalization became dominant. The cult was turned into
an extreme example of alienating the people's social power into fetishized
political authority, finally leading to the worship of the self-created icons of
power.[41]

Actor-based models emphasize the role played by Mao Zedong himself
and highlight questions of legitimacy, charismatic rule, and manipulation.
In most accounts, the cult is portrayed as a tool serving the immediate
political purposes of either Mao Zedong or "intriguers" such as Lin Biao,
Kang Sheng, or the "Gang of Four."[42] There can be no doubt about the
utilitarian motives or personal vanity that drove Mao and his sycophants
toward fostering the cult as a tool for political ends, but strictly functionalist definitions fail to account for the variety of the cult phenomenon. The
Cultural Revolution is probably one of the best examples to show that the
political sphere cannot be reduced to an analysis of certain political structures or individual intentions alone.

The most elaborate interpretations of the Mao cult and its relation to
charismatic rule are to be found in Frederick Teiwes' book *Leadership,
Legitimacy, and Conflict in China* and Wang Shaoguang's *Failure of
Charisma*. Teiwes unfolds an analysis of recent Chinese politics based on
Max Weber's distinction between traditional, rational-legal, and charismatic rule. According to Teiwes, Mao's rule changed between all three
forms of domination over time, as charismatic rule during the early

---

[39] For the latter case, see Göran Aijmer, "Political Ritual: Aspects of the Mao Cult during the
Cultural Revolution," in *China Information* 11.2/3 (1996), 215.

[40] Maurice Meisner, *Marxism, Maoism, and Utopianism: Eight Essays*, Madison: University
of Wisconsin Press, 1982, 165.

[41] Ibid., 183.

[42] See, for example, Martin, *Kult und Kanon*, 10–12.

Cultural Revolution in particular turned out to be inherently unstable and was subject to increasing routinization, just as Weber had predicted. Mao Zedong's legitimacy, according to Teiwes, rested on the interrelation of personal abilities, such as his strategic brilliance, and especially the *"demonstrated success at a time of revolutionary crisis."*[43] It was this revolutionary legitimacy, the previously unimaginable success of the Chinese communist movement, that gained Mao respect among his fellow CCP leaders. Since the acceptance of the leader's legitimacy among the party elite represented *"the* crucial factor for survival in Leninist systems,"[44] the demonstrations of unquestioning loyalty during the Rectification campaign in 1942–3 among the CCP top echelon provided the background against which the propagation of a personality cult became possible in the first place. By interpreting the cult as a "synthetic"[45] form of charismatic rule basically aimed at the lower-level party members and the populace, Teiwes underlined the constructivist character of personality cults, the creation of a myth to serve political ends that the CCP leadership did not necessarily believe in.

Wang Shaoguang, on the other hand, in a case study on the Cultural Revolution in Wuhan, focused on the popular dimension of the cult. Relying on rational choice theory, Wang did not contest the emotional efficacy of the cult in securing popular support, but he differentiated between an emotional and a cognitive aspect of charismatic rule to demonstrate that the symbols of the cult were not unambiguously accepted. Instead, he emphasized how they became subject to constant reinterpretation. Despite their emotional affection toward Mao Zedong, the Chinese, according to Wang, remained "rational true believers"[46] who strategically placed their personal interests above the common interests sketched out in Mao's nebulous directives. By emphasizing the strategic appropriation of the cult rhetoric and symbols, Wang Shaoguang tried to wrest the subject from the common descriptions of the cult as an irrational craze beyond the confines of scientific explanation.

This book has in many ways been shaped and informed by the results of the aforementioned scholarship, yet it takes a slightly different approach to analyze the Cultural Revolutionary leader cult. It is the aim of this book to disentangle the complex historical processes of shaping, sustaining, and

---

[43] Frederick C. Teiwes, *Leadership, Legitimacy, and Conflict in China: From a Charismatic Mao to the Politics of Succession*, Armonk, NY: M. E. Sharpe, 1984, 48.

[44] Ibid., 45.

[45] Ibid., 46.

[46] Wang Shaoguang, *Failure of Charisma: The Cultural Revolution in Wuhan*, Oxford, New York: Oxford University Press, 1995, 280.

adapting the Mao cult during the Cultural Revolution with a primary focus on the importance of its rhetoric and rituals. The CCP's restrictive archive policies and the resulting lack of primary sources have contributed to the domination of narratives written by victims of the regime, many of whom relied on the cult's excesses to reveal the inhumanity of the CCP dictatorship.[47] The cult therefore has commonly been portrayed either as a craze for which no one seems to be accountable or as a crude tool of intoxication and brainwashing.[48] Such views, based on a totalitarian concept of CCP rule, fail to account for the internal dynamics and changes of the cult. They do not explain the rise of new forms of worship, the power of symbolic representations, and the ways the cult was created and transmitted among the different layers of state, party, and populace. This book thus will pay equal attention to official sponsorship of the cult and its midlevel or local adaptation and reception, an effort that has been made possible through newly available sources, including archival and quasi-archival documents.

The modern personality cult here is primarily analyzed as a phenomenon of authoritarian political communication, as both an intended means to secure party unity and as the unintended consequence of patron–client relationships forged in a political system without clearly defined rules of ascent. The employment of personalized symbols serving as a focus of loyalty in many ways resembles a rudimentary form of what in modern business parlance could be termed "branding," the creation of a powerful image to represent a vast organization.[49] The emotional potency of personalized politics can be found under whatever rule, irrespective of its democratic or authoritarian character, as German social democrat Eduard Bernstein noted already in the early 1910s. Bernstein used the example of the bourgeoning worship of Ferdinand Lassalle within the

---

[47] See the examples quoted in Lu Xing, *Rhetoric of the Chinese Cultural Revolution: The Impact on Chinese Thought, Culture, and Communication*, Columbia: University of South Carolina Press, 2004. Lu's work mainly relies on Red Guard discourse and published recollections. The book is thus helpful for analyzing patterns of remembrance rather than contemporary political circumstances. This holds especially true for the chapter on the Mao cult.

[48] "It was through the Yenan Terror that Mao accomplished another most important goal: building up his own personality cult. [...] This worship had nothing to do with spontaneous popularity; it stemmed from terror. Every step in the construction of his cult was choreographed by Mao himself." See Jung Chang and Jon Halliday, *Mao: The Unknown Story*, New York: Alfred A. Knopf, 2005, 268f., 423f.

[49] See, as well, Daniel Leese, "The Mao Cult as Communicative Space," in *Totalitarian Movements and Political Religions* 8.3/4 (2007), 623–39. For a comparison of Nazi, fascist, and communist branding strategies, see Steven Heller, *Iron Fists: Branding the 20th-Century Totalitarian State*, London: Phaidon Press, 2008.

General German Workers' Association in the early 1860s to claim that the socialist movement had greatly benefited from the cult's cohesive power:

> It would, however, be altogether a mistake to deny the fact that this cult for the personality of Lassalle did, for a long time, greatly help the movement. ... Most persons like to see a cause, which, the more far-reaching its aims at any given moment, must seem the more abstract, embodied in one individual. This craving to personify a cause is the secret of the success of most founders of religions, whether charlatans or visionaries, and in England and America it is a recognised factor in political party-struggles.[50]

In the world of business, brands are employed to generate emotional bonds, possibly even loyalty to a specific firm. Resonant images come to represent large entities and are to secure support through customers or voters. Present-day marketing strategists therefore consider brands to be "the most important and sustainable asset"[51] of any kind of organization, commodity, or even nation. Although mass media techniques can be applied to propagate all of the aforementioned categories, the branding of a certain commodity that has to fulfill specific needs is much easier than the branding of a huge organization or even "nation branding." The multitude of tasks associated with a government complicates the building of trust in the veracity of claims, which can be gained only through repeated interaction over time. The failed efforts of the U.S. government after 9/11 to "brand America" by means of public relations techniques in the Middle East are just one example.[52]

The success of a brand in systems allowing for competition is not determined by propagation efforts alone but by the level of acceptance that the brand enjoys among the populace. The product associated with a certain brand has to satisfy a certain need and to keep in touch with changes through constant service or product innovation. The power of brands thus ultimately lies with the customers, as they continue to buy the firm's products only if their expectations are constantly exceeded or at least met. The branding of a commodity within a market system, like the

---

[50] Eduard Bernstein, *Ferdinand Lassalle as a Social Reformer*, London: Swan Sonnenschein, 1893, 188f.

[51] Rita Clifton and John Simmons (eds.), *Brands and Branding*, Princeton, NJ: Bloomberg Press, 2004, 2.

[52] Asked why the U.S. government shortly after 9/11 had employed public relations specialist Charlotte Beers to sell American foreign policy, Secretary of State Colin Powell replied: "There is nothing wrong with getting somebody who knows how to sell something. We are selling a product. We need someone who can rebrand American foreign policy, rebrand diplomacy. [Besides] she got me to buy Uncle Ben's rice." See Naomi Klein, "America Is Not a Hamburger: President Bush's Attempts to Rebrand the United States Are Doomed," in *The Guardian*, 14 March 2002.

campaigns to boost the image of a political candidate in an electoral competition, thus differs in important aspects from the CCP dictatorship. Once the party had assumed power, there was no way of opting for a different competitor. The question therefore remains why an all-powerful party-state should employ personality cults after all and not rely on impersonal national symbols to stir up public emotion.

The answer to this question involves several layers of explanation. The Mao cult, as has just been discussed, was created amid a situation of internal and external competition in the late 1930s and early 1940s. The constant battles with the better-equipped Guomindang forces and the ensuing propaganda warfare necessitated the creation of an image that could compete with the cult fostered around Chiang Kai-shek. The rise of the early Mao cult in many ways was a mirror image of the Chiang cult, itself modeled on the cult of Sun Yat-sen. Yet the CCP methods of exegetical bonding were a unique blend of the Soviet model, the Confucian text-centered tradition, and practical experience.

Once Mao's legitimacy had been firmly established, the cult could gain certain aloofness without interfering in day-to-day politics. Its sphere was basically confined to commemorative events and ritualized formulae. This equilibrium could become disrupted, for example, by the influx of a rapidly increasing party membership, a split within the Politburo, or dramatic policy failures such as the Great Leap Forward that contradicted the officially proposed view through lived experience. At such times of crisis, the need to strengthen emotional bonds could become necessary again by comparing the present situation favorably with the past or by relying on renewed waves of rectification and exegetical bonding that had to be strictly supervised. It thus functioned best in hierarchical organizations such as the People's Liberation Army (PLA). However, the CCP was in a position to enforce its view to obtain ritualized compliance irrespective of personal belief.[53] The loss of true belief in the message of the cult and its imagery therefore did not necessarily hamper the cult's effectiveness as a

[53] In his important study on small groups and political rituals based on émigré interviews in Hong Kong in the late 1960s, Martin K. Whyte already described the working of these processes in detail. The CCP relied on activists to communicate party policies within local settings and, by fostering enthusiasm or adding peer pressure, the party was remarkably successful in strengthening its organization capacities. Yet he also mentioned the dangers of mere "acting as if," especially after the initial enthusiasm invoked by the Maoist mass campaigns wore down. Effectiveness in terms of social control, communication, and political mobilization thus did not necessarily guarantee changes in individual attitude. See Martin King Whyte, *Small Groups and Political Rituals in China*, Berkeley: University of California Press, 1974, 234f.

means of rule, as the cynical leader cults of Saddam Hussein, Kim Jong-il, or Hafez al-Assad reveal.[54]

Besides the branding dimension, another important factor contributing to the rise of personality cults in communist dictatorships was posed by the system's structural deficit to provide formal rules of political ascent and succession. As Graeme Gill has shown in his analysis of Soviet leader cults, individual success within the party bureaucracy depended to a large extent on networks of vertical and horizontal loyalties. In this context, the leader cult served a dual function. By promoting the cult of an important leader, lower-level cadres could signal their loyalty and effectively create a system of patronage. Political leaders vying for power within the Politburo thus recruited a number of loyal followers, who would support the leaders' policy lines as long as they in turn could hope for political ascendancy or at least for protection during inner-party struggles. An important ingredient of the cult, besides providing a common symbol to represent the CCP organizational apparatus, was thus its function as a "non-bureaucratic form of communication between apex and lower-rungs of the bureaucratic hierarchy."[55] The emergence of these patron–client relationships did not necessarily have to be restricted to the top level but could instead result in plural cults flourishing at the same time – for example, on the provincial level.

Irrespective of the personal abilities of the leader himself, the political system thus encouraged asymmetric types of communication between the apex and lower rungs of the party hierarchy and eased the formation of what M. Rainer Lepsius, following Max Weber, has called "charismatic relationships."[56] He singled out as main criteria of such charismatic relationships personal devotion among the followers, the dissolution of normative standards, and the creation of a community based on emotion and loyalty rather than on formal rules.[57] This aspect is of supreme importance, as it offers an explanation regarding why seemingly irrational behavior and language came to assume such an important role among the cult's followers. By defining Max Weber's ideal type of charismatic leadership not solely through individual traits of character but through the

---

[54] See Lisa Wedeen, *Ambiguities of Domination: Politics, Rhetoric, and Symbols in Contemporary Syria*, Chicago: University of Chicago Press, 1999.

[55] Graeme Gill, "The Soviet Leader Cult: Reflections on the Structure of Leadership in the Soviet Union," in *British Journal of Political Science* 10 (1980), 183.

[56] M. Rainer Lepsius, "The Model of Charismatic Leadership and Its Applicability to the Rule of Adolf Hitler," in *Totalitarian Movements and Political Religions* 7.2 (2006), 175.

[57] See, as well, Apter and Saich, *Revolutionary Discourse*, 11f.

structures of charismatic relationships that the leader was able to maintain, Lepsius brings into focus the dynamics of the leader cult. Personal charismatic qualities were not necessarily required for the establishment of a leader cult, but they could greatly enhance its acceptance.

The creation of a leader's superior cult image relied on numerous personal and institutional interests and only seldom worked as unambiguously as the omnipresent cult symbols make believe. The representation of the CCP through the image of Mao as savior of the Chinese nation proved instrumental in increasing internal cohesion and external appeal, yet unless the image remained under firm party control, it always bore the danger of being hijacked for contradictory purposes. This threat was generally counterbalanced through various measures, most importantly through the reliance on what Timothy Cheek has termed the "directed public sphere"[58] controlled by the CCP Propaganda Department and the Ministry of Culture. The discussion of controversial political issues in public was discouraged in order to prevent alternative readings of official state symbols. The effectiveness of transmitting the cult through newspapers, schoolbooks, and radio broadcasts was only possible within a highly regulated media apparatus and by employing a strictly regulated language. The uniformity of expression granted through the monopoly of the state media enabled the regime to imprint its hegemonic interpretation of reality to dominate the public sphere in ways inconceivable in a democratic system. The character of the Chinese broadcasting apparatus during the Mao period thus can be characterized as a device to provide an integrated, "correct" worldview with a ritualized meaning.[59]

The CCP paid enormous attention to the control of the works and image of Mao Zedong and repeatedly intervened against the unauthorized printing and distribution of his speeches and pictures. Mao himself was highly aware of his symbolic power and was furious about quotations being used out of context.[60] The choosing of the right words and phrases was a highly political matter in the People's Republic, as the party had to demonstrate its legitimacy by adapting quotes from the Marxist-Leninist

---

[58] Timothy Cheek, "Introduction: The Making and Breaking of the Party-State in China," in Timothy Cheek and Tony Saich (eds.), *New Perspectives on State Socialism in China*, Armonk, NY: M. E. Sharpe, 1997, 7.

[59] See Michael Holmes, *Communication Theory: Media, Technology, Society*, London: Sage, 2005, Chapter 5.

[60] Compare Roderick MacFarquhar, Timothy Cheek, and Eugene Wu (eds.), *The Secret Speeches of Chairman Mao: From the Hundred Flowers to the Great Leap Forward*, Cambridge, MA: Council on East Asian Studies/ Harvard University, 1989, 395.

canon and simultaneously reduce ambiguous meanings.[61] After all, the CCP had to secure a uniform implementation of its policies through roughly 20 million party members in a state with a population of more than 745 million people at the outset of the Cultural Revolution. The doctrinal authority of the CCP thus resulted in enormous attention being paid to words and symbols, irrespective of the personal role of Mao Zedong. Furthermore, it sharpened the readership's awareness of the equation of changes in vocabulary with changes in power relations.

The advantage of such a formalized system of language for the researcher lies in the possibility of using quantitative research methods to search for breaks within the semantic web. Formulations such as "cult of the individual" were subjected to continual revision and, if no longer considered to be embodying Marxist-Leninist truths, would vanish within a day from public discourse. The highly restricted mode of political communication underwent a dual change during the Cultural Revolution. On the one hand, the official media acquired a uniformity and formalization of expression that exceeded all previous periods. By 1968, the number of articles in the *People's Daily* had been drastically reduced, equaling roughly 40 percent of the number of articles published in 1960. Furthermore, half of the articles immediately referred to Mao Zedong and his thought. There was little choice but to join publicly in the cult rhetoric if one did not want to risk the danger of being ostracized. Fear and terror strongly contributed to the rise of the patterns of communication characteristic of the cult of the individual.

On the other hand, nonofficial media and uncensored documents began to circulate during the tumultuous period between 1966 and 1968 that contested the officially proposed views. Alternative interpretations and information-gathering activities among the Red Guards developed in previously unthinkable dimensions and temporarily broke the uniformity of the directed public sphere. With the implosion of the party apparatus, claims to power had to be negotiated according to their proximity to Mao Zedong Thought. As a consequence, a multitude of actors employed the symbols and rhetoric of the cult for different purposes, or, in the terms of Joseph Esherick and Jeffrey Wasserstrom, "political ritual" was turned into "political theater."[62] The result was seldom fundamental opposition

---

[61] See Michael Schoenhals, *Doing Things with Words in Chinese Politics: Five Studies*, Berkeley, CA: Center for Chinese Studies, 1992, especially Chapter 1.

[62] Joseph W. Esherick and Jeffrey N. Wasserstrom, "Acting Out Democracy: Political Theater in Modern China," in *Journal of Asian Studies* 49.4 (November 1990), 835–65.

to central policies; instead, the performances served as means to negotiate power within highly specific local settings. The boundaries between the political and the apolitical, between public and private, underwent continual changes and spread the cult into areas that the party leadership never intended them to reach. Therefore, the period is an excellent example of the capacity of the cult symbols "to take on non-ordinary meaning[s]"[63] and to function in contexts where they did not belong.

A final danger of elevating a living leader's image as brand symbol was presented by the threat that the leader might employ his image to turn against inner-party rivals or even against the Leninist party organization as such. The forging of charismatic relationships that cut across bureaucratic hierarchies within the party and the successful installment of Mao Zedong as a brand symbol beyond party confines enabled him to rally forces both inside and outside the CCP by way of what Joel Andreas has called "charismatic mobilization," the ability to mobilize people "without the benefits or constraints of formal organization."[64] Although the employment of the cult in inner-party struggles had been a salient feature since the very beginning, the Cultural Revolution was unique insofar as Mao aimed at the destruction of the very system he had helped to create. While Mao was highly successful in disrupting bureaucratic routines and in mobilizing the masses, he ultimately failed to provide an alternative vision of how to govern China. The instrumentalization of his image led to a thorough erosion of trust and the emergence of political structures after his death that represented the very opposite of what he had originally intended to achieve with the Cultural Revolution. The present "socialism with Chinese characteristics" in his opinion would probably just have been a flattering misnomer for revisionism.

The book is divided into three parts following a roughly chronological order. Since the origins of the Mao cult, as briefly sketched in this introduction, reach back much further than the accustomed starting point of the Cultural Revolution in 1966, Part One begins by tracing the theoretical discussions on the concept of the "cult of personality" in China in the years after Stalin's death in 1953. By showing how the CCP on different levels tried to grapple with the consequences of Khrushchev's secret speech and de-Stalinization policies, the transnational character of the personality cult

---

[63] Judith Butler, *Excitable Speech: A Politics of the Performative*, New York: Routledge, 1997, 161.

[64] See Joel Andreas, "The Structure of Charismatic Mobilization: A Case Study of Rebellion during the Cultural Revolution," in *American Sociological Review* 72 (2007), 437.

phenomenon is revealed. Part Two covers the emergence of the specific forms of the Cultural Revolutionary Mao cult in the early 1960s. The focus is on the aspects of charismatic mobilization and the rise of the specific cult rhetoric and rituals in the PLA. This part of the book provides a short history of the cult's primary token, the Little Red Book, before turning toward the "spectacles of worship" in the autumn of 1966. It furthermore details the multifarious instrumentalizations of the cult symbols during the high tide of the Red Guard Mao worship in 1966–7 by way of looking at one specific Red Guard organization, United Action (*liandong*). Part Three, finally, deals with the shift from employing the cult as a means of charismatic mobilization toward its propagation and enactment as a means to secure discipline and compliance. Following the destruction of the party bureaucracy, the cult was instrumental in enforcing submission to state authority either through military training or the omnipresent Mao Zedong Thought Study Classes. During this period the most obscure rituals of worship emerged, including "quotation gymnastics" (*yulu cao*) and loyalty dances, but the cult and its manifestations resisted strict party control, as the massive drive toward commodification and sacralization reveal. The third part concludes with the attempt to curb the outer manifestations of the cult after 1969 and briefly sketches its further development up to Mao's death and beyond. Because of the scarcity of archival sources on the 1970s, especially with regard to the reception side, the period after 1969 is unfortunately dealt with in much less detail and will, I hope, be supplemented by future research. The same holds true for a multitude of other aspects related to the cult that deserve closer analysis but cannot be covered here, including the influence of the cult in artistic production, music, theater, and literature.[65]

The period covered by this book loosely ranges from Stalin's death in 1953 until the passing of the 1981 *Resolution on Party History* and is somewhat at odds with narrow definitions of the Cultural Revolution, the periodization of which has become an issue of long-standing dispute in itself.[66] Undisputed, however, is the fact that great differences exist between the tumultuous Red Guard phase from 1966 to 1968, the period of PLA domination between 1969 and Lin Biao's death in 1971, and the

---

[65] For recent accounts that touch on the subject, see Paul Clark, *The Chinese Cultural Revolution: A History*, Cambridge: Cambridge University Press, 2008, and Richard King (ed.), *Art in Turmoil: The Chinese Cultural Revolution 1966–76*, Vancouver: UBC Press, 2010.

[66] Jonathan Unger, "The Cultural Revolution at the Grass Roots," in *China Journal* 57 (2007), 109–37.

years 1972 to 1976 that recently have been termed the "twilight of the Cultural Revolution."[67] The Mao cult cuts across all these divides. Although the most important period is clearly presented by the years 1966 to 1969, the internal periodization follows a different timeline, most clearly visible in the shift from employing the cult as a means of mobilization toward fostering compliance in late 1967. As we look at repeated interactions between elite politics, the midlevel bureaucracy, and grassroots implementation over time, the Mao cult regains the historicity that is all too often neglected and thus shall be linked to the growing body of historical research on modern personality cults.

---

[67] Frederick C. Teiwes and Warren Sun, *The End of the Maoist Era: Chinese Politics during the Twilight of the Cultural Revolution 1972–1976*, Armonk, NY: M. E. Sharpe, 2007.

PART ONE

COMING TO TERMS WITH THE "CULT OF THE INDIVIDUAL"

In the late hours of 5 March 1953, Joseph Stalin died. The official announcement drafted in the name of the CCP Central Committee expressed the enormous grief his death had inflicted upon the Communist Party of the Soviet Union (CPSU) and the course of the world revolution. For the CCP, it was likewise a loss "the tragic consequences of which could not be fathomed."[1] The Chinese public had been well informed about the changing health situation of the "great leader of the world revolution," since the CCP had regularly published accounts in the media and ordered to post daily bulletins about Stalin's condition at major public places.[2] During the official commemoration ceremony, Mao Zedong himself laid down a wreath of flowers in honor of the deceased at the Gate of Heavenly Peace, which had been decorated with Stalin's portrait, and called upon the Chinese to turn their grief into renewed strength for the revolutionary cause. For three days, all of China was to commemorate the dead. All flags were to be lowered, all public institutions closed. The leader of world communism had died and despite his frequent quarrels over the correct path of the Chinese Revolution with the CCP leadership and Mao Zedong in particular, his commemoration could leave no doubt about the importance and influence Stalin had exerted on the communist movement. The enormous consequences of Stalin's death were

---

[1] "Zhongyang guanyu quandang he quanguo renmin daonian Sidalin qushi de zhishi" [CCP Center Instruction Concerning the Mourning of Stalin in the Whole Party and Nation], 7 March 1953, Hebei Provincial Archives (HPA) 855-2-266.

[2] "Guanyu you guan Sidalin tongzhi huanbing qijian de xuanchuan ying zhuyi de shixiang" [Items to Be Observed in Propaganda Work during the Period of Comrade Stalin's Illness], 5 March 1953, HPA 855-2-266.

not only reflected within the party leadership but led to discussions among the lower-ranking cadres and the populace as well. Doubts were uttered as to whether the Soviet–Chinese alliance could carry on as it had before and questions were asked regarding how the socialist states could continue to attract further members without Stalin's personality.[3] By means of frequent propagation and regular study sessions, the local party committees were to counter the rising tide of skeptics and to stop the spreading of rumors about what would happen now that the helmsman of the world revolution had died.[4]

The death of Stalin presents a major turning point in the history of the communist movement. As Stalin had failed to install an eminent successor, the Soviet Union's leading role in the world communist movement came to be questioned from various sides. Long-standing communist party leaders and successful state founders such as Mao Zedong were not easily impressed by figures such as Stalin's interim successor Georgi Malenkov. That it was to take only a decade, however, until the widely celebrated bloc unity would fall apart and the Soviet Union and China openly contended as leaders of world communism was only possible against the backdrop of Khrushchev's secret speech. The assault on Stalin's legacy and its national and international reverberations left a deep imprint on the history of the CCP and CPSU alike.

---

[3] "Hebei shengwei guanyu zhengque xuanchuan Sidalin qushi dengqing ge zhong hunluan sixiang de zhishi" [Hebei Provincial Committee Instruction Concerning the Correct Propagation of Stalin's Death and the Clearing-Up of All Types of Confused Thinking], 19 March 1953, HPA 855-17-158.

[4] The state-owned Xinhua bookstores, for example, started large-scale commemoration sales of Stalin's *Collected Works*. See Hebei sheng Xinhua shudian (ed.), *Hebei tushu faxing zhi* [Hebei Book Distribution Gazetteer], vol. 2, unrevised manuscript, 1990, 170.

The Secret Speech and Its Impact

Three years after Stalin's death, the Twentieth CPSU Congress convened in Moscow. The secret speech that First Party Secretary Nikita Khrushchev delivered on 25 February 1956 shattered Stalin's image as omniscient and wise leader of the communist movement and revealed the crimes committed during his rule. The Soviet Central Committee's attitude toward Stalin and his legacy had by no means been straightforward after his death. Only in late 1955 had it been agreed upon that a commission was to investigate Stalin's role in the Great Terror of 1936–7, when Stalin had consolidated his monocracy by having millions of potential opponents killed or sent to work camps. The commission's findings were incorporated into a long report, which the Central Committee, after a controversial dispute, decided to read out on the last day of the Twentieth CPSU Congress to the Soviet delegates only.[1]

Neither the Chinese delegation (headed by Marshal Zhu De and including Deng Xiaoping, Tan Zhenlin, Wang Jiaxiang, and the Chinese ambassador to the Soviet Union, Liu Xiao) nor representatives of other communist parties had been given prior notice about its content. Khrushchev's four-hour speech combined the prepared report with a number of impulsive impromptu remarks. He set out by fiercely attacking Stalin for having elevated himself above the party: "[I]t is impermissible and foreign to the spirit of Marxism-Leninism to elevate one person, to transform him into a superman possessing supernatural characteristics,

---

[1] For a review of the CPSU's approach to demythologizing Stalin and its difficulties, see Polly Jones, "From Stalinism to Post-Stalinism: De-Mythologising Stalin, 1953–56," in *Totalitarian Movements and Political Religions* 4.1 (2004), 127–48.

akin to those of a god. Such a man supposedly knows everything, sees everything, thinks for everyone, can do anything, and is infallible in his behavior."[2] Without elaborating on the theoretical notion of the cult within Marxist philosophy, Khrushchev mainly dealt with individual cases and postmortem rehabilitations of old cadres killed during the Great Terror. Despite his great services to the party, Khrushchev exclaimed, Stalin had failed to differentiate between enmity toward the exploiting classes and diverging opinions among communists. He had credited himself with having played the decisive role in all victories of the Soviet Union while fostering an image of utmost modesty in public. Khrushchev demonstrated this by way of quoting changes that Stalin personally had made to the manuscript of the *Short Course on the History of the CPSU [Bolsheviks]*. He had alienated himself from both the party and the people and finally come to rely solely on pictorial or cinematographic representations of reality.

Khrushchev's speech equated the "cult of the individual" with breaking the principle of collective leadership and facilitating despotism, terror, and mass repressions, along with omnipresent flattery to Stalin's genius. He called upon the party to abolish personality cults once and for all, although caution would have to be taken. The Soviet populace had become accustomed to reading the semiotic displays of power in terms of leadership struggles. If all *kolkhozes* named after current party leaders were to be renamed, this would incite negative consequences. Khrushchev tried to ensure that no word of the speech leaked out to the Western press: "We should know the limits; we should not give ammunition to the enemy; we should not wash our dirty linen before their eyes."[3] Given the attendance of 1,500 Soviet delegates and the massive reprint of the speech in the following weeks for study purposes all over the country, this hope turned out to be illusory.

NATIONAL AND INTERNATIONAL REVERBERATIONS

The secret speech has been called the most daring and reckless action Khrushchev took in his entire life.[4] Its national and international repercussions, however, proved to be disastrous for the unity of the communist movement. By combining personal assaults with misgivings mainly in the

---

[2] Thomas Rigby (ed.), *The Stalin Dictatorship: Khrushchev's "Secret Speech" and Other Documents*, Sydney: Sydney University Press, 1968, 23.

[3] Ibid., 83.

[4] William Taubman, *Khrushchev: The Man and His Era*, New York: Norton, 2003, 274.

legal sector of the Soviet system, Khrushchev neither provided an authoritative statement on how to evaluate Stalin's historical role nor sketched out the systemic changes that would have to be taken in order to overcome the defects of Stalin's legacy. These inadequacies were soon voiced as the speech was read out to party members all over the Soviet Union. The Soviet Presidium had upon Khrushchev's request sent the speech on 5 March 1956, the third anniversary of Stalin's death, to all party committees for study purposes. The red-covered booklets, imprinted with "not for the press," were read to more than seven million party members during the following weeks. Although some hesitant criticism of the cult was voiced, reports and letters from the provinces revealed popular support for the "traditions 'invented' by the cult."[5] In some provinces, the author of the secret speech was attacked for dismantling the cult and even called a cretin and a moron.

Rumors about the content of Khrushchev's speech soon leaked to Western media. Of special importance was the reprint of the speech by the Polish Workers' Party. The first secretary of the Polish Workers' Party, Stefan Staszewski, remembered his unauthorized printing and distribution of the speech's full text in late March 1956: "I personally handed a copy hot off the press, to Philip Benn, the Le Monde correspondent, and to [Sidney] Gruson from the Herald Tribune and to Flora Lewis from the New York Times."[6] The Chinese delegation, according to the remembrances of Wu Lengxi, head of the Xinhua News Agency, had been informed by a member of the Soviet Liaison Office about the content of the speech two days after the congress had ended. The report had been read to the delegation once in a verbal translation. They had not been allowed to copy it down and therefore it left only a vague and distorted impression on the delegates.[7] The impact of the speech and the beginning of de-Stalinization became obvious as well during a visit that Zhu De, as head of the Chinese delegation, paid to Stalin's hometown in Georgia on 7 March 1956 amid massive protests that Stalin's birthday be commemorated as usual.[8]

---

[5] Jones, "Post-Stalinism," 135.

[6] Teresa Toranska, "Them": Stalin's Polish Puppets, New York: Harper & Row, 1987, 174.

[7] The Chinese chief interpreter at the congress, Shi Zhe, recalls that immediately after the speech a copy was handed out to the Chinese delegation, but does not provide further details. See Shi Zhe and Li Haiwen, ZhongSu guanxi jianzheng lu. Shi Zhe koushu [Witness to Sino–Soviet Relations: Recollections of Shi Zhe], Beijing: Dangdai Zhongguo chubanshe, 2005, 207.

[8] On the demonstrations, see Sergei Khrushchev, Nikita Khrushchev and the Creation of a Superpower, University Park: Pennsylvania State University Press, 2000, 163.

The Chinese response to Khrushchev's speech was published on 5 April 1956 and has been regarded as being extraordinarily late, indicating either disapproval of the article's content or at least tensions within the Chinese Politburo about how to reply.[9] Recently published accounts, however, reveal that the article was not only written within a very short span of time but also that the CCP leadership unanimously supported its content. According to the remembrances of Wu Lengxi, it was not until parts of the secret speech were published by the *New York Times* in mid-March that the Chinese leadership received a complete version of the speech.[10] The *New York Times*, however, did not print the text until 5 June, a day after the U.S. government had officially released it. It seems quite possible that the Chinese obtained a copy of the internal Soviet reprint either directly from the Soviet Union or through one of its Eastern European embassies.

On 17 March, Mao Zedong convened a meeting of the Central Secretariat in the Yinian Hall adjacent to his living quarters in Zhongnanhai. The translation of the speech had been distributed to the members of the secretariat the previous day through the institution in charge of the party's paper flow, the CCP General Office. Upon Mao's request, a number of other high-ranking cadres had joined the discussion, among them Yang Shangkun (head of the CCP General Office); Hu Qiaomu (Mao's former political secretary and deputy head of the Central Propaganda Department); the former ambassadors to the Soviet Union, Zhang Wentian (vice-minister of foreign affairs) and Wang Jiaxiang (in his capacity as head of the CCP Liaison Department in charge of handling affairs with other communist parties); as well as Wu Lengxi himself. As most of the participants had not yet been able to read the translation completely, they agreed only on the urgency of responding to the speech in an appropriate way.

Mao summarized his impression of the speech as having "removed a lid"[11] by proclaiming that not everything Stalin or the Soviet Union had done in the past had always been correct. On the other hand, Khrushchev had "poked a hole" into the armor of the communist movement because

---

[9] See Donald S. Zagoria, *The Sino–Soviet Conflict, 1956–1961*, New York: Atheneum, 1964, 43.

[10] Wu Lengxi, *Shinian lunzhan, 1956–1966. ZhongSu guanxi huiyilu* [A Decade of Polemics, 1956–1966: A Memoir of Sino–Soviet Relations], vol. 1, Beijing: Zhongyang wenxian chubanshe, 2000 [1999], 4.

[11] Wu Lengxi, *Yi Mao zhuxi. Wo qinshen jingli de ruogan zhongda lishi shijian pianduan* [Remembering Chairman Mao: Fragments of Certain Major Historical Events Which I Personally Experienced], Beijing: Xinhua chubanshe, 1995, 4.

the report contained great mistakes both in terms of form and content. During the following week, Mao twice convened enlarged meetings of the Politburo and added the experience of the party's foremost propagandists – Lu Dingyi (head of the Central Propaganda Department); Deng Tuo (chief editor of the *People's Daily*); Mao's former secretary, Chen Boda (director of the CCP Political Research Office); and Chen's deputy, Hu Sheng – to the aforementioned group in order to discuss the impact and appropriate answer to Khrushchev's speech. As far as Wu's recollections reveal, Mao seems to have dominated the meetings by sketching out the content of the reply and settling for the form of an editorial. An official resolution would have carried too much weight given the ongoing impact the speech had caused in capitalist and socialist countries alike. Furthermore, the CPSU had not yet made the speech public. Chen Boda was assigned to draft the article with the assistance of the Central Propaganda Department and the Xinhua News Agency, which collected all major articles on the subject from foreign news agencies. Chen finished the first draft on 29 March 1956 and, upon request from Deng Xiaoping, discussed it with Lu Dingyi, Hu Qiaomu, Hu Sheng, and Wu Lengxi.[12]

Meanwhile, the Twentieth Congress had become a lively topic among local cadres as well. With the exception of the secret speech, the proceedings of the congress had been made public through translations from the CPSU organ *Pravda*. By mid-March, however, the question of what effectively constituted a personality cult had through nonofficial communication channels become a frequently discussed subject. A secret cable sent by the Hebei Provincial Propaganda Department to the Hebei Provincial Committee and the Central Propaganda Department on 26 March stated that most party members supported the congress's decisions. Yet a number of specific problems had arisen that the Provincial Propaganda Department had not been able to answer. The distinction between fostering a personality cult and cherishing the historical role of individual leaders remained especially troublesome. The report quoted a section from Anastas Mikoyan's speech to the Twentieth CPSU Congress that had been cited by local cadres for failing to provide a clear criterion:

---

[12] Roderick MacFarquhar, in his seminal account of the period, which even thirty-five years after its publication still represents the standard reference work, identifies Hu Qiaomu as the main author of the editorial, based on an account of Liu Shaoqi's wife, Wang Guangmei. See Roderick MacFarquhar, *Contradictions among the People, 1956–1957*, London: Oxford University Press, 1974, 43. Hu, however, drafted the follow-up editorial, "More on the Historical Experience of the Dictatorship of the Proletariat," in late December 1956; see Chapter 2.

"'Lenin's genial expression about the laws of the development of the society is an extraordinarily precious source for a correct understanding of many present phenomena. Without Lenin, it would be impossible to understand them' [. . .]. This sentence in itself is already tantamount to worshipping the individual. Its standpoint is not historical materialism."[13] While the ideological predicament among cadres grew more complicated, the provincial and local propaganda departments signaled their strong need for a definite answer to these questions. On 30 March 1956, the *People's Daily* published a translated *Pravda* editorial entitled "Why Personality Cults Violate the Spirit of Marxism-Leninism,"[14] which made the topic of the secret speech an openly debated issue. With thirty-five references to the "cult of the individual," the article firmly rooted the translation *geren chongbai* in Chinese political discourse.

Two days later, on 1 April 1956, Chen Boda sent the revised draft version of the reply to Mao Zedong. Mao ordered it to be distributed to the rest of the Politburo and sketched out in detail the Politburo members' responsibilities until the proposed publication.[15] Upon Mao's request, the Politburo discussed the article under Liu Shaoqi's guidance and added a few further corrections. Liu pointed out that not all of Stalin's mistakes should be interpreted as a consequence of the "cult of the individual" but rather should be explained along the lines of failing to distinguish between subjective views and objective circumstances. The term *geren chongbai* did not seem to be very appropriate to Liu in conveying the meaning of religious superstition associated with the Russian *kul't lichnosti*. Liu advocated the term *geren mixin* instead, with its clearly pejorative connotation of superstitious belief in an individual leader.[16] However, as the translation had already become standardized, a change in vocabulary did not seem mandatory.

---

[13] "Hebei shengwei xuanchuanbu guanyu ganbu dui Sugong di ershi ci daibiao dahui de sixiang qingkuang jianbao" [Hebei Provincial Committee Propaganda Department Bulletin Concerning Opinions among Cadres with Regard to the Twentieth CPSU Congress], 26 March 1956, HPA 864-1-157.

[14] "Weishenme geren chongbai shi weifan Makesi Liening zhuyi jingshen de" [Why Personality Cults Violate the Spirit of Marxism-Leninism], in *Renmin ribao*, 30 March 1956, 3.

[15] Zhonggong zhongyang wenxian yanjiushi (ed.), *Jianguo yilai Mao Zedong wengao* [Mao Zedong's Post-1949 Manuscripts], vol. 6, (1956.1–1957.12), Beijing: Zhongyang wenxian chubanshe, 1992, 59.

[16] Wu, *Shinian lunzhan*, 1, 20f. Wu is mistaken in pointing out that *geren mixin* became the standard translation after December 1956. This did not happen until mid-1958.

Deng Xiaoping insisted on adding more analysis about the reasons for the emergence and continuing influence of the cult. After all, Khrushchev's speech had failed to explain whether the cult had been the reason or the consequence of Stalin's actions. Deng further advised to point out the precautions taken by the CCP against the rise of similar phenomena in China. After a final discussion, Mao decided upon the headline "On the Historical Experience of the Dictatorship of the Proletariat" and added the subtitle "Written by the Editorial Department of the *People's Daily* on the Basis of the Discussion Which Took Place at an Enlarged Meeting of the Political Bureau of the Central Committee of the Communist Party of China." Even the title thus was to express that China did not have to cope with the problem of a personality cult. The article was broadcast by the Xinhua News Agency the same evening and appeared in print in the *People's Daily* the following day.[17] Despite the hurried circumstances of its compilation and distribution, the editorial presented a systematic attempt to historicize the cult as a political phenomenon and to explain its emergence with reference to historical materialism.

ON THE HISTORICAL EXPERIENCE OF THE DICTATORSHIP OF THE PROLETARIAT

The article focused on three main purposes: first, to limit the speech's doctrinal damage caused by lifting the discussion to the level of Marxist-Leninist theory; second, to attempt to evaluate preliminarily Stalin's historical role; and third, to outline the preventive measures taken by the CCP in dealing with the problem of the cult. The discussions at the Twentieth Party Congress were interpreted as courageous self-criticism despite the ferocious attacks the report had incited in the Western media. After all, the Soviet comrades had nothing to lose "except their errors,"[18] as the editorial, in obvious analogy to the *Communist Manifesto*, put it. This unique honesty of the dictatorship of the proletariat should not be interpreted as weakness but rather as strength. Since the Soviet Union had been the first state in the world to establish the dictatorship of the proletariat, it had not been able to benefit from the experiences of any predecessors. But "whatever the mistakes, the dictatorship of the proletariat is, for the popular

---

[17] One day later, the article was also broadcast in Russian after chief translator Shi Zhe had supervised a rapid translation prepared by the staff of the *Sino–Soviet Friendship Paper*; see Shi and Li, *ZhongSu guanxi*, 209f.

[18] Editorial Department of the *People's Daily*, *On the Historical Experience of the Dictatorship of the Proletariat*, Beijing: Foreign Languages Press, 1959, 2.

masses, always far superior to all dictatorships of the exploiting classes, to the dictatorship of the bourgeoisie."[19] The role of Stalin was to be ana-lyzed in a comprehensive way. His merits as successor to Lenin, as military leader in the Second World War, and as proponent of industrialization and agricultural collectivization had gained him the status of an "outstanding Marxist-Leninist fighter."[20] Unfortunately, the enormous success had diz-zied Stalin's mind. He had failed to engage further in criticism and self-criticism, lost contact with the masses, and violated the principle of collec-tive leadership. Stalin had fallen victim to subjectivism and one-sidedness, allowing the cult of the individual to take hold of him. The cult itself was explained as the resurrection of the tradition of patriarchy and tsar worship:

> The cult of the individual is rooted not only in the exploiting classes but also in the small producers. As [it] is well known, patriarchy is a product of small-producer economy. After the establishment of the dictatorship of the proletariat, even when the exploiting classes are eliminated, when small-producer economy has been replaced by a collective economy and a socialist society has been founded, certain rotten, poisonous ideological survivals of the old society may still remain in people's minds for a very long time. "The force of habit of millions and tens of millions is a most terrible force" (Lenin). The cult of the individual is just one such force of habit of millions and tens of millions. Since this force of habit still exists in society, it can influence many government functionaries, and even such a leader as Stalin was also affected by it. The cult of the individual is a reflection in man's mind of a social phenomenon, and when leaders of the party and state, such as Stalin, succumb to the influence of this backward ideology, they will in turn influence society, bringing losses to the cause and hampering the initiative and creativeness of the masses of the people.[21]

By interpreting the cult as an outgrowth of patriarchy, as a "foul carry-over from the long history of mankind," the Politburo tried to overcome the major weakness of Khrushchev's speech: the failure to root the cult in Marxist-Leninist orthodoxy and to provide an answer to the questions about the reasons for its development and its consequences for the Soviet system. Without providing explicit references to the *Collected Works* of Marx and Engels, the article invoked the relative autonomy of the super-structure vis-à-vis the economic base. The cult was to be interpreted as an outgrowth of the former practice of tsar worship, yet it derived its specific potency from Stalin's acceptance of this social phenomenon and the lack of

---

[19] Ibid., 4f.
[20] Ibid., 7.
[21] Ibid., 9. Original English translation.

"inner-party democracy." This twist explained the importance attached to psychological aberrations and legal deficiencies in the following argument, which no longer dealt with the historical setting or limitations of the leadership's unrestricted power but rather with strategies for avoiding alienation between leaders and populace.

In order not to give a wrong impression about the ongoing importance of leaders in revolutionary movements, the article strongly echoed the arguments first expounded by Georgi Plekhanov in 1898 in his work *On the Role of the Individual in History*. Plekhanov had argued that a leader's greatness was not based on the capacity to alter the course of history at will but rather on the ability to articulate the great and predetermined social conflicts of the time: "He is a hero. But he is a hero not in the sense that he can stop or change the natural course of things, but in the sense that his activities are the conscious and free expression of this inevitable and unconscious course."[22] Stalin's deviation from the right path of socialism should not result in the downplaying of the role of leaders or in major changes within the socialist system but rather in a return to the Maoist concept of the "mass line."[23] By keeping close contact with the masses and by consequently distinguishing the correct ideas from among the plethora of opinions and transforming these into coherent policy guidelines, the party and its leaders would help to propel the correct and inevitable course of history forward.

The article supported the CPSU in its struggle against the cult of Stalin in order to destroy blind faith in dogmatic viewpoints. Yet the article revealed clearly that the CCP had taken over the explanatory task that would have been expected from Moscow before introducing the novel theoretical concept of "personality cults" without informing the rest of the communist camp. The argument that the existence of a personality cult was due to ideological remnants seemed to make sense within the newly founded, largely rural People's Republic of China, but it did not merit equal explicatory value in the case of the Soviet Union nearly forty years after the Russian Revolution. The speech had indeed "poked a hole" into the communist ideological armor, and the CPSU's failure to provide an

---

[22] Georgi Plekhanov, *Lun geren zai lishi shang de zuoyong* (On the Role of the Individual in History), Moscow: Waiguowen shuji chubanju, 1950, 43f. Plekhanov's essay had been translated into Chinese and reprinted repeatedly since 1948. The largest editions were printed immediately before the onset of the Cultural Revolution in 1964 and 1965.

[23] Mao Zedong, "Some Questions Concerning Methods of Leadership," in *Selected Works* 3, 119.

interpretative framework led to questioning not only of Stalin's role but also of party rule in general, as Mao had foreseen.

In the name of the CCP Central Committee, usually referred to as CCP Center or CCP Central (*Zhonggong zhongyang*) in official documents, all local party committees were ordered to circulate and discuss the article within and outside party circles in order to obtain a correct knowledge about the cult of the individual and the Stalin question.[24] In a complementary circular, the Central Propaganda Department advised the localities on the method of study and how to deal with problems that might arise.[25] The provincial party committees passed the circulars on to the district and city committees with even more information about the temporal extent of the study period and the exact content. The study was to be terminated at the end of April 1956 and was to focus on the article, leaving *Pravda* editorials for additional self-study. The local cadres were advised to schedule reading times for party members and to guide the following discussions decisively in order to secure the outcome. Individual self-criticism was not deemed necessary. Study for nonparty members was to be arranged according to local conditions. By early May, the local and city committees were requested to submit a concluding report to the provincial propaganda departments about the progress of the study and the difficulties encountered.[26]

The study of the article brought forth a number of problems. The Hebei Provincial Propaganda Department, in a concluding report sent to the Provincial Party Committee and the Central Propaganda Department on 25 May, stated that the primary goal of sharpening cadre awareness of the dangers presented by personality cults had been "basically fulfilled." Yet the discussions had made clear that a number of problematic questions had arisen that had not received satisfying answers so far. The report specified six main areas of problems encountered and asked for a central directive about how to address them correctly:

[24] "Zhongyang guanyu xuexi he taolun si yue wu ri renmin ribao 'Guanyu wuchan jieji zhuanzheng de lishi jingyan' yi wen de tongzhi" [CCP Center Notice Concerning the Study and Discussion of the 5 April *People's Daily* Editorial "On the Historical Experience of the Dictatorship of the Proletariat"], 4 April 1956, HPA 855-18-509.

[25] "Guanyu xuexi 'Guanyu wuchanjieji zhuanzheng de lishi jingyan' yi wen de buchong tongzhi" [Additional Notice Concerning the Study of the Editorial "On the Historical Experience of the Dictatorship of the Proletariat"], 6 April 1956, HPA 855-18-509.

[26] "Hebei shengwei guanyu xuexi he taolun 'Guanyu wuchanjieji zhuanzheng de lishi jingyan' yi wen de tongzhi" [Hebei Provincial Committee Notice Concerning the Study and Discussion of the Editorial "On the Historical Experience of the Dictatorship of the Proletariat"], 8 April 1956, HPA 855-18-509.

1. [How are we to] estimate correctly the importance of a leader [without] aggrandizing the individual? [How are we to] distinguish between love for the leader and a personality cult? For example, some cadres from Zhangjiakou didn't dare to shout "Long live Chairman Mao" during the Labor Day parades, afraid of committing the error of worshipping the individual.

2. Concerning the question of Stalin, [many cadres] think that the other members of the Soviet Party Center definitely share responsibility; therefore, why are Stalin's faults exposed in public while the others do not make public self-criticisms?

3. Those cadres who haven't heard the secret speech always request to be informed about Stalin's actual faults. Some cadres say that unless [we] come out with actual evidence, [we] won't be able to convince them.

4. Are Stalin's works still considered to be part of the canonical works, [and] what is the criterion for works to be part of the Marxist-Leninist canon? At what place is the viewpoint of worshiping the individual to be found within the *Short Course on the History of the CPSU* (especially in Chapters 7 and 8)? Further, is the *Short Course on the History of the CPSU* still to be used as teaching material until new materials have become available?

5. Can Stalin still be mentioned alongside Marx, Engels, and Lenin?

6. What is the correct viewpoint concerning the question of a peaceful transition of capitalist countries to socialism and the question of the inevitability of war in this respect?[27]

The questions were aimed at the very heart of the problem and sharply revealed the ambiguity of the definition characterizing cults as rotten relics of feudal heritage. The implementation of Marxism-Leninism had so far been based on the claim of representing the most advanced scientific theory. The emergence of personality cults, however, showed the continuing existence of elements of rule that could not be justified with reference to rational modes of governance but were based on genuine faith in a proposed dogma.

The difficulties of the CCP and all other communist parties to come to terms with the cult of the individual were due both to systematic defects of vanguard party rule and the successful reliance on powerful imagery to increase internal unity and external appeal. Although the cult's dangerous potency had been recognized by cadres such as Liu Shaoqi, who was principally opposed to the employment of personal images to represent

---

[27] "Hebei shengwei xuanchuanbu guanyu xuexi he taolun 'Guanyu wuchanjieji zhuanzheng de lishi jingyan' yi wen de baogao he qingshi" [Report and Instruction of the Hebei Provincial Committee Propaganda Department Concerning the Study and Discussion of the Editorial "On the Historical Experience of the Dictatorship of the Proletariat"], 25 May 1956, HPA 864-1-157.

the abstract truths of Marxism-Leninism, the immediate gains of implementing Mao's image in propaganda warfare against Chiang Kai-shek and inner-party rivals had been considered to be of greater value. The emergence of the modern personality cult as historical phenomenon in China had thus been an offspring of immediate political maneuvering and not the consequence of theoretical elaboration. It was to take another two years until Mao Zedong himself came to grasp the crucial importance of supplementing his own cult theoretically.

NATIONAL SYMBOLS

The question of the cult of personality not only disrupted the education of cadres but became a relevant subject in the preparations on Labor Day (1 May) and National Day (1 October). The parades had always been of great importance to the CCP's public display of power.[28] After the founding of the People's Republic in 1949, decisions about the scale and organization of festivities had been the subject of central documents (*Zhongfa*) giving meticulous advice on the correct order of slogans and the arrangement of public imagery. A week after the establishment of the People's Republic, the CCP had first announced a general guideline on where to display the images of state leaders. In all party buildings, the portraits of Marx, Engels, Lenin, Stalin, and Mao should be on display. In the offices of state organs and organizations, the portraits of Sun Yat-sen and Mao Zedong were to be placed,[29] although portraits of Sun were not deemed mandatory.

All major celebrations were awarded different imagery. On 1 July, the traditional founding date of the CCP, the Central Secretariat members Mao Zedong, Liu Shaoqi, Zhou Enlai, and Zhu De appeared in all newspapers, while in public places the gallery of the Marxist founding fathers, including Mao, was considered appropriate.[30] On 1 August, the day commemorating

---

[28] For a general overview, see Chang-tai Hung, "Mao's Parades: State Spectacles in China in the 1950s," in *China Quarterly* 190 (2007), 411–31. See as well Wu Hung, *Remaking Beijing: Tiananmen Square and the Creation of a Political Space*, London: Reaktion, 2005, especially Chapters 2 and 3.

[29] "Zhongyang guanyu xuangua lingxiu xiang de guiding" [CCP Center Regulations Concerning the Display of Leader Portraits], 7 October 1949, in Zhonggong zhongyang xuanchuanbu bangongting and Zhongyang dang'anguan bianyanbu (eds.), *Zhonggong gongchandang xuanchuan gongzuo wenxian xuanbian* (ZGXG) [Selection of Documents on CCP Propaganda Work], vol. 3, 1949–56, Beijing: Xuexi chubanshe, 1996, 1.

[30] "Zhongyang guanyu 'qi yi' jinian jie baozhi kandeng lingxiu xiang de zhishi" [CCP Center Instructions Concerning the Publication of Leader Portraits on "1 July"], 26 June 1950, in ZGXG 3, 89.

the founding of the Red Army, the portraits of Mao and Marshal Zhu De were printed side by side in the newspapers. During the public celebrations, however, the pictures of Mao and Stalin were to be displayed "slightly higher" than the respective images of the army leaders.[31] On Chinese National Day, the only picture to be displayed on the podium itself was to be the image of Mao Zedong, but not just any kind of Mao portrait:

> [All localities] should use the picture that has been published in the newspapers on 1 August, [showing Mao] looking leftward. The picture is already being manufactured in large quantities by the Xinhua bookstores. Portraits that have previously been used in different localities showing [Mao] open-mouthed or looking downward are all to be done away with and not displayed again.[32]

Labor Day was the last of the four major events that achieved official standardization. The 1952 guidelines with regard to how Labor Day was to be celebrated listed the following order of portraits to be carried by the crowds: "The first row from left to right: Marx, Engels, Lenin, Stalin; the second row Mao Zedong, Liu Shaoqi, Zhou Enlai, Zhu De,"[33] to be followed by the leaders of various other countries. Ten days later, however, the order was significantly changed. An additional circular now placed Sun Yat-sen and Mao Zedong in the first row; Liu, Zhou, and Zhu in the second row; and the Marxist founding fathers in the third row followed by other communist leaders.[34]

The meticulous orders relayed through central documents were of limited impact for cities without national importance. In cities with a population of less than half a million, it was considered to be sufficient to display Mao's image as the most important symbol of the new state in

---

[31] "Zhongyang guanyu qingzhu ba yi gua lingxiu xiang de guiding" [Regulations of the CCP Center Concerning the Display of Leader Portraits When Celebrating 1 August], 22 July 1950, in ZGXG 3, 102.

[32] "Zhongyang guanyu guoqing jinian banfa de guiding" [CCP Center Regulations Concerning the Arrangement of National Day], 8 September 1950, in ZGXG 3, 116f. See further "Hebei shengwei guanyu guoqingri qingzhu banfa de zhishi" [Hebei Provincial Committee Instructions Concerning the Celebration of National Day], 15 September 1950, HPA 855-1-46.

[33] "Zhongyang guanyu 'wu yi' jie xuanchuan yaodian he jinian banfa de tongzhi" [CCP Center Notice Concerning the Propagation and Commemoration of Labor Day], 17 April 1952, in ZGXG 3, 356-7.

[34] "Zhongyang guanyu 'wu yi' youxing shi lingxiu xiang pailie shunxu de buchong tongzhi" [Additional Notice of the CCP Center Concerning the Arrangement of Leader Portraits during the "Labor Day" Parade], 27 April 1952, in ZGXG 3, 358.

public places, schools, cinemas, and traffic hubs.[35] To ensure that the leader portraits were not "manufactured in a rough and slipshod fashion,"[36] the distribution of portraits had been exclusively assigned to the state-owned Xinhua publishing houses because having the portraits printed by private publishing houses had posed numerous problems of quality both in terms of form and content. Not only had traditional calendar paper and floral designs been used for printing, often the correct order of the portraits had been mixed up and CCP cadres had been included in collections with noncommunist state leaders. The titles of the portraits, a matter of great political importance, had sometimes been flawed, especially when printing the names of foreign communist leaders. Kim Il-sung thus had been wrongly assigned the nonexisting position as "Chairman of the North Korean Ministerial Assembly," and occasionally even the names of Lenin and Stalin had been confused.[37]

The slogan "Long live the great leader of the people of the world, Stalin!" had always assumed the final and most important position during all parades. Mao Zedong, as leader of the Chinese Revolution, had even during the celebrations of Chinese National Day conceded this honor of the superior position to Stalin as a question of principle. Stalin's death disrupted this equilibrium. During the preparations for Labor Day 1953, portraits and portable posters of his successor Malenkov had to be produced in a hurry,[38] but Malenkov was not awarded the same honors as Stalin and assumed the position as first among equals among the ranks of the foreign communist leaders.[39] Instead, the image of Mao Zedong as the most experienced leader of the world revolution now assumed the central position.[40] The changes within the Soviet leadership during the following two years further aggravated the problems. They both weakened the

---

[35] "Zhongyang guanyu xuangua lingxiu xiang de tongzhi" [CCP Center Notice Concerning the Display of Leader Portraits], 23 December 1954, HPA 855-17-215.

[36] Ibid.

[37] "Zhonggong zhongyang pizhuan zhongxuanbu guanyu yinshua he faxing lingxiu xiang wenti de baogao" [Central Propaganda Department Report Approved and Transmitted by the CCP Center Concerning the Question of Printing and Distributing Leader Portraits], 31 July 1953, HPA 855-2-266.

[38] "Hebei shengwei guanyu jinian 'wu yi' jie de tongzhi" [Hebei Provincial Committee Notice on Commemorating "Labor Day"], 18 April 1953, HPA 855-17-158.

[39] "Zhongyang guanyu 'wu yi' jie xuanchuan yaodian he jinian banfa de tongzhi" [CCP Center Notice Concerning the Propagation and Commemoration of "Labor Day"], 10 April 1954, HPA 855-17-255.

[40] "Zhongyang guanyu 1953 nian guoqingjie jinian banfa de tongzhi" [CCP Center Notice Concerning the Commemoration of National Day 1953], 12 September 1953, in ZGXG 3, 575f.

credibility of a strong communist leadership in the eyes of the Chinese Politburo and presented the provincial and local committees with enormous difficulties when trying to organize the parades. The correct order of foreign leader portraits kept changing until, finally, local committees were ordered not to hand out any foreign leader portraits to the marching crowd.[41]

After Khrushchev's secret speech, the question of public imagery had to be reviewed in the context of the cult of personality. On 13 April 1956, in a central document approved of by Liu Shaoqi, the Central Propaganda Department transmitted the order of the CCP Center on how to celebrate Labor Day. It gave precise instructions about the slogans to be used. "Long live Chairman Mao" retained the final position.[42] The question of leader portraits proved to be more complicated. A separate document was circulated on 18 April that listed the portraits that were to be displayed and carried during the parades. Besides those of Marx, Engels, and Lenin, the portrait of Stalin was still to be displayed. The pictures of Mao Zedong and Sun Yat-sen as representatives of the Chinese Revolution were to remain prominent but were to be separated both from one another and the gallery of the founding fathers of Marxism-Leninism. During the parade, the portraits of other foreign and Chinese politicians were to be shown as well, including Liu Shaoqi, Zhou Enlai, Zhu De, and Chen Yun.[43]

On 27 April, a complementary directive interdicted the display of any kind of portrait on Labor Day, either at the meeting place itself or as portraits carried by the crowd. Only in places such as Tiananmen Square, where portraits had already been put in place a few days earlier, were they to be kept during the festivities in order not to confuse the public.[44] Again the demand for clarification from provincial and local party committees was enormous. As the symbolic display of power was by no means an arrangement to be taken lightly, various petitions and

---

[41] "Hebei shengwei qingshi guoqingjie taixiang shunxu wenti" [Hebei Provincial Committee Instruction Concerning the Order of Portraits on National Day], 30 August 1955, HPA 855-3-787.

[42] "Zhongyang guanyu 1956 nian 'wu yi' jie xuanchuan neirong he jinian banfa de tongzhi" [CCP Center Notice Concerning the Propagation and Commemoration of May Day 1956], 13 April 1956, HPA 855-9-3983.

[43] "Zhongyang guanyu jinian 'wu yi' jie huichang gua xiang he youxing shi na xiang banfa de tongzhi" [CCP Center Notice Concerning the Display of Portraits in the Assembly Hall and the Carrying of Portraits during the Parade Commemorating "May Day"], 18 April 1956, HPA 855-9-3983.

[44] "Zhongyang guanyu 'wu yi' jie gua xiang de buchong tongzhi" [CCP Center Additional Notice Concerning the Display of Portraits on "May Day"], 27 April 1956, HPA 855-9-3983.

questions were sent to the party leadership asking for new regulations. On 25 June, the CCP Center therefore announced:

1. From today on, there will be no uniform rule regarding the display of portraits in institutions (including party, government, and people's organizations) or in public places. Whether or not to display portraits and whose portrait to display should be decided individually by the local authorities according to local conditions.
2. As for the problem of displaying portraits during activities connected to foreign policy, a separate decision will be made by the Ministry of Foreign Affairs according to local conditions.[45]

Never had the former meticulous arrangement of portraits been so liberalized. Although the directive was not to be interpreted as a call to exchange Mao's pictures with capitalist leaders' portraits, it loosened the former extremely tight regulations. The extent to which the CCP Center decided to liberalize its control over the symbolic display of power in 1956 has often been severely underestimated. Yet liberalization became obvious in the attitude toward the regulation of the state media in general. A case in point is the reduction of party supervision of the *People's Daily*.[46] On 1 August, the CCP Center approved of the circulation of a self-critical report drafted on 20 June 1956 and submitted by the editorial staff of the *People's Daily*.[47] Circulated as Central Document *Zhongfa* [56] 124, the report stated that the *People's Daily* had so far been regarded solely as the paper of the party and therefore neglected the views of the masses. Representing the official view "in every word and sentence"[48] was not only deemed to be impossible but to carry a negative influence on party politics as well.

The circular explicitly encouraged the printing of articles with opinions contrary to the official view and called upon provincial and district newspapers to pay more attention to local politics in their coverage. The report revealed statistical data on staff, organization, circulation numbers, and readership of the *People's Daily* that up to that date had been kept as a

---

[45] "Zhongyang guanyu gua xiang wenti de tongzhi" [CCP Center Notice Concerning the Question of Displaying Portraits], 25 June 1956, HPA 855-9-3983.

[46] For a valuable account of the situation at the *People's Daily* in mid-1956 and the role played by editor-in-chief Deng Tuo, see Timothy Cheek, *Propaganda and Culture in Mao's China: Deng Tuo and the Intelligentsia*, Oxford: Oxford University Press, 1998, 145–8.

[47] "Zhongfa [56] 124, Zhonggong zhongyang pizhuan Renmin ribao bianji weiyuanhui xiang zhongyang de baogao" [Report of the Editorial Board of the *People's Daily* to the Center Approved and Transmitted by the CCP Center], 1 August 1956, HPA 855-9-3983.

[48] Ibid., 1.

state secret.⁴⁹ In May 1956, a total of 879,000 copies had been printed, of which less than 1 percent (6,800 copies) were sent abroad, mostly to the Soviet Union.⁵⁰ The report further listed the news items that the readership was especially fond of, according to the opinions expressed in letters to the editor. In May 1956, the average number of letters received by the editors had been roughly eight hundred a day. According to this feedback, the readership especially liked well-written editorials, critical reports about model units, and reports relying on actual work experiences, short stories, and comics, whereas standard formulae about party meetings, highly complex reports stemming from the party administration, and mere statistical reproductions of articles published by the Telegraph Agency of the Soviet Union (TASS) were held in low regard. The internal report concluded by offering information on major foreign papers. These included the *Times* (London), the *New York Times*, the Japanese *Asahi Shimbun*, and the French Communist Party's newspaper *L'Humanité*, all of which were presented as models for the Chinese press to learn from.

Given the general trend of liberalization, the issue of the cult became a frequently debated subject in local and provincial newspapers. The China Youth Publishing House edited short booklets for educational purposes on the dangers of the personality cults, with print runs of one hundred thousand copies each.⁵¹ In the party newspapers, the cult featured prominently, with some seventy articles mentioning the subject in the *People's Daily* in 1956 and about twenty in the newly founded *Liberation Army News*. Most of these articles were translations of how the CPSU and other communist parties had dealt with the consequences of the cult. But among the articles were a few which reflected upon the Chinese consequences in particular. On 3 July 1956, the *People's Daily* published a short article on its last page entitled "On Independent Thinking."⁵² It pointed out two principal dangers of independent thinking, both of which were closely linked to the means of education: dogmatism and the cult of the individual. It linked dogmatism to the traditional style of education through emulating classical works, denying any validity to new thoughts. Although this was a thinly veiled critique against blindly following the experiences of the Soviet

⁴⁹ On the difficulties of obtaining any statistical data on the *People's Daily* as a foreign correspondent in the 1960s, see Jacques Marcuse, *The Peking Papers: Leaves from the Notebook of a China Correspondent*, New York: Dutton, 1967, 108ff.
⁵⁰ "Zhongfa [56] 124," 8f.
⁵¹ See, for example, Sun Changxian, *Fandui geren chongbai* [Oppose Personality Cults], Beijing: Renmin chubanshe, 1956.
⁵² Xuan Zhu, "Tan duli sikao" [On Independent Thinking], in *Renmin Ribao*, 3 July 1956, 8.

Union, the second danger dealt with the tendency to mistake "thinking about oneself" with independent thinking. The author pointed out that this trend of thought might lead to the promotion of personality cults around high-ranking leaders and sycophancy among the followers. Although the first danger was said to have been eliminated, the second was implicitly recognized as being more dangerous at that time.

The fact that such criticism could be published in the party's leading newspaper in mid-1956 is a clear indication of the thoroughgoing impact the secret speech had incited in China. The summer and autumn of 1956 witnessed a period of liberalization and opportunity that might have resulted in the creation of a unique communist public sphere. Lu Dingyi, head of the Central Propaganda Department, in a speech on the role of science in the socialist system, advocated the strengthening of intellectual exchange with capitalist countries and proposed to learn from their experiences to advance the development of the Chinese sciences.[53] Chinese scientists should be allowed to attend conferences abroad and to make themselves a name through their intellectual achievements. The political climate seemed favorable for such a turn. However, the Eighth Party Congress in September 1956, which is widely recognized as a congress of moderation, already bore the core for a renewed strengthening of the vanguard role of political leaders, and the staunchest defender of this renewal was none other than the newly elected secretary general, Deng Xiaoping.

In a preliminary outline for the media coverage of the congress, the CCP Center explicitly restricted the printing of congratulatory telegrams, cadre interviews, or other "welcoming news."[54] Furthermore, no photos of individuals were to be published besides the official picture of the old and new members of the Politburo Standing Committee. Liu Shaoqi delivered the political report and made frequent references to "comrade Mao Zedong" instead of using the accustomed "Chairman Mao." Liu did not mention "Mao Zedong Thought" in the report, but stressed the principle of collective leadership instead. According to Liu, the high prestige that Mao Zedong enjoyed as helmsman of the Chinese Revolution derived from the fact that he knew how "to integrate the universal truth of Marxism-Leninism with the actual practice of the Chinese Revolution, but also [... that he] firmly believes in the strength and wisdom of the

---

[53] *Xuanjiao dongtai* [Trends in Propaganda and Education] 20, 26 October 1956, 1–4.
[54] "Zhongfa [56] 133, Zhonggong zhongyang guanyu dang de di ba ci quanguo daibiao dahui xuanchuan baodao gongzuo de tongzhi" [CCP Center Notice Concerning the Propaganda Coverage of the Eighth Party Congress], 3 September 1956, HPA 855-9-3893.

masses, initiates and advocates the mass line in party work, and stead-fastly upholds the party's principles of democracy and collective leadership."[55]

The only speaker to comment on the question of the cult in detail was Deng Xiaoping in his comments on the revision of the party constitution. Deng emphasized the importance of the Twentieth CPSU Congress. It had shown the serious consequences deriving from the deification of leaders, a phenomenon that, owing to its long history, could not be uprooted in a short period of time: "The Twentieth Congress of the CPSU has thrown a searching light on the profound significance of adhering to the principle of collective leadership and of combating the cult of the individual, and this illuminating lesson has produced a tremendous effect not only on the CPSU but also on the communist parties of all other countries throughout the world."[56] The CCP, according to Deng, had already taken appropriate measures against the public glorification of individual leaders. He reminded the audience of a resolution passed at the Second Plenum of the Seventh Party Congress in March 1949, suggested by Mao Zedong himself, which had prohibited the celebration of leaders' birthdays and the naming of streets, towns, and enterprises after individual party leaders: "The Central Committee has always been against sending to the leaders messages of greetings or telegrams reporting successes in work. Likewise, it has been against exaggerating the role of leaders in works of art and literature."[57] Nevertheless, the CCP should remain alert against tendencies toward the worship of individuals given the dangerous and long-standing influence of leader worship.

As a first measure, the congress's delegates adopted the revised consti-tution in which the two references to "Mao Zedong Thought" had been dropped. Instead, the party was to be "guided by Marxism-Leninism [and] Comrade Mao Zedong's works."[58] There is no indication that Mao at this point objected to these changes as it was later alleged during the Cultural Revolution. He had himself on a number of occasions deleted the phrase "Mao Zedong Thought" and replaced it with "Mao Zedong's works" during the early 1950s.[59] He had furthermore voted against the sending of

[55] *Eighth National Congress of the Communist Party of China: Documents*, Beijing: Foreign Languages Press, 1981, 108f.
[56] Ibid., 202.
[57] Ibid., 211.
[58] Ibid., 228.
[59] Zhonggong wenxian yanjiushi (ed.), *Mao Zedong wengao* 4, 238.

gifts and the construction of statues in his name.[60] The omission of the references from the constitution thus did not signal a weakening of Mao's position.[61]

Yet the Politburo, despite the anti-cult rhetoric, failed to provide clear guidelines regarding the occurrence of personality cults. At the congress, Deng Xiaoping even claimed: "Love for the leader is essentially an expression of love for the interests of the party, the class and the people, and not the deification of an individual."[62] The limits of liberalization were posed by critical comments about the CCP leadership as representatives of the mass line, and the comments thus officially sealed the ambiguity of cults in disguise of a dialectic principle. Cults were permissible as long as they served the stability of party rule but were considered harmful if an individual elevated himself above party constraints. The Leninist vanguard party along with Mao Zedong's well-established preeminence in the CCP's governing bodies thus provided the structural foundations for the renewed rise of personal worship that was further aggravated by Mao's appraisal of the international situation in the wake of Khrushchev's secret speech.

---

[60] Zhonggong wenxian yanjiushi (ed.), *Mao Zedong wengao* 1, 362.
[61] See Pang Xianzhi and Jin Chongji, *Mao Zedong zhuan (1949–1976)* [Biography of Mao Zedong, 1949–1976], vol. 1, Beijing: Zhongyang wenxian chubanshe, 2003, 535.
[62] *Eighth National Congress*, 211.

2

The Dual Nature of Commodities

In mid-October 1956, the Central Propaganda Department reorganized its internal documentation of national and international developments for the CCP top leadership. The establishment of a highly regulated public sphere had resulted in the necessity to rely on internal party journals reflecting both international developments and trends within popular opinion.[1] The publication of the Propaganda Department's journal on international affairs, the *Propaganda Work Bulletin* (*Xuanchuan gongzuo tongxun*), was terminated and the relevant news items from now on were integrated into the *Trends in Propaganda and Education* (*Xuanjiao dongtai*) that formerly had been a platform for national developments only. It was to cover important developments "within and outside the party, national and international,"[2] for its readership, ranked provincial secretary or above. The *Trends* were usually published two or three times a week and contained highly diverse items reflecting the input from the provincial and local propaganda departments.

In its issue of 26 October 1956, the *Trends* published a report about the reverberations from the Eighth Congress based on survey data provided by local propaganda departments in the Shanghai and Tianjin municipalities. The general perception of the congress among cadres had been excellent, probably even too good. Commenting on the leadership within the communist movement, cadres had made remarks such as "in the past it's been

---

[1] Published works on the nature of popular opinion reports in the early People's Republic are scarce so far. For a stimulating collection of essays on the experiences of other dictatorships, see Paul Corner (ed.), *Popular Opinion in Totalitarian Regimes: Fascism, Nazism, Communism*, Oxford: Oxford University Press, 2009.

[2] *Xuanjiao dongtai* 20, 1.

with Stalin as principal, from now on it should be with Chairman Mao as principal."[3] Critical comments had been made about handling the question of the personality cult. Deng Xiaoping, in his political report, had claimed that the CCP had opposed leader cults throughout. This was deemed incorrect since every large meeting still sent a "gratulatory telegram" (*zhijing dian*) to Mao Zedong, not because of the CCP Chairman's vanity but owing to requests of local leaders eager to demonstrate their allegiance. The *Trends* quoted CCP members who claimed it would have been sufficient to admit that "in the past this kind of wrong thinking existed, but now it has already been changed."[4]

At the same time, the reverberations of Khrushchev's secret speech within the international communist movement became visible. Demands for greater autonomy from Moscow resulted in upheavals in Poland and shortly afterward in Hungary. The Chinese position toward both countries varied considerably.[5] The newly chosen Gomulka government in Poland was perceived as loyal to the communist cause and its goal of searching for a national way of building socialism was a viewpoint the CCP had argued for ever since the Comintern days. Upon hearing of Moscow's plans to intervene by military means in Poland, China's leadership reacted swiftly. Mao on 20 October 1956 summoned the startled Soviet ambassador, Pavel Yudin, to his bedroom and made him relay to Khrushchev the Chinese disapproval of the Soviet measures. He further was to hint at the possibility of Chinese assistance to Poland in case of armed conflict.[6] During an enlarged Politburo meeting the same afternoon, Mao Zedong, after having received a Soviet report that indicated the possible use of force, strongly opposed Soviet "big power chauvinism" and upon Soviet invitation sent a Chinese delegation, headed by Liu Shaoqi and Deng Xiaoping, to circumvent the danger of armed conflict by means of shuttle diplomacy.

The situation in Poland was settled without the use of military force, but Gomulka's example had stimulated demands for greater autonomy in Hungary. The resistance of the regime under the leadership of Ernö Gerö to any kind of liberalization led to conflicts in Budapest and the unofficial replacement of Gerö with Imre Nagi on 23 October. Under the direction of Soviet Politburo member Anastas Mikoyan, the Hungarian Workers'

[3] Ibid., 4.
[4] Ibid., 6.
[5] See Lorenz M. Lüthi, *The Sino–Soviet Split: Cold War in the Communist World*, Princeton, NJ: Princeton University Press, 2008, 54ff.
[6] Wu, *Shinian lunzhan 1*, 39.

Party chose János Kádár as official successor the following day and ordered the military's suppression of the growing wave of strikes and demonstrations. The Chinese leadership perceived a fundamental difference between the developments in Poland and Hungary. In the case of Poland, the modification of socialism according to national conditions was seen as justified. The Hungarian uprising, however, was perceived as an attempt at capitalist resurrection, triggered by intellectuals such as the "Petöfi Circle" with the assistance of Western espionage agents and the media. The CCP Center therefore called upon its emissaries in Moscow to opt for continuing military influence of the Soviet Union in Hungary.

The events in Eastern Europe and the simultaneous Suez crisis caused Mao Zedong to reevaluate his views on the Twentieth CPSU Congress. Khrushchev's speech had not only led communist parties to destroy blind faith in the Soviet Union in search for their own way of building socialism but it had also fueled a worldwide trend of criticism. This trend had to be opposed by analyzing the changes that had occurred within the international communist movement in the light of recent developments. Wu Lengxi was ordered to supervise a two-volume collection of all statements or articles from other communist parties pertaining to the problems raised in the secret speech. The CCP leadership was to gain an overview about the most pressing questions that needed to be answered. Special notice was given to Josip Tito's scathing critique of the Soviet handling of the Hungarian uprising and Stalinism in general, which he had delivered in Pula on 11 November 1956 while the CCP was holding the Second Plenum of the Eighth Congress. Mao demanded a full translation of the speech besides the press reports he had received in the Xinhua News Agency's internal *Reference Materials (Cankao ziliao)*, a large-scale collection of all relevant items from internal and foreign observers edited twice daily by the Xinhua News Agency for the party's top leadership only. The reports derived from the large web of Xinhua correspondents who provided the leadership not only with official news items but also with intelligence on popular opinion.[7] During the plenum, the change in Mao's perception of the general situation became more pronounced. He characterized Lenin and Stalin as the two swords of socialism, the latter of which had already

---

[7] "Zhonggong zhongyang guanyu Xinhuashe jizhe caixie Neibu cankao ziliao de guiding" [CCP Center Regulations Concerning the Employment of New China News Agency Journalists for Internal Reference Coverage], July 1953, in Zhongyang xuanchuanbu bangongting (ed.), *Dang de xuanchuan gongzuo wenjian xuanbian* (DXG) [Selection of Documents on Party Propaganda Work], vol. 1 (1949–66), Beijing: Zhonggong zhongyang dangxiao chubanshe, 1994, 138.

been discarded by Khrushchev. Given the recent developments in Eastern Europe, he sensed a fundamental danger for all communist states that the other sword, Leninism and the Leninist party organization, was about to be discarded as well.

Public discussions in the meantime dealt with similar questions. A lengthy report in the *Trends in Propaganda and Education*, relying on intelligence gathered by the Beijing Party Committee, mentioned more than fifty different opinions among cadres, intellectuals, workers, and students concerning the events in Poland and Hungary. The party media had in conformity with the TASS articles branded the upheaval as a "reactionary riot," but some observers had asked: "If its nature has been reactionary, why did so many people join in the protests?"[8] According to the internal intelligence, the nature of the conflict remained unclear, but simplistic explanations blaming imperialist traitors or spies were rejected as unsatisfactory. Few people claimed that the Soviet intervention had been a necessity; rather, bewilderment about the developments after Stalin's death was mentioned. "How come that as soon as Stalin is dead, so many accidents happen one after another, just like having released all air from a car's wheels?"[9]

The *Trends* further mentioned the influence of the Twentieth Congress as a source of the upheaval because it had enabled democratic organizations to raise their heads again and possibly led to a mistaken evaluation of government leaders. "Opposing the cult of personality," according to one cadre, had become "a bit overheated."[10] The most frequently expressed criticism, however, was directed against the coverage of the events in the Chinese media. The lack of reports preceding the events had made them seemingly appear out of thin air. As no official explanations about the developments were provided, individuals sent letters to the Central Propaganda Department and other CCP institutions to demand a more detailed and rather objective coverage of the current events. "Khrushchev's report at the Twentieth CPSU Congress concerning the question of Stalin has been made public in capitalist countries, while quite a number of [Chinese] cadres and party members still don't know [what he said].[11]

---

[8] *Xuanjiao Dongtai* 25, 4 November 1956, 1.
[9] *Xuanjiao Dongtai* 26, 7 November 1956, 3.
[10] *Xuanjiao Dongtai* 25, 2.
[11] Ibid., 5. See further *Xianjiao dongtai*: 26, 40. A week later, members of an unidentified Christian church in China interpreted the recent developments in Eastern Europe and the French–Anglo invasion in Suez as indicators of the approaching Armageddon; see *Xianjiao dongtai*, 11 November 1956, 28.

Criticism of the CCP remained the exception. The intelligence reports by early November 1956 instead revealed a differentiation between the socialist regimes in Eastern Europe that had been imposed from above after World War II and the specific Chinese situation where CCP rule had been the result of a successful fight against the Japanese invaders and the Guomindang. There are only a few cases mentioned in the *Trends* that reveal an immediate correspondence to the Hungarian upheaval.[12] In most reports, the Hungarian crisis was employed to remind the CCP leadership of the need to improve the people's material conditions, such as food supply, housing, and wages, without calling for an overthrow of the present system.[13] Generally speaking, by late 1956 the internal intelligence available to the CCP top leadership offered no indication that fundamental dissent or cleavages existed among the masses. Quite to the contrary, the reports could serve to augment viewpoints calling for a liberalization of the public sphere, as the CCP could obviously count on broad public support.

MORE ON THE HISTORICAL EXPERIENCE OF THE DICTATORSHIP OF THE PROLETARIAT

In a series of consecutive Politburo meetings from 25 November 1956 onward, the CCP Politburo discussed recent trends within the communist movement. Most of the meetings were held in Mao's private bedroom in the Fengzeyuan compound in Zhongnanhai. Three members of the Politburo did not take part, or only seldom took part, in the discussions. Owing to his advanced age, Red Army veteran Zhu De did not attend the meetings, which, to accommodate Mao's irregular sleeping habits, were convened until late in the night. Chen Yun and Lin Biao did not attend the meetings either, Chen because of his focus on economic issues, and Lin owing to a peculiar long-term illness. Even the formal arrangement of the meetings imposed restrictions on a critical assessment of personality cults, as the remembrances of Wu Lengxi reveal:

> When the meetings were convened in Mao's bedroom, Mao often wore his pajamas, half leaning on the head of the bed and half lying on it. The rest of the Politburo Standing Committee members formed a half-circle around the bed. Usually Comrade Xiaoping would sit on the right end of the bedside, near Mao's tea table, as he was a little hard of hearing; he thus sat close to hear the Chairman speaking. The others, from right to

---

[12] *Xuanjiao dongtai* 25, 6.
[13] *Xuanjiao dongtai* 29, 15 November 1956, 4.

left, normally were: Peng Zhen, Shaoqi, the Premier, Wang Jiaxiang, Zhang Wentian, Chen Boda, Hu Qiaomu, and me sitting on the left edge near the small book table at the foot of Mao's bed.[14]

During the four Politburo sessions convened in late November 1956, the questions of how to achieve socialism, the role of Stalin, and a differentiation of the contradictions in present world affairs were debated. Mao emphatically claimed that Stalin's policies had generally been sound. Although Stalin's faults, such as disrupting parts of the legal system and the constitution but "not all of it,"[15] were to be criticized, the dictatorship of the proletariat was to be exempted. Attempts to weaken communist party rule or to question the superiority of the communist system as in Hungary should be swiftly circumvented and, if necessary, suppressed.

The situation thus differed considerably from that of the immediate aftermath of the secret speech and called for a new official appraisal to provide guidance for CCP members. Mao again opted for an editorial. This time, Hu Qiaomu was to prepare a first outline.[16] Hu finished his task within three days, and after a discussion with Wu Lengxi and Mao's secretary Tian Jiaying on 3 December 1956, he prepared the first draft of the article. Mao was closely involved in the process of editing the draft and advised Hu even in terms of rhetorical strategy. Since criticism of Stalin was currently overwhelming, the article was to assess Stalin's faults first and to discuss his achievements toward the end. Otherwise, it would be unacceptable to most foreign readers at that time. The article was to make clear that Khrushchev's criticism had given rise to a wave of right-wing revisionism trying to denigrate the achievements of the October Revolution. This criticism had not only blasted the image of Stalin as omniscient leader of the communist movement, but also endangered the crucial role of Leninism for the stability of the communist system. The Politburo discussions about the article continued through another six sessions until the end of the month, with Mao setting the agenda. Finally, on 27 December, the last corrections were made to the draft. Mao proofread every single page before finally announcing it ready for print on 28 December at 9 A.M. The article was made public via the Xinhua News

---

[14] Wu, *Yi Mao zhuxi*, 17.

[15] Ibid., 19.

[16] Wu Lengxi, "Tong Jiaying gongshi de rizi" [Days of Working Together with Comrade Jiaying], in Dong Bian, Zhang Deshan, and Zeng Zi (eds.), *Mao Zedong he ta de mishu Tian Jiaying* [Mao Zedong and his Secretary Tian Jiaying], Beijing: Zhongyang wenxian chubanshe, 1996, 117.

Agency the same evening and appeared in print in the *People's Daily* the following morning.

The editorial was considerably longer than its predecessor and set out to explore four major topics: the political situation of the Soviet Union, the role of Stalin, the dangers of dogmatism and revisionism, and the need for maintaining unity among all communist parties. All of the arguments were closely linked. By proving the general line of the CPSU to be basically correct, the editorial had to explain Stalin's mistakes without discrediting the Soviet Union or socialism as a whole. The editorial thus set out to claim that the mistakes Stalin had committed in his later years were no indication of the Soviet system being outmoded, as it had been argued in the Western media. Quite the contrary, the mistakes had been committed despite the correctness of the system: "No system, however excellent, is in itself a guarantee against serious mistakes in our work. ... [E]ven under a good system it is still possible for people to commit serious mistakes and to use a good state apparatus to do evil things."[17]

Stalin's blind faith in his personal wisdom was criticized, but in general terms his achievements were said to outweigh his shortcomings. Attacks on "so-called Stalinism" or "Stalinist elements," as recently made by Tito, should therefore be interpreted as referring back to communism and Marxism-Leninism itself. The change in outlook between the arguments presented in the April and December editorials becomes most obvious in the section on dogmatism and revisionism. Dogmatism had previously been defined as blindly following Soviet experiences and been named the gravest fault of the CCP. It now came to play a much smaller role. Differences among the national applications of socialism according to given circumstances were still claimed to be necessary in order to build powerful party-states, but these differences should not justify an attack on the universal truths of Marxism-Leninism itself on the pretext of criticizing dogmatism. Yet this had precisely been the effect of Khrushchev's speech: "Because Stalin and the former leaders in some other socialist countries committed the serious mistake of violating socialist democracy, some unstable people in the communist ranks, on the pretext of developing socialist democracy, attempt to weaken or renounce the dictatorship of the proletariat, the principles of democratic centralism of the socialist state, and the leading role of the Party."[18] The dictatorship of the proletariat

---

[17] Editorial Department of the *People's Daily*, *More on the Historical Experience of the Dictatorship of the Proletariat*, Beijing: Foreign Languages Press, 1959, 35f.

[18] Ibid., 47f.

should not be confused with Western democratic models or the dictatorship of the bourgeoisie. The concentration of power at the top was deemed necessary in order to fight against the enemies of communism and to eradicate counterrevolutionary remnants. "If there is a kind of democracy that can be used for anti-socialist purposes and for weakening the cause of socialism, it certainly cannot be called socialist democracy."[19] The communist countries should stand united against the danger of frictions deriving from a misuse of the attacks against Stalin and dogmatism.

While the article as such presented a much more sophisticated argument regarding the present situation and the role of Stalin, the "cult of the individual" no longer appeared as part of the explanation.[20] Structural deficits of the system were played down in favor of a primarily psychological explanation that emphasized Stalin's personality. The danger of a split within the communist movement owing to the inept handling of Stalin's heritage came to assume primary importance. Collective leadership and democratic centralism were to provide a safeguard against the rise of similar phenomena in China. The reactions from lower-level party members to the secret speech, however, had proven that cult building did not solely derive from the aberrational psyche of the supreme leader but that the cult perpetuated itself through the fostering of charismatic relationships within the party apparatus and the specific mode of party rectification the CCP had come to rely on since the Yan'an days. The prior elevation of Mao Zedong and his works as a means to fight off inner-party contenders for power now proved to be a major obstacle in overcoming the defects associated with the cult of the individual.

CONTRADICTIONS AMONG THE PEOPLE AND WITHIN THE PARTY

Although the internal intelligence reports did not give the CCP reason to fear an immediate loss of power, retaining tight organizational and ideological control proved to be difficult owing to the large increase in numbers of the CCP membership. By June 1956, membership had

---

[19] Ibid., 49.

[20] Kang Sheng, in an internal meeting in March 1957, pointed out this crucial difference: "'On the Historical Experience' and 'More on the Historical Experience' are basically the same. But there is one major difference, the first mentions the problem of opposing the cult of the individual, the second does not invoke that phrase." Li Xuekun and Zhang Peihang, "Dangnei geren chongbai de lishi kaocha. Jian bo Kang Sheng de zaoshen miulun" [Historical Exploration of Inner-Party Personal Worship, Refuting Kang Sheng's Absurd God-building Theory], in *Dangshi yanjiu* 2 (1981), 23.

surpassed 9 million. The common way of fostering a united ruling stratum had been rectification campaigns, the organized group study of canonical texts. Rectification had been a regular part of party life in the early years of the People's Republic.[21] Thus it was not uncommon that in commemoration of the upcoming fifteenth anniversary of the Yan'an Rectification campaign the CCP Center on 17 June 1956 circulated a document concerning the renewed need to fight subjectivism and dogmatism within the party.[22] The document, approved of by Liu Shaoqi personally, heralded the Yan'an campaign as a glorious achievement that had managed to establish a link between the universal truths of Marxism-Leninism and Chinese practice. Unlike during the original campaign, the document not even once referred to the influence of Mao Zedong, who previously had been praised as the symbol and mastermind behind the Sinification of Marxism.[23] Just like the contemporary instructions on the placement of leader imagery or the media coverage of the Eighth Party Congress, toning down the leader cult remained a prevailing issue in 1956 and took place within a general climate of media liberalization.

Demands calling for a liberalization of the media had been strongly voiced in China in the aftermath of the Twentieth CPSU Congress, and the complaints had been relayed to the CCP leadership through the internal intelligence reports. Given the leadership's impression that CCP rule enjoyed popular support, Mao had opted for a relaxation of the regulations governing the strictly controlled public sphere and even allowed for critical viewpoints to be published in the party media. In August 1956, along with the aforementioned internal circular in which the *People's Daily's* editorial staff offered a self-criticism for having failed to incorporate the wishes of the readership, the CCP encouraged the individual subscription of newspapers instead of the former workunit (*danwei*)-based regulation. This caused significant changes within the media landscape. The previous ratio between workunit and private subscription of newspapers had been 4:1. Within two months, the ratio nearly reached equilibrium.[24] This change also became visible with regard to circulation

---

[21] Compare Frederick C. Teiwes, *Politics and Purges in China: Rectification and the Decline of Party Norms, 1950–1965*, Armonk, NY: M. E. Sharpe, 1979.

[22] "Zhongyang guanyu xuexi 'Gaizao women de xuexi' deng wu ge wenjian de tongzhi" [CCP Center Notice Concerning the Study of "Reform our Study" and Five Other Documents], 17 June 1956, HPA 855-9-3983.

[23] Raymond F. Wylie, "Mao Tse-tung, Ch'en Po-ta and the 'Sinification of Marxism,' 1936–38," in *China Quarterly* 79 (1979), 447–80.

[24] *Xuanjiao dongtai* 21, 30 October 1956, 7.

numbers. A survey of the forty-one most important central and provincial newspapers revealed that circulation had risen by only 1.9 percent between August and October 1956, from 4,417,074 to 4,502,257 copies, but there had been relative changes. While the *People's Daily* had remained nearly constant with about 800,000 copies, the *Guangming Daily*, a paper mainly directed at intellectuals, had gained 31.4 percent in two months. Similar gains of market share were reported from papers directed at a young readership, such as the *China Youth Daily* with an increase of 28 percent; simultaneously, most worker and peasant newspapers experienced a disproportionate decline. The most dramatic decline had been experienced by the *Sino–Soviet Friendship Paper*, which lost 23.4 percent of its former 153,315 subscribers in just three months. A pronounced liberalization of the media was thus clearly noticeable and affected the formerly cemented structures of the media landscape. Critical comments against party policies or against individual leaders, however, remained the exception.

Another liberalizing move taken by the CCP shortly afterward was to widen the scope of persons entitled to read the Xinhua News Agency's internal publication *Reference Information (Cankao xiaoxi)*, which carried items from capitalist news agencies. As the articles featured by *Reference Information* were often considered to be blatantly wrong, there was no way of placing them in the regular party media. An official party directive issued on 18 December 1956 highlighted that cadres down to the county level should be able to assess critically the speciousness of the capitalist viewpoints themselves. The reason for widening the scope of the readership rested with the CCP's positive assessment of the present situation and the increase in political awareness among intellectuals and cadres.[25] The nature of the articles was to range from "reactionary" to "progressive" and was to be confined to news and commentaries to guarantee minimal overlap with the public media. Not to be included were items with "extremely negative"[26] content or materials that might

---

[25] "Zhonggong zhongyang guanyu kuoda 'Cankao xiaoxi' dingyue fanwei de tongzhi" [CCP Center Notice on Extending the Range of Subscribers to "Reference Information"], 18 December 1956, in ZGXG 3, 1198.

[26] "Zhongyang xuanchuanbu dui Xinhua tongxunshe guanyu 'Cankao xiaoxi' gaiban kuoda faxing hou bianji fangzhen de yijian de pifu" [Response of the Central Propaganda Department to the New China News Agency's Opinion Concerning the Editorial Guidelines after the Changes and Widening of Circulation of "Reference Information"], 12 March 1957, in ZGXG 4, 17ff.

give rise to "rumors."[27] On 16 January 1957, the Central Propaganda Department circulated complementary directions from the Xinhua News Agency in order to specify the concrete procedures.[28] As the only way to obtain *Reference Information* was via mail subscription, the local party committees were to select the local institutions that were to be added to the circulation list. Yet although the reach of the paper was to be broadened considerably, local committees had to take precautions to ensure that the newly added institutions complied with the prescriptions of the CCP Center and did not make the contents available to the general public.

The most important stimulus for a liberalization of the public sphere was provided by Mao's famous speech "On the Correct Handling of Contradictions among the People," which he delivered before an enlarged Supreme State Conference meeting on 27 February 1957.[29] The speech drew together several threads Mao had been pondering since Khrushchev's secret speech and mirrored a significant change in outlook. Mao set out to explain why, even after a successful socialist revolution and the extermination of most enemies, opposition to party policies remained. Mao proposed to differentiate between "antagonistic" contradictions between friend and foe, and "non-antagonistic" contradictions among the people. Although antagonistic relations tended to disappear in a socialist society with the extinguishing of its enemies, non-antagonistic contradictions remained, owing to one main reason: the continuing differences between the slow-changing superstructure and the economic base. Mao pointed at phenomena rooted in feudal and capitalist ideology such as the accumulation of wealth, as well as problems arising from the process of socialist transformation. Here the formation of new privileged strata such as the economic experts or possibly even the CCP itself could be perceived. The nature of the contradiction thus had to be clearly determined in order to understand the present situation. The Hungarian uprising, for example,

---

[27] "Zhongyang pizhuan zhongyang xuanchuanbu guanyu jin yi bu kuoda 'Cankao xiaoxi' yuedu fanwei de baogao" [Central Propaganda Department Report Commenting on and Circulated by the CCP Center Concerning the Further Widening of "Reference Information's" Scope of Readership], 10 October 1958, in ZGXG 4, 119f.

[28] See "Zhongyang xuanchuanbu pizhuan Xinhuashe guanyu kuoda Cankao xiaoxi faxing fanwei de jidian buchong yijian" [Additional Opinions of the New China News Agency Circulated and Commented on by the Central Propaganda Department Concerning the Widening of Reference Information's Scope of Distribution], 16 January 1957, HPA 855-4-1045.

[29] For a translation of Mao's speaking notes, as opposed to the highly edited print version published by the *People's Daily*, see MacFarquhar, Cheek, and Wu (eds.), *Secret Speeches of Chairman Mao*, 131–80.

had been characterized by antagonistic contradictions between a small number of counterrevolutionaries aided by foreign intelligence and the socialist system supported by the broad masses. The riots had been fomented to overthrow the system. Recent criticism and strikes that had occurred in China should not be treated the same way. Although they mirrored strands of capitalist ideology – that is, a supreme interest in material gains – the main thrust, according to Mao, had been directed against bureaucratism and thus was clearly of a non-antagonistic nature. Therefore, no military suppression of these contradictions among the people was to take place. The only way to overcome the gap between the prevailing capitalist mentalities and the economic reality rested in continuing persuasion and education, or, rather, intellectual education and "remolding," a phrase he mockingly compared with the American "brainwashing": "Some people become afraid as soon as they hear the word remolding. We have such people. This thing, remolding, the Americans call it brainwashing. We call [it] remolding. I think the Americans are the real brainwashers, Americans can really do a good job of washing [brains]. We here are a bit more civilized."[30]

In Mao's opinion, Stalin's failure to distinguish between antagonistic and non-antagonistic contradictions had been his greatest fault. After having secured his power, Stalin thus had no longer adhered to the basic principles of dialectics as laid out by Lenin[31] and instead implemented a rule by fiat and dogmatic one-sidedness. He had proposed a static and "metaphysical" view on social developments, resulting in a biased perception of contradictions, thus proving himself to be "30% bourgeois, 70% Marxist."[32] Not only Stalin had failed to grasp the importance of dialectics, the same could be said with regard to his successors and their treatment of the Stalin question or recent events such as the Hungarian uprising:

> Do you think the Hungarian Incident was good or bad? I say [it] was both good and bad. Of course it was bad, since they had disturbances. But Hungary did one very good thing; the counterrevolutionaries really helped us. Since the end of the Hungarian Incident, things have become more secure than before. Hungary now is better than the Hungary of the past when there were no disturbances – all in the socialist camp have learned [from Hungary's experience]. Thus I say the Hungarian Incident

---

[30] Ibid., 155.
[31] Vladimir I. Lenin, "On the Question of Dialectics (1915)," in *Collected Works*, vol. 38, Moscow: Progress, 1972, 355–64.
[32] MacFarquhar, Cheek, and Wu (eds.), *Secret Speeches*, 173.

has a dual character, both good and bad. An anti-Soviet, anti-communist current has arisen in the world. ... How do we look on it? Naturally, I think it's not good. Secondly, [it] is good; this is a good thing. Because imperialist anti-Sovietism and anti-communism steels the Communist Party. ... How should we look on the criticism of Stalin? We [humans] are also commodities of dual character. The criticism of Stalin has a two-sided nature. One side has real benefit, one is not good. To expose the cult of Stalin, to tear off the lid, to liberate people, this is a liberation movement; but his [i.e., Khrushchev's] method of exposing [Stalin] is incorrect; [he] hasn't made a good analysis, clubbing [him] to death with a single blow. On the one hand, this provoked the Hungarian and Polish incidents. But he [Stalin] had his incorrect side.[33]

Mao's idea of a "dual nature of commodities," which even included humans as symbols of a certain movement, was no genuine scientific concept derived from Marxist theory. It rather shifted the focus of attention to the differentiation between theoretical concepts and the political exploitability of historical events. By anticipating the aspect of international and domestic reaction, Mao's idea enabled political manipulation to come to the fore. From here it was only a small step to interpret the "cult of personality" as a commodity of dual character itself, which could become useful not only as a medium of integrating the party but as well as a way of charismatic mobilization to circumvent party institutions by appealing to the masses directly. What made the original version of the speech so exceptional was the fact that Mao did not exempt party members from the accusation of harboring feudal or capitalist thoughts, especially on economic issues. Mao therefore stressed the necessity of letting different views, "flagrant flowers and poisonous weeds,"[34] be voiced publicly in order to ferret out correct perceptions from incorrect ones. The need to harvest the poisonous weeds would arise once in a while, but only by the endless dialectical process of criticism and temporary unity would Marxism be able to advance further.

What distinguished Mao from his colleagues was his hatred of bureaucratic routines and the danger he perceived to arise from privileged strata. He thus envisioned that non-party members should take an active public role in determining the correct path to communism and that rectification of CCP members should not be restricted to internal party institutions. Provincial and local party committees therefore faced difficult situations as they struggled to make sense of Mao's speeches of 27 February and a

---

[33] Ibid., 177f.
[34] Ibid., 170.

follow-up on 12 March before the CCP's National Conference on Propaganda Work with a similar emphasis on allowing critical opinions to be voiced in the public sphere. Without the detailed announcements that usually meticulously defined the timing and scope of the campaigns, anticipating the next step became guesswork. Although many high-ranking cadres had been witness to Mao's speech, no official print version had been distributed and the state media did not disclose further information either.[35]

The Hebei Party Committee convened a Provincial Propaganda Conference in mid-April, in order to sum up and clarify the most pressing issues that had arisen since Mao's speech. The discussions revealed a complete disagreement over the effective meaning of the speech and the scope of applying it in day-to-day politics. Most questions that were brought up by the conference's participants dealt with the nature of antagonistic and non-antagonistic contradictions. How was the main contradiction within the superstructure to be defined properly after socialism had by and large been achieved? Was it the contradiction between socialism and capitalism, between advanced and backward elements within society, or rather the contradiction between the objective circumstances and the subjective consciousness?[36]

Most cadres had welcomed the distinction between antagonistic and non-antagonistic contradictions, but applying the distinction according to local conditions proved to be nearly impossible. A large number of rural cadres reported the recent growth of contradictions owing to shortages of grain. A cadre from Feng County in Hebei reported eighty-nine cases of violent clashes between rural cadres and brigade members within the last three months alone. Sharp contradictions had further arisen over the question of the treatment of prisoners. Since prisoners were legally entitled to get 63 pounds of food per month, a number of people had purposely violated the law "because in detainment one still eats better than at home."[37] But what kind of contradiction did this imply? The questions

---

[35] Mao later was to criticize the *People's Daily* heavily for not having complied with his wishes to immediately publish his 12 March speech; see Wu, *Yi Mao zhuxi*, 41f. On the much more complicated reasons for the delay and Deng Tuo's role as scapegoat, see Cheek, *Propaganda and Culture*, 177–82.

[36] "Zhonggong Hebei shengwei bangongting you guan sixiang gongzuo de yixie wenti de huiji" [Recollections of the Hebei Provincial Party Committee Office Concerning a Few Problems in Ideological Work], 14 April 1957, HPA 864-1-187.

[37] Zhonggong Hebei shengwei bangongting, "Quansheng xuanchuan gongzuo huiyi fenzu taolun de wenti huiji 1" [Recollections of Problems Discussed in Subgroups at the Provincial Propaganda Work Meeting 1], 16 April 1957, HPA 864-1-187.

of how and where to let people "bloom" or "contend," as Mao had termed his policies referring to the classical expression to "let a hundred flowers bloom and a hundred schools of thought contend," remained highly unclear. The same applied to the question of who was to lead the movement. Or, as a local report from the Hebei Provincial Committee put it, "Chairman Mao's remark about leading and at the same time not leading is a very dialectic expression, and very profound as well, but in the concrete situation of a unit, three possible scenarios may occur: the party takes the lead, people outside the party take the lead, or no one assumes leadership."[38]

When the Rectification campaign, commonly known as the "Hundred Flowers campaign," finally got under way on a nationwide scale during a five-week period between May and June 1957, the questions regarding how to specify its exact aims and methods remained unanswered. Mao's speech had been made available to the party committees as broadcast, but as the Hebei Provincial Propaganda Department reported, a number of local cadres had not made it public, either because they believed there were "no contradictions within their legislation" or because they feared "if we make it public and the masses know about it, anarchy will result."[39]

The cult of the individual and the international debates were not among the main topics of criticism. In fact, most local discussions did not even mention the issue of the cult. During the end of the fourth week of criticism, part of a translation of Khrushchev's secret speech from the New York *Daily Worker* was posted at Beijing University's Democratic Plaza and stimulated criticism against the party, dogmatism, and the attitude of local cadres pretending to be "born saints."[40] Criticism of high-level cadres or of Mao himself remained the exception, but the bitterness expressed by intellectuals against party leadership and the disadvantages of the socialist system, as well as the mounting tide of institutional havoc in local party cells, caused Mao to change his evaluation regarding the urgency of combating dogmatism and revisionism. In a speech on 25 May 1957 to the Communist Youth League, Mao Zedong emphasized that the Chinese

---

[38] Ibid., 5.
[39] "Zhonggong Hebei shengwei xuanchuanbu guanyu dangqian dangnei wai ganbu yixie sixiang qingkuang xiang shengwei ji zhongyang xuanchuanbu de baogao" [Report of the Hebei Provincial Party Committee Propaganda Department to the Provincial Party Committee and the Central Propaganda Department Concerning the Current Ideological Situation within and outside the Party], 24 May 1957, HPA 864-1-187.
[40] Roderick MacFarquhar, *The Hundred Flowers Campaign and the Chinese Intellectuals*, New York: Praeger, 1960, 93f.

Communist Party remained the core of leadership of all Chinese people: "All words and deeds departing from socialism are completely wrong."[41] Although Mao acknowledged the ongoing danger of dogmatist or simplistic "leftist" standpoints, he now claimed the real danger to consist of efforts of revisionist and capitalist elements to overthrow the party: "Now we should start paying attention to criticize revisionism."[42]

The reasons for the termination of the Hundred Flowers campaign in early June 1957 after only five weeks' time have been the subject of many debates, and understanding this termination is indeed crucial for grasping Chinese political development in the following two decades. Mao Zedong himself defended his policy of blooming and contending against a mounting rise of inner-party critics as a device to "lure snakes out of their holes." Shanghai Party Secretary Ke Qingshi, known for his loyalty to Mao Zedong, even claimed that from now on similar campaigns would be conducted on a regular basis. Most works relying on a totalitarian conception of CCP rule have tended to substantiate this theory as expounded by Mao himself after the actual event and described the Hundred Flowers campaign as just another example of the Chairman's viciousness.[43] The analysis of multilevel inner-party documents, as conducted here, however, leads to a contrary understanding. The Hundred Flowers campaign was only the culmination of a fifteen-month process of liberalization that had started with Khrushchev's secret speech and led to a pronounced stance toward enabling critical discussions in the media. As internal top-level intelligence reports reveal, the CCP leadership in the mid-1950s had no reason to perceive that its rule was widely unpopular, although cleavages based on class background, job status, and residential location existed.[44]

The failure of the Hundred Flowers campaign was mainly due to the incompatibility of its attempt at unspecified party rectification within a bureaucratic system of top-down communication.[45] Previous repression campaigns had cautioned intellectuals, and these restraints could not be easily dismissed by a series of incoherent speeches that were even contradicted by the slow response of party newspapers to relay the messages to a wider audience. Although Mao commanded enough authority to voice

[41] Zhonggong wenxian yanjiushi (ed.), *Mao wengao* 6, 488.
[42] Ibid., 469.
[43] Chang and Halliday, *Mao*, 416ff.
[44] See Elizabeth Perry, "Shanghai's Strike Wave of 1957," in Cheek and Saich (eds.), *New Perspectives*, 234–61.
[45] See, as well, Andreas, "Charismatic Mobilization," 437.

opinions contrary to the established system of bureaucratically instituted communication, his voluntaristic approach to liberalization placed those in responsible offices in a difficult position, as they had to transform his reasoning into political directives without a clear sense of direction, as the local responses reveal. The Hundred Flowers campaign was no preconceived coup to root out counterrevolutionaries but a failed attempt to liberalize the directed public sphere.

THE ANTI-RIGHTIST CAMPAIGN

The failure of the rectification campaign led to a self-generated political crisis of faith in the ability of the CCP's governance, and the responsibility was clearly to be placed on Mao. He thus faced two "credibility gaps":[46] The campaign had tarnished his image as omniscient helmsman of the Chinese Revolution among party members, and the campaign's indecisive enactment led non-party members to question his authority over the CCP. By subduing all sources of resistance, Mao's claim that the Hundred Flowers campaign had been a well-arranged trick to reveal the true identity of counterrevolutionaries and vaguely defined "Rightists," who had managed to slip the net of the CCP cleansing in the early days of the People's Republic, was to be substantiated. The Anti-Rightist campaign set out with demonstrating the antagonistic nature of certain criticism that had broken forth in the previous five weeks. The state media therefore made a point of republishing those comments that had been directed against the CCP and in a few cases even against Mao himself. A number of articles made lengthy quotations from discussions held by representatives of the few formally existing Chinese democratic parties in the preceding weeks. The most critical public account of Mao Zedong had been provided by members of these democratic splinter parties, such as Chen Mingshu, who had publicly attacked Mao's "Bismarckian temper" and "one-sided judgments."[47] It remains questionable, however, whether the reprinting of these verbal assaults should be interpreted as a subtle revenge instigated by cadres such as Peng Zhen and Liu Shaoqi, who had previously opposed Mao's approach of letting noncommunists rectify the party and now saw

[46] MacFarquhar, *Contradictions among the People*, 278.
[47] "Chen Mingshu gongran wumie Mao zhuxi. Minge zhongyang xiaozu yizhi tongchi Chen Mingshu kuangwang wuzhi" [Chen Mingshu Openly Slanders Chairman Mao. The Central Leadership Group of the Revolutionary Committee of the Chinese Guomindang Unanimously Denounces Chen Mingshu's Arrogance and Shamelessness], in *Renmin ribao*, 15 July 1957, 2.

their judgment to have been correct.[48] Red Guard sources indeed reveal a number of harsh remarks that Peng Zhen made about Mao's approach to liberalize the party press. Among the most important is a quote emphasizing Mao's role as a "tool" or rather popular brand symbolizing the CCP:

> Stalin considered himself perpetually and absolutely correct. The result was, that he was seized by the 20th Congress and smashed to smithereens, and in many places in the world his pictures were taken down and even torn up. As one can see, all men make mistakes; what differs is the size and nature of the mistakes. ... The cadres in our party are all tools of the party. The problem is how should a tool like Comrade Mao Tse-tung be *better* used.[49]

Yet the publication of dissenting opinions in the state media was no singular phenomenon born from a personal grudge during a period of disorder. In a circular from 1 August 1957, issued in the name of the CCP Center (and thus increasingly Mao himself), the reprint of assaults on the party, the people, and socialism as a pedagogical means to expose the counterrevolutionary word- or thought-crimes of the bourgeois Rightists was explicitly encouraged.[50] Furthermore, only two weeks before the bulk of articles appeared in the *People's Daily*, Wu Lengxi, upon Mao's request and under his close supervision, had taken up the post as the paper's editor-in-chief. Mao by this time was clearly in charge of propaganda work. Wu's task had been to strengthen the "class character of the news" by conforming to the standpoint that only the CCP represented the interests of the people and therefore was entitled to voice them publicly. Mao clearly pointed out that there was no such thing as objective news coverage: "Capitalist papers publish only items that are beneficial for them, nothing that would be harmful to their interests. ... Khrushchev's secret report accusing Stalin has been covered extensively by the capitalist papers but in our papers not one single character was published."[51] The right to utter criticism from now on again became a question of political standpoint.[52]

---

[48] MacFarquhar, *Contradictions among the People*, 283ff.

[49] Ibid., 270.

[50] Zhongguo renmin jiefangjun guofang daxue dangshi dangjian zhenggong jiaoyanshi (ed.), *Zhonggong dangshi jiaoxue cankao ziliao* [Reference Materials for the Teaching of Party History], vol. 22, Beijing: Guofang daxue chubanshe, 1980, 265.

[51] Wu, *Yi Mao zhuxi*, 36.

[52] "Shi bu shi lichang wenti?" [Is It a Question of Standpoint?], in *Renmin ribao*, 14 June 1957, 1, and "Zai lun lichang wenti" [Discussing the Question of Standpoint Again], in *Renmin ribao*, 29 June 1957, 1.

The failed Rectification campaign led Mao to rephrase his conception of the present situation of contradictions among the people. At the Third Plenum of the Eighth Congress in October 1957, he defined the main contradiction in the People's Republic to be the struggle between the two roads of socialism and capitalism. The struggle against persons having committed crimes against "the party, the people, or socialism" expanded the original timeframe from the expected four weeks to nearly a year. Among the offenders were mostly intellectuals, but the campaign gained force within the CCP as well. On 29 June 1957, the CCP Center estimated that all in all 4,000 Rightists would have to be dealt with. By mid-1959, the official statistics reported more than 460,000 persons who had been persecuted (not including those within the military sector),[53] among them high-ranking party members such as Pan Fusheng, first secretary of Henan province, and Wang Jing, secretary of Liaoning province.[54] The social background was no longer the sole determining factor of whether or not a person could be defined a Rightist, but rather the attitude taken toward the party, the people, and socialism. From now on, the enemy could loom everywhere, hidden within the populace. Only the critical observation of conduct and speech of every individual was to reveal clues about a person's true nature.

Against the background of the crackdown on alleged Rightists and the reassuming of strict control over the media, praises of the party as representative of the people appeared more frequently. A justification for praising the party was provided in a *People's Daily* article. The author analyzed the different meanings certain expressions could assume, depending on the speech context. Under feudal rule, "praising virtue" had referred to the acquiescent and loyal subject of the ruler, singing the praises of his oppressors. Opposition to the status quo therefore had acquired a positive connotation. Under socialism, however, the terms had come to take on the opposite meaning. "Why is this? It is because the standpoint is different.... Now the status quo has been created by the people themselves, it is principally good; moreover now there are numerous things that deserve

---

[53] "Muqian quanguo youpai fenzi de gaizao qingkuang" [Current National Situation of Rightists Undergoing Reform], in Zhongyang gong'anbu (ed.), *Gong'an gongzuo jianbao* 67 [Public Security Work Bulletin], 20 September 1959, 2. Thanks to Michael Schoenhals for providing me with this source.

[54] For the situation in different provinces, see Han Gang, "Zhengfeng yundong he fanyoupai douzheng" [Rectification Movement and Struggle against Rightists], in Guo Dehong, Wang Haiguang, and Han Gang (eds.), *Quzhe tansuo (1956–1966)* [Complicated Explorations (1956–1966)], Chengdu: Sichuan renmin chubanshe, 2004, esp. 170–9.

to be praised."[55] A true communist should still despise the praises publicly accorded to him, as he had to be aware that one had to distinguish between the truly felt praise of the party as the "benefactor" or "savior" of the people and "sugar–coated bombs" of mischievous Rightists.

In October 1957, Mao made his second and last trip abroad, when he traveled to Moscow to take part in the festivities to celebrate the fortieth anniversary of the October Revolution. The question of Stalin was not among the major topics of the ensuing discussions. Mao, in high spirits, followed Khrushchev's announcement of overtaking the United States in steel production within the next fifteen years by claiming the same for China with regard to Great Britain. In his three speeches to the conference, Mao called the Soviet measures against the cult "wise" and made a number of flattering references to Comrade Khrushchev, all of which were deleted in the published version of his speech.[56] Mao's last rhetorical demonstrations of communist bloc unity, however, could not mask the fact that he had become increasingly dissatisfied with both the Soviet handling of the Stalin question and Stalin's concept of socialist development itself with its primary focus on industrialization. Mao instead delved into the search for a uniquely Chinese way of building communism by advocating an economic policy of "leaps," as Lenin had laid it out in his treatise on dialectics, which deeply influenced Mao's own understanding of economic development. It provided Mao with a rationale to do away with the model of the Soviet Union and to experiment with the forces of "self-movement" by revoking the theory of the mass line that had been a hallmark of the Yan'an days. By summing up the experiences of the masses in the economic sphere, the vanguard party was to distinguish the correct path and to boost the morale of the population. The cult of the individual was to play an important part in this increasingly utopian search for a uniquely Chinese path of development.

[55] Ruo Shui, "Lun 'ge gong song de' he 'fandui xianzhuang'" ["On 'Singing the Praises of' and 'Opposing the Status Quo'"], in *Renmin ribao*, 11 July 1957, 5.
[56] Michael Schoenhals, "Mao Zedong: Speeches at the 'Moscow Conference,'" in *Journal of Communist Studies* 2.2 (1986), 110f.

3

Redefining the Cult

The first half of 1958 was a period of constant travel and consecutive conferences for the CCP leadership. In his speeches during this period, Mao repeatedly returned to the topic of dogmatism. He emphasized the necessity to overcome slavish respect for the Soviet model and "experts" in general. Instead of placing supreme attention on the cultivation of heavy industry that had shaped the Chinese understanding of economic development in the early years of the People's Republic, policies were shifted in the direction of agricultural collectivization. By means of instigating a "Great Leap Forward," China was to skip the period of socialism (and capitalism) made possible through the "emancipation of thinking and the destruction of superstition" (*jiefang sixiang, pochu mixin*), one of the most prominent slogans of the Great Leap Forward. The destruction of superstition was to be made possible through the cultivation of a worship of "truth," the nearest approximation of which was defined as Mao Zedong Thought. As this chapter is to show, Mao during the Great Leap postulated a dialectical relationship between leader cults and intellectual emancipation,[1] a distinction that was to give rise to the first public expounding of his cult since the Yan'an days.

In March 1958, the Politburo met in Chengdu, the capital of Sichuan province. In a series of speeches, Mao stressed the priority of spontaneously acquired truth over arduously accumulated knowledge by invoking a pantheon of religious leaders, scientists, and philosophers ranging from Jesus and Buddha to Marx and Darwin. According to Mao's reasoning, they all had made their path-breaking discoveries at an early age, unspoilt

---

[1] Michael Schoenhals, *Saltationist Socialism*, Ph.D. dissertation: Stockholm, 1987, 177, n. 6.

by long years of education. Furthermore, they had persistently clung to their insights once they had discovered the truth. Mao compared this trait of character to the past development of the CCP. The Chinese Revolution had succeeded against Stalin's advice and had been denounced by Stalin as a fake revolution. After the founding of the People's Republic in 1949, Soviet help had been necessary but it had also fostered dogmatism and bureaucratism; it had stifled creativity and the ability to think comparatively. After destroying superstition in foreign models, Mao claimed that there could be only one object worthy of future worship: truth itself.

Returning to the subject of the dual nature of commodities, he criticized the influence of a dogmatist cult: "Whenever heroes appear on stage they look extraordinary; Stalin is that kind of man. Chinese people used to be slaves and it appeared that they would continue that way. Whenever a Chinese artist painted a picture of me with Stalin, I was always shown shorter than Stalin. [The artist] was blindly subdued under the spiritual shadow of the Soviet Union."[2] Although Mao was adamant about Stalin's culpability for serious mistakes in his estimates concerning the course of the Chinese Revolution, he detested Khrushchev's criticism of Stalin, which Mao considered one-sided and failing to distinguish between the correct and incorrect aspects of Stalin. A number of Stalin's thoughts had been "comparatively correct or basically correct"[3] and the worship of his person therefore should not be condemned. "They don't display his portrait, we do."[4] After all, the cult's main objective did not rest with the worship of a person but with the embodied truth. Mao therefore advanced his own theory of personality cults, which again made use of his conception of the dual nature of commodities:

> There are two kinds of personality cults. One [kind of cult] is correct, for example we have to worship the correct things of Marx, Engels, Lenin, and Stalin and to worship them forever. Not to worship them is not possible. Truth is in their hands, why shouldn't we worship them? We believe in truth as truth derives from objective circumstances. Members of a squad must worship their squad leader. Not to worship is impossible. Another kind of cult is incorrect, without adding one's own analysis, blindly obeying, this is just not right. ... The problem does not rest with the cult of the individual but with whether it represents the truth or not.

[2] "Mao Tse-tung's Speeches at the CCP Chengtu Conference (Part 1)," in *Issues and Studies* 11 (1973), 97.

[3] "Mao Tse-tung's Speeches at the CCP Chengtu Conference (Part 2)," in *Issues and Studies* 12 (1973), 108.

[4] Ibid., 97f.

If it represents the truth, it should be worshipped. If it does not, even collective leadership won't work.[5]

Mao's distinction between truthful and nontruthful personality cults has led party historians to wonder how this seasoned dialectician could have come up with such a crude theory.[6] However, the report also included a different, mainly functional aspect of personality cults, amalgamated within Mao's meandering reasoning, that pointed at the political foundations of his argument. Mao defined Khrushchev's secret speech as mainly driven by political purposes. Khrushchev accordingly had come to understand the political potency of the cult as an extrabureaucratic source of power that did not rely on its recognition within the party elite. But, as Mao later told Snow, Khrushchev never really managed to foster a sufficient cult himself and thus could be purged all too easily by his Politburo comrades. At Chengdu, Mao further revealed that the attempts at cult building by former CCP leader and "north-eastern king" (*dongbei wang*) Gao Gang had represented an eighth-degree political earthquake. By fostering his own power base in Manchuria and establishing immediate relations with Stalin, Gao, according to Mao, had threatened China's political stability. The dictatorship of the proletariat therefore had to remain firmly in the hands of those representing truth. Mao asserted the correctness of his own position by quoting Lenin: "Some people opposed Lenin, saying that he was a dictator. Lenin replied flatly, it is better for me to be a dictator than it is for you."[7] Mao's speech thus presented a warning not to take the secret speech as pretext for an attack on his authority by way of arguing against personality cults in general: "Some people are very interested in opposing personality cults. ... There are also two aims behind opposing personality cults: one is to oppose incorrect cults, and one is to oppose the worship of others, demanding one's own worship instead."[8]

Mao's conception of personality cults operated on different levels. While theoretically he was willing to concede the existence of feudal remnants and to acknowledge implicitly similarities between CCP rule and the traditional mandate of the emperors, the impact of the secret speech had provided him with ample proof about the dangers of

[5] *Mao Zedong sixiang wansui* [Long Live Mao Zedong Thought], n.p.: 1969, 162.
[6] Xu Jianhua, "Mao Zedong tongzhi you fandui geren chongbai dao jieshou geren chongbai de guocheng" [Comrade Mao Zedong and the Process from Opposing Personality Cults to Accepting Personality Cults], in *Dangshi yanjiu* 5 (1984), 72–8.
[7] "Mao: Speeches at Chengtu 1," 97.
[8] *Mao Zedong sixiang wansui*, 162.

debunking prominent symbols. The emotional expediency of the cult in stirring up public support and enthusiasm for his own policy directives made it an indispensable tool if he wanted to retain a powerful link to the masses outside of the regular channels of the party bureaucracy. The cult had furthermore proven its functional importance within internecine party struggles more than once in the past and should therefore not be done away with too easily.

THE GREAT LEAP FORWARD

With the shunning of the policy to emulate Soviet experiences, there was no longer a commonly recognized model of development. Besides the vague repository provided by the general principles of Marxism-Leninism, no clear indicator existed on how to proceed toward future communism. A perpetuated system of trial and error and the propagation of successful model experiences through the mass media were to circumvent the danger of going it alone. But the experiences of the mass line needed to be analyzed and distinguished by a vanguard party under a constantly correct leadership. There can be no doubt that Mao believed himself to be the only person within the CCP capable of mastering the task as helmsman of the Chinese Revolution. His call for vehement criticism of those in offices of power, "to dare to take the risk of being cut to pieces so as to pull the emperor from the horse,"[9] therefore operated under certain constraints. Mao repeatedly emphasized that the correct views on present developments did not automatically derive from the tenure of high-level party offices like that of the CCP Chairman:

> An individual is sometimes right and sometimes wrong. Follow him, when he is right and do not follow him when he is wrong. One must not follow without discrimination. We follow Marx and Lenin, and we follow Stalin in some things. We follow whoever has the truth in his hands. *Even if he should be a manure carrier or a street sweeper, as long as he has the truth he should be followed.*[10]

The retrospective definition of truth proved to be much easier than during day-to-day political work. Mao would often joke about his own intellectual odyssey from classical Confucianist viewpoints to Marxism-Leninism and thus acknowledge that he himself had not been immune against

---

[9] "Mao: Speeches at Chengtu 2," 111.

[10] Quoted in Roderick MacFarquhar, *The Origins of the Cultural Revolution: 2. The Great Leap Forward, 1958–1960*, New York: Columbia University Press, 1983, 54f. Emphasis in the original.

holding wrong opinions. But by 1958, Mao was no longer prepared to accept criticism from his Politburo comrades if it presented a threat to his personal authority, as Minister of Defense Peng Dehuai was to experience a year later at the Lushan Plenum after having placed the blame for the excesses of the Great Leap Forward at Mao's feet. Political power ultimately remained superior to questions of theoretical consistency.

Among Mao's followers, the semantic subtleties and distinctions between different types of cults were clearly seen as referring to the deceased forefathers of communism or future communist leaders and not to Mao Zedong himself. As early as 1956, Mao had proposed to step back to the second row of leadership and to enable his potential successors to gain firsthand experience in running the party-state. The position as state and party chairman thus should not be seen as eternally tied to Mao personally. The promulgation of a correct personality cult at the Chengdu conference nevertheless brought forth a wave of massive flattery. Ke Qingshi, the first secretary of the Shanghai Party Committee and a major proponent of the steel drive during the Great Leap Forward, proposed to follow the CCP Chairman blindly even to the point of superstitious belief.[11] In the same year, Kang Sheng, Mao's former security chief from the Yan'an days and by 1958 alternate member of the Politburo, announced that Mao Zedong Thought should be regarded as the "apex" (*dingfeng*) of present-day Marxism-Leninism. A few months later, at the Second Plenum of the Eighth Congress in May 1958, a local party cadre was quoted as follows:

> We have to completely eradicate superstition and achieve a true liberation of thought, a great revolution of thought. With respect to Mao Zedong Thought, the problem of superstitious belief does not exist. In the past, particular stress has been placed on the study of the original works of Marx, Engels, Lenin, and Stalin while the study of Mao Zedong's works has remained insufficient; from now on, the cadres have to read them and should primarily study them. This is living dialectics, living Marxism.[12]

All phraseology dealing with the notion of superstition was semantically closely linked to a blind acceptance of the Soviet model. The study of Mao Zedong Thought therefore a priori ruled out the possibility of bearing resemblance to any kind of superstitious belief in the individual. The small

[11] Cong Jin, *Quzhe fazhan de suiyue* [Years of Tortuous Development], Zhengzhou: Henan renmin chubanshe, 1989, 117.
[12] Lin Yunhui, "Ershi shiji liushi niandai geren chongbai de qiyuan" [The Origins of the Personality Cult in the 1960s], in *Dangshi bolan* 11 (2005), 36.

group from Mao's home province of Hunan at the Second Plenum expressed this equivalence in clear terms: "[F]ollowing Mao Zedong from the bottom of our hearts is not worship of the individual or superstitious belief in the individual but the worship of truth; the decades of revolution and construction have proven that Chairman Mao is the representative of truth."[13]

Mao had repeatedly requested to raise the political consciousness of the populace and advocated the publication of communist magazines for both a party-internal readership and the general public to stimulate thinking about the harmful impact of bourgeois influences in the superstructure. Even after the failure of the Hundred Flowers campaign, Mao searched for ways to encourage public criticism against bureaucratism and decadence at lower party levels. It seemed necessary to create a kind of atmosphere that would make people dare to "talk and act big."[14] A correct personality cult could help to foster this kind of lively, emotional climate in which everyone, given his or her proletarian standpoint, would dare to attempt to remove mountains like in the story *"Yugong yi shan,"* which was to become one of the "three constantly read articles" (*lao san pian*) of the Cultural Revolution. But without belief, without the recognition of the fundamental truths of Marxism-Leninism and the destruction of the ideological remnants of the old society, communism would never be achieved. Therefore, a blind belief in and staunch defense of communism should arm the populace on the uncertain road ahead.

The result was what Michael Schoenhals has termed "emancipation by proxy."[15] By combining the cohesive functions of the cult with a higher objective, the destruction of superstitious belief in the Soviet model, the Chinese leadership regarded the cult as a means to attain a greater good. It was aimed at discovering a uniquely Chinese path to communism and not implemented as a device of rule in the first place. Quintessentially, the cult at this stage therefore could be described as an attempt at what Karl Popper termed "utopian social engineering."[16] In high spirits, "cherishing every minute,"[17] as Mao had expressed in one of his most often quoted poems, the Chinese were to destroy the depressing atmosphere of blindly following the Soviet model and to sketch out their own path to communism.

---

[13] Ibid., 36.

[14] "Mao: Speeches at Chengdu 2," 111.

[15] Schoenhals, *Saltationist Socialism*, 23–5, 39.

[16] Karl R. Popper, *The Open Society and Its Enemies*, vol.1, Princeton, NJ: Princeton University Press, 1963 [1945], 157–68.

[17] Mao Zedong, *Mao Tsetung Poems (Chinese-English)*, Beijing: Shangwu yinshuguan chuban, 1976, 92f.

The drive of enthusiasm Mao had envisioned rooting out the causes of dogmatism and bureaucratism resulted in a competition to produce completely fictive numbers of both agricultural statistics and cultural artifacts in order to signal adherence of the provincial cadres to the party Center. Consequently, cult building resumed on a large scale during the Great Leap Forward. Examples are to be found both in the mythical language employed when describing Mao's visits to model communes and the difficulties that the CCP Center faced in keeping the localities from reviving "bourgeois" forms to express their gratitude. In late 1957 already, the CCP Center had been obliged to confirm its previous policy forbidding the naming of places, streets, and factories after present leaders.[18] An examination of painted wall-slogans in villages on behalf of the Hebei Provincial Government in June 1959 had revealed the existence of numerous incorrect and boasting slogans that had to be amended.[19] Mao Zedong himself at the Shanghai Conference in April 1959 heavily criticized the all-pervasive tendency of lying and later warned against the reappearance of the "five styles" (egalitarianism, commandism, blind leadership, pomposity, and superior attitude) among party cadres. He even called for a binary compilation of examples of good and bad persons, who during the first year of the Leap had either given in to the boasting or withstood the tides. The signs were clearly in favor of trimming the excesses of the Great Leap. The tendency of "empty boasting" as evident in the reports on the people's communes was to be replaced by a description according to the facts.

By the time the Lushan Plenum was convened in July 1959, Liu Shaoqi had attained the position as state chairman. Mao retained the much more powerful position as CCP Chairman. Liu's new position did not effectively alter the Mao-centered politics, as the Lushan crisis in July 1959 was to reveal. The sharp criticism of the Great Leap Forward, as presented in a personal letter by Peng Dehuai to Mao on 14 July 1959, had a dramatic impact on the further development of the cult. The letter evaporated Mao's conciliatory attitude toward correcting his mistaken policies. Peng's status as PLA leader and the inherent danger of losing the army as a power base, a threat that has to be seen against the backdrop of the affair around Soviet Minister of Defense Georgi Zhukov, led Mao to make a drastic response.

---

[18] "Zhongfa [57] 39, Zhonggong zhongyang guanyu jinzhi yong geren mingzi zuo diming, jieming, he qiye deng mingzi de tongzhi" [CCP Center Notice Concerning the Prohibition of Turning Personal Names into Place Names, Street Names, and Factory Names], 20 November 1957, HPA 855-4-1045.

[19] Hebei sheng xuanchuanbu (ed.), 1958–1965 dashiji [Major Events of the Years 1958–1965], 21 February 1966, n.p., 9.

He accused Peng and others of forming a "military club" and trying to usurp power and had him stripped of his command. The crisis, provoked by Mao's anger, reinvigorated the policies of the Great Leap that the party had been about to correct. Their continuation ultimately resulted in an agonizing famine in which tens of millions of Chinese peasants starved to death.[20]

As Peng had enjoyed great respect within the armed forces, Mao had to replace him with a commander of similar prestige on whose personal loyalty he could count. Marshal Lin Biao proved to be the ideal choice. He was the youngest of the ten PLA marshals, known for his military genius and absolute loyalty to Mao. Owing to health reasons of uncertain nature, Lin had kept a low profile during the first decade of the People's Republic but had been elected member of the Standing Committee of the Politburo and CCP vice-chairman in February 1958. Lin's decision to take over the responsibilities of such a crucial office was due in large part to Mao's constant requests. As soon as he had been installed in his new position, Lin Biao immediately set out to overcome any signs of doubt in Mao's authority by reinvoking the Yan'an-style rectification of troop morals through exegetical bonding and the public championing of Mao Zedong's works. Liu Shaoqi joined Lin Biao in the renewed efforts of cult building. At a conference on 9 September 1959, Liu accused a number of party members such as Peng Dehuai of trying to follow the example of the Twentieth CPSU Congress and attempting to oust Mao Zedong. Again, as in 1943 when his support had been crucial for the acceptance of the Mao cult as brand symbol of the CCP, Liu now portrayed himself as staunch supporter of the cult:

> I have always advocated the "cult of the individual," but one can argue whether the term "cult of the individual" is appropriate or not. What I mean is that I have always advocated Mao's leadership authority. ... I am still advocating it and I will continue to build the "personality cults" of comrades Lin Biao and Deng Xiaoping. If you don't agree with me, I will continue regardless; I don't necessarily have to rely on other people's support.[21]

The cult of the individual, in Liu's opinion, was a term awkwardly synonymous with the prestige of Mao Zedong as symbol of the party and thus the Chinese Revolution. The creation and nurturing of the powerful image

---

[20] Frank Dikötter, in his recent history of the famine, cites internal sources with a death toll of at least 45 million deaths, Frank Dikötter, *Mao's Great Famine: The History of China's Most Devastating Catastrophe, 1958–62*, London: Bloomsbury, 2010, 333.

[21] Cong, *Quzhe fazhan*, 305f.

had to be advanced in the interest of the party. Given the difficulties of ascertaining the correct path to communism and the danger posed by factional warfare, the cult remained important and had to be substantiated through minor cults around possible successor figures. The unanimity of the CCP leadership was best conveyed by a strong and positive depiction of collective leadership in the press, while possibly religious overtones or similarities between CCP and emperor rule would be declared to be ideological remnants and vanish over time. With the dismissal of Peng Dehuai, the sustaining of a "correct" cult within the party steadily gained ground. In September 1960, the fourth volume of Mao Zedong's *Selected Works* was published, accompanied by media celebrations and study campaigns. While in China the Mao cult thus had been well established and theoretically justified, the issue had not been settled on the international stage. It turned out to be one of the main ideological reasons for the increasing rift between China and the Soviet Union.

THE SINO–SOVIET RUPTURE AND THE WAR OF WORDS

The Sino–Soviet relationship had been steadily deteriorating since Khrushchev's secret speech. The rift had two principal reasons. The first reason was based on matters of political line. The CCP and a small minority of other communist parties, including those in Albania, North Korea, and Indonesia, objected to Khrushchev's concept of peaceful coexistence and advocated unremitting struggle against imperialism and its "running dogs." Ideological differences further existed about the question of the cult, the existence of which, according to the CCP, had weakened the socialist camp. Finally, Soviet criticism of the Great Leap Forward and the Soviets' supposed neutrality regarding the Indo–Chinese border clashes in the autumn of 1959 had deepened animosities. The second reason was of a more personal nature and linked to the role played by Khrushchev himself. Communication in foreign affairs, as Pierre Bourdieu once remarked, has to retain a high degree of codification given the risks involved in the case of failure.[22] Khrushchev however, not quite the diplomat, frequently criticized others personally with his sharp, impromptu remarks. At a conference in Warsaw in February 1959, he had in a private talk referred to Mao as "an elderly, crotchety person, rather like an old shoe, which is

---

[22] Pierre Bourdieu, *Language and Symbolic Power*, Cambridge: Polity Press, 1991, 78.

just good enough to put in a corner to be admired,"[23] and at Bucharest in 1960, he had even proposed to display a portrait of Peng Dehuai. The strained personal relationship between Mao and Khrushchev made a cessation of enmities unlikely as long as both parties retained their leading personnel.[24]

The breach became clearly visible with the publication of the article "Long Live Leninism" in the journal *Red Flag* in April 1960. The commemoration of Lenin's ninetieth birthday was taken as an opportunity to attack the Soviet failure to grasp the continuing importance of Leninist theory, especially class analysis and class struggle. In August 1960, the Soviet Union withdrew its technical experts from China, and ideological clashes continued at conferences in Bucharest and Moscow during the following year. At the Moscow conference in November 1960, the Chinese delegation, after long discussions, formally signed the conference communiqué that included a positive reference to the secret speech and its attack on the cult: "Marxist-Leninist Parties ... work indefatigably for the strengthening of their bonds with the Party membership ... and do not allow the cult of the individual, which shackles creative thought and initiative of Communists."[25]

The question of the cult became virulent after the Twenty-Second Congress of the CPSU was convened in Moscow in October 1961. It decided upon the removal of Stalin's sarcophagus from public display and the burning of his remains. During his speech to the congress on 17 October 1961, Khrushchev sharply criticized Enver Hoxha, first secretary of the Central Committee of the Albanian Labor Party, for his failure to live up to his former agreement on the policies of de-Stalinization. The remarks were simultaneously a thinly veiled attack on the rising cult of Mao Zedong since the Lushan Plenum. Hoxha replied on 7 November 1961 with a vehement, highly personal criticism of Khrushchev. He emphasized the Albanian Labor Party's continued commitment to opposing the "sickening belief"[26] in personality cults or other violations of the legal sphere, but this was not to diminish the "love and respect" for the legitimate leaders of the masses.

---

[23] MacFarquhar, *Great Leap Forward*, 268.
[24] See as well Sergey Radchenko, *Two Suns in the Heavens: The Sino–Soviet Struggle for Supremacy, 1962–1967*, Washington: Woodrow Wilson Center Press, 2009, 91.
[25] See Appendix Q in John Gittings, *Survey of the Sino–Soviet Dispute: A Commentary and Extracts from the Recent Polemics 1963–1967*, London: Oxford University Press, 1968, 367.
[26] "Enwei'er Huocha tongzhi de jianghua (zhi yi)" [Comrade Enver Hoxha's Speech (Part 1)], in *Renmin ribao*, 17 November 1961, 5.

Hoxha gave the interpretation a further twist by claiming that ulterior motives lay at the heart of Khrushchev's secret speech. He claimed that Khrushchev was "using the so-called criticism of Stalin's cult of the individual" to achieve non-Marxist goals by way of propounding revisionist theories that weakened the awareness among the working class of continuing class struggle. The "combating the so-called cult of the individual" (*fandui suowei geren mixin*) had been turned into a bugbear to threaten leaders of communist parties not complying with Khrushchev's revisionist course. Furthermore, Hoxha accused Khrushchev of deliberately shaping his own personality cult in the Soviet Union as "great military strategist" and "architect" of the victory over fascism. The single aim of the empty talk on personality cults should thus be seen in Khrushchev's efforts to install revisionist and even imperialist "elements" in positions of leadership in order to carry out his destruction of Leninism.

Most of Hoxha's lengthy speech was published ten days later in the *People's Daily*, including the crucial section on the "combating the so-called cult of the individual." A highly restricted internal circular pointed out that the CCP would currently refrain from making a public statement on the issue but would continue to reprint the views of both sides in the party newspapers. In small group discussions within local party cells, the basic unity of the socialist camp should be emphasized. The political instructors were further to differentiate between the CPSU leadership and the Soviet populace in general. Toward the latter, a much more cordial attitude should be adopted. To express the basic correctness of the Albanian standpoint, a commentary was to be published under a pseudonym in the *People's Daily*: "To do it this way is effective in unmasking the errors of revisionism, to sustain the correct standpoint in order to educate the people."[27]

The abridged TASS version of Khrushchev's speech to the congress had been reprinted in the *People's Daily* on 20 October 1961, supplemented six days later with the full text of his remarks against Albania. Yet the speech's content, which had been relayed to CCP members through internal news organs, had already become widely known because the internal party publications were not treated with sufficient secrecy: "Sometimes [the reports] are first read by the mail correspondents and the cleaning and the mail-delivery personnel before they finally reach the designated

---

[27] "Zhongfa [61] 717, Zhongyang guanyu Su-A guanxi wenti de zhishi" [CCP Center Instruction Concerning the Question of Soviet-Albanian Relations], 17 November 1961, HPA 855-6-2033.

reader. Some people furthermore just leave their *Reference Information* anywhere so that it can be read by anyone."[28] The local cadres were requested to pay more attention to matters of secrecy and to prohibit "unprincipled" discussions regarding matters of foreign policy, especially with foreign residents and visitors. All questions should be answered by relying on the formulations that had been employed by the leading party comrades. Still the Chinese populace paid "vivid attention"[29] to the Twenty-Second CPSU Congress and its proceedings, as the internal intelligence bulletins reveal. Students in particular were reported to have been discussing Sino–Soviet politics all night. They further had sent letters to the CPSU Central Committee and tried to convince foreign students of the correctness of the Chinese standpoint regarding the cult.

The breaking point that was finally to trigger the Sino–Soviet rupture was the signing of the nuclear test-ban treaty among the Soviet Union, the United States, and Great Britain in July 1963. The situation had already been tense in the previous months, despite a short period of rapprochement during the Cuban Missile Crisis. The criticism had not ceased, but it had been focused on Albania and Yugoslavia serving as proxies. The consequences of an open schism within the international communist movement and the loss of the Soviet Union's nuclear shield for China in particular muffled public rhetoric on both sides to a certain extent. Internal communication during a series of communist party conferences, however, took on ever more rigid, even comical forms. The Chinese side proved to be more apt in employing quotes from the Marxist-Leninist canon to bolster its arguments, leading Khrushchev to exclaim at the Sixth Congress of the German Socialist Unity Party on 16 January 1961: "These people imagine that to engage in endless swearing and cursing at imperialism is to do what will best help the socialist countries. This is a sort of voodoo belief in the power of curses and incantations."[30] Both sides had clarified their standpoints in an exchange of letters preceding a possible meeting in mid-1963. The CPSU Central Committee, in a letter of 30 March 1963, emphasized

---

[28] Ibid.

[29] "Zhongfa [61] 739, Zhongyang pizhuan Dongbeiju 'Guanyu ganbu, qunzhong yilun Sugong ershi'er da youguan wenti shi ying zhuyi shixiang de tongzhi'" [Northeastern Bureau Notice Approved and Transmitted by the CCP Center Concerning Certain Items to Be Observed with Regard to Opinions Voiced by Cadres and the Masses about Problems Related to the Twenty-Second CPSU Congress], 25 November 1961, HPA 855-6-2033.

[30] Alexander Dallin, Jonathan Harris, and Grey Hodnett (eds.), *Diversity in International Communism: A Documentary Record, 1961–1963*, New York: Columbia University Press, 1963, 750.

the importance of peaceful coexistence and a growing living standard as well as the danger of a thermonuclear war, rather than the theory of unremitting class struggle. The growing care for the well-being of the Soviet populace, however, should not be interpreted as a sign of going soft on imperialism.[31] The CPSU took a clear stand against capitalist politics and possible Trojan horses carrying bourgeois ideology into the Soviet system while simultaneously engaging in further cultural contact with capitalist countries. The CPSU requested the CCP to eliminate the personality cult in order to show how the bonds and viewpoints shared by the fraternal parties had already been strengthened. A unified communist bloc would be the only way of preventing the dangers ahead.

The Chinese side took more than two and a half months to prepare its response. Unlike in the Soviet case and similar to the process of writing the other aforementioned editorials, Mao Zedong as Chairman of the CCP, personally supervised the process of drafting the answer to the Soviet letter by a newly established Anti-Revisionist Writing Group that included the party's foremost propagandists and up-and-coming "scholar scribes" (*xiu-cai*). Other high-ranking leaders, including Liu Shaoqi, Zhou Enlai, and Deng Xiaoping, were all deeply involved in the discussions. The group prepared a collection of materials to facilitate a profound refutation of the Soviet claims to represent the true legacy of Marxism-Leninism. The quantitative output of the scholarly undertaking was truly astounding. The collections of materials that served as background for the writing of the open letter and the following nine polemics included indices of quotations from all major works of the Marxist-Leninist canon as well as Mao Zedong's own works, totaling more than 4 million characters.[32] The letter was drafted by Chen Boda and the Leftist writers Wang Li, a former *Red Flag* editor who was to play a major role in the first years of the Cultural Revolution, and Fan Ruoyu, deputy editor-in-chief of *Red Flag*.[33] The draft was finalized on 14 June 1963 and published three days later in the *People's Daily*. The answer, twice as long as the Soviet letter, listed twenty-five specific problems that set the agenda for a meeting between both sides. It presented a scathing critique of the CPSU's standpoints. Section 20 specifically dealt with the question of the cult and invoked Leninist party principles to substantiate the claim that the CPSU was about to subvert the

---

[31] *The Polemic on the General Line of the International Communist Movement*, Beijing: Foreign Languages Press, 1965, 515.

[32] Wu, *Shinian lunzhan* 2, 591.

[33] Wang Li, *Xianchang lishi. Wenhua da geming jishi* [On the Scene of History. Chronicle of the Great Cultural Revolution], Hong Kong: Oxford University Press, 1993, 20.

relationship between leaders and masses. The only aim behind the frequent mentioning of the cult was to be seen, just as Hoxha had argued, in its function as a tool to topple disobedient leaders of fraternal parties while simultaneously fostering worship around Khrushchev at home.[34]

The Soviet reply in the form of an open letter dropped all diplomatic niceties and declared the CCP to be incapable of dealing with the realities of a changing world. By clinging to orthodox viewpoints expressed in a completely different context, the Chinese verbal "camouflage"[35] seemingly ignored the fundamental issues at stake, such as the questions of war and peace, colonialism, or overcoming the cult ideology. In fact, the Chinese case should be seen as the first example of an open proclamation of a leader cult within the communist movement: "It is hard fully to ascertain the Chinese comrades' motivation in upholding the personality cult. ... It should be observed that even at the height of the personality cult in our country, Stalin himself was forced, at least in words, to reject this petty-bourgeois theory, saying that it stemmed from the Socialist-Revolutionaries."[36] Given the hostile attitude on both sides, the failure of the meetings between high-ranking delegations held in Moscow in mid-July was predictable. The bilateral talks were adjourned and the polemics resumed immediately.

Four days after the return of the Chinese delegation to China, the Soviet Union signed the partial nuclear test-ban treaty on 25 July 1963 with the United States and Great Britain that had been discussed parallel to the CCP–CPSU talks in a much more cordial atmosphere. China had become completely isolated with the exception of a few loyal allies such as Albania and been kept out of the nuclear club. The open rupture between China and the Soviet Union spurred enormous propagandistic activities. Unlike the CPSU, the CCP had published all critical remarks in the *People's Daily* and had even reprinted the Soviet Union's open letter in full on 20 July. The refutation of the Soviet arguments had thus become a question on which the credibility of the CCP rested at home and abroad, and was accordingly treated as a matter of ideological principle. While both sides during

---

[34] The Albanian media continued their attacks against the so-called opposition to personality cults through the period of the polemics, and major articles were reprinted in China; see, for example, A'erbaniya "Renmin zhi sheng bao" bianjibu, *Chedi jielu Heluxiaofu jituan guanyu suowei fandui 'geren mixin' de weixian yinmou* [Thoroughly Expose the Dangerous Intrigue of the Khrushchev Clique Concerning the So-called Opposition to "Personality Cults"], Beijing: Renmin chubanshe, 1964.

[35] *Polemic*, 539.

[36] Ibid., 563.

extensive visits lobbied for support among developing countries, the war of words was conducted on the Chinese side by a large group of the party's most gifted scribes, which had been formed ad hoc and divided into different sections that drafted the famous "Nine Comments" (*jiu ping*) to refute the intellectual contents of the open letter of the Soviet Union. The comments were published between 6 September 1963 and 14 July 1964 in the *People's Daily*. The small group in charge of the supervision of the different sections under the leadership of Kang Sheng and Wu Lengxi first discussed the drafts with Deng Xiaoping, who would then send them to Mao Zedong, Liu Shaoqi, and Zhou Enlai. After their remarks had been included, each article was scrutinized in a Politburo session before it was distributed via print media and radio stations.[37]

The second comment, entitled "On the Question of Stalin," provided the final Chinese statement on the cult up to the Cultural Revolution. Mao Zedong personally corrected the draft three times before it was published on 13 September 1963. The comment rejected the allegations voiced in the CPSU letter as nonargumentative pathos and proceeded in dialectical fashion to prove the correctness of the Chinese standpoint. In its first argument, the CCP tried to prove that the criticism of Stalin was not only directed against the person of Stalin himself but against the dictatorship of the proletariat in general. By claiming a thirty-year period of the personality cult, Khrushchev had left the impression that the Soviet populace had not been liberated from serfdom through the October Revolution but had in fact continued to live under an even worse threat than feudalism. The second main argument dealt with the inconsistency of Khrushchev's own position. Not only had he been part of the system ("In the position of an accomplice to a 'murderer' or a 'bandit'? Or in the same position as a 'fool' or an 'idiot'?"),[38] but he also had continuously praised Stalin. Worst of all, while openly denouncing the personality cults of others, Khrushchev had even at the Twenty-Second CPSU Congress been entitled as "cosmic father,"[39] a clear indication of the double talk involved on his side. What, therefore, had been his motivations for delivering the secret speech?

> To put it bluntly, it is nothing but the following:
> 1. On the pretext of "combating the personality cult," to counterpose Stalin, the leader of the party, to the party organization, the proletariat, and the masses of the people;

---

[37] Wu, *Shinian lunzhan* 2, 538f.
[38] *Polemic*, 126.
[39] Ibid., 134.

2. On the pretext of "combating the personality cult," to besmirch the proletarian party, the dictatorship of the proletariat, and the socialist system;
3. On the pretext of "combating the personality cult," to build [himself] up
   and to attack revolutionaries loyal to Marxism-Leninism so as to pave
   the way for revisionist schemers to usurp the party and state leadership;
4. On the pretext of "combating the personality cult," to interfere in the
   internal affairs of fraternal parties and countries and strive to subvert
   their leadership to suit themselves;
5. On the pretext of "combating the personality cult," to attack fraternal
   parties which adhere to Marxism-Leninism and to split the international communist movement.

The "combat against the personality cult" launched by Khrushchov [sic]
is a despicable political intrigue. Like someone described by Marx, "He is
in his element as an intriguer, while a nonentity as a theorist."[40]

By quoting other revisionists who had been critical of Stalin and his cult,
most notably Trotsky, the implementation of the cult as an instrument of
political intrigue was to become obvious. The CCP argued that a final
verdict on how to evaluate Stalin would probably not be reached in the
present century.[41] The attempts of Khrushchev to slander Stalin's memory,
however, would be futile. "Khrushchev was able to utilize his privileged
position to remove the body of Stalin from the Lenin Mausoleum, but try
as he may, he can never succeed in removing the great image of Stalin from
the minds of the Soviet people and of the people throughout the world."[42]

WORSHIP OR SUPERSTITIOUS BELIEF

A quantitative survey of articles published in the *People's Daily* that
mention the cult of the individual closely mirrors the national and international reverberations of the secret speech. The data reveal a drastic bifur-
cation. The term *geren chongbai*, first used as translation for the "cult of
the individual" in 1953, steeply rises in public usage after Khrushchev's
secret speech. With the end of the Hundred Flowers campaign in June
1957, it declines in similar fashion and vanishes nearly completely from
public discourse by 1959. Mao's differentiation between two types of
personality cults at Chengdu had left newspaper editors and party propagandists with a semantic problem. As *geren chongbai* now referred to
both a correct and an incorrect variant of cult, one of the two types of the
cult had to be renamed. In an article published in the *People's Daily* on 25

[40] Ibid., 133.
[41] Zhonggong wenxian yanjiushi (ed.), *Mao wengao* 10, 369.
[42] *Polemic*, 137f.

December 1958, the question of correct translations from the Russian vernacular was made explicit. The author, Lin Ling, singled out a number of expressions that did not exactly match the Russian original and thus failed to denote their exact object of reference, sometimes causing considerable harm. The original meaning of the Russian *kul't lichnosti* was declared to be "transforming an individual into a worshiped icon." Therefore, the translations *geren mixin* (superstitious belief in the individual) or *geren mobai* (prostration before an individual) were said to capture the quasireligious meaning much more precisely than the term *chongbai*, indicating reverence in general.[43] In future, the expression *geren mixin* should therefore be made use of in order not to negate the veneration of eminent and respected persons owing to "an unfortunate result of a lack of thoughtfulness during the time of translation."[44]

As Figure 1 reveals, the term *geren chongbai* by and large vanished from public discourse with the onset of the Great Leap Forward. Instead, the following years witnessed the rise of the new translation for personality cults, *geren mixin*, referring to incorrect cults. The term was employed particularly often during the fierce debate accompanying the split in Sino–Soviet relations, which the CPSU itself compared to a scholastic dispute. As noted previously, superstition became closely linked to the incorrect cult and a dogmatic following of the Soviet model. The notion of *chongbai*, on the other hand, retained its ambivalent status and was massively revived during the Cultural Revolution when "boundless veneration" and "eternal veneration" came to be part of the standard vocabulary. The new translation of *geren mixin* was seldom used in its positive form. Most common was the negative usage "opposing the so-called cult of the individual" first adopted by Enver Hoxha in his 1961 speech. The polemics in 1963–4 resulted in roughly sixty articles mentioning the topic per year. But by the time of the Cultural Revolution, when the cult of Mao Zedong was just about to get started in a way that would dwarf even the Stalin cult in its heyday, both terms referring to the cult by and large disappeared from CCP discourse. The cult as historical phenomenon was not dependent on its theoretical explanation in the media but gained force through a variety of new mechanisms to be dealt with in more detail in Part Two of this book.

[43] Lin Ling, "Cong 'an lao fenpei, an xu fenpei' de zhengyi xiangqi de" [Thinking about the Correct Translation of "Each According to His Ability, Each According to His Needs"], in *Renmin ribao*, 25 December 1958, 8.
[44] Ibid., 8.

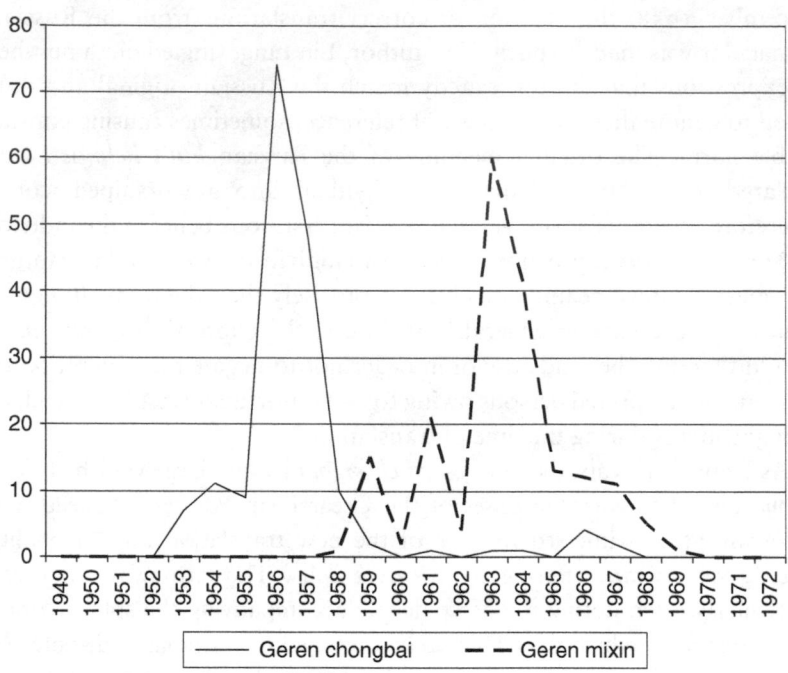

FIGURE 1. Translations of the "cult of the individual" in the *People's Daily*, 1949–72

The constant redefinition of the cult had succeeded in eliminating its original pejorative connotation and had turned the cult into a dialectical means to promote the destruction of superstitious belief in foreign models. Praise of the party and its leaders was no longer propagated as harmful but as a necessary means to promote unity and to attract followers in the global fight against imperialism. After Khrushchev's demotion within the CPSU Central Committee on 14 October 1964, the term nearly vanished completely from Chinese discourse.[45] The cult around Mao Zedong, on the other hand, became ever more extravagant. During the National Day Parade on 1 October 1964, for the first time a Mao statue, 10 meters

[45] A denouement that had seemed possible after Khrushchev's fall evaporated after the Soviet minister of defense, Rodion Malinovsky, during a reception at the Kremlin on 7 November 1964, approached Chinese Marshal He Long, member of the Chinese delegation to Moscow, and asked when China would finally would get rid of Mao like the CPSU had disposed of Khrushchev. See Zhonggong zhongyang wenxian yanjiushi (ed.), *Zhou Enlai nianpu, 1949–1976* [Chronicle of the Life of Zhou Enlai, 1949–1976], vol. 2, Beijing: Zhongyang wenxian chubanshe, 1997, 686.

high, was carried amid a sixteen thousand–man strong guard of honor, while huge models of hogs, ducks, and cabbage were displayed to symbolize the success of the People's Republic's economic policies.

Simultaneously with the public announcement of Khrushchev's demise, China's first nuclear bomb detonated in the desert near Lop Nor. The successful explosion massively enhanced China's status in world politics as China no longer depended on the Soviet Union's nuclear shield, the extent of which Mao had long remained skeptical. The same evening, Mao, Zhou Enlai, and other party leaders in the Great Hall of the People celebrated the CCP's dual fortune by attending the third public staging of the song and dance epic *The East Is Red*. The production had been meticulously supervised by Premier Zhou Enlai himself and was to present the "unification of politics and art, of form and content."[46] It started with a recital: "In the Mao Zedong era, the Chinese people are happy, the land is beautiful. But how can we forget the sufferings of the past? How can we forget our Long March under the guidance of Chairman Mao!" By presenting party history in the form of a heroic epic, the performance reinvigorated the image of Mao as the radiating sun that had been the earliest element of graphic and self-chosen depiction in the party newspaper *Liberation Weekly* back in June 1937. The epic was restaged in all major Chinese cities during the following years, and the televised version, produced upon Zhou Enlai's request, gained enormous attention. The sunflower motif came to be a standard iconographical feature of the Mao cult. Up to this day, sunflowers and not dragons or other traditional signs of the emperor's court decorate the golden roof tiles on top of the Gate of Heavenly Peace.

By late 1964, China had become a nuclear power and the CCP had self-confidently claimed its doctrinal authority within the Sino–Soviet dispute. International prospects seemed promising, although the critical situation in Vietnam triggered the buildup of a massive relocation of industry toward the so-called Third Front, which was to provide the CCP with a safe industrial power base in case of an invasion. The main danger that Mao perceived thus was internal. In numerous speeches after Khrushchev's demise, he warned local cadres about the possible rise of revisionism at the CCP Center, carried forth by a "Chinese Khrushchev." If even the motherland of socialism had fallen prey to revisionism after the death of Stalin, similar incidents might occur in China as well. Mao therefore closely watched the moves of his potential successors and pondered new possibilities of immunizing China against the revisionist threat. The

---

[46] Ibid., 668.

biggest antirevisionist insurance in Mao's opinion was provided by the political training in the PLA under Lin Biao's supervision, which was based on the constant heightening of vigilance to unmask hidden enemies and wrong thoughts. The PLA work style and thus the Mao cult were advocated as the model for the whole nation in 1964 and spread the cult to every part of society. The campaign to "Learn from the PLA" prepared the grounds for Mao's all-out attack on his own party two years later, when guarded by the "spiritual nuclear bomb" (*jingshen yuanzidan*)[47] of Mao Zedong Thought, China was to delve into the Cultural Revolution.

---

[47] The first public mention of the term had been in the *Liberation Army News* editorial on 1 August 1960 recalling the thirty-third anniversary of the founding of the PLA.

PART TWO

CHARISMATIC MOBILIZATION

The personality cult fostered around Mao Zedong had started prior to the founding of the People's Republic and had developed in close rivalry with the projected image of Chiang Kai-shek as sole legitimate national Chinese leader. However, only after Stalin's death and Khrushchev's secret speech had the cult been turned from an unquestioned employed device of rule into a theoretical concept in need of explanation. Although the roots of the first Mao cult traced back to Yan'an, the Cultural Revolutionary leader cult was clearly shaped by the forms of worship developed in the PLA under the auspices of Lin Biao after 1959. The ritualization of behavior and speech by way of framing conduct according to short quotations from Chairman Mao had a huge impact on the further development of the cult. Mao consciously employed the cult in the mid-1960s to mobilize the masses against the party bureaucracy. With the destruction of the Leninist party system and clear hierarchies, however, the aims and strategies of employing the cult and its symbols came to vary increasingly. The ensuing cult anarchy revealed the variety in which out-of-context citations could be invoked and the futility of steering a political campaign through the manipulation of symbols alone.

The following three chapters deal with the rise of ritualistic Mao worship and its instrumentalization as a means of charismatic mobilization. The "lively study and application" (*huoxue huoyong*) of Mao Zedong's works in the PLA provided the basic patterns of conduct. The campaign followed no master plan but was shaped by the proven effectiveness of its measures in overcoming the consequences of the devastating Great Leap Forward within the army. One of the byproducts of the campaign for the lively study and application of Mao Zedong Thought was the Little Red

Book, the cult's best-known icon. Chapter 5 provides an overview of the complex creation of the "Mao bible," commonly attributed to Lin Biao, and reveals the unsystematic fashion of its emergence. Finally, the efforts to mobilize the youth against revisionist tendencies within schools, universities, and the party by way of rendering inchoate fragments of Mao Zedong Thought the only criterion of truth are discussed. Gigantic spectacles of worship, such as the reception of some 12 million Red Guards in Beijing, spread the Cultural Revolution and the Mao cult to every corner of China. The lack of clearly communicated aims of the movement, however, also resulted in the emergence of differing opinions and the employment of the cult symbols for varying objectives, as will be shown with regard to the Red Guard organization named United Action.

4

Lively Study and Application

The major difference between the correct leader cult advocated by Mao Zedong in Chengdu 1958 and its successor after the first Lushan Plenum the following year is to be observed with respect to the object of worship. At the Chengdu conference, Mao had advocated a worship of truth that postulated a dialectical relationship between leader cults and intellectual emancipation. After Lushan, the identity of opposites, of worship and intellectual emancipation, evaporated. References to Chairman Mao and Mao Zedong Thought skyrocketed in the media, especially in PLA publications. The cult, even by Mao's standards, was turned into an incorrect cult by asking for the worship of an individual at the expense of others. Its primary function was no longer intellectual emancipation but securing personal loyalty, party unity, and control over the army. Peng Dehuai's resistance to the public leader cult had been taken as a proof of his factional activities. His successor, Lin Biao, therefore came to champion the cult whenever possible in order to avoid Peng's fate and to use the cult's cohesive power to curb the devastating impact of the Great Leap Forward.

Lin Biao remains one of the most enigmatic politicians of modern-day China. A widely acclaimed military strategist and hero of the Anti-Japanese War, Lin had after the Communist victory withdrawn from the public stage under the pretense of healing the consequences of an injury he had suffered back in 1938. After having been reelected as member of the Politburo in 1956, Lin became CCP vice-chairman in 1958. Given his extraordinary revolutionary credentials as the youngest of the ten Chinese marshals, Mao's choice of Lin Biao as successor to Peng Dehuai was not questioned among the party's top leadership. Lin had proven outstanding personal loyalty in the past and Mao's choice was a clear indication of his desire to guarantee the political stability of the PLA.

Lin Biao has previously been credited with being the mastermind behind the Mao cult and with having invented its most prominent symbol, the Little Red Book, for reasons of personal ambition. These viewpoints have also been enshrined as the official party line by the 1981 "CCP Resolution on Party History." Recent scholarship has contested the portrayal of Lin Biao as a plotting careerist trying to usurp power.[1] Instead, he is described as a neurotic tactician, rather disinterested, probably even incapable of engaging in regular political work. By taking on a number of real and faked symptoms of illness, including the fear of heat, wind, and rain, Lin Biao secluded himself from politics in the first decade after the founding of the People's Republic. There can be no doubt about Lin's wariness regarding the reality of CCP collective leadership even in the 1950s, which Frederick Teiwes aptly described as "court politics."[2] The discussions conducted in Mao's bedroom on whether China had to deal with the problem of a personality cult are a telling example.

Lin Biao was an astute observer of Mao's ruling techniques. In 1949, Lin had already written in a private note: "First he will fabricate 'your' opinion for you; then he will change your opinion, negate it, and re-fabricate it – Old Mao's favorite trick. From now on I should be wary of it."[3] After assuming political office, Lin tried to keep away from the pitfalls of politics by minimizing contact with other members of the CCP leadership, by taking long recreational breaks and by refraining from proposing any policy directives without Mao's explicit consent. Even if he had personal opinions on a subject matter, he would modify his standpoint as soon as word about a definite statement of Mao's was heard. By adopting the strategy of "raising high" (*gaoju*) the banner of Mao Zedong Thought and "closely following" (*jin'gen*) Mao's political line, Lin tried to circumvent the danger of being retrospectively held accountable for independent viewpoints that at the time had been sanctioned or at least been

---

[1] See Frederick C. Teiwes and Warren Sun, *The Tragedy of Lin Biao: Riding the Tiger during the Cultural Revolution, 1966–1971*, Honolulu: University of Hawaii Press, 1996; and Jin Qiu, *The Culture of Power: The Lin Biao Incident in the Cultural Revolution*, Stanford, CA: Stanford University Press, 1999.

[2] Frederick C. Teiwes, *Politics at Mao's Court: Gao Gang and Party Factionalism in the Early 1950s*, Armonk, NY: M. E. Sharpe, 1990.

[3] Yu Houdao, *Gongheguo lingxiu, yuanshuai, jiangjun jiaowang shilu* [Records of the Interactions among PRC Leaders, Marshals, and Generals], Chengdu: Sichuan renmin chubanshe, 2001, 4.

tolerated by Mao, as it frequently had happened and was to continue to happen in party history. However, Lin Biao also knew how to instrumentalize the Mao cult to outmaneuver political rivals in the military.

Despite Lin Biao's prominence in basically every work on the Cultural Revolution, his role in propagating the Mao cult has seldom been given adequate attention. Fragmentary bits and pieces of his speeches pre- and post-1966 are taken at random to illustrate his character as a "hypocrite, careerist, [and] intriguer."[4] To understand the rise of the Mao cult during the Cultural Revolution and its specific forms, a closer analysis of the "lively study and application" of Mao Zedong Thought in the PLA is necessary. It will be argued that Lin Biao effectively employed the cult within the army's internal conflicts and used it as a medium to signal his loyalty to Mao Zedong. However, he was neither the only one trying to strengthen a charismatic relationship with Mao nor was he particularly apt at manipulating phrases.[5] The skillful art of political maneuvering was not a sphere he commanded as easily as he mastered military tactics.

POLITICAL EDUCATION IN THE PLA

The task of political education in the army had after 1949 been assigned to the General Political Department, one of the three main units below the Central Military Commission, the other two being the General Staff and the General Logistics Department. The implementation of policy directives was supervised through a joint leadership of both military unit leaders and political commissars who headed the political committees established at all levels. In the early 1950s, a number of military academies and institutes for education and military research were established to provide training for the political commissars and other high-level military cadres. In 1956, the Nanjing PLA Political Academy headed by Marshal Luo Ronghuan replaced its predecessors and became responsible for the education of the PLA's leading personnel. Its objective was to familiarize high-level military cadres with the basics of political work, to strengthen party spirit, and to advance the modernization of Chinese forces.[6] By 1958, the Political Academy had educated more than 170,000 cadres in CCP history, CPSU

---

[4] Ibid., 2.

[5] According to Lin's own statement, he was a rather inarticulate man, see Schoenhals, *Doing Things with Words*, 4.

[6] "Zhongguo renmin jiefangjun tongjian" bianji weiyuanhui (ed.), *1927–1996. Zhongguo renmin jiefangjun tongjian (PLA tongjian)* [1927–1996: People's Liberation Army Comprehensive Handbook], vol. 2, Lanzhou: Gansu renmin chubanshe, 1997, 1703.

history, political economy, and theory, and thus continued the influence of the Soviet model.

The reverberations of the secret speech and the ensuing alienation from the Soviet Union led parts of the PLA leadership to question the former model. Slavishly following the Soviet experiences was declared to be an expression of dogmatism hindering the creative power of the Chinese military tradition. After returning from the Chengdu conference, Lin Biao was informed about controversial opinions on how to deal with dogmatism in military training. Some participants advocated the continuing importance of systematically studying the Soviet military experiences and not to confuse critical assessment with dogmatism. Lin in turn urged Mao to place the topic of dogmatism high on the agenda of the upcoming enlarged meeting of the Central Military Commission in May that had been decided upon at Chengdu. At the meeting, Lin Biao, in his first speech after 1949 that is still available for research, proclaimed the necessity to destroy superstition in foreign models and bookish worship of the Marxist classics. He further emphasized the importance of uniting the universal truths of Marxism-Leninism with the practice of the Chinese Revolution, as Mao Zedong had done in the past: "The military works of Comrade Mao Zedong are military science. They have creatively developed the theories of Marxism-Leninism in the military realm and we should therefore study them well. Yet we should not only study but should create. Only when these two aspects are linked together has the study succeeded."[7]

All instances of rhetorical extravagancy that are commonly cited to expose Lin's viciousness are taken from contexts of immediate conflict. A good example is the quarrel about the direction of political study with Tan Zheng, who had taken over Marshal Luo Ronghuan's responsibilities as head of the General Political Department in December 1956. At a military conference in May 1959, Tan had argued that Mao's opposition to dogmatic study was not coterminous with abandoning the study of theory altogether. Debating current problems without having established a theoretical fundament, according to Tan, bore the danger of "intellectual confusion."[8] Tan argued against bridging difficult concepts with simplistic

---

[7] Quoted from Lin Biao, "Zai quanjun gaoji ganbu huiyi shang de jianghua" [Speech at an All-Army High-Ranking Cadres Conference], May 1958, in Yi Lin futongshuai wei guanghui bangyang wuxian zhongyu weida lingxiu Mao zhuxi (YLF) [With Vice-Commander Lin as Glorious Example Boundlessly Loyal toward the Great Leader Chairman Mao], vol. 1, Beijing: n.d., 272f.

[8] *PLA tongjian* 2, 1800.

slogans[9] or neglecting the importance of changed circumstances. He therefore advocated the systematic study of Mao Zedong Thought. But what angered Lin most was that Tan even sought Mao's opinion on the matter while asking for guidance on a related issue.[10] The fact that Tan established an exclusive line of communication with Mao led Lin Biao to fear that his publicly fostered image as closest student of the Chairman would be contradicted.

Although Tan gave in shortly thereafter, Lin remained skeptical about his reliability because he had proven to place matters of content above personal loyalty. The removal of Tan Zheng from the General Political Department remained a difficult task since Tan had powerful supporters such as Luo Ronghuan. During an enlarged meeting of the Central Military Commission in September and October 1960 on the eve of the campaign to celebrate the publication of the fourth volume of Mao's *Selected Works*, the political climate had become expedient enough to criticize anyone on grounds of hindering the advancement of Mao Zedong Thought. In his speech to the conference, Lin Biao elaborated on his concept of a correct working style and criticized those who had opposed his idea of a "living" application of Mao Zedong Thought.[11] He raised the stakes of Mao Zedong Thought even higher by declaring it to represent the "peak of modern-day thought."[12] All those who had not complied with his working style were thus placed under the Damocles sword of having opposed Mao Zedong. Tan was accused of having come close to harboring an "independent kingdom" (*duli wangguo*) and of having formed a sectarian group.[13] By elaborating on the danger of capitalist restoration and the necessity to raise class consciousness through political education, Lin catered to Mao's idea of a return to the frugal, politicized military style advocated during the Yan'an period. Tan was demoted to deputy rank and would later be incarcerated for nine years during the Cultural Revolution for his "counterrevolutionary crime" of opposing Mao Zedong Thought.

---

[9] Junshi kexueyuan junshi lishi yanjiubu (ed.), *Zhongguo renmin jiefangjun liushi nian dashiji (1927–1987)* [Major Events in Sixty Years of the PLA (1927–1987)], Beijing: Junshi kexue chubanshe, 1988, 578.

[10] Zhonggong wenxian yanjiushi (ed.), *Mao wengao 9*, 177.

[11] Lin Biao, "Zai quanjun gaoji ganbu de huiyi shang" [Speech at an All-Army High-Ranking Cadres Conference], October 1960, in YLF 1, 322.

[12] Ibid., 340.

[13] Junshi kexueyuan, *Jiefangjun liushi nian*, 588.

A SHORTCUT TO MARXISM

The unsystematic character of Mao's *Selected Works* presented cadres in charge of political education with difficulties. The two basic ways of circumventing the restrictions imposed by the writings themselves were either to widen the spectrum by including other works of the Marxist-Leninist canon or to emphasize the study of certain key concepts only and to adapt them through constant repetition. Lin Biao took the latter approach to extremes. While he was not the inventor of the "lively study and application" of Mao Zedong Thought,[14] he was determined and in a position to carry it further than anyone else. In his first speech as minister of defense, before an assembly of high-ranking military officers in September 1959, Lin Biao dealt at length with the question of political study. He acknowledged the importance of the Marxist-Leninist classics ("if we don't study Marxism-Leninism this is tantamount to a doctor not studying medicine"),[15] but instead of arduously reading through the whole canon with its references to foreign names and places, he proposed a theoretical shortcut:

> How should we study Marxism-Leninism? I propose to you, Comrades, to mainly study the works of Comrade Mao Zedong. This is a shortcut to studying Marxism-Leninism. Comrade Mao Zedong comprehensively, creatively developed Marxism-Leninism. We study Comrade Mao Zedong's works because [they are] easy to study and can be applied as soon as we have studied them. To study well is an extremely useful thing.[16]

By early 1960, the shortcut to Marxism was reduced even further as Lin proposed to study Mao's works by way of learning to recite only the most important sentences.[17] The advice, derived from a personal habit of collecting quotations of important Chinese philosophers on flash cards and memorizing them for later usage, was to have a profound influence on the development of the Cultural Revolutionary Mao cult. Instead of achieving systematic knowledge of Mao's works or even of the Marxist-Leninist

---

[14] The name of the campaign had been brought up by Xu Rongxin, a squad leader of unit 159, as a method to improve the quality of military training during the Great Leap Forward; see Wang Jining, "Zhanshu dongzuo yao huojiao huoxue huoyong" [Tactical Movements Should Be Lively Taught, Lively Studied, and Lively Applied], in *Jiefangjun bao*, 11 July 1958, 1.

[15] YLF 1, 276.

[16] Ibid., 276.

[17] Lin Biao, "Zai quanjun gaoji ganbu huiyi shang de jianghua (jielu)" [Speech at an All-Army High-Ranking Cadre Conference (Excerpt)], February 1960, in YLF 1, 306.

canon itself, his followers came to employ fitting quotations as an ultimate means of persuasion by invoking the authority of the CCP Chairman.

The methods employed under the aegis of Lin Biao reveal continuity with the policies of his predecessor in many aspects except for the style of political study.[18] Lin's notion of studying theory was based on the premise that theory was not necessarily to be understood by cognitive means but rather to be acknowledged in a ritualized fashion through a process of habitual action. In April 1961, while inspecting troops, Lin Biao had distinguished between education by means of performing examples to be emulated by others (*shenjiao*) and by means of verbal instructions (*yan-jiao*),[19] both of which should be practiced on a regular basis, much like one practices table tennis by playing. Verbal education was to supplement the physical training by providing the soldiers with an intellectual compass, with fitting quotations applicable under any situation. The dual education was to develop into a natural conduct of the soldiers in order to prevent the rise of doubts. If using the notion of ritual to explain Lin's style of political education, one should distinguish between the aforementioned types of habitual action that came to be increasingly formalized from transcendent notions of ritual that are often employed in anthropological usages of the term. Even during the Cultural Revolution, rituals in the sense of religious worship remained the exception. Lin was highly aware of the formative power of habitual action and the close interdependence of form and content. In a speech about the drill of troops in 1944, he had already argued for the importance of achieving a spirit of unanimity by standardizing successful experiences of drill, ceremony, and military order. The working style of an army should not be disregarded as empty formalism.[20]

The emphasis on political study originated from a sharp assessment of the present situation characterized by the catastrophic situation in the countryside and Mao's endorsement of cult building. The dismissal of the highly respected Peng Dehuai had severely undermined the prestige

---

[18] David Shambaugh has pointed out the difference between the image fostered by Lin and the actual military spending that continued to rise continuously under his aegis; David Shambaugh, "Building the Party-State in China, 1949–1965: Bringing the Soldier Back In," in Cheek and Saich (eds.), *New Perspectives*, 144f. This conforms to Lin's habit of advocating political study in public, while even in October 1960 he declared that between 60 and 80 percent of time should be spent with military and not political training in order not to transform the PLA into a "fake army." See YLF 1, 330f.

[19] Lin Biao, "Shicha budui shi de zhishi (jielu)" [Instructions while Inspecting the Troops (Excerpt)], April 1961, in YLF 1, 373.

[20] Lin Biao, "Jinnian zenyang lianbing" [How to Drill Troops This Year], 18 October 1944, in YLF 1, 92f. See further YLF 1, 338.

of the party and Mao Zedong personally within the PLA. The dramatic consequences of the Great Leap Forward in late 1959 were noticed even in the Central Bureau of Guards, the unit entrusted with guarding the party leadership. The internal *Bulletin of Activities* recorded "unrest in thought and instability in feeling,"[21] as well as criticism of the party's agricultural policies among the young soldiers, most of whom had a rural background themselves. Reports about the dramatic food situation reached the recruits via correspondence with their families or trips to relatives. Soldiers quoted commune members from their home villages as saying "[a]t present what the peasants eat in the villages is worse than what dogs ate in the past," or rhetorically asked whether "Chairman Mao [is] going to allow us to starve to death."[22]

These trends would potentially endanger the stability of the PLA if ideological work did not catch up. Lin Biao developed two basic strategies to counter these trends. The first was a codex of general conduct, the "three-eight working style" (*san ba zuofeng*), named after two inscriptions Mao had made in 1939 for the Anti-Japanese Military and Political University in Yan'an (*Kangda*), of which Lin had been director for a couple of months. The working style was mainly aimed at easing top-down communication and at having orders carried out "vigorously and speedily."[23] It was to prevent the dangers posed by an undisciplined and slow response under conditions of nuclear threat. The second approach was termed the "four firsts" (*si ge diyi*), which meant placing the human factor, political and ideological work, and living thought above military weapons, nonpolitical and nonideological work, and dogmatism. By transforming Mao Zedong Thought into a "spiritual nuclear bomb," a loyal and politically stable army was to be secured through constant remolding. Lin thus subscribed to Mao's modified view of the interaction between super- and infrastructure:

> Marxism-Leninism is materialism, but this materialism is a dialectical materialism. It accepts the primary nature of matter and the secondary nature of the mind. But here some people often make the mistake of equating primary nature with primary importance. This is a big error.... Under certain conditions spiritual things surpass material things, surpass the power of matter. Spiritual things can also transform into material

---

[21] *Bulletin of Activities* 1 (1 January 1961), in J. Chester Cheng (ed.), *The Politics of the Chinese Red Army: A Translation of the Bulletin of Activities of the People's Liberation Army*, Stanford: Hoover Institution on War, Revolution, and Peace, 1966, 13.

[22] Ibid., 13.

[23] YLF 1, 301.

strength ... like after the explosion of a nuclear bomb, when it releases an enormous power.[24]

The details of implementing Lin Biao's "invention,"[25] however, remained vague and provided political commissars with possibilities to come up with model soldiers or units that had excelled in the application of the abstract maxims. The ensuing campaign of "lively study and application" was thus characterized by numerous exchanges between the central and local levels. Successful models were taken up by the *Liberation Army News* and, through redistribution via the media networks, were circulated throughout the whole army as worthy of emulation.

The wider significance of the campaign to study and apply Mao Zedong Thought in the military after 1959 lies with respect to the strategies that were devised to secure its success amid the turbulences of the Great Leap Forward. Many of the devices had already been employed during earlier rectification movements, but never with the extreme focus on quotations of Mao Zedong. All of the measures were to retain their importance on a much larger scale during the PLA-dominated phase of the Cultural Revolution. The most important strategies consisted of restricting access to unofficial sources of information possibly contradicting the prescribed views, of unifying perception and description of the present situation by means of exegetical and emotional bonding, and finally, of implementing a system of incentives that awarded eager students of Mao's teachings publicly through the propagation of political model heroes.

INFORMATION CONTROL AND EXEGETICAL BONDING

Because of the rural background of most of its recruits, the PLA was especially vulnerable to the effects of the famine. Although only the military top leadership, entitled to read the Xinhua News Agency's *Internal Reference* (*Neibu cankao*), was informed about the national scale of starvation, the news about people dying in the villages and local cadres using brute force to try to keep the peasants from rebelling reached the soldiers by a varied range of communication channels. The most frequent way of transporting information, as mentioned previously, was via family

---

[24] Ibid., 326f.
[25] Mao completely endorsed the "four firsts," calling them a "great creation" and "invention"; see Li Zhisui and Anne F. Thurston, *The Private Life of Chairman Mao: The Memoirs of Mao's Personal Physician Dr. Li Zhisui*, New York: Random House, 1994, 412.

letters or visits from relatives. Other sources of information included local media that tended to be less severely controlled than the central media. In mid-1960, therefore, all Hebei provincial party cadres were specifically addressed to start secret examinations of the local publishing organs and to pay more attention to the supervision of local newspapers and broadcasting units. After all, even foreign intelligence agencies were said to have increasingly focused on local media in order to understand the "ever growing successes"[26] of the Great Leap Forward. Occasional reports related to the famine and diseases stemming from malnutrition or reports on unsuitable sources of food in provincial-level internal party organs were criticized in a similar fashion.[27]

As a first measure, the influx of noncensored information via family ties and personal networks was restricted. All army units and especially those stationed in disaster areas were to pay adequate attention to letters and visits, and to "take the initiative in preventing the soldiers from being harmed by bad influences."[28] The prevention, however, was not to proceed by means of restrictive measures such as the confiscation of family letters or the rejection of visiting relatives, as it had occasionally been conducted in the past. Rude action was deemed to be incapable of exerting a long-term positive effect on the behavior of the soldiers or to improve the declining image of the PLA among the general populace. Instead of using force, the political committees were to proceed by turning critical situations into examples of living education. Family letters and the sentiments expressed in them were to be taken seriously. The situation was to be explained by blaming the famine on the harmful influence of natural disasters and the deviations of a number of local cadres from the correct

[26] "Hebei shengwei xuanchuanbu guanyu zai xinwen chuban bumen kaizhan baomi de jiancha he jinxing ganbu renyuan shencha qingli gongzuo de tongzhi" [Hebei Provincial Committee Propaganda Department Notice on Starting a Secret Inspection in the News and Publishing Department and on Conducting Examination and Cleansing Work among the Cadre Personnel], 19 July 1960, HPA 864-1-229.

[27] Among the eighty-three internal publications circulated in Hebei province in 1960, sixty-eight were abolished due to a paper shortage, redundancy, or the leakage of state secrets. A prominent case was the *Substitute Food Bulletin* (*Dai shipin jianbao*), which in its eighth issue had covered the situation in Yu County near Zhangjiakou, where 80 percent of the county's roughly 13,600 sick people had suffered from the coarse ingredients of the "substitute" foodstuff. See "Hebei shengwei xuanchuanbu guanyu zhengdun shengji neibu kanwu de qingkuang he yijian xiang shengwei baogao" [Report of the Hebei Propaganda Department to the Provincial Party Committee Concerning the Situation of and Opinions on Reorganizing the Provincial Internal Publications], 25 March 1961, HPA 864-1-249.

[28] Cheng, *Politics*, 15.

line. By convincing the common soldiers of these views, ambiguous thinking was to be replaced through a uniform and positive evaluation of the
"Three Red Banners" (referring to the Great Leap, the people's communes,
and the CCP general line of socialist construction) and the soldiers' passive
acceptance to be turned into active and self-conscious propagation of the
party's interpretation of the events. This type of exemplary education,
according to a contemporary report, proved to be ten times more effective
than the usual frontal classroom lectures.[29]

The instruments by which the communist conversion was to be achieved
were manifold and specified according to the different ranks within the
army. While the military leadership was to continue with self-study and
small group discussions, the search for effective models brought forth new
forms of exegetical bonding at the lower ranks that emphasized the emotional aspect. The Lanzhou Military Region had, after conducting a rectification of working styles among party cadres in July 1960, employed a
method to strengthen the proletarian class standpoint; this method was
commonly referred to as "two remembrances, three investigations" (*liang
yi, san cha*).[30] On Lin Biao's request, the report of the Lanzhou Military
Region was promoted throughout the army in a number of trial spots. Liu
Zhijian, deputy director of the General Political Department since October
1957, during a telephone conference on 7 January 1961 described the
experiences in the trial spots as highly satisfying. Within a short period
of time (usually three to four weeks), the educational movement had raised
the soldiers' class awareness and fueled "fervent love" for the socialist
cause.[31] The participants, according to the report, had compared their
present situation with the bitterness of the past and had come to feel
gratitude toward the party, despite the present hardships. Guided by
Mao Zedong Thought, the soldiers were able to overcome their "numb
feelings for peace,"[32] further correct their attitude toward duty, and
become a unified force. Based on the experiences of 412 trial units, the

---

[29] *Bulletin of Activities* 7, 1 February 1961, in Cheng, *Politics*, 211.

[30] "Jiazhang liandui sixiang gongzuo de yi ba yaoshi. Ji Lanzhou budui de yiku yundong"
[A Key to Strengthening Ideological Work in the Companies. On the Remembering
Bitterness Campaign in the Lanzhou Armed Forces], in *Jiefangjun bao*, 28 September
1960, 2. The method of employing comparisons and remembrances to justify present
policies had been previously used within the military; see, for example, Junshi kexueyuan,
Jiefangjun liushi nian, 564.

[31] *Bulletin of Activities* 4, 11 January 1961, in Cheng, *Politics*, 97.

[32] Ibid., 97.

emotional bonding was implemented as the core of political work in all army units in the first months of 1961.

A report of the Beijing Military Region describes the highly theatrical performances and the necessary preparations in detail. The subordinate companies and platoons were first to understand the situation within the unit, to analyze the specific grievances, and to search for trustworthy models with flawless work records and good verbal expression. Because the success of the movement rested to a large extent on the credibility of the employed models, they were not to be "manufactured or simulated for the occasion,"[33] but to be nurtured with care. The general guidance was to be provided by the army's political committees while the political and administrative personnel in the military regions remained responsible for the training of the lower-level cadres. A few short writings of Mao Zedong, most notably "In Memory of Norman Bethune" and "Serve the People," both stories about martyrs for the socialist cause, became the key texts of the movement.

The campaign itself proceeded in three basic steps. The first phase was to arouse passions by remembering past hardships and to use the historical experiences of the CCP to remember the oppression of the Chinese nation. As the success was highly dependent on the setting and the choice of models, the cadres were advised to employ solemn decoration and distinguished models and to look after the material well-being of the participants. The meetings were to be an occasion of great sadness and thus to take place in a disciplined manner; however, cadres were not to insist on formalities such as the weeping of the participants as demonstration of their sincerity:

> [T]he atmosphere of remembering hardships should not seem compulsory. However, since remembering the hardships is a serious business, there must be a certain atmosphere (such as writing and shouting slogans) but this should not be overdone, such as eating "hardship rice" [*chi yiku fan*]. It would also be a mistake if during the meeting of "remembering the hardship" no one were allowed to wear shoes with nails, to come in and go out, and to be excused to go to the lavatory. Neither should there be any excessive stress on "weeping." Weeping is quite natural if it arises from emotional stress but it should not be used as a standard; there should be no regulation such as "no dismissal of the meeting until the weeping stage is reached."[34]

---

[33] Ibid., 109.
[34] Ibid., 103.

From the stage of remembering hardships, the political commissars were to channel the hatred toward the imperialist aggressors and internal class enemies. Popular means included oral presentations, the study of Mao writings dealing with class analysis, and recent newspaper articles. By "taking revenge," the participants were to be enabled to realize the two major reasons behind the past oppression: capitalist exploitation and private ownership. After the commissars had traced the reasons back to the regime of Chiang Kai-shek and his U.S. supporters, the soldiers were to uproot the sources of hardship by unmasking capitalism and U.S. imperialism as the "big boss of all the world's reactionaries."[35] The catharsis, finally, was to be reached by comparing the past favorably to the present, based on the reading of Mao articles on frugality and proletarian solidarity.

This living education was to lead individuals to find the "source of sweetness" in the correct leadership of the CCP and Mao Zedong. To achieve this goal, local instructors were to employ all possible materials. Movies, comics, big character posters, performances, invited talks by workers who had suffered during the old regime, exhibitions, or on-the-spot inspections of model communes presented legitimate forms of persuasion. In a final step, everyone had to investigate his or her own class standpoint, fighting spirit, and work record, and try to model his or her life on the given examples. The employment of specific enemies on which the hatred could be channeled presented a possible outlet for the experienced frustrations and thus a source of releasing aggressions. But Lin Biao himself quickly realized the destructive potential aroused through the comparisons. In January 1961, he therefore forbade participants to project the generated class hatred onto individual cadres for their personal wrongdoings or to criticize them publicly.[36] The violent language that was employed to achieve the emotional bonding was not to result in destruction but to be transformed into fervent love for the Chairman and the CCP. No such restrictions would apply during the Cultural Revolution a few years later.

The disciplinary and clearly functional character of the "two remembrances" movement reportedly did not hamper its efficiency, even within companies where the majority of the soldiers' families had been affected by the famine. The success of the campaign, according to acting Chief-of-Staff Luo Ruiqing, was to be seen in linking day-to-day military problems with Mao Zedong Thought, as he reported to Mao and Lin Biao after an inspection of several provinces in March 1961. Luo astutely observed

---

[35] Ibid., 110.
[36] *Bulletin of Activities* 7, 1 February 1961, in Cheng, *Politics*, 205.

that most comparisons of the present sweetness referred back to the period of the land reform, whereas remarks about the Great Leap Forward were "inclined to be abstract and without substance."[37] Luo's observations revealed the limits of propagandistic activities and the necessity to root the exegetical bonding in genuinely positive experiences in order to stimulate popular feeling. In the final report, which was endorsed and transmitted by the Central Military Commission on 30 March 1961, the campaign was described as the turning point of implementing living education among the troops.[38] The movement had been successfully accomplished in 90 to 95 percent of the primary units and had reminded the young soldiers, who were born in hardship and had grown up in the "sweetness" of socialism, of their class origins. Only a small number of persons, according to the reports, still did not realize the superiority of the present living conditions and would have to be remolded over time.

Among the examples chosen to substantiate the success of the campaign and to show unrelenting hatred of class enemies was the example of a young soldier named Lei Feng. Born to a poor peasant household in Wangcheng district in Hunan province, Lei's father was said to have been buried alive by the Japanese, his brother had been persecuted to death by Guomindang capitalists, and his mother had committed suicide after being assaulted by a landlord.[39] Lei Feng's story moved the audiences and instilled fierce hatred against the numerous enemies. He was to rise to nationwide fame after his premature death in the following year at age twenty-two. By mid-1961, the remembrance campaign had been successfully completed and the army entered a new stage on the path of political education: the cultivation of model units and soldiers.

EMULATING INDIVIDUALS AND COLLECTING EXPERIENCES

The emotional bonding had been effective in countering the immediate impact of the famine on troop morale but it was no instrument that could be employed continuously without weakening its impact. A well-managed, repeated socialist education therefore had to rely on a multitude of techniques to achieve its objectives. After the break with the Soviet Union, the search for national traditions and models worthy of emulation was encouraged. The works of Mao Zedong presented a natural choice for a

[37] See *Bulletin of Activities* 11, 2 March 1961, in Cheng, *Politics*, 278.
[38] *Bulletin of Activities* 15, 5 April 1961, in Cheng, *Politics*, 413.
[39] Ibid., 413.

successful model of adapting Marxism-Leninism to Chinese conditions. The relics of the cult of Mao Zedong in the early 1940s and his acceptance among the party leadership now proved to be crucial for the emergence of the new Mao cult. While Mao's works provided the intellectual framework, the local and provincial party organs had to search for local model experiences with a possibly nationwide appeal.

Campaigns to elevate certain individuals could rely on a number of earlier traditions in the People's Republic, most notably the cultivation of different kinds of "activists" (*jijifenzi*) in state factories, the PLA, or the Youth League. The distinguishing of activists had been one of the main instruments of the CCP to secure a stratum of like-minded successors who both provided information on local conditions and helped in taking over responsibilities from the chronically understaffed party secretaries. Other sources were the frequent public competitions and assemblies in the PLA or the Youth League and the awarding of trophies for excellence in military training, theoretical study, and the displaying of communist morals. Most prominent in the years leading up to the Cultural Revolution was the "four good–five good" (*si hao–wu hao*) competition in the PLA. The designation had come to be used in the mid-1950s already, although the specific content changed slightly over time. The campaign gained nationwide importance during the Great Leap Forward and from early 1961 came to serve as a way of strengthening discipline within a self-perpetuating, merit-based system of incentives. The "five good" designations referred to individual behavior, namely, to be good in politics, military training, style of work, fulfillment of tasks, and physical education. The parallel "four good" campaign was aimed at companies and requested them to be good in fostering political work and unbookish ideas, in military training, in the display of a good life, and in the display of a good work style.

Although the twin campaign was advocated throughout the army in 1961, the exact criteria for how to measure success or the respective targets to be reached remained vague. The units were asked to develop specific criteria for awarding the designations and to ensure that they could be achieved after several attempts.[40] In April 1962, the General Political Department announced the results of the "four good" campaign in 1961. Over 5,800 "four good" companies and local-level units had been designated; 520,000 individuals had been awarded the title of "five good" soldier; and 185,000 soldiers had been awarded titles as distinguished

---

[40] *Bulletin of Activities* 14, 29 March 1961, in Cheng, *Politics*, 390f.

gunmen, grenadiers, or technical experts.[41] In the following year, the campaign continued on a regular basis and titles began to be awarded according to a standardized system of rating provided by the General Political Department.

The campaign to emulate Lei Feng, the most famous subject of all Chinese model campaigns and commonly employed to characterize the growing Mao cult prior to the Cultural Revolution, was part of these attempts to secure discipline and political awareness. Lei Feng's prominent role in the "two remembrances" movement had already granted him a high media profile before his alleged premature and tragic death on 15 August 1962 after being accidentally killed by a falling telephone pole that had been run into by a truck. The early perishing of the model soldier caused the leadership of his former unit in Shenyang to prepare a study campaign to learn from Lei's experiences on 18 January 1963. Three days later, the Ministy of Defense awarded the title "Lei Feng unit" to Lei's former company. The *Liberation Army News* on 8 February printed an editorial entitled "Become Good Soldiers of Mao Zedong Thought like Lei Feng," and by early March, the civilian party press, most notably *China Youth*, spread the example of the selfless soldier of utmost loyalty to Mao Zedong throughout China.[42] Selections from his diary, authentic or not, were published along with a number of verses in his memory written by CCP leaders. Other model soldiers were to follow and the "Good Eighth Company on Nanjing Road" (*Nanjing lushang hao ba lian*) became the first collective to be awarded nationwide attention. The whole country was to study the experiences of the PLA, and thus the influence of Lin Biao's style of political work extended beyond the confines of the army.

CONTEMPORARY CRITICISM

The destruction of superstition in foreign models and overarching awe regarding Western military theory had been a near-consensus among the military leadership. The acceptance of Lin's working style, however, was not unanimous. The formulation and supervision of political work within the PLA had formally been the prerogative of the General Political Department and the Political Academy under the leadership of Luo

---

[41] *PLA tongjian* 2, 1866.
[42] A short overview about the haphazard manner of the planning of the campaign can be found in Roderick MacFarquhar, *The Coming of the Cataclysm, 1961–1966*, Oxford, New York: Oxford University Press and Columbia University Press, 1997, 338f.

Ronghuan, upon whose loyalty Mao placed enormous trust.[43] Luo had in a talk on revising work methods in April 1958 already argued that regardless of whether the study documents consisted of CCP Center directives, Chairman Mao's works, or classical Marxist-Leninist writings, the important point was to develop the spirit of the work and not just be able to recite a few fitting quotes.[44] The danger of an overt stress on application, as Luo argued, derived from potentially wrong application if the basic truths of Marxism-Leninism had not been understood. Especially after the demotion of his long-time trusted colleague Tan Zheng, Luo, who had taken up the responsibility as head of the General Political Department again on 3 January 1961, opened a salvo of criticism at Lin's proposed style of study and the impression that the development of Marxism-Leninism had reached its peak with Mao Zedong Thought. The most dangerous aspect of the working style proposed by Lin Biao, in Luo's opinion, remained the repetition of catchphrases without the ability to relate them to the spirit of Marxism-Leninism or Mao Zedong Thought. Luo especially criticized Lin's directive of "studying with problems in mind" from late October 1960: "If we study with problems in mind, this way we have to look for answers in Mao's *Selected Works*. This is not very appropriate. If for example two people have a disagreement and a problem occurs, how shall we find an answer from Mao's *Selected Works*? We should continue to study standpoint, viewpoint, and method."[45]

Within the civil administration, Deng Xiaoping voiced similar criticism. In a speech before a party meeting in Tianjin on 25 March 1960, Deng specifically addressed the question of how to propagate Mao Zedong Thought correctly by listing a number of problems in current propaganda work:

> First, the main problem at present is that Mao Zedong Thought is being used in a vulgar fashion. Everything is said to be Mao Zedong Thought. For example, if the [number of] customers in a shop increases slightly, one calls it a development of Mao Zedong Thought; practicing table tennis has likewise been called an application of Mao Zedong Thought. Second, Marxism-Leninism itself is very seldom being talked about. ... Why should we address this problem? Because according to our correct understanding of Mao Zedong Thought, on the one hand, one has to support

---

[43] See his comment to Wang Li in 1963 that the three people he trusted most were Luo Ronghuan, Deng Xiaoping, and Chen Yun, quoted in Jin, *Culture of Power*, 60.

[44] Huang Yao, *Luo Ronghuan nianpu* [Chronicle of the Life of Luo Ronghuan], Beijing: Renmin chubanshe, 2002, 780.

[45] Ibid., 816.

and defend Marxism-Leninism; on the other hand, we have to develop Marxism-Leninism. Mao Zedong Thought and Marxism-Leninism are the same thing. Mao Zedong Thought supports the universal truths of Marxism-Leninism and has added a lot of new content to the treasure trove of Marxism-Leninism. Therefore, one should not try to separate Mao Zedong Thought from Marxism-Leninism, as if they are separate things. ... If one speaks of Mao Zedong Thought and does not mention Marxism-Leninism, it appears to be an appraisal of Mao Zedong Thought but in reality it means diminishing its effectiveness.[46]

Deng's criticism was specifically directed against Lin's shortcut to Marxism and the formulaic appraisal of Mao Zedong Thought. Here two fundamentally different ways of approaching the theoretical heritage of Marxism-Leninism collided. While Deng Xiaoping held steadfast to the principal truth of Marxist theories and genuinely searched for ways of adapting reality to the communist model, Lin Biao's approach was much more instrumental. Lin had come to understand the strategic advantages Mao Zedong had gained in the past by selectively modifying certain concepts and thus eliminating other sources of legitimacy. Deng's pondering about collective leadership in his speech in Tianjin provided another example of his insistence of how things should be done according to theory without taking into account the modus vivendi that had come to dominate CCP politics:

> There further exists the problem of collective leadership; this should also be mentioned during certain party meetings. We practice collective leadership. Mao Zedong is a representative of this collective leadership. He is the leader of our party. His rank and position are different from normal members of the collective leadership, but under no conditions can Comrade Mao Zedong be separated from the CCP Center. Instead, one should look at Mao as a member of the party's collective leadership and thus speak about his position within our party according to the facts. Comrade Mao Zedong respects collective leadership. Yesterday he said that phrases should conform to realities, for if they do not conform to reality they stand on feet of clay. We should adopt this kind of spirit in order to succeed in the propagation of Mao Zedong Thought.[47]

Lu Dingyi took up Deng Xiaoping's characterization of Mao Zedong Thought in two speeches in April 1961 and specifically addressed the possible "vulgarization" of Marxism-Leninism, a phrase that without quoting its source came to be the cardinal accusation against the by then disbanded CCP Propaganda Department and the Ministry of Culture

[46] ZGXG 4, 184f.
[47] Ibid., 184f.

during the Cultural Revolution. Lu warned of teaching the younger generation a highly simplified view of difficult matters. The phrase "Mao
Zedong Thought" was not to be freely attached to all kinds of phenomena:
"if we attach this label, anything can be 'Mao Zedong Thought'. ...
Placing labels resembles the Boxer movement, [which thought] after reading a spell that no knifes could harm them."[48]

At a Central Military Commission meeting on 30 April 1961, Luo
Ronghuan immediately confronted Lin Biao by pointing out that the
sentence "studying Mao's *Selected Works* with problems in mind" should
be reconsidered since "this sentence has a shortcoming."[49] Upon Lin's
inquiry regarding what specifically was to be changed, Luo answered that
the focus should be directed at the content and spirit of Mao's works and
advised that the sentence should be dropped from the discussed document.
Unable to take up the dispute with his long-time political commissar, Lin
Biao declared the meeting to be over and stormed out even before Luo had
finished his answer, in which he advocated the classical Maoist triad of
standpoint, viewpoint, and method. The enmity that Lin's failure to stand
up to Luo at the meeting engendered ended two years later when Luo
Ronghuan prematurely died, aged sixty-one, on 16 December 1963. Mao
Zedong the same evening praised Luo's outstanding loyalty, integrity, and
indomitable spirit of straightforward criticism instead of spreading rumors
behind his back. Thus even during the Cultural Revolution, Luo was not
posthumously criticized. After Luo's death however, Lin no longer had a
comparable adversary in the PLA and started to build a network of loyal
cadres who would back his political views and try to materialize Lin's
directives on political study. Thus it was no coincidence that merely a
month after Luo's death the first internal version of the Mao cult's primary
token, the Little Red Book, was compiled and distributed.

---

[48] *Da pipan ziliao xuanbian. Lu Dingyi fangeming xiuzhengzhuyi jiaoyu yanlun zhaibian*
[Selection of Criticism Materials: Extracts from Lu Dingyi's Counterrevolutionary
Reactionary Utterances on Education], Shanghai: "Neikan" fanxiubing, May 1967, 2.
[49] Huang, *Luo Ronghuan nianpu*, 835.

5

The Little Red Book

The history of the *Quotations from Chairman Mao Tse-tung* is probably the most astounding publishing tale ever. The estimated number of official volumes printed between 1966 and 1969 ranges just over a billion, second only to the Holy Bible in terms of circulation numbers and this figure even excludes local prints, foreign language editions, internal army volumes, and innumerable mimeographed or handwritten collections.[1] Up to Lin Biao's death in September 1971, the Little Red Book was translated into thirty-six languages, including Braille script, and published around 110 million times abroad. Besides the official versions of the *Quotations*, up to 440 local editions have been noted. During the decade of the Cultural Revolution, all in all some 10.8 billion Mao texts or posters were printed by the state, making Mao the best-selling author ever, especially if the 783 million Mao items published between 1949 and 1965 are included.[2] The stunning success of the works of Mao Zedong and most importantly the Little Red Book played a crucial role in the unfolding of the Cultural Revolution and the rise of its specific rhetoric. This chapter provides a short history of the compilation and distribution of the Little Red Book

---

[1] San Mu, "Guanyu 'Wenge' qianhou Mao Zedong zhuzuo de chuban shimo" [The Story of Publishing Mao Zedong's Works in the "Cultural Revolution" Period], in *Shehui kexue luntan* 1 (2004), 89. The estimated circulation number of the Bible according to the *Guinness Book of World Records* (2006) is 2.5 billion since 1815.

[2] The estimate is based on the numbers published in the Ministry of Culture's internal news organ *Culture Trends* (*Wenhua dongtai*). See Liu Gao and Shi Feng (eds.), *Xin Zhongguo chuban wushi nian jishi* [Recollections about Fifty Years of Publishing in New China], Beijing: Xinhua chubanshe, 1999, 97.

against the background of political events up to the Politburo meeting in May 1966.

Lin Biao has often been portrayed as the mastermind behind the compilation of the *Quotations*.[3] Lin's ritualistic style of studying and applying quotations instead of arduously working through the Marxist-Leninist classics clearly played an important role in shaping the process that finally led to the book's compilation but, as will be shown, he was only marginally involved in determining the book's specific form and content. During an inspection of troops in April 1961, Lin Biao had requested that the *Liberation Army News* frequently reprint quotes from Mao Zedong to help ensure that "every soldier at any time, under any condition can immediately receive guidance from Chairman Mao's Thought."[4] Occasional quotes had started to appear in the *Liberation Army News* from November 1960 onward. The citations were taken from various sources and included Lu Xun's works, entries from revolutionary martyrs' diaries, and quotations from Mao Zedong and Lin Biao. From 1 May 1961 onward, Mao quotations started to appear daily in the army newspapers' headlines. The task of retrieving a suitable Mao quote to supplement the main gist of the editorial rested with the *Liberation Army News* Reference Material Department and the staff in charge of the card collection of Marx, Engels, Lenin, Stalin, and Mao quotes. The usage of specific formulae to render an argument authoritative had been a universal feature in Marxism-Leninism, but the necessity to come up with a suitable Mao citation on daily issues presented the editorial board with great difficulties. The text corpus to choose from encompassed the authoritative and published volumes one through four of Mao's *Selected Works*, covering the period between 1926 and 1949. Besides offering general remarks on the style of work or study, the need for selfless perseverance to communist ideals, a frugal lifestyle, and constant vigilance against the rise of enemies, the texts could hardly provide guidance for the questions posed by de-Stalinization or the economic havoc caused by the Great Leap Forward.

As no concordance or general index of Mao Zedong's works had been compiled to that date, Li Yimin, editor-in-chief of the *Liberation Army News*, on behalf of his staff asked Luo Ronghuan in his capacity as head of the General Political Department about how to deal with the necessity to follow Lin Biao's requests strictly, especially on how to come up with a

---

[3] See, for example, Yan Jiaqi and Gao Gao, *Turbulent Decade: A History of the Cultural Revolution*, Honolulu: University of Hawaii Press, 1995, Chapter 11.

[4] YLF 1, 373.

suitable quote for issues on which Mao had never officially been on the record. Luo's answer was pragmatic. He advised to study the spirit of Mao's directives on newspaper work, most importantly his "Talks to the Editorial Staff of the *Jinsui Daily*," and not to turn Mao's writings into holy scripture.[5] The editor did not dare to adopt a standpoint as independent as that of the old marshal. Deputy editor-in-chief Tang Pingzhu was ordered to study the experiences of other newspapers faced with the same dilemma and was delighted to hear about a method employed by the *Tianjin Daily*. There the most famous passages of Mao's *Selected Works* had been copied and thematically arranged in a card box.[6] Finding a suitable quote thus was much easier. Tang ordered four staff members to copy the whole catalogue. The task was completed within a week and eased the search for fitting Mao quotes considerably. The arrangement according to topics in the card boxes, an idea imported from Tianjin, provided the fundament of the later compilation of the Little Red Book.

The frequent changes of policy line may explain the enormous popularity the quotes enjoyed not only in the PLA but among party cadres as well. If a local report could be justified by invoking the authority of Chairman Mao, the danger of being exposed as having fostered an "independent kingdom" or of having followed an incorrect line was reduced considerably. The campaign to learn from the PLA, unique within the socialist camp in urging the party to learn from the army, further fueled attempts in the civilian realm and the state bureaucracy to model themselves after the examples of military study activists. The Daqing oilfield and the agrarian production brigade of Dazhai were the first civilian units that rose to nationwide fame for their success in adapting the study methods within a new field. The provincial propaganda departments were therefore especially keen on tracking successful examples of study in counties or local brigades and stepped up the efforts to raise the Marxist-Leninist knowledge of party members and populace.

The Hebei Provincial Committee in March 1964 decided upon new guidelines with regard to the study of Marxist theory. While high-ranking cadres had to work through a thirty-volume collection of selected Marxist-Leninist works, edited by the Central Propaganda Department, county-level secretaries were advised to finish the reading of Mao's *Selected Works* in two years' time. Many counties therefore had reinvigorated the Study

---

[5] Huang, *Luo Ronghuan nianpu*, 836.

[6] See Wei Meiya, "'Mao zhuxi yulu' chuban jiemi" [Solving the Mystery of Publishing the *Quotations from Chairman Mao*], in *Dangshi bolan* 7 (2004), 5.

Chairman Mao's Works Reading Groups established during the Great Leap Forward and meticulously listed the reading progress of every member.[7] Cadres below the county level were to read a collection, edited by the Hebei Provincial Committee, entitled *Classes, Class Struggle, Oppose Revisionism, and Prevent Revisionism*, which consisted primarily of short Mao texts and newspaper articles.[8] Among the general populace, the situation varied according to the efforts of the local cadres in taking the lead in study. However, the increased knowledge of Mao's writings among the masses had also raised the intellectual stakes for many cadres. If villagers discovered that cadre behavior deviated from the basic guidelines laid out in Mao's works, the cadres were sometimes "put in an awkward position."[9] Knowledge of Mao quotations thus theoretically provided a means of empowerment.

Because the *Selected Works* were not accessible to everyone, the quotation excerpts from the *Liberation Army News* were frequently copied in personal notebooks and supplemented through individually found Mao "treasures,"[10] quotations cited in other places. The media assumed an important role in setting examples of successful study. Squad leaders such as Liao Chujiang rose to prominence through their continuing efforts to propagate Mao Zedong Thought through innovative means. In Liao's case, it was the transformation of the army's instructional blackboards into "Quotations boards" that could be carried along when conducting marches or training sessions.[11] Others compiled collections on specific topics such as *Methods of Study* or *Mao on Politics*. The idea to compile an official collection of Mao quotations thus followed deliberately from the recitation style of study.

[7] See "Nangong xianwei zhongxin xuexi xiaozu xuexi Mao zhuxi zhuzuo de qingkuang (chugao)" [The Situation of Studying Chairman Mao's Works in the Nangong County Committee Central Study Group (Preliminary Draft)], 3 April 1964, HPA 864-1-335.

[8] "Hebei shengwei xuanchuanbu guanyu dangqian ganbu, qunzhong xuexi Mao zhuxi zhuzuo qingkuang de huibao" [Hebei Provincial Committee Propaganda Department Report Concerning the Current Situation of Cadres and the Masses in Studying Chairman Mao's Works], 19 April 1964, HPA 864-1-335, 1.

[9] Ibid., 8.

[10] "Zhongguo gongchandang Hebei sheng weiyuanhui guanyu taolun 'Mao zhuxi yulu' yangben yijian de baogao" [CCP Hebei Provincial Committee Report on the Discussion of Different Versions of the "Quotations from Chairman Mao"], 10 February 1966, HPA 855-20-1618, 1.

[11] Wu Qisi and Li Bin, "Heiban bao. Huo sixiang jiaoyu de zhendi" [Blackboard Newspapers: The Front of Lively Thought Education], in *Jiefangjun bao*, 16 January 1965, 2.

There is no hint that Lin Biao himself ordered the publishing of a compilation as it has been commonly alleged. Neither was the reprint of booklets containing short passages to boost troop morale a CCP invention since similar devices had already been employed, among others, by the Guomindang and various Republican era warlords.[12] The project was first made subject of discussion at the General Political Department work conference in December 1963, when Tang Pingzhu presented the idea to his editorial staff to publish Mao quotations in book form for inner-army use. The proposal was greeted with great enthusiasm and Tang ordered his staff to come up with an exemplary work before the end of the conference. Within two weeks' time, the first printed issue, entitled *200 Quotations of Chairman Mao*, was handed out to the conference participants on 5 January 1964 and the project received approval. The number of subject areas was enlarged and sixty-seven quotations were added to the final conference volume that appeared on 10 January with a short preface issued in the name of the General Political Department.[13] During the following four months, the first draft version was revised upon the suggestions of study activists such as Liao Chujiang and other military specialists in the field of Mao Zedong Thought. The draft was then sent to the Central Military Commission and found enthusiastic approval. The book was ordered to be distributed to all military cadres along with one copy supplied to every squad.

On 16 May 1964, the first regular print edition of the *Quotations from Chairman Mao* appeared, classified as "internal" military reading. Its size, in accordance with feedback from study activists, had been reduced to neatly fit into the pockets of military uniforms. The *Quotations* appeared in two print versions: an ordinary edition with a white paper cover imprinted with red characters for the ordinary readership, and a special edition clad in a red plastic covering.[14] Party leaders, including Mao Zedong, Zhu De, and Zhou Enlai, got hold of their private copies through their secretaries. The General Political Department preface had been updated to read 1 May 1964 and was further supplemented by an inscription by Lin Biao. The *Liberation Army News* had requested that he write four short phrases from Lei Feng's diary: "Read Chairman Mao's books, listen to Chairman Mao's words, act according to Chairman Mao's

---

[12] Martin, *Kult und Kanon*, 30.
[13] Wei Meiya, "'Mao zhuxi yulu' bianfa quancheng xunzong" [Complete Account of the Compilation of *Quotations from Chairman Mao*], in *Yanhuang chunqiu* 17.8 (1993), 15.
[14] Liu and Shi, *Xin Zhongguo chuban*, 91.

instructions, and be a good fighter for Chairman Mao." Lin Biao, however, for reasons unknown, stopped short after the third phrase and declined to add the last phrase. Tang Pingzhu finally gave instructions to publish the calligraphy as it was. Only after the book had been distributed, a number of letters from different readers alerted the editors that Lin Biao had not only skipped a sentence but also misspelled the character "ting" ("listening") by adding a superfluous dot. As the books had been distributed to every squad already, the mistake was removed only in the second edition in 1965.

Meanwhile, other collections of Mao texts had been published. In June 1964, the People's Press, under the title of *Selected Readings from Mao Zedong's Works* (*Mao Zedong zhuzuo xuandu*), published a two-volume edition of Mao texts aimed at party cadres, while the Youth Press simultaneously published a collection of mostly abbreviated essays under the same title for a worker and peasant readership. The volumes included four previously unpublished Mao texts, among them the only recently rediscovered 1930 piece "Oppose Book Worship" and the famous "Where Do Correct Ideas Come From." The texts proved important in revising the first edition of the *Quotations* according to a large number of letters that had been sent to the *Liberation Army News* editorial board by its readers. Most requests dealt with pleas to add specific topics. Zhou Enlai's wife Deng Yingchao, for example, had asked to include a section on women. Only in a few cases were deletions requested. Kang Sheng and Mao's secretary Tian Jiaying alerted the editors about three quotations that, despite having originated with Mao, had been published under a different name and therefore were to be dropped in subsequent editions.[15]

The editors in charge of the quotation compilation even conducted fieldwork in the Beijing Garrison to consult famous study activists and to learn about further modifications brought forth at the grassroots level. A Mao Zedong Thought activist named Kong Xiangxiu advised to add a section on the relevance of Mao Zedong Thought within present world affairs by adapting phrases from the 1960 Central Military Commission resolution and Lin Biao's speeches.[16] As a result of the field trip, therefore, the foreword was revised to include an evaluation of Mao Zedong Thought:

> Comrade Mao Zedong is a great Marxist-Leninist of our time. Mao
> Zedong Thought is creatively developed Marxism-Leninism in the era

[15] See Mao Zedong, "Zai shicha ge difang gongzuo shi de jianghua" [Speech Given during the Inspection of Local Work Experiences], November 1965, in CRDB.

[16] Wei, "'Mao zhuxi yulu' chuban jiemi," 8.

in which imperialism is heading for total collapse and socialism is advancing to worldwide victory.... Mao Zedong Thought is the highest and most lively Marxism-Leninism.[17]

The last sentence upon Chief-of-Staff Luo Ruiqing's interference was omitted later, a "crime" that during the Cultural Revolution was taken as a primary example of Luo's opposition to Mao Zedong. The revised draft, now encompassing 33 sections and 427 quotations, found the approval of the General Political Department leadership and Marshals Lin Biao, He Long, Nie Rongzhen, Liu Bocheng, and Ye Jianying. Mao Zedong himself seems to have been rather fond of the edition as well. In a talk with local cadres in November 1965, he compared its scope with the short but influential works attributed to Laozi and Confucius. On 1 August 1965, commemorating the thirty-eighth anniversary of the founding of the PLA, the second edition of the *Quotations* was published. Again its circulation was restricted to inner-military use only. All volumes had been covered in red plastic, giving the book its distinctive appearance; the size had been reduced even further to fit the needs of the soldiers. With a slight modification in the foreword, most notably its attribution to Lin Biao and the interchanging of numerous adjectives with superlatives, the Little Red Book was to be reprinted in December 1966 and spread to every corner of China.

The success of the army volume in 1965 stimulated the compilation of quotation editions within other institutions. But only two other attempts had the necessary institutional background to rival the army volume. With the approval of the CCP Central Secretariat, the Central Propaganda Department, the Ministry of Culture, and the People's Press started collaborating on another version of quotations in April 1965. Furthermore, according to a notice from Luo Ruiqing's successor as chief-of-staff Yang Chengwu to Liu Zhijian, deputy head of the General Political Department, Mao Zedong himself requested Chen Boda to produce an authoritative collection of quotations with the help of his editorial department at the *Red Flag* journal.[18] A fourth version aimed at readers with limited reading skills, entitled *A Hundred Quotations of Chairman Mao*, had upon the Central Propaganda Department's request been compiled by the *People's Daily* in November 1965 but never appeared in print.

The CCP General Office in early 1966 submitted all three volumes to the provincial committees to consult their opinion. The army volume, already known to all cadres, was commonly referred to as the "small-sized

---

[17] Ibid., 16.
[18] The quoted document is said to be dated 28 December 1965; see ibid., 20.

volume"; the final proof version of the People's Press, due to its larger size, was known as the "middle-sized volume"; and the untitled manuscript, written under Chen Boda's aegis with more than 300,000 characters as opposed to the 88,000 in the army volume, came to be known as the "large-sized volume."[19] The replies sent by the provincial committees emphasized the enormous popularity that the *Quotations* enjoyed. Some people had been able to get their copies from the army; others had fabricated their own versions. The main benefit, according to reports, was its practical format, which allowed workers and peasants to carry it with them to work and to consult it whenever necessary. Furthermore, the short citations could easily be remembered and allowed even those unable to read whole essays by Mao Zedong to understand some of his key points.

The Hebei Provincial Committee in its reply encouraged the official reprint of two different quotation volumes aimed at different audiences. A comprehensive volume based on a revised version of Chen Boda's script was to be published as reference material for all institutions and party cadres above the county level. A shorter edition for local-level cadres and the general populace was either to be extracted from this long version or to rely on the "middle-sized volume."[20] The army edition, which was to gain nationwide supremacy shortly thereafter, was explicitly not chosen as a model for further publication. Yet the small edition also included a few strong points that struck the provincial committee as advantageous, especially the foreword to provide guidance with respect to the contemporary relevance of Mao Zedong Thought and the practical format that allowed readers to carry the volume along with them constantly. Both advantages were explicitly pointed out by the provincial committee, which requested that they be included in future editions. The committee further advised that future editions include more quotations from recent speeches of Mao Zedong until the fifth and sixth volumes of Mao Zedong's *Selected Works* were to appear in print. The report specifically singled out the subjects of opposing revisionism, the "ten great relationships" defined by Mao in 1956, and class struggle as subjects in need of further clarification. After all, many of Mao's more recent speeches had already been distributed as study documents and thus had become "part of the common language of cadres and masses,"[21] but had not been included in the official canon of Mao writings.

---

[19] See "Zhongguo gongchandang Hebei sheng weiyuanhui guanyu taolun 'Mao zhuxi yulu' yangben yijian de baogao," 2.

[20] Ibid., 3.

[21] Ibid., 7.

Even before all reports had reached the CCP General Office, Deng Xiaoping and Peng Zhen called a meeting on 29 January 1966 at the Diaoyutai Guesthouse compound to discuss the questions pertaining to which edition of the quotations should be regarded as authoritative. The participants included the leadership of the Central Propaganda Department: Lu Dingyi; Xu Liqun; Yao Zhen; Mao's former secretary Tian Jiaying; and Shi Ximin, a former secretary of the Shanghai Party Committee, who had just been appointed to run the day-to-day business of the Ministry of Culture under its new head, Lu Dingyi. After a critical review of the strengths and weaknesses of the three versions, Deng Xiaoping decided to start revising the middle-sized edition for print, which after all had been compiled on behalf of the CCP cultural establishment.[22] This specific edition of quotations never appeared, though. The purge of high-ranking officials – which had started with the fall of Yang Shangkun as head of the CCP General Office in charge of the party's paper flow in November 1965, followed a month later by the dismissal of Luo Ruiqing as PLA chief-of-staff, and was to continue until the demotion of Liu Shaoqi and Deng Xiaoping at the Eleventh Plenum of the Eighth Congress in August 1966 – left the top leadership busy with issues other than the compilation of Chairman Mao's *Quotations*. The huge excess demand for the quotations, due to both the book's supposed guidance function and the hype created especially within the army, however, did not cease.

The first edition of the *Quotations* had been based on an estimated print number of 4.2 million books. The original target of supplying each squad with one book only, however, turned out to be insufficient. The demand among the soldiers necessitated a tripling in numbers and the setting up of a separate structure to distribute the books within the army. By the time the second edition appeared in August 1965, the book had been printed 12.1 million times and the demand kept adding pressure on the Liberation Army Publishing House, whose workers were already working in shifts around the clock. To release some pressure, General Political Department Deputy Liu Zhijian approached Luo Ruiqing to discuss the possibility of distributing paper molds to local, non-army printing plants. Luo accepted the proposal, as did Central Propaganda Department head Lu Dingyi, Kang Sheng, and Marshal He Long in separate decisions regarding local requests during September 1965. On 19 November, the CCP General Office phoned the *Liberation Army News* to communicate Mao Zedong's approval of handing out paper molds to the Anhui Party

[22] Liu and Shi, *Xin Zhongguo chuban*, 96.

Committee.[23] Even before Deng Xiaoping decided upon the middle-sized volume as future standard, the reprint of the rival army edition was thus well under way. Yet the reason did not derive from a centrally planned decision but mostly had to be attributed to popular demand.

Until the Cultural Revolution, the *Quotations* played no role in the calculations of the Ministry of Culture's plans for allocating paper and other resources. By February 1966, some 75 million copies of the *Selected Readings* had been printed and, according to the ministry's statistics, had basically fulfilled the needs of the targeted groups.[24] The situation concerning the *Selected Works*, however, remained far from satisfying. Since the founding of the People's Republic, roughly 10 million sets of Mao's *Selected Works* had been distributed as well as 610 million single speeches and texts. According to the ministry's internal news organ *Culture Trends* (*Wenhua dongtai*), the total number of printed Mao texts and books in the same period had been 783 million.[25] With the beginning of the study campaign to learn from the PLA and the increasing effect of the Socialist Education Movement in the countryside, however, the demand for the four-volume set exceeded the supply provided by the state-owned Xinhua bookstores, especially in rural areas.

The distribution of books in rural areas had been an issue of long-standing difficulty for the CCP's publishing organs. The Xinhua bookstores had in 1953 extended the reach of book selling beyond their own branches by creating a "double-track" (*shuang gui*) system, requiring department stores as well as local sales and marketing cooperatives to sell books on a commission basis of 8 percent.[26] These "commission agents" relied on a newly created supply chain and proved highly successful in widening the spectrum of customers. By 1956, for example, 147 cooperatives had been established in Hebei province; through their local branches, these cooperatives reached 82 percent of the populace and increased book sales by 56 percent in the first six months of 1956 alone. The situation in remote villages, however, remained difficult. In July 1957, mobile sales units were established in 118 Hebei districts, leading to further increases. These structures were revived after the Great Leap Forward, when, after 1962,

---

[23] Wei, "'Mao zhuxi yulu' bianfa," 18.

[24] "Zhongfa [66] 118, Zhongyang tongyi wenhuabu dangwei guanyu 'Mao Zedong xuanji' yinzhi faxing gongzuo de baogao" [Report on the Approval of the CCP Center to the Ministry of Culture's Party Committee Concerning the Printing and Distribution Work of the *Selected Works of Mao Zedong*], 21 February 1966, HPA 855-20-1336.

[25] Liu and Shi, *Xin Zhongguo chuban*, 97.

[26] Hebei sheng, *Hebei tushu faxing zhi* 2, 118ff.

mobile sales personnel were specifically trained for this task. The distributional structures facilitated rising sales numbers during the early 1960s but were not always able to cope with the demand engendered, as a notice posted by the Xinhua News Head Office on 10 July 1964 revealed, after announcing the publication of Mao Zedong's *Selected Readings*:

> Beginning at dawn and continuing the whole day, the stream of phone calls and customers in the bookstores of Tangshan, Baoding, Shijiazhuang, and Zhangjiakou did not cease. In Baoding, the shop served more than one thousand customers a day. Some readers from villages walked more than a dozen kilometers to buy their books. In front of many sales departments, readers would start queuing at 6 A.M.[27]

The situation in other parts of the country was similar. In 1965, the People's Press had received over 2,500 letters, of which 63 percent were written in an unsuccessful effort to order the *Selected Works*. According to the demands sent in by the local branches of the Xinhua bookstores and investigations conducted in four cities, the national supply fell short by at least another 11 million copies just to supply the most important units, such as party organs, schools, and workplaces. As it seemed impossible to print the same number of *Selected Works* in one year that had been printed since the founding of the People's Republic, the Ministry of Culture fixed as the goal for 1966 5 million sets that were to be published in two periods.[28] It further advised the bookstores to serve the most important customers first, simultaneously urging the local printing factories to keep up the high standard of quality. Temporarily unsatisfied customers should not be angered, for example, by referring to the greater importance of the internal distribution of Mao works within the party and the army, but were to be alerted about the general political situation, especially the need to counter Soviet revisionism in word and deed, to understand potential inconveniences caused by paper shortages.

In the meantime, on 13 March 1966, the Ministry of Culture sent a preliminary report to the Central Propaganda Department and the CCP Center about the state of printing and distribution of the *Quotations*.[29]

---

[27] Ibid., 172.

[28] "Zhonghua renmin gongheguo wenhuabu guanyu 'Mao Zedong xuanji' faxing gongzuo de tongzhi" [Ministry of Culture Notice Concerning the Distribution of the *Selected Works of Mao Zedong*], 3 March 1966, HPA 1030-2-325.

[29] "Zhongfa [66] 182, Zhongyang pizhuan wenhuabu dangwei guanyu 'Mao zhuxu yulu' yinzhi faxing gongzuo de qingshi baogao" [Report of the Ministry of Culture Party Committee Approved and Transmitted by the CCP Center Concerning the Printing and Distribution Work of *Quotations from Chairman Mao*], 23 March 1966, HPA 855-20-1336.

Although the book continued to be distributed internally only, the enhanced capacities engendered by the spreading of printing molds to local plants, while leading to an increase of 28 million copies in total, had not been able to cope with the demand of party cadres and the populace. The Central First Light Industry Ministry had supplemented another 5,100 tons of paper, equaling 51 million copies, but still the demand remained extreme. The reaction to local print requests to hand out printing molds to local plants had further led to inefficiencies in allocating the copies, as some units were receiving their samples both through local and central channels, thus further reducing the limited resources. To solve the problem, the Ministry of Culture drew a sharp distinction between the central units to be supplied by the Beijing Municipal Party Committee and local units. Based on this distinction, local units were to receive their share according to the schedules of the respective ministries of culture under the supervision of the local party committees. The actual distribution was to take place through the Xinhua bookstores. The internal prices were to be adjusted according to local conditions, but not to exceed 3 to 4 jiao. To curb the possibly disruptive impact of the mechanisms of a free market allocation on the already strained publishing schedules, there should be "no notice within the papers, no advertising, no public displays, and no sale to foreigners. A small amount may be used for outlet sales."[30] Quality standards should remain high, despite the fact that the book was to be regarded as internal study material only. The report, finally, confirmed the erstwhile continuation of publishing two different editions: a slightly more expensive plastic-cover edition and the cheaper paper-bound edition. The CCP Center approved of the report ten days later.

Meanwhile, the State Council's Foreign Affairs Department issued a circular to make all foreigners return their *Quotations* copies because the book did not represent a comprehensive collection of Mao Zedong Thought and was to be considered for internal education only. According to the State Council, the Little Red Book therefore was not to be read in the presence of foreigners or mentioned in conversations, yet collecting the copies that had already been given to foreigners turned out to be difficult. For example, a student at Nankai University in Tianjin had donated his volume to a Vietnamese exchange student planning to translate it upon his return home. It took the intervention of the university

[30] Ibid.

president to regain the copy.[31] On 20 April, the Central Propaganda Department loosened the tight regulations considerably. It had been impossible to regain all copies and the efforts occasionally had resulted in tarnishing the image of Mao. Therefore, in the future, wrote the Central Propaganda Department, all "foreign experts and exchange students can request to borrow or possibly buy a copy of the *Quotations from Chairman Mao* at their respective units."[32] Copies already handed out should not be recollected but the book should be distributed only following an explicit request. Furthermore, while handing out copies, local staff were to explain the special nature of the book as internal study material.

To facilitate a unified process of distribution, the People's Press on 22 April contacted the small group revising Mao Zedong's writings under Kang Sheng's leadership and obtained permission to take over responsibility for supplying the local printing plants with paper molds.[33] The People's Press thus took over the monopoly from the Liberation Army News Publishing House after having failed to secure the success of the Central Propaganda Department's own version of Mao quotes. The *Quotations* continued to be distributed as internal reading. However, local party committees were still to decide such matters as whether to print the frontispiece or to include a Mao portrait, as well as what the book's exact price would be and which local distribution methods would be used. Material requirements were defined in detail[34] and the prices were calculated at 0.6/0.32 yuan for the respective editions, slightly above the manufacturing costs.[35]

---

[31] "Hebei sheng wenhuaju pizhuan sheng renwei waiban guanyu lin bu xiang waiguoren zengsong 'Mao zhuxi yulu' de tongzhi" [Notice of the Hebei Personnel Department Foreign Affairs Office Approved and Transmitted by the Hebei Culture Bureau on Temporarily Not Giving *Quotations from Chairman Mao* to Foreigners], 21 March 1966, HPA 1030-2-325.

[32] "Zhongyang xuanchuanbu guanyu waiguo zhuanjia, liuxuesheng xu yao 'Mao zhuxi yulu' de wenti de tongzhi" [Central Propaganda Department Notice on the Problem of Foreign Experts and Students Plainly Wanting the *Quotations from Chairman Mao*], 20 April 1966, HPA 864-2-340.

[33] "Guanyu zongzheng ban 'Mao zhuxi yulu' fuzhi gongxing shi" [Concerning the Matter of Reproducing Molds for the Central Political Department's *Quotations from Chairman Mao*], 22 April 1966, HPA 1030-2-322.

[34] No spot whatsoever was to appear on the page with Mao's portrait. See "Hebei renmin chubanshe guanyu 'Mao zhuxi yulu' de yinzhi guige he yinzhuang zhiliang yaoqiu" [Hebei People's Press Concerning the Printing Standards and Binding Quality Demands of the *Quotations from Chairman Mao*], 1 May 1966, HPA 1030-2-322.

[35] "Mao zhuxi yulu shi wan chengben jisuan dan" [Cost Calculation for One Hundred Thousand Copies of Quotations from Chairman Mao], April 1966, HPA 1030-2-322.

After transferring the task of allocating resources efficiently to the local party committees, the provincial leaders of the People's Press and the printing factories were to decide upon targets and print numbers, which were then fixed by the local ministries of culture and divided among the different cities within a province. Because of the lack of sufficiently modern printing facilities and the task of publishing the works of Mao Zedong, up to July 1966 they had only been printed in twelve provinces. After all, the publication of Mao's works, even the internal *Quotation* copies, was considered a highly political and solemn task, not to be hampered by mechanical deficiencies. In Hebei and Tianjin, the estimated number of *Quotations* copies added up to 12 million. Production was divided among thirteen printing plants according to local capabilities. Since the enormous number of books required additional labor force, especially to help with the binding, 835 temporary workers were employed, each one expected to handle 50 books a day.[36] The increase of paper supply was to be handled by reducing the allocation of resources to the printing of other books and newspapers, given China's continuing shortage of paper. The printed copies were to be delivered straight to the provincial Xinhua bookstores, from which the distribution within the different regions was to proceed. For county-level bookstores, this meant that they had to hire additional personnel to supply the many villages and smaller townships that lacked a proper bookshop. During 1966, the Xinhua bookstores in Hebei hired an additional 1,049 workers to help with the sale and distribution of Mao works throughout the province.[37]

The huge excess demand for the *Quotations* had been triggered by various factors. The increase of political study campaigns – such as the Socialist Education Movement to reinvigorate communist morals in rural areas or the nationwide campaign to learn from the PLA – provided a political background without which the demand could never have grown on such a large scale. But other factors contributed as well. By providing the populace with a point of reference, the *Quotations* turned out to offer a possibility of empowerment for non-party members. The secretive nature

---

[36] "Jifa [66] 62, Hebei shengwei pizhuan sheng wenhuaju dangzu guanyu 'Mao zhuxi yulu' yinzhi faxing gongzuo de qingshi baogao" [Report of the Provincial Cultural Bureau Party Group Approved and Transmitted by the Hebei Provincial Committee Concerning the Printing and Distribution Work of the *Quotations from Chairman Mao*], 24 April 1966, HPA 855-20-1618.

[37] "Jifa [67] 2, Guanyu chongshi he jiaqiang Mao zhuxi zhuzuo faxing renyuan de tongzhi" [Notice on Augmenting and Strengthening the Distribution Personnel for Chairman Mao's Works], 16 January 1967, HPA 907-7-389.

with which the book was published, the difficulties of obtaining it, and the design shaped by rudimentary customer feedback all worked together in creating a cult object sought after by soldiers, party members, and the general population alike. The incredible excess demand put the planned economy to a severe test and led to a massive rechanneling of nearly all resources within the publishing sector to the reprint of Mao works. By 30 June 1966, the Ministry of Culture announced that until the end of 1967, a total amount of 200 million *Quotations* copies should be printed, along with some 23 million sets of the *Selected Works*. Thus by mid-1966, almost the entire publishing sector concentrated on the printing of Mao's writings at the expense of every other print item, including schoolbooks. The enormous popularity of the book further enhanced the glorious image of Mao Zedong while simultaneously the Cultural Revolution slowly took shape through purges of high-ranking CCP cadres.

DEBATING LOYALTY

Between 4 and 26 May 1966, the CCP Politburo met for an enlarged session in Beijing to discuss the cases of the previous chief-of-staff, Luo Ruiqing; the head of the CCP General Office, Yang Shangkun; Beijing First Secretary Peng Zhen; and Lu Dingyi, head of the Central Propaganda Department. During the meeting, the carefully orchestrated purges that had started with the fall of Yang Shangkun in November 1965 for having bugged Mao's personal carriage during the Great Leap reached its temporary apex with the debunking of the whole leading body of the departments in control of the state media. Since Khrushchev's fall in October 1964, Mao had occasionally pondered the danger of a coup d'état. The reasons for Mao's doubt regarding the reliability of the party apparatus had first been incited by his public clash with his long-term successor, Liu Shaoqi, in 1962 about the relative importance of political faults for the fatal outcome of the Great Leap Forward, for which Mao did not want to be held accountable alone. He thus reemphasized the importance of class struggle and insisted that the dangers posed by capitalist influence should be talked about "every year, every month, and every day."[38]

By the mid-1960s, Mao was convinced that the party bureaucracy itself turned out to be the primary breeding ground for a capitalist restoration, including the CCP Central Committee. In an informal talk with local party

---

[38] Mao Zedong, "Zai ba jie shi zhong quanhui shang de jianghua" [Speech at the Tenth Plenum of the Eighth Party Congress], 24 September 1962, in CRDB.

leaders on 13 January 1965, Mao alerted them about the possibility of revisionism appearing within the Central Committee. He brought up the topic again during a central work conference of the CCP in September and October 1965, renewing the emphasis on the continuing existence of classes and antagonistic contradictions within socialism. Mao's growing paranoia about the possibility of a purge, similar to Khrushchev's fate a few months earlier, strengthened his belief in the necessity to replace his successor. To avoid the fate of Stalin, Mao considered ways of securing his revolutionary legacy by rendering a new generation of communists immune from the lures of capitalism. This would work only by changing the present system of education and replacing it with a new mode that was to rely on physical work and active class struggle as opposed to book worship and the generation of specialists.

The search for incriminating passages from political speeches and articles to reveal capitalist sprouts in the CCP and PLA leadership proved to be a viable instrument in outmaneuvering the defenses of the communist bureaucracy. Mao himself fostered this trend by acting on a divide-and-rule strategy. He increasingly circumvented the formal communication channels to achieve his goals and instead relied on extrainstitutional groups and individuals such as Kang Sheng, Chen Boda, or his own wife, Jiang Qing, all of whom depended solely on his personal favor, to facilitate his directives. Mao's physical absence from the capital shrouded his opinions in mystery even to the cadres in the Politburo Standing Committee and required them to take on responsibility in delicate issues that Mao often had provoked himself. Culture turned out to be the most ambiguous field and thus was predestined for the detection of hidden sentiments and class standpoints. Mao encouraged and three times personally revised the attack of a radical Shanghai intellectual, Yao Wenyuan, on a theater piece about the upright Ming dynasty official Hai Rui, written half a decade earlier on Mao's behest by the vice-mayor of Beijing and famous historian, Wu Han.[39] Yao Wenyuan's polemic attacked the portrayal of Hai Rui as defender of peasant rights against the arbitrary cruelty of the feudal system. Historical materialism, according to Yao, did not allow for individuals to transcend the restrictions inflicted upon them by their class background. Hai Rui had opposed arbitrary cruelty but remained a

---

[39] Zheng Qian, "Dui xinbian lishiju 'Hai Rui ba guan' de pipan" [The Criticism of the New Historical Play *Hai Rui Dismissed from Office*], in Guo Dehong, Wang Haiguang, and Han Gang (eds.), *Shinian fengyu (1966–1976)* [Ten Years of Troubled Times (1966–1976)], Chengdu: Sichuan renmin chubanshe, 2004, 4ff.

"loyal servant" of his feudal authorities. The play should therefore be considered a "poisonous weed"[40] as a vivid expression of the necessity to continue class struggle in the superstructural realm.

Yao's polemic served a number of related purposes. It expressed Mao's dissatisfaction with his potential successors and especially their failure to implement policies according to his wishes. Although the CCP leadership still bestowed Mao with the necessary honors and kept him meticulously informed, he complained about being left out of the loop on important decisions. He further expressed his dissatisfaction with the party bureaucracy in general and the handling of propaganda in particular, since it lacked vividness, theoretical content, and class character. The polemic provided a welcome opportunity to attack the stronghold of the Beijing party circle around Peng Zhen and Lu Dingyi, responsible for the dissemination of party propaganda. The article was first published by the newspaper *Wenhui bao* in Shanghai on 10 November 1965 but did not receive major attention in other parts of the country. The Shanghai People's Press, on Mao's request, turned the article into a small brochure to be distributed by the Xinhua bookstores before the *People's Daily* on 30 November finally printed the article along with a commentary revised by Peng Zhen and Zhou Enlai that encouraged differing opinions to be voiced within the sphere of culture. The resistance to the reprint of the article provided Mao with the proof needed to step up the attacks, mainly through scribes formerly employed in the CCP Anti-Revisionist Writing Group. The situation grew increasingly tense over the following months, as criticism against high-ranking party officials was stepped up.

The events finally culminated during the enlarged Politburo meeting held in Beijing in May 1966. The former Beijing party leadership was accused of fundamental errors in political line and of having plotted capitalist restoration. Lin Biao two days later took up the notion of a coup d'état and delivered an extraordinary speech to his Politburo comrades by reminding his audience about the importance of retaining power and securing the continuation of the proletarian dictatorship. He invoked recent coups ("eleven coups per year have been the average"[41]) and warned not to feel too secure once power had been wielded from the hands of the capitalist classes. The cases of Khrushchev in the Soviet

---

[40] Yao Wenyuan, "Ping xin bian lishiju 'Hai Rui ba guan'" [Critique of the New Historical Play *Hai Rui Dismissed from Office*], in *Wenhui bao*, 10 November 1965.

[41] Lin Biao, "Zai zhongyang zhengzhiju kuoda huiyi shang de jianghua" [Speech at the Enlarged Meeting of the Central Committee Politburo], 18 May 1966, in CRDB.

Union and Imre Nagy in Hungary should be taken as vivid examples of a possible reoccurrence of revisionism. A thorough revolutionization of thought and unremitting class struggle in the superstructure thus had become inevitable. Lin drew examples from astronomy to microbiology in order to substantiate his premise of struggle as the founding principle of life.[42] "If you don't beat them, they will beat you; if you don't kill them, they will kill you."[43] China should thus beware not to "change color" like the Soviet Union did after the rise of Khrushchev.

Lin did not provide factual proof for his accusations against his former comrades. Instead, he postulated the unquestioning recognition of the supreme role of Mao Zedong, his thought, and the vivid propagation of both to be the watershed between real and fake communists. All of the accused, according to Lin, had at one point or another obstructed the propagation of the Chairman's thought in order to wrest this "mighty weapon" from the hands of the masses. He thereafter presented himself as stoutest supporter of Mao Zedong by setting out with a eulogy that surpassed all that had previously been given and was to set the standard for the rhetoric of worship during the Cultural Revolution.

> Chairman Mao is the founder of our party, the creator of our national revolution, the great leader of our country and party; he is the greatest Marxist-Leninist of present times. Mao Zedong creatively, comprehensively, and with genius has inherited, defended, and developed Marxism-Leninism and elevated Marxism-Leninism to a new stage.... The sayings, articles, and the revolutionary practice of Chairman Mao show his great proletarian genius. There are people who do not admit genius. This is not Marxism. One cannot negate genius.[44]

To oppose the constant propagation of the teachings of Mao Zedong was considered a heinous crime and the final proof for detecting enemies who had infiltrated the CCP. The latent danger that Mao might one day share Stalin's fate was made immediately clear in the frequent allusions Lin made to Mao's health and in the threat with which he ended his four-hour speech:

> We now support Chairman Mao and a hundred years after Chairman Mao we will still uphold Chairman Mao [sic]. Mao Zedong Thought will continue to be passed on forever.... [Throughout the days] that Chairman Mao lives, ninety years, over a hundred years, he will always be the highest leader of our party. His words will always be the guideline

[42] Roderick MacFarquhar and Michael Schoenhals, *Mao's Last Revolution*, Cambridge: Belknap Press of Harvard University Press, 2006, 38f.
[43] Lin, "Zai zhongyang zhengzhiju kuoda huiyi," in CRDB.
[44] Ibid.

of our actions. Whoever opposes him, the whole party will punish and the whole nation will suppress. If someone should ever deliver a Khrushchev-style report behind his back, this person clearly is an intriguer, a great bastard, and the whole party will punish him, the whole nation will suppress him. Mao Zedong Thought will be a general truth forever; it will always remain the compass of our actions. It will always be the common treasure trove of the Chinese people and the revolutionary people of the whole world. It will always radiate its glory.[45]

Lin's speech narrowed the definition of the correct class standpoint down to a single criterion: the adherence to and propagation of Mao Zedong Thought. Those who had failed to display a sufficiently supportive attitude toward Mao or even had criticized aspects of his writings were placed under the suspicion of treason. By declaring Mao Zedong Thought to be sacrosanct, Lin Biao ensured that anyone who ever had been on the record with a critical remark of Mao, his writings, or the style of study as advocated by Lin would be considered a potential traitor and usurper. The search for incriminating materials in old speeches and articles such as phrases critical of Mao Zedong thus became the single most important source for attacks in the early stages of the Cultural Revolution. As the class standpoint "materialize[d] in the words and deeds of a person,"[46] speech, acts, and deeds were closely monitored for deviances from the canon of Mao's works and gave rise to Manichaean distinctions between "red" and "black" lines either supporting or opposing Mao. The cleavages that were brought forth by these distinctions shattered the unity of the CCP to the foundations and placed personal loyalty to the Chairman above loyalty to the party, the nation, or Marxism-Leninism.

It seems difficult to explain why Liu Shaoqi and other CCP leaders watched and presided over the demise of the Beijing party leadership. The new and highly flexible criteria brought forth by Lin Biao could be applied to nearly anyone wielding the power of interpretation. Yet Mao's revolutionary legitimacy obviously had been so thoroughly established that open deviance was beyond question. A primary example is offered by Premier Zhou Enlai, who jumped on the train three days later by completely endorsing Lin's speech in his own address to the meeting. He not only accepted the overwhelming importance of class struggle in the

---

[45] Ibid.
[46] Fang Qiu, "Bu neng huibi yaohai wenti. Ping Wu Han tongzhi 'guanyu "Hai Rui ba guan" de ziwo piping'" [One Cannot Avoid the Crucial Questions: Critique of Comrade Wu Han's "Self-Criticism Concerning *Hai Rui Dismissed from Office*"], in *Renmin ribao*, 7 April 1966, 6.

superstructure but echoed the praise of Mao's genius. Zhou further credited Lin Biao with having detected the opposition to the study of Mao's works to be the primary evidence distinguishing true from fake supporters. In the last part of his speech, Zhou added a further viewpoint that is probably most revealing of the attitude of a large faction among the long-standing CCP members. By elaborating on the necessity of keeping revolutionary integrity, Zhou invoked party discipline even to the point of agreeing to preside over the organization's self-destruction: "We shall follow Chairman Mao. Chairman Mao is our leader today and he will be our leader in one hundred years. Those who did not uphold their integrity in their later years and are guilty of treason shall be liquidated with one stroke."[47] Zhou's words were primarily directed at the former CCP leader Qu Qiubai, who had recanted communist doctrines and whose ashes were soon afterward removed from the martyrs' cemetery at Babaoshan. Yet Zhou only echoed an extended historical discussion about the Taiping "loyalty king" Li Xiucheng and the question of whether he had surrendered to the enemy forces after defeat. Mao had characterized his behavior as surrender and coined the expression, "loss of integrity in the later years is unworthy of being taken as an example" (*wan jie bu zhong, bu zu wei xun*).[48] The preservation of communist integrity, genuine conviction in the continuing legitimacy of Mao Zedong as founder of the People's Republic, or simply fear may have inhibited the majority of the CCP leadership from failing to oppose the purge of their comrades. With Lin Biao's speech and its acceptance by the Politburo in May 1966, Mao's position had become virtually unassailable or, as Lin Biao phrased it, "every sentence [of Chairman Mao] is the truth; one sentence [of his] surpasses ten thousand of ours."[49] To indulge in performances of loyalty or revolutionary integrity thus became necessary if one did not want to find oneself being excluded from the ranks of the people.

[47] Zhou Enlai, "Zai zhongyang zhengzhiju kuoda huiyi shang de jianghua" [Speech at the Enlarged Meeting of the Central Committee Politburo], 21 May 1966, in CRDB.

[48] Gao Wenqian, *Wannian Zhou Enlai* [Zhou Enlai's Later Years], New York: Mingjing chubanshe, 2003, 111.

[49] See Lin, "Zai zhongyang zhengzhiju kuoda huiyi," in CRDB. Lin Biao at a military conference on political work in January 1966 made first use of these phrases; see Lin Biao, "Zai quanjun zhengzhi gongzuo huiyi shang de baogao zhong de zhongyao zhishi" [Important Instructions during a Report at the All-Army Political Work Conference], 24 January 1966, in CRDB.

6

Spectacles of Worship

The image that in public memory is most closely associated with the Cultural Revolutionary Mao cult is probably the image of Mao Zedong standing on top of Tiananmen reviewing millions of enthusiastic Red Guards. Like no other event, these eight "mass receptions" between August and November 1966 have come to symbolize the cult's charismatic force to mobilize the Chinese youth. Despite the prominence of the mass receptions both in memoirs and scholarly literature, neither the specific circumstances nor the incredible logistical background have been subjected to closer examination. This chapter provides a tentative outline of the characteristics, organization, and impact of the Red Guard Mao worship and the "exchange of experiences" or "great link-up" (*chuanlian*) that spread the seeds of the Cultural Revolution nationwide. Finally, the chapter examines strategies of employing cult symbols to oppose the policies of the Central Cultural Revolution Group (CCRG) around Jiang Qing. To explore these strategies, the chapter looks at the case of a specific Red Guard organization, called United Action (*liandong*), which achieved redoubtable fame in the first year of the Cultural Revolution.

The call for mobilization would not have incited a similar effect if Mao's public image had not been raised through incessant study campaigns and media coverage, not only in the *Liberation Army News* but also in the party's mouthpiece, the *People Daily*. Mao's profile had by no means been low since the start of the campaign to learn from the PLA in 1964, but up to this point, the propagation of his cult had mainly been confined to advocating new ways of studying and applying Mao Zedong Thought. Revolutionary activists and martyrs such as Lei Feng, Ouyang Hai, or Wang Jie received lavish attention for displaying the basic characteristics of the "new communist man": selfless duty and unwavering determination. Personal praise of Mao Zedong had been confined to the reprint of letters and poems that were usually introduced by quoting foreign enthusiasts.

There was no law comparable to the Nazi *Gleichschaltungsgesetz*, the forcible coordination of the mass media according to standards offered by the Propaganda Department. Self-censorship and what in the German case has been called "working towards the *Führer*"[1] presented the common reaction. Self-censorship of content and a remodeling of appearance based on the example of the *Liberation Army News* had been conducted in various broadcasting units, as, for example, an internal investigation of the *Beijing Daily* in May 1965 reveals.[2] By early 1966, the *People's Daily* had already come a long way in the direction of emphasizing the importance of the CCP Chairman. References to Mao Zedong Thought had increased tenfold compared to three years earlier. Figure 2 reveals the dramatic increase in references to Mao Zedong Thought at the outset of the Cultural Revolution, when references nearly quadrupled within half a year.

The attention paid to the activities of other state leaders and especially the choice of photographic material had until June 1966 partially counterbalanced the verbal dominance of Mao Zedong. Liu Shanqi's numerous state visits abroad in the first half of 1966 were prominently covered and showed, among others, his wife Wang Guangmei during a visit to Indonesia in the traditional *Qipao* dress at the side of the state chairman. Yet after the May 1966 Politburo meeting, the staging of the cult in the party media was massively stepped up, after Mao had replaced the leading bodies of the *People's Daily* with his former secretary, Chen Boda, who immediately took up the task to denounce revisionist trends and false authorities and to champion the wise leadership of Mao Zedong

Although by mid-1966 Mao's image was omnipresent in the party media, chances actually to see Mao had been minimal and basically confined to those activists entitled to take part in the parades on Labor Day or National Day. Mao's public appearances during the eight mass parades therefore constituted an unprecedented chance to get a look at the man

---

[1] See Ian Kershaw, "'Working towards the Führer': Reflections on the Nature of the Hitler Dictatorship," in Ian Kershaw and Moshe Lewin (eds.), *Stalinism and Nazism: Dictatorships in Comparison*, Cambridge: Cambridge University Press, 1997, 88–106. See as well MacFarquhar and Schoenhals, *Mao's Last Revolution*, 47.

[2] The report compares the relative percentage of articles dealing with Mao Zedong Thought and its application. Beijing ribao bangongshi (ed.), *Kan Jiefangjun bao xiangdao de jige wenti* [Look How the *Liberation Army News* Thought of a Few Questions], 28 May 1965.

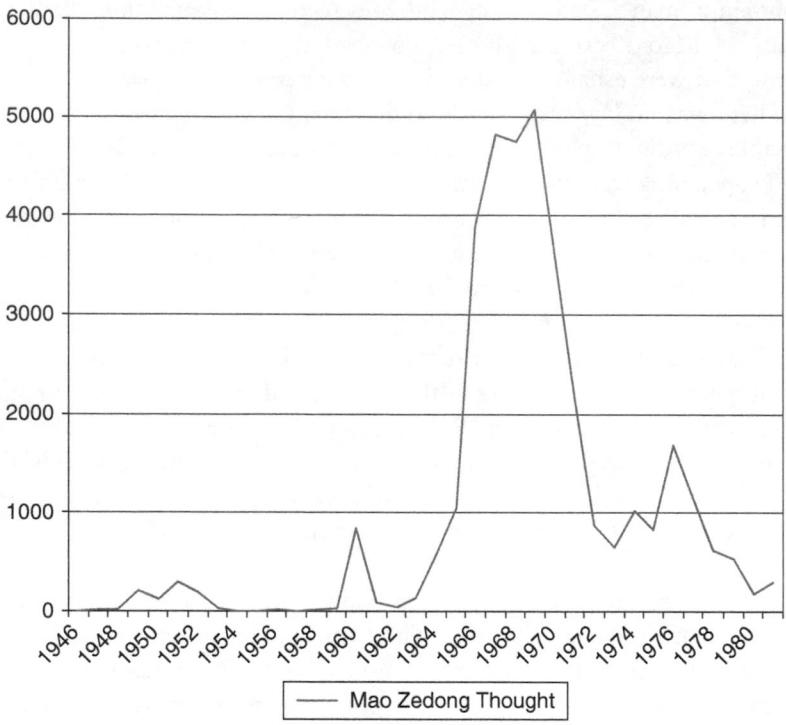

FIGURE 2. References to Mao Zedong Thought in the *People's Daily*, 1946–81

who, in the words of Lin Biao, had "developed Marxism-Leninism with genius, creatively and comprehensively and has brought it to a higher and completely new stage."[3] The first reception took place on 18 August 1966 on Tiananmen Square and included roughly one million students and citizens from all over China. Many students had traveled from different provinces to the capital to learn about the experiences of the Cultural Revolution. Although a reception hosted by Chen Boda had been advertised, Mao's partaking in the event had not been predicted. But as rumors spread among the students that Mao was to participate in the assembly, a large crowd gathered already during the night and at dawn witnessed a scene that a journalist in the *People's Daily* described in the following words:

> This morning at 5 A.M., as the sun had just spread its first beams of light from the Eastern horizon, Chairman Mao informally appeared on

[3] Lin Biao, "Foreword to the Second Edition of Quotations from Chairman Mao Tse-tung," in *Quotations from Chairman Mao Tse-tung*, Beijing: Foreign Languages Press, 1966, I.

Tiananmen Square .... Chairman Mao wore a grass-green army uniform. On the Chairman's military cap glistened a single red star.
Chairman Mao crossed the Gold Water Bridges in front of the Gate of
Heavenly Peace and walked directly amongst the masses. He shook hands
with many of the surrounding people and further waved his hand as a
salute to the revolutionary masses on the Square. At that moment, the
Square boiled over, everyone raised their hands over their heads and
jumped in the direction of the Chairman, loudly calling and clapping
their hands. Many people clapped their palms until they turned red; many
people shed tears of excitement and gladly expressed: "Chairman Mao
has come! Chairman Mao has come among us!" On the Square, tens of
thousands of people loudly called: "Long live Chairman Mao! Long live!
Long, long live!" One wave of hurrahs surpassed the other, shaking the
sky above the capital.[4]

Accustomed to the exaggerated formulations and the splendor of communist parades, the jubilant rhetoric disguises the fact that Mao's early-
morning appearance on Tiananmen Square presented nothing less than a
disaster for the organizers and security staff. Mao's attendance had only
very briefly beforehand been communicated to the organizing staff around
Premier Zhou Enlai. Yet Mao appeared much earlier than anticipated. He
had not slept the whole night and, according to one of his bodyguards, he
had requested to wear a military uniform while attending the parade only
after hearing that Red Guards constituted the majority of the crowd. As
Mao had not worn a uniform in decades, his staff had to search for a
member of the Beijing Garrison with a similar physique. Finally, a cadre
named Liu Yuntang was found whose uniform apparently fitted Mao
rather well.[5] Around 4 A.M., Mao set out to the Square. By the time he
arrived, most of the security staff arranged by Zhou Enlai had not yet made
it since the parade was not scheduled to get started for hours to come. Mao
nevertheless climbed Tiananmen shortly past 5 A.M. and after having been
welcomed with ferocious applause decided to greet the masses in person.
The worst nightmare of his security staff started to unfold. Mao's appearance among the masses caused tumultuous havoc and only due to the quick
action of his staff members, who shoved Mao on a viewing stand surrounded by a metal fence near the Gold Water Bridges, was the CCP

---

[4] "Mao zhuxi he Lin Biao, Zhou Enlai deng tongzhi jiejian le xuesheng daibiao bing jianyue
le wenhua da geming dajun de youxing" [Chairman Mao, Lin Biao, Zhou Enlai, and Other
Comrades Received Student Representatives and Inspected the Cultural Revolutionary
Mass Parade], in *Renmin ribao*, 19 August 1966, 1.

[5] Zhang Huicang and Ye Jiefu, "Wo suo qinli de Mao zhuxi ba ci jiejian hongweibing"
[My Personal Experiences of Chairman Mao's Eight Red Guard Receptions], in *Dangshi
bocai* 2 (2006), 32.

Chairman saved from being crushed by the jubilant masses.[6] With tremendous efforts, the reluctant Mao was guided back to Tiananmen and waited for the formal opening of the meeting at 7:30 A.M.

The assembly itself passed smoothly, but Mao's sudden appearance had exhilarated the masses to an extent that the speeches of Chen Boda (who referred to Mao for the first time as "great leader, great teacher, and great helmsman"), Lin Biao (adding the "great supreme commander"), and Zhou Enlai were incessantly interrupted by calls of "Long live Chairman Mao!" Lin Biao in his coarse voice called upon the students to smash capitalist mentalities and to establish a new proletarian culture by "changing the people's souls and implementing a revolutionization of thought" under the guidance and command of the "greatest genius of the world,"[7] Chairman Mao. To bridge the gap between the rather quiet atmosphere among the party leadership on top of the gate and the roused masses, Zhou Enlai, with Mao's consent, had the commander of the Beijing Garrison, Fu Chongbi, select 1,500 of the most prominent Red Guards, and after a security inspection allowed them to climb the gate.[8] They were arranged on the eastern and western sides of the platform and after an instruction from Zhou Enlai, the CCP Chairman arrived to greet them in person, with a cordon of security personnel and media staff to document the scene. The prospect of seeing Mao up close and even shaking hands with him resulted in tumultuous scenes. Mao, like a pop star, had to autograph numerous Little Red Books while different Red Guards breached the security cordon, wielding ribbons imprinted with the names of their organizations. At least two students managed to attach their armbands to his left arm. After removing a ribbon imprinted with "Mao- Zedongism Red Guards," Mao accepted the ribbon of a Beijing Normal University Girls' Middle School student, Song Binbin, who for this act and the following short discussion about the change of her insufficiently "revolutionary" name (*Binbin* means "suave" or "refined" in Chinese) into Song Yaowu (that is Song "be martial"), unwittingly was to become a media star. After over six hours of mainly waving hands to the masses, the party leadership finally left the rostrum.

During the eight mass receptions, Mao Zedong reviewed approximately 12 million people.[9] The arrangement of the assemblies changed constantly

---

[6] Lü Hong, "Wo ren hongweibing jiedai congzhan zhanzhang de rizi" [My Days as Head of the General Red Guard Reception Station], in *Yanhuang chunqiu* 12 (1998), 46.

[7] Lin Biao, "Zai qingzhu wenhua da geming qunzhong dahui shang de jianghua" [Speech at a Mass Assembly Celebrating the Cultural Revolution], 18 August 1966, in CRDB.

[8] Zhang and Ye, "Wo suo qinli," 33.

[9] Compare *Xuexi ziliao* [Study Materials], Beijing: Neibu kanwu, 1969, 190–4.

and was aimed at saving time to keep Mao from becoming fatigued while simultaneously allowing a maximum number of revolutionaries a close look at the Chairman. Due to criticism that Mao had not been distinguishable by the crowds in the far parts of Tiananmen Square, the second parade on 31 August was arranged differently. Mao set out in an open car from the Great Hall of the People and appeared on top of Tiananmen only after this *tour d'honneur* through the masses. The main concern of the organizers remained Mao's safety. After the fourth parade on National Day had resulted in considerable chaos, when Mao's convoy had been brought to a stop by the masses on its way to the Great Hall of the People, the fifth parade consisted of a 25 kilometer drive along the stretch of the present-day eastern and northern third ring road. Thus 1.5 million Red Guards were "received" in just one hour.

Despite the growing efficiency in accommodating Mao's wish to arouse the masses at minimal personal involvement, Zhou Enlai kept experimenting. As it had been impossible to staff the whole 25 kilometer route with the normal three-layered safety cordon of PLA soldiers and selected Red Guards, the sixth parade was conducted on Tiananmen Square again. This time, 2 million Red Guards were paraded past Tiananmen in six thousand trucks. The advantage of the trucks was that the outbursts of excitement would not lead to casualties among the weakest participants, who occasionally had been trampled to death under the feet of the jubilant masses.[10] But again, unexpected difficulties appeared, since, unlike during the practice session, the Red Guards when passing Tiananmen all scrambled to one side of the trucks to get a better view of Mao and thus forced the drivers to reduce speed to avoid risking an accident.[11] Therefore, the traditional style of the mass receptions was revived in the two last assemblies on Tiananmen Square and finally at the airport in the western suburbs.

Compared to the fascist spectacles of power, the mass receptions in 1966 are characterized by their anarchic quality. The organized leader cult of the Nazis relied heavily on rhetorical devices and decorum to create an atmosphere conducive to render the individual willing to serve the leader to the very end. Clear-cut aims and a stringently racist worldview provided a certain coherence to the speeches that Hitler or his chief propagandist Joseph Goebbels would carefully practice before going on stage. The leader as charismatic orator played a fundamental role in the fascist leader cult, an element that is completely missing in the Cultural Revolutionary Mao worship. Mao never addressed the masses in public besides uttering

---

[10] Lü, "Congzhan," 46.
[11] Zhang and Ye, "Wo suo qinli," 35.

short couplets later relayed by the media. The short greetings and speeches at the mass rallies usually presented by Lin Biao, Zhou Enlai, or Chen Boda were not prone to incite public adoration either. The silent presence further added to Mao's mystery and aloofness and eased the projection of all kinds of personal qualities to the CCP Chairman. Mao effectively became the supreme but empty symbol of the movement.

Nevertheless, the mass receptions had a tremendous effect on the Cultural Revolution. Mao openly declared his support for the Red Guards by receiving them in the capital and thus provided them with symbolic legitimacy to set out on their crusade against old culture, habits, and thought. The mobilizing effect was further enhanced through images of the mass receptions that were not only reprinted in newspapers but also staged on television and in movie theaters all over the country. The personal encounter, however marginal it actually might have been, whipped up a tremendous emotional response. The cult at this stage was not only a media phenomenon but also one with immense popular appeal. Contemporary Red Guard diaries and later recollections express utmost joy and elation upon getting to see Mao in person.[12] Unlike the internal party cult of the Yan'an period that elevated Mao as brand symbol of Chinese communism to foster unity or the proclaimed worship of truth during the Great Leap Forward, the Red Guard worship in many ways resembled the modern hype of celebrity stardom. The Red Guards represented a new generation who had grown up in an environment that placed supreme emphasis on the importance of Mao as founder of the state and ultimate source of revolutionary wisdom and were yet untainted by political disenchantment. Several memoirs have therefore later emphasized that this type of "totalitarian socialization" misled a whole generation into mindlessly following Mao's directives.

Immediately after the first reception, some of the Red Guards set out on their mission to destroy anything that presumably represented capitalist or feudalist influences, as Lin Biao had called for in his speech to the first assembly. Beijing was to become an "extremely revolutionarized, extremely militarized"[13] capital. The most visible consequence was the alteration of all slogans, street names, and shop names that could be associated with feudalist or capitalist culture. A loosely knit alliance even requested to change the name Beijing into "The East Is Red City" and to replace the ornamental

---

[12] See, for example, Bei Guancheng, "I Saw Chairman Mao!!!" in Michael Schoenhals (ed.), *China's Cultural Revolution 1966–1969: Not a Dinner Party*, Armonk, NY: M. E. Sharpe, 1996, 148f.

[13] "Wuchan jieji wenhua da geming de ganglingxing wenjian" [A Programmatic Document of the Great Proletarian Cultural Revolution], in *Hongqi* 10, 9 August 1966.

columns and lions in front of Tiananmen with copper statues of Mao Zedong.[14] The Red Guards did their best to determine what the new revolutionized culture of Mao Zedong Thought was to look like. During public oath-taking rallies, they swore their unquestioning loyalty to Chairman Mao and promised unceasing efforts to liberate the suppressed classes from the yoke of capitalism. The Red Guard organization Red Flag at the former Middle School No. 26 presented a list of one hundred examples of how to destroy the old culture and establish the new one, including the following:

1. It is the duty of the resident committees to oversee that every street and lane sets up quotation boards, that every household and family puts up Mao portraits and quotation posters.
2. In public parks there should be more quotation boards; the foremost duty of every bus driver and train attendant should be to propagandize Mao Zedong Thought and Mao's *Quotations*. [...]
5. Every person should have a *Quotations* volume, always carry it, constantly study it, and always act according to it. [...]
7. The existing bicycles and pedicabs have to attach quotations plates; on cars and trains Chairman Mao's portraits have to be displayed and Chairman Mao's quotations have to be lacquered [on the sides].[15]

With the exception of Mao quotes and imagery, however, little consensus was to be found as to what effectively constituted the new culture The militarization of conduct and speech was followed by a new dress code, making worn-out green army uniforms sought for insignia of revolutionary conviction. Besides the adornment with military caps, red ribbon straps, and broad buckled leather belts, red colored books were a requisite accessory of the new, martial army style. As the *Quotations* had remained an internal army publication so far, most students had to put up with a copy of Mao's *Selected Readings* or the *Selected Works* in the early stages of the movement, as can clearly be distinguished in newspaper photographs of the early rallies. Nevertheless, the *Quotations* quickly became one of the most effective weapons of the Red Guards. By setting up temporary "inspection offices" in the streets, the Red Guards could question pedestrians about their knowledge of Mao's works; if they failed to come up with sufficient quotations, they were harassed at will. The Mao cult that came to dominate public space thus developed less on behalf of orders from the state bureaucracy but derived to a large extent from

---

[14] Zhonggong wenxian yanjiushi (ed.), *Zhou Enlai nianpu* 3, 70.
[15] "Mao Zedong zhuyi xuexiao" (yuan ershiliu zhong) hongweibing (hongqi), *Po jiu li xin yibai lie* [100 Examples of Destroying the Old and Establishing the New], August 1966, in CRDB.

grassroots organizations. Among the central directives, the renaming of all "chairmen" (*zhuxi*) into "directors/heads" (*zhuren*) to emphasize the uniqueness of Mao's position[16] and the order to replace all other public imagery with Mao's picture on 27 August 1966 are noteworthy.[17]

The destruction of old culture took on rampant forms after the first mass reception. On the evening of 18 August, Zhou Enlai had to call in a battalion of the Beijing Garrison to stop students from breaking into the Forbidden City.[18] The unfocused violence could be directed against any kind of object, even against a plantation of apple trees on the pretension of "removing revisionist roots."[19] Although material objects, ranging from classical paintings to religious imagery, were targeted, the main thrust was directed against representatives of the "five black elements" (landlords, rich peasants, counterrevolutionaries, "bad elements," and Rightists) who had served as scapegoats in most political campaigns since the founding of the People's Republic. In Beijing's southeastern Chongwen district, between 24 August and 2 September alone a total of 137 persons were beaten to death.[20] Red Guards brought another 735 persons to the Chongwen branch to be taken into custody, mostly on the pretext of possessing capitalist items. Despite the brevity of the period of randomly searching houses and arresting people, the anarchic violence proved to be highly effective in creating a climate of terror that discouraged attempts to retain a critical stance toward the Cultural Revolution.

The detainment of "bad elements" and "fake Red Guards" had been one of the aims of the newly formed Western District Picket Corps, an elite Red Guard organization that been established in an assembly of thirty-one middle schools on 25 August.[21] The tradition of picket corps in assisting the local steering of mass movements had been a frequently employed measure of the CCP. The Western District Picket Corps encompassed

---

[16] "Zhonggong zhongyang guanyu ge renmin tuanti 'zhuxi' gaicheng 'zhuren' (zhaiyao)" [CCP Center on Replacing the Title of "Chairman" with "Director" in All People's Organizations (Summary)], 26 August 1966, in CRDB.

[17] "Zhongfa [66] 444, Guanyu guaxiang wenti de tongzhi" [Notice Regarding the Question of Displaying Portraits], 27 August 1966. Although the title can be traced in archives, the original document has so far not been available for research.

[18] Zhonggong wenxian yanjiushi (ed.), *Zhou Enlai nianpu* 3, 50.

[19] See Beijing shi Fengtaiqu difangzhi bianzuan weiyuanhui (ed.), *Beijing shi Fengtaiqu zhi* [Beijing City Fengtai District Gazetteer], Beijing: Beijing chubanshe, 2001, 49.

[20] Beijing shi gong'anju Chongwen fenju (ed.), *Beijing Chongwen gong'an shiliao* [Beijing Chongwen Public Security Historical Materials], vol. 2, Beijing: Neibu kanwu, 2000, 675.

[21] The Western branch was followed on 9 September by an Eastern branch and a Haidian branch. Picket Corps also emerged in other Chinese cities, such as Wuhan, Shanghai, and Guangzhou, in September 1966.

roughly one thousand members with a core of some two hundred activists, most of them teenage students from middle schools. In its founding proclamation, the Picket Corps presented itself as the "nucleus force" of the Red Guard movement and defined the propagation and defense of Mao Zedong Thought as its main goal.[22] The establishment and increasing influence of the Picket Corps would not have been possible without the support of the state bureaucracy. The tumultuous outrage of destroying old culture had led the State Council and security organs to ponder institutionalized options for gaining influence over the Red Guard movement. Two days after the first parade at Tiananmen Square, Yong Wentao of the Beijing Municipal Secretariat and political commissar of the Shenyang Military Region approached Wang Renzhong, vice-chairman of the CCRG and former first secretary of the Central South Bureau, with the question of how to establish closer supervision of the Red Guards. As a result, six hundred PLA soldiers were assigned the duty of helping the Red Guards establish liaison stations.[23]

As most of the Picket Corps students originated from high-ranking cadre families, they seemed to provide the state bureaucracy with a welcome possibility to guarantee the safety of party leaders and central institutions while linking up with the perceived vanguard of the Cultural Revolution. The State Council and especially its secretary, Zhou Rongxin, provided the Picket Corps with material resources, including cars, phones, and armbands.[24] The material support secured a short-term superiority over other student organizations, most notably the "minority faction"[25] of university students that on 6 September had formed its own leadership organization, the so-called Third Headquarters. The Third Headquarters, led by Zhu Chengzhao of the Beijing Geological Institute and Qinghua University student leader Kuai Dafu, quickly became the main opponent of

[22] Shoudu hongweibing jiuchadui xicheng fendui zhihuibu, *Shoudu hongweibing jiuchadui (xicheng fendui) xuangao chengli* [Manifesto on the Establishment of the Capital Red Guard Picket Corps (Western District Detachment)], 25 August 1966, in CRDB.

[23] "Ba fangeming zuzhi 'Xi jiu' na chulai shi zhong. Xicheng jiuchadui zuixinglu" [Drag the Counterrevolutionary Organization "Western Pickets" Out to Confront the Masses: Crime Record of the Western District Picket Corps], in *Dongfanghong bao*, 9 March 1967, reprinted in NRGM 9, 3231.

[24] See "Liandong de qianshen. 'Xicheng jiuchadui' de zui'e shi" [A Precursor of United Action: A History of the Crimes of the "Western District Picket Corps"], in Hongweibing Shanghai silingbu (ed.), *Polan "liandong,"* Shanghai: Neibu kanwu, May 1967, 33.

[25] On the complicated political reasons behind Red Guard factionalism, see Andrew Walder, *Fractured Rebellion: The Beijing Red Guard Movement*, Cambridge: Harvard University Press, 2009.

the Picket Corps and gained the support of the CCRG, which in turn provided the Third Headquarters with information and material subsidies. Yet the factional disputes reached their climax only after November 1966. During the first months of the Cultural Revolution, the invitation to revolutionary masses from all over the country to visit the capital and learn from the experiences of the Cultural Revolution shook the organizational capacities of the state at its foundations and kept students busy with traveling all over the country in order to foster rebellion and raise the flag of Mao Zedong Thought.

EXCHANGING REVOLUTIONARY EXPERIENCES

The parade of 18 August and its media coverage in print and film had been a huge success in terms of charismatic mobilization. The result had been the formation of Red Guard organizations nationwide and the kindling of revolutionary activism. The instrumental value of staging mass receptions of the CCP Chairman in Beijing, the "center of world revolution,"[26] was made evident further through the large number of students who upon their own initiative had traveled to the capital in order to get a glimpse of Mao. On 5 September, students and revolutionaries were officially invited in the name of the CCP Center to travel to the capital.[27] During an average period of four days, the visitors, in organized fashion, should get acquainted with the situation in different key institutions such as Qinghua University, participate in the Cultural Revolutionary activities, and be given a reception by "leading cadres of the Party Center."[28] Travel and accommodation were to be provided for by the state and provinces.

The instigation of free travel to exchange experiences caused a massive change in China's transportation schedules. Up to November 1966, some

---

[26] The popular phrase was declared unscientific in "Zhongfa [68] 72, Zhonggong zhongyang, zhongyang wenge guanyu 'shijie geming de zhongxin' lun de zhongyao tongzhi" [Important Notice of the CCP Center and the CCRG Concerning the Theory of the "Center of World Revolution"], 18 May 1968, in CRDB.

[27] "Zhongfa [66] 450, Zhonggong zhongyang, guowuyuan guanyu zuzhi waidi gaodeng xuexiao geming xuesheng, zhongdeng xuexiao xuesheng daibiao he geming jiaozhigong daibiao lai jing canguan wenhua da geming yundong de tongzhi" [Circular of the CCP Center and the State Council on Organizing the Revolutionary College Students, Representatives of the Revolutionary Middle School Students, and Representatives of the Revolutionary Staff in the Provinces to Come to Beijing for Observing the Cultural Revolutionary Movement], 5 September 1966, in CRDB.

[28] Ibid.

10 million "revolutionary successors" visited the capital and had to be fed and accommodated. Even after the official termination of free travel on 20 November, roughly half a million travelers arrived on foot as well as some six hundred thousand representatives of different revolutionary communes who traveled to the capital to ask for official guidance.[29] Simultaneously, large numbers of students from the capital traveled throughout the country to kindle the flames of revolution, enjoy revolutionary tourism, or establish communications with other organizations. Furthermore, child crusaders with Mao pictures and banners set out on heroic missions to reenact the Long March or to visit the "sacred places" (*geming shengdi*) of the communist revolution, which besides the capital included sites within the former revolutionary base areas, Jinggangshan, Ruijin, Zunyi, and Yan'an, as well as Mao's birthplace Shaoshan (see Map 2). The instigation of exchanging revolutionary experiences resulted in an unparalleled widening of the revolutionary activities since many students displayed much more revolutionary fervor in distant places than at home, where they had to consider other interests involved.

The whole movement to exchange experiences, which more than any other factor contributed to the spreading of the Mao cult and the nationwide attacks against old culture, ironically would not have reached similar dimensions without the extreme efficiency of the state organs in charge of its organization. Immediately after the first parade, Zhou Enlai, with the aid of the State Council Secretariat, discussed the creation of a new body to facilitate the reception of the masses. The result was the formation of the General Reception Station under the leadership of Lü Hong, a member of the National Defense Institute. Different work groups were placed in charge of the travelers' material well-being, while roughly four thousand reception points in all major units and travel hubs of the city conducted the practical implementation of these guidelines.

Accommodating the incoming masses posed the next great difficulty. The first tent city was built on the grounds of the Altar of Heaven. It was erected within seventeen days and provided shelter for approximately four hundred thousand people. But especially around National Day, the numbers grew exorbitantly. Between September and November 1966, 130,000 students on average arrived at the Beijing railway station daily, while some

---

[29] Yuan zhonggong Beijing shiwei waidi geming shisheng jiedai weiyuanhui (ed.), *Beijing shi jiedai lai jing chuanlian de geming shisheng he hongweibing gongzuo zongjie* [Summary of the Beijing City Reception of Revolutionary Teachers and Students from Other Places Traveling to the Capital and of Red Guard Work], September 1967, 2.

MAP 2. "Sacred Places" of the Revolution: Beijing, Jinggangshan, Ruijin, Zunyi, Yan'an, and Shaoshan

120,000 people left from the Yongdingmen station that had been assigned to departing trains.[30] In October, the numbers doubled and at their most extreme, 3 million people had to be accommodated at the same time. To solve the problem, all citizens were required to help via the street committees by taking in groups of students. Zhou Enlai even opened the party compound of Zhongnanhai to lodge one hundred thousand persons temporarily. The departments in charge of food and supplies contributed large sums of material, approximately 50 million kilograms of food alone, as well as clothing and medical services; they furthermore organized travel during the allotted four days in the capital.[31] All in all, about one million people were involved in providing accommodation and service during the high tide of exchanging experiences in the capital.[32]

Although the chance of being received by Mao Zedong made Beijing clearly the main attraction, cities such as Shanghai witnessed a steadily growing number of incoming students as well, though comparatively late. The city leadership on 19 August 1966 had held its own assembly to welcome the Cultural Revolution, although later reports accused the

[30] Yuan zhonggong, *Beijing*, 26.
[31] Ibid., 10.
[32] Ibid., 2ff.

local party committee of taking advantage of nightfall and heavy rain to withdraw inside the building while they "arranged roughly ten persons of the guarding corps in two groups, which then took shifts in climbing the reviewing stand and on behalf of the leadership waved to the parading troops."[33] While the influx of students in Beijing reached its apex in the first weeks of October, especially around National Day, the number of students in Shanghai started to rise drastically only from mid-October 1966 onward. The city therefore did not establish an organization similar to Beijing's General Reception Station until 18 October, when the students could no longer be accommodated by the provisional liaison offices of the Shanghai Student Federation and the Railway Department. The Shanghai Party Committee finally created a small group for organizing to cope with an estimated total of three hundred thousand to five hundred thousand students. Within two weeks, the estimates were already outdated, as the growing restrictions on accepting students in Beijing and Guangzhou made Shanghai an attractive haven. On 15 October, the State Council announced a temporary reduction in the number of students allowed to visit the capital, but to no avail. Therefore, the CCP Center and the State Council, in a directive of 31 October 1966, declared that between 1 and 5 November 1966 all trains boarded by Red Guards and heading in the direction of Beijing would be canceled in order to bring relief to the chaotic railway scheduling that had led to endless delays in public transport.[34]

Despite its late establishment, Shanghai's reception work proved to be very effective, unlike in the barren area of the Jinggangshan, where Mao had first established a Soviet area back in 1927 and that came to be one of the main destinations of revolutionary travel. Here, as in Shanghai, the number of traveling students reached its peak in November, when an estimated two hundred thousand students stayed in the immediate vicinity of the mountains due to rumors that Mao Zedong would appear at a reception

---

[33] Shanghai shi gong'anju geming zaofan lianhe zhihuibu and Zhengzhibu zaofandui (eds.), *Chedi jielu shi gong'anju jiu dangzu yuyong gongju. Jiu wenge bangongshi de taotian zuixing 2* [Thoroughly Expose the Hired Tools of the Old City Public Security Bureau Party Organization: The Heinous Crimes of the Old Cultural Revolution Management Office, Part Two], September 1967, 16. Thanks to Michael Schoenhals for sharing this source.

[34] Chen Donglin, *Neiluan yu kangzheng. "Wenhua da geming" de shi nian (1966–1976)* [Civil Disorder and Resistance: The Ten Years of the "Cultural Revolution" (1966–1976)], Changchun: Jilin renmin chubanshe, 1994, 173.

at Jinggangshan.[35] The coming winter and the growing scarcity of food had to be relieved through military grain transports. A partial evacuation of the mountains caused the surrounding military districts major difficulties as many Red Guards refused to be driven away and some of them even died after going astray in the surrounding woods.[36]

The maximum number of incoming students in Shanghai was reached shortly after the official termination of the movement to exchange experiences. On 22 November 1966, according to the statistical data provided by the Shanghai Reception Office (see Table 1), exactly 997,692 students stayed in Shanghai, many of them making a stopover on their way to their home provinces, others hoping to spend the winter.

An investigation of four trains arriving in Shanghai on 25 November revealed that over 70 percent of the students violated the central directive to return immediately to their study units. Many students had simply not gotten off the train in time or traded their tickets to facilitate their travels. Others simply refused to leave the city according to schedule and enjoyed playing basketball and cricket in their host units.[37] To offer the students an incentive to get their return tickets, the Shanghai Reception Small Group on 27 November came up with the ingenious idea that every student willing to return to his or her study unit would be presented with a "Chairman Mao Quotations Stele" (*Mao zhuxi yulubei*), a glass stele with an inscribed red-golden inlay. The creative employment of cult tokens proved to be effective. Nearly 240,000 students got their return tickets the same day and most students soon followed.[38] By mid-December, Shanghai had by and large been relieved of the pressure of incoming students and three months later the reception facilities were completely disbanded.

---

[35] Zhao Feng, "*Zhong*"*zi xia de yinying. Wenhua da geming zhong de guai xianxiang* [Shadows under the "Loyalty" Sign: Weird Phenomena during the Cultural Revolution], Beijing: Chaohua chubanshe, 1993, 28f.

[36] See Hu Ping and Zhang Shengyou, "Lishi chensi lu. Jinggangshan hongweibing da chuanlian ershi zhounian cha" [Historical Reflections in Memory of the Twentieth Anniversary of Red Guards' Great Exchange of Experience Trips to the Jinggang Mountains], in Zhou Ming (ed.), *Lishi zai zheli chensi. 1966–1976 nian jishi* [Here History Is Lost in Thought: True Record of the Years 1966 to 1976], vol. 5, Taiyuan: Beiyue wenyi chubanshe, 1989, 43, 53.

[37] Jin Dalu, "Shanghai jiedai waisheng hongweibing de wu ge jieduan" [The Five Phases of Receiving Red Guards from Other Provinces in Shanghai], in *Qingnian yanjiu* 9(2005), 45.

[38] Ibid., 46.

TABLE I. *Number of students traveling to and from Shanghai,
August–December 1966*

Date	Arrivals	Departures	Number of Students in Shanghai	Cumulative Total
15–25.8.1966	352	0	n/a	352
1.9.1966	2,514	406	n/a	8,079
17.9.1966	> 13,500	n/a	> 50,000	> 134,500
20.10.1966	50,671	22,207	202,620	374,851
25.10.1966	79,301	> 38,000	> 347,000	1,056,145
1–3.11.1966	238,559	109,596	568,587	1,801,186
14.11.1966	96,526	75,421	764,495	2,698,276
22.11.1966	71,898	80,658	997,691	3,511,127
28–29.11.1966	58,792	220,763	526,909	3,778,740
12.12.1966	n/a	n/a	115,405	4,035,825

Shanghai shi jiedai gedi geming xuesheng bangongshi (ed.), "'Waidi xuesheng lai Hu qingkuang fanying' jianbao" [Bulletin on the "Situation of Students from Other Parts of the Country Coming to Shanghai"], Shanghai, August–December 1966.

THE CASE OF UNITED ACTION

Between 9 and 28 October 1966, the CCP central and regional leadership met in Beijing to discuss the current situation and prospects for the Cultural Revolution. The conference gave the movement a new turn by shifting attention from the destruction of old thought and culture toward the uprooting of "power holders within the party taking the capitalist road." For the first time, Liu Shaoqi and Deng Xiaoping were criticized by name for having suppressed the revolutionary masses and for having failed to implement antirevisionist policies while being in charge of day-to-day party politics. According to Mao's estimate, the movement had roughly passed its zenith and should carry on for another five months or longer before he could feel safe that the country would remain on track so that he himself would not share Stalin's fate once he went to "see Marx."[39]

Yet the movement, rather than winding down, grew increasingly violent. The CCRG had on various occasions criticized the elite Red Guard Pickets Corps in public. Instead, it openly favored the former minority faction organized as the Third Headquarters and thus contributed to the growing factionalism between different Red Guard groups. In late 1966,

[39] Zhonggong wenxian yanjiushi (ed.), *Mao wengao* 12, 143.

a number of middle school students established the Capital Red Guard United Action Committee (often called simply United Action), the last stand of what now came to be referred to as the Old Red Guards. With the termination of the movement to exchange experiences in late November, many of the former Picket Corps members who had traveled through China returned to the capital. Dissatisfied with the change in direction in October that had brought the Third Headquarters to the fore of the leadership's attention, the middle school students were angered by the lack of support from members of the CCRG such as Qi Benyu and Guan Feng who had come to take on most liaison work responsibilities.

The first visible consequences of the Old Red Guards' growing disenchantment with the course of the Cultural Revolution, and especially the role played by the CCRG around Jiang Qing, were a number of big character posters critical of the present situation. Li Hongshan, a student at the Beijing Forestry Institute, gained fame with his daring call to cut ties with the CCRG and to act out the revolution without protection from above. He further was involved in the painting of huge slogans on the viewing stands at the northern end of Tiananmen Square on 2 December that read "The Central Cultural Revolution Group enacts a reactionary capitalist line."[40] But the CCRG was not the only body coming under attack. Liu Zhenzhong and Zhang Licai, two students of the Beijing Agricultural Institute Middle School, publicly questioned the validity of Lin Biao's style of rendering Mao Zedong Thought sacrosanct. In an open letter posted at Qinghua University on 15 November under the pseudonym Yilin Dixi, they challenged the replacement of the Marxist-Leninist canon with Mao Zedong Thought as advocated by "dear Comrade Lin Biao, our deputy commander-in-chief and Chairman Mao's single closest comrade-in-arms and successor,"[41] by heavily quoting Stalin and Mao Zedong himself in support of their position.

The different strands of criticism merged in the formation of United Action, which in its founding declaration of 5 December revived Mao's dictum of the right to rebel against "a new type"[42] of capitalist roaders

---

[40] Bu Weihua, "Pipan 'zichanjieji fandong luxian'" [Criticizing the "Reactionary Capitalist Line"], in Guo, Wang, and Han (eds.), *Shinian fengyu*, 106.

[41] Yilin Dixi, "Gei Lin Biao tongzhi de yifeng gongkai xin" [An Open Letter to Comrade Lin Biao], 15 November 1966, in CRDB. For the English translation, see Schoenhals (ed.), *China's Cultural Revolution*, 161.

[42] Shoudu hongweibing lianhe xingdong weiyuanhui (ed.), "Shoudu hongweibing lianhe xingdong weiyuanhui xuanyan" [Proclamation of the Capital Red Guard United Action Committee], 5 December 1966, in CRDB.

who intimidated and suppressed the masses. Its members swore to be loyal to the party and Chairman Mao and "to prepare measures immediately to crush all acts opposing Mao Zedong Thought."[43] The best way to prove organizational capacities through the various Red Guard groups was the arrangement of large-scale assemblies. To prove their unquestioning loyalty to the CCP Chairman, United Action members planned their first large-scale event to take place on Mao's birthday, 26 December. Back in Yan'an in the 1940s, Mao had forbidden his followers to celebrate his birthday. The date thus had never been of particular prominence up to the Cultural Revolution. Now, however, United Action, by holding a convention in the assembly hall of the Beijing Exhibition Center, instrumentalized the date for staging their loyalty to Mao.

Despite later allegations, the meeting was not intended to generate far-reaching criticism of the CCRG. It was an attempt to display the organization's continuing relevance as well as its willingness to engage in discussion with the CCRG, possibly even to conduct self-criticism.[44] As none of the CCRG's scheduled speakers turned up and thus publicly demonstrated their opposition to United Action, the atmosphere grew tense. Former Picket Corps members recalled the brutalities experienced when being detained by the Ministry of Public Security. Others publicly declared, "Some leaders of the CCRG should not become too presumptuous."[45] The screening of two specific movies further boosted their confidence. The first, showing Mao's reception of the Red Guards in August 1966, recalled the high tide of the Middle School Red Guards' influence. The second movie, *The Secretary of the County Committee* (*xianwei shuji*), showed a meeting during which the appearance of Central Military Commission members was greeted with ferocious applause while the CCRG members received a rather hostile reception by the audience. The assembly on Mao's birthday thus turned out to become the first large-scale demonstration of opposition to the politics of the CCRG.

In the following days and months, United Action members started attacking the CCRG, local public security bureaus, and members of the Third Headquarters either with brute force or by employing symbolic

---

[43] Ibid.

[44] Xu Youyu, *Xingxing sese de zaofan. Hongweibing jingshen suzhi de xingcheng ji yanbian* [Rebels of All Stripes: A Study of Red Guard Mentalities], Hong Kong: Zhongwen daxue chubanshe, 1999, 188.

[45] "Liandong neimu" [Inside Story of United Action], in *Dongfeng*, August 1967, 4, reprinted in NRGM 10, 3978.

devices such as slogans, chants, and rumors. When breaking into an assembly of the Third Headquarters on 4 January, United Action members seized the microphone and claimed, "The Chairman has returned to the capital. ... The CCRG has split into two factions, 6 A.M., Instruction of the Chairman,"[46] thus causing a great disturbance by invoking Mao's authority. The "six o'clock instruction" had been invented by United Action members at Beijing University Middle School immediately after the 26 December meeting and spread along with other rumors, such as "Mao Zedong has criticized Jiang Qing," throughout the city.[47]

United Action members' criticism of the CCRG did not incite a wider response among the populace, although they kept their attacks up until the summer of 1967 and staged further protests against their criminalization. The large share of responsibility that rested with United Action members for the violence against perceived class enemies during the Red August of 1966 alienated a wider audience. The political leadership condemned United Action as "reactionary group" in a *Red Flag* editorial in February 1967, and many of its members, some of whom today are upcoming, highly prominent fifth-generation party leaders, were detained by the public security organs and only released upon Mao's intervention on 22 April. Despite its efforts to reorganize or to regain the support of the CCRG,[48] United Action was marginalized and in one of its strongholds, 1 August Middle School, a permanent exhibition entitled "Strike down United Action" was established. The enormous importance that came to be attached to the exhibition rested less with the organization itself than with the political instrumentability of United Action as examples of Liu Shaoqi's and Deng Xiaoping's "reactionary capitalist line."[49] With the fall of United Action, the attacks on the "backstage bosses," Liu and Deng, were stepped up. When the CCRG collectively visited the exhibition on 8 March 1967, Kang Sheng, upon wandering through the spacious garden

---

[46] "Liandong neimu," 6, reprinted in NRGM 10, 3980.

[47] Shoudu hongweibing chedi cuihui "liandong" geming lianluo weiyuanhui and Beijing gangyuan fuzhong kanglianjun (eds.), *Liandong fan Mao Zedong sixiang zuixing 50 lie* [Fifty Examples of United Action Crimes of Opposing Mao Zedong Thought], May 1967, 6.

[48] Hongdaihui zhengfa gongshe wenge jianxun bianjibu (ed.), "Liandong dongtai" [United Action Platform], in *Wenge jianxun zengkan* 62, 6 May 1967, 4.

[49] Shoudu dazhuan yuanxiao hongdaihui and Cuihui fangeming zuzhi "Liandong" zhanlanhui (eds.), *Cuihui fangeming zuzhi "Liandong" zhanlanhui. Neirong jieshao* [Destroy the Counterrevolutionary Organization United Action Exhibition: Explanation of Contents], August 1967.

and exquisite architecture, remarked, "Here one can see at one glance from which divide United Action and revisionism have emerged."[50]

By the end of 1966, the twists in policy line as well as the growing rivalry for political support and power among the mass organizations resulted in a drastic change in the character of the cult. Instead of inciting charismatic mobilization, the cult was increasingly instrumentalized to justify the attacks on opposing organizations or to purge high-ranking communist cadres. Stimulated by CCRG members, special groups were formed to investigate past speeches and actions of CCP leaders in order to produce incriminating evidence. Committees made up of various Red Guard organizations from late January onward started to compile quotes under headlines such as opposition to Mao Zedong, Lin Biao, the CCRG, the Cultural Revolution, the Great Leap Forward, and other topics. By printing the "correct viewpoints" of Marxism-Leninism, Mao Zedong Thought, and Lin Biao quotations in opposition to the incriminating evidence, the committees could thus encourage the interpretation of every deviation as potentially a counterrevolutionary crime. As any critical word previously voiced now represented a political time bomb that could decide the future fate of an individual, the active employment of cult rhetoric and symbols in factional struggles as a safeguard against possible accusations replaced the former pop-star–like Mao craze during the autumn of 1966. From 1967 onward, the cult increasingly came to be employed by local groups for specific purposes, ultimately resulting in cult anarchy.

The purge of party committees that had started with the establishment of the short-lived Shanghai Commune in January 1967 came to destroy the organizational foundations of the party-state, the local party cells and committees. The steering of the Cultural Revolution therefore had to rely even more on symbolic devices such as speeches and study meetings to communicate the newest directions of the CCP Center. With the call to seize power from all capitalist roaders within the party, China descended into the most chaotic period since the founding of the People's Republic, and the cult was to play an ever more important role.

---

[50] "Zhongyang wenge canguan ba yi xuexiao 'liandong zuixing zhanlan' shi de jianghua" [Speeches by the CCRG while Visiting the "Crimes of United Action Exhibition" in the 1 August School], 8 March 1967, in CRDB.

PART THREE

CULT AND COMPLIANCE

The first months of 1967 witnessed a drastic widening of the impact of the Cultural Revolution. Middle and high school students had played a dominant part in the early stages of the movement. Now it spread within production units and the countryside after official restrictions had been lifted in December 1966. The CCP leadership effectively allowed for the creation of rival organizations that resulted in violent clashes about resources of power, such as party institutions, propaganda devices, and military equipment. At the same time, Red Guards were to participate in short term military training to secure the concordance of their thoughts and actions with the aims of the Cultural Revolution. The parallel trends of employing the cult for disciplinary functions and the increasing lack of state control fostered multiple ways of instrumentalizing Mao Zedong's image for different purposes. Although up to this point the main way of expounding the cult had been Maoist rhetoric, the physical presence of Mao icons, including statues, badges, and images, now grew indomitable, despite the efforts of the CCP Center to restrict the spreading of what was referred to as "formalism" (xingshi zhuyi). The open-textured nature of the revolutionary symbols invoked in different settings was revealed with increasing clarity from mid-1967 onward. To regain control over the factionalized patchwork of revolutionary groups and to quell the growing civil unrest, the CCP returned to the methods of emotional and exegetical bonding. Basically, every Chinese citizen had to take part in the guided study of Mao texts that was organized from central study classes down to household study classes within families.

This third part of the book demonstrates how the mobilizing force of the cult was superseded by its disciplinary function, when the Cultural

Revolution turned from a mass movement into "moving the masses."[1] After tracing the measures of military force used to end the nearly complete cult anarchy in the first half of 1967, this part discusses the specific forms of rhetorical and ritual worship. Both the language of flattery and the rituals of worship developed under highly specific circumstances and flourished only during a short period of time. They were expressions of loyalty within a climate characterized by utmost instability and fear and reveal the performative nature of Cultural Revolutionary rhetoric and ritual. The last chapter finally provides a brief overview of the extended process of curbing the most visible traces of the Mao cult, especially after the Ninth Party Congress in 1969. The impact of the Lin Biao affair on the credibility of the cult and popular reaction currently cannot be dealt with in similar detail, since the archival stacks on, for example, participation in the "Criticize Lin Biao and Confucius" campaign remain closed. The devastating impact that the death of the personality cult's most ardent supporter had on the cult, however, is not to be underestimated.[2] Although the visible traces of the cult were reduced, the fundamental mode of communication remained stable, even beyond the death of Mao Zedong, and thus allowed for renewed leader cults to appear in China until the present.

[1] Tang Shaojie, *Yi ye zhi qiu. Qinghua daxue 1968 nian "bairi da wudou"* [One Leaf Knows the Autumn: The "One Hundred–Day Great Armed Struggle" at Qinghua University], Hong Kong: Zhongwen daxue chubanshe, 2003, 260.
[2] See, as well, Teiwes and Sun, *End of the Maoist Era*, 31ff.

7

Ambiguous Symbols

The silent appearances during the eight receptions of the revolutionary masses had elevated the image of Mao Zedong as the "great helmsman, great leader, great commander, and great teacher" of the Chinese Revolution to previously unfathomed heights. Simultaneously, the CCP's most prestigious brand symbol had become devoid of a clear-cut message. Mao had not provided the movement with a blueprint of how the Cultural Revolution was to be conducted, nor had he delivered any speeches in public that would have offered a coherent vision of his aims. Party cadres and masses could only rely on the often vague official guidelines published in the party press and either risk offering their interpretation or wait for the seldom impartial exegesis conducted by members of Mao's camarilla. During the course of the movement, the instrumental character of the cult serving as a means to mobilize the masses and to strike down holders of party offices came to be widely recognized. The raids of high party officials' homes had supplied Red Guard organizations with original Mao texts that had not been censored and reworked by the party authorities. By publishing his often coarse and musing comments, deleted in the official versions, these texts added a number of new aspects to the sacrosanct image of Mao fostered in the party media and provided the base for interpretations focused on immediate political instrumentability. The loss of the party's exegetical monopoly led to the emergence of contradictory and conflated usages of Mao's image and words by different groups, of "waving the Red Flag to knock down the Red Flag" (*dazhe hongqi fan hongqi*). Regaining control necessitated the reestablishment of authoritative guidelines about which texts and policy lines were to be studied.

With the party organizations rendered by and large defunct, the only way of establishing order was reliance on the organizational capacities of the PLA.

"THREE SUPPORTS, TWO MILITARIES"

The first measure to unify the perception of the present situation and to regulate the behavior of the Red Guard organizations was presented by the instigation of short-term military training.[1] Mao Zedong, in a comment to Lin Biao in mid-December 1966, had requested to strengthen the principles of the "four firsts" and the "eight rules of discipline" among the students. During a period of twenty days, advanced military activists in the study of Mao Zedong Thought were ordered to refashion the outlook of the Red Guards in congruence with the newest party directives. As a result, between 20 January and 10 February 1967, 4,105 military cadres conducted military training for some 22,685 students in five of the country's most prestigious universities.[2] The study activists had not been specifically trained for this task and started out according to the modus of inner-military political education. A short booklet compiled by an "East Is Red Institute" in December 1966 and republished for military training in January 1967 provides a clue on how political education work was conducted.[3] In a series of stream-of-consciousness–like texts and graphs, the primary contents of Mao Zedong Thought and political education were taught along with general rules of correct behavior. Furthermore, the military cadres made use of the whole arsenal of techniques of "lively study and application" that had been refined over the years and ranged from comparisons between past and present, over visits to revolutionary model communes and cultural performances. Military training became popular for a short time among middle school students, while leaders of

[1] "Zhongfa [67] 2, Zhonggong zhongyang, guowuyuan guanyu dui da zhong xuexiao geming shisheng jinxing duanqi junzheng xunlian de tongzhi" [CCP Center and State Council Notice on Practicing Short-Term Military and Political Training for University and Middle School Revolutionary Teachers and Students], 31 December 1966, in CRDB.

[2] "Zhonggong zhongyang pizhuan Mao zhuxi guanyu yuan xiao he dang, zheng, jun, min jiguan junxun de zhishi ji liang ge fujian" [Instructions of Chairman Mao Concerning Military Training in Universities and Colleges as Well as in Party, State, Military, and Civil Institutions Approved and Transmitted by the CCP Center, with Two Appendices], 19 February 1967, in CRDB.

[3] Dongfang hong zhanxiao (ed.), *Xuexi jiefangjun zhengzhi gongzuo jingyan* [Studying the Experiences of PLA Political Work], n.p., December 1966. For an identical document published by a different group, see Schoenhals (ed.), *China's Cultural Revolution*, 65–75.

large university factions such as Kuai Dafu soon criticized the restraining behavior of military cadres and, with reference to the widely criticized work teams that had been sent to universities by Liu Shaoqi in the summer of 1966, accused the soldiers of behaving "even more like work teams than the work teams themselves."[4]

Mao approved of the disciplinary efforts. He had a report about the experiences of the Tianjin Yan'an Middle School distributed nationwide, where the establishment of study classes through the military had been used as the groundwork for the unification of the contending factions.[5] The scope of military involvement was thus widened considerably. In April 1967, no less than 53,000 PLA cadres were involved in conducting military training in some 3,091 educational units.[6] In his comment on the Tianjin experiences, Mao had advised to proceed by establishing trial units first and then to implement "three-in-one combinations" as new leadership bodies made up jointly of representatives of revolutionary cadres, the PLA, and the masses as the new guiding principle in all units. Mao's short comment, made public on the first anniversary of the report's internal circulation on 8 March 1968, was retrospectively declared to be his "great strategic plan" (*weida zhanlüe bushu*)[7] on how to unite the contending factions successfully. But as the need for the report's renewed publication a year later, along with clear instructions to speedily put the described measures into practice, revealed, the contemporary implementation was not overwhelmingly successful.

The military training was only a small part of the importance the PLA assumed in early 1967. The call for power seizures in the early days of January had made the political situation increasingly desperate. During the first three weeks of January 1967, unchecked struggles for power among competing factions occurred all over the country. The main objects of

[4] Zhonggong wenxian yanjiushi (ed.), *Zhou Enlai nianpu* 3, 151.

[5] "Zhongfa [67] 85, Zhonggong zhongyang zhuanfa Mao zhuxi pizhuan de 'Tianjin Yan'an zhongxue yi jiaoxueban wei jichu shixian quanxiao da lianhe he gonggu, fazhan hongweibing de tihui' ji fujian" [CCP Center Transmits Chairman Mao's Comments on "The Experiences of the Tianjin Yan'an Middle School in Establishing a School-Wide Great Alliance Based on Teaching Classes and the Stabilization and Development of the Red Guards," with an Appendix], 8 March 1967, in CRDB.

[6] Deng Lifeng, "'San zhi liang jun' shulun" [Treatise on the "Three Supports, Two Militaries"], in *Dangdai Zhongguoshi yanjiu* 8.6 (2001), 50.

[7] See Zhonggong wenxian yanjiushi (ed.), *Mao wengao* 12, 250f, and "Mao zhuxi guanyu wuchanjieji wenhua da geming de weida zhanlüe bushu de zhishi" [Chairman Mao's Instruction Regarding the Great Strategic Plan for the Great Proletarian Cultural Revolution], in *Renmin ribao*, 8 March 1968, 1.

struggle were naturally resources of power: political institutions, broadcasting networks, military equipment, monetary institutions, and storage
facilities. Mao requested that the PLA assist truly revolutionary masses in
their attempts to seize power, without offering advice on how to distinguish "truly" revolutionary masses from their counterparts. The choice of
local commanders was therefore basically restricted to the "freedom of
choosing which error to commit."[8] Support from the military presented
local factions with the ultimate legitimacy needed to seize power. In cases
where the local PLA commanders openly came to support a majority
faction, as occurred in Heilongjiang, Shanxi, and Guizhou provinces,
revolutionary committees headed by military personnel were established
within weeks. The revolutionary committees established in the early stages
varied considerably in size from those to be formed after 1967, as they
could accommodate a larger number of members from competing factions.
Thus the Heilongjiang Revolutionary Committee consisted of a working
staff of 1,470 members whereas the Hubei Revolutionary Committee
established a year later received approval for only 200 of the proposed
1,500 staff through the CCP Center.[9]

The growing chaos did not remain without criticism from within the
party. On 16 February 1967, during a meeting of the occasional caucus
that had come to replace the Politburo, veteran cadres such as Tan
Zhenlin, Chen Yi, and Ye Jianying sharply attacked the policies of the
Cultural Revolution and especially the tactics of the CCRG to purge old
cadres one by one. Yao Wenyuan and fellow radical Zhang Chunqiao
relayed the minutes of the so-called Huairen Hall meeting to Mao
Zedong the same night. Mao reacted brusquely. He called a meeting of
the Politburo, which turned out to be its last formal gathering before it
came to be replaced by the informal Central Caucus (*Zhongyang
pengtou huiyi*) and made it clear that whoever attacked the CCRG
criticized him personally. Like many times before, Mao called upon his
perceived opponents to assume power and to try their luck ruling China

---

[8] Li Ke and Hao Shengzhang, *"Wenhua da geming" zhong de renmin jiefangjun* [The PLA
during the "Great Cultural Revolution"], Beijing: Zhonggong dangshi ziliao chubanshe,
1989, 243.

[9] Huang Yongqiang, "Geming weiyuanhui jigou qingkuang (Shenyang junqu canmou
Huang Yongqiang tongzhi jieshao)" [The Situation of the Revolutionary Committee
Institutions (Explained by Shenyang Military District Staff Officer, Comrade Huang
Yongqiang)], in Shandong sheng weisheng fangyizhan hongqi gongshe xuanchuanzu
(ed.), *Dou pi gai canzheng ziliao* [Materials on Participating in Struggle-Criticism-
Reform], n.p., 1968, 31.

while he and Lin Biao would once more climb the Jinggang Mountains and build a new army.

Meanwhile, the Central Military Commission between 26 February and 25 March met in Beijing to discuss the impact of the new tasks of the PLA. On 19 March 1967, a directive was passed that defined the tasks as "three supports, two militaries" (*san zhi, liang jun*) – namely, the support of the Left, workers, and peasants, as well as military training and supervision. After the crushing of the party-state, the PLA had to assume regulatory functions in all parts of society. Although supporting the Left clearly caused the most political trouble, assisting workers and peasants in the process of production required by far the largest number of men and the greatest amount of resources. In March and April 1967, over one hundred thousand soldiers joined civilian units to supervise industrial production[10] and even more soldiers were deployed to help in agriculture. Simultaneously, military control was to be established in all important units, including broadcasting stations, transportation units, and military research institutes, leading to the obscure situation of military control in military institutions such as the PLA General Political Department.

By May 1967, military control had come to be extended to 7,752 units and special protection had been granted to another 2,145 units.[11] Without the PLA's omnipresent efforts to restore order, the People's Republic would no longer have been able to keep up with performing even the most basic functions. Until the disbanding of the campaign in 1972, some 2.8 million soldiers came to take part in the "three supports, two militaries."[12] Lin Biao on 20 March 1967 contrasted the involvement of the PLA during the Cultural Revolution with previously fought wars or major epidemics. Despite the present unrest and seemingly chaotic situation, Lin asserted, the losses had been the "tiniest, tiniest, tiniest," compared to previous campaigns, and the success had been the "greatest, greatest, greatest."[13] The violent phase of the Cultural Revolution, however, was just about to get started.

---

[10] Deng, "'San zhi liang jun' shulun," 46.

[11] Deng Lifeng, "Renmin jiefangjun de 'san zhi liang jun'" [The PLA's "Three Supports, Two Militaries"], in Guo, Wang, and Han (eds.), *Shinian fengyu*, 196.

[12] Ibid., 176.

[13] Lin Biao, "Zai jun yishang ganbu huiyi de jianghua" [Speech at a Cadre Meeting at the Level of the Army Command or Higher], 20 March 1967, in CRDB.

MONUMENTS OF BELIEF AND CULT ANARCHY

Despite its growing influence, the PLA from April 1967 onward came under increasing political pressure for having failed to support the revolutionary masses correctly. Immediate criticism of the PLA had up to this point been rarely voiced; now military leaders were replaced on grounds of having suppressed revolutionary mass organizations. Attacks on military district headquarters and theft of weapons became increasingly common. By August 1967, some 1,175 cases of theft had been reported and the stolen items included 21,600 rifles and 78 anti-aircraft guns.[14] In Hunan, 28 tons of gunpowder had been stolen from a military factory, and the PLA officially had limited possibilities of countering the attacks because the use of any kind of weapon against the masses, except for brandishing the "spiritual nuclear bomb," the Little Red Book, and shouting quotations, had been strictly forbidden.

The volatile situation made the employment of the cult and its icons an important instrument to prove a faction's revolutionary credentials. While in the past public declarations had been the most important way of demonstrating allegiance, the upcoming first anniversary of the Cultural Revolution and many of its important directives provided the background for commemorative activities. By May 1967, the factions started to build large-scale Mao statues, without initial support or funding from the state leadership, to demonstrate their revolutionary credentials. The first statue was unveiled on the campus of Qinghua University on 4 May 1967. The link with the May Fourth Movement, which might have been an alternative point of commemoration, was only briefly cited in the speeches. The statue had been built upon the decision of the Qinghua Jinggangshan Regiment within little more than four weeks. The official announcement placed similar emphasis on the nobility of its objective and the determination of its builders: "We Jinggangshan people love the great leader Chairman Mao the most! We want to eradicate the old revisionist Qinghua and construct a new communist Qinghua! We precisely want to greatly enhance Mao Zedong Thought and establish the absolute authority of Chairman Mao in a big way!"[15]

The chosen height of the statue was not arbitrary; it was 7.1 meters. The number could be read as both a symbol for the party's traditional

---

[14] Deng, "Renmin jiefangjun," 183.
[15] "Mao zhuxi yongyuan liushuai women qianjin. Ji Mao zhuxi quanshen juxing suxiang de luocheng" [Chairman Mao Forever Commands Us Forward: Remembering the Completion of the Large Full-Length Statue of Chairman Mao], in *Jinggangshan*, 6 May 1967, 5f.

founding date, 1 July, or of the homophonous word for "uprising." The construction process was declared a test of political determination and relied heavily on the help of other students, teachers, and workers, numbering up to five thousand altogether, not all of whom took part in construction work, though. Cultural performances such as singing quotation songs, liaison work with other organizations (especially those skilled in artwork), and searching for relevant photographic source material were other ways of supporting the progress. Lin Biao contributed an inscription of the "four greats" (teacher, leader, commander, and helmsman) that was engraved in the monument's socket. The instrumental value of establishing statues as symbols of firm belief in Mao Zedong Thought was often directed against immediate rivals within the universities. In the case of Qinghua University, it was the "Jinggangshan April 14th" faction that had come to contest the supremacy of the Jinggangshan Regiment.[16] The rivalry finally resulted in armed conflicts, the "hundred-day armed struggle," until order was restored on campus in mid-1968.

The use of statues to demonstrate loyalty spread rapidly among other universities. The already existing statues provided models that were scrutinized in great detail by special delegations. Most organizations, however, tried not to simply copy the models but to distinguish their own statue through various means. The first statue cast with aluminum at the Beijing Mining Institute was considered a huge innovation. It was unveiled on Mao's seventy-fourth birthday, 26 December 1967, and presented the ultimate combination of revolutionary numerology. The statue itself was 7.1 meters high, and thus incorporated the previously mentioned symbolism. In addition, the socket on which it was placed was exactly 5.16 meters, in remembrance of the 16 May directive that had ultimately presented the starting point of the Cultural Revolution. Yet the final clue was the combined height: 12.26 meters, an acronym for Mao's birthday.[17] The statue's ingenious design proved to be an ongoing inspiration for later construction; the dimensions were taken up during the second wave of building Mao statues in mid-1968 in the name of the newly established revolutionary committees, resulting in the standard height of 12.26 meters for most Mao statues.

[16] On the two factions, see Joel Andreas, "Battling over Political and Cultural Power during the Chinese Cultural Revolution," in *Theory and Society* 31 (2002), 492ff.

[17] "Wo yuan longzhong juxing lüzhu Mao zhuxi xiang luocheng dianli" [Our University Solemnly Celebrates the Completion of the Large-Sized Aluminum-Cast Chairman Mao Statue], in *Dongfang hong*, 26 December 1967, 1, reprinted in Zhou Yuan (ed.), *Hongweibing ziliao: A New Collection of Red Guard Publications* (RGM), Part I. *Newspapers*, vol. 6, Oakton, VA: Center for Chinese Research Materials, 1999, 1223.

Given the examples of the Kims in North Korea or Saddam Hussein in Iraq, the construction of leader statues is commonly understood as an expression of totalitarian state power and the cherishing of personal vanities. In the Chinese case, the circumstances are more complicated. As mentioned before, Mao Zedong had in the early stages of the People's Republic on a couple of occasions interdicted the setting up of statues and other visible phenomena of a leader cult. The cult, in Mao's opinion, was clearly of instrumental value. It could be employed to attract followers and to oppose rivals within the CCP, but Mao did not indulge in its aesthetic representations. Even after he had effectively legitimated a "cult of truth" as a nonbureaucratic form of rule in 1958, he remained aware of the differences between true loyalty and mere performances. In a talk with Ho Chi Minh in June 1966, he proudly claimed that, unlike in Vietnam, where everyone had grown accustomed to calling "long live" in Ho's presence, a similar custom had not persisted in China:

> I advise you, not all of your subjects are loyal to you. Perhaps most of them are loyal but maybe a small number only verbally wish you "long live," while in reality they wish you a premature death. When they shout "long live," you should beware and analyze [the situation]. The more they praise you, the less you can trust them. This is a very natural rule.[18]

If Mao conducted the kind of private analysis he had advised Ho to undertake in the face of exaggerated praise, his conclusion must have been that he could count on Lin Biao's personal loyalty irrespective of his public utterances. Just a month after his meeting with Ho, Mao, in a famous letter to his wife, Jiang Qing, expressed mistrust in the use of the cult terminology employed by Lin Biao within the public sphere and declared that the instigation of the cult had been conducted against his will: "This is the first time in my life that I have conceded to other people against my own will regarding matters of principle."[19] He declared to have been employed as a twentieth-century Zhongkui, a legendary demon fighter, to counter the threat of revisionism. If the letter is authentic,[20] Mao displayed a very clear understanding of how his image had been used as a revolutionary brand symbol to stir up public emotion. The cult thus was to be endured at that time despite the fact that it represented a major nuisance.

---

[18] Mao Zedong, "Zai Hangzhou tong Hu Zhiming tongzhi de jianghua (jielu)" [Talk with Comrade Ho Chi Minh in Hangzhou (Abstract)], 10 June 1966, in CRDB.

[19] Mao, Zedong, "Gei Jiang Qing de xin" [Letter to Jiang Qin], 7 August 1966, in CRDB.

[20] The authenticity of the letter has repeatedly been questioned; see, for example, Chen Xiaoya, "Mao Zedong gei Jiang Qing de xin zhenwei bian" [Is Mao Zedong's Letter to Jiang Qing Authentic or Fake?], in Ding Kaiwen (ed.), *Chongshen Lin Biao zui'an* [Reassessing the Criminal Case of Lin Biao], New York: Mingjing chubanshe, 2004, 614–20.

By mid-1967, the instrumentalization of cult symbols had been rendered beyond Mao's immediate control. He seems to have taken notice of the new trend to build statues only in early July. On 4 July 1967, the "Briefings on Letters and Complaints during the Cultural Revolution 280," an internal publication compiled by a section of the CCP General Office Secretariat that relayed general trends of popular opinion to the CCP leadership, reported the wave of establishing Mao statues. Mao reacted on the recent phenomenon by commenting on the back of the report: "This kind of phenomenon wastes manpower and money; what is useless, is harmful. If it is not stopped, it will stir up a proneness to boasting and exaggeration."[21] He furthermore encouraged stopping the issuing of his previously unpublished speeches, especially at the Beijing Mining Institute. Even after the local Red Guards had been reprimanded, they had continued to edit their "Long live Mao Zedong Thought" collections by sending staff to Changsha, the capital of Mao's native province Hunan, to have it printed there.[22] Upon Mao's comments, Central Document (*Zhongfa*) [67] 219 was drafted at a meeting of the Central Caucus on 12 July and issued the following day:

> The strongly voiced request of the broad revolutionary masses to erect Chairman Mao statues truly derives from their boundless hot love towards the great leader Chairman Mao. But, creating Mao Zedong statues is a grave political question. Every statue has to guarantee a high political and artistic quality in order to be passed on to the following generations. This is only possible, if it is carried out at the right time and place under the united supervision of the CCP Center. The current hectic activity of numerous mass organizations is inclined not only to produce economic losses but political losses as well. ... Furthermore, in various places previously unpublished speeches of Chairman Mao have been issued, even comments to other persons and poetry have been included. The CCP Center reaffirms: All speeches, articles, documents, and poems of Chairman Mao that have previously not been made public shall not be reproduced, printed, and distributed without the previous permission of Chairman Mao and the CCP Center.[23]

Interestingly, Lin Biao had shortly beforehand assessed the present situation as well and had come to quite different conclusions. Upon witnessing the upsurge of activities to construct Mao statues, he perceived the military to be lagging behind in public worship and thus sensed the danger of losing the PLA's and

---

[21] Zhonggong wenxian yanjiushi (ed.), *Mao wengao* 12, 368.

[22] Ibid., 369, n. 1.

[23] For the renewed issuing of the Central Document, see "Zhongfa [67] 219, Zhonggong zhongyang guanyu jianzao Mao zhuxi suxiang wenti de zhishi" [CCP Center Notice Concerning the Question of Constructing Chairman Mao Statues], 13 July 1967, in CRDB.

his own avant-garde role as the best students of Mao Zedong Thought. On 28 June, Lin advised the General Political Department and the General Logistics Department to follow the recent trend of constructing Mao statues.[24] Preparations had begun after the instruction had been sent to all units on 1 July. Lin usually sent all of his decisions past Mao for approval beforehand, but this time he waited another ten days before he submitted a draft. Mao returned the document to Lin with a reference to the forthcoming central document. Although Lin usually was highly astute in anticipating Mao's judgment, this time he failed to sense accurately that the commodification of the cult had gone too far, in Mao's opinion. The employment of cult symbols by all factions supplied them with a degree of symbolic power that resisted immediate intervention from above and thus angered Mao. The mechanisms brought forth by a system that had come to rely solely on personal loyalty and reliance on Mao Zedong Thought rendered CCP control over the cult ever more difficult, as even Lin Biao was to experience.

Shortly before advising the building of Mao statues within the PLA, Lin had tried to cope with the increasing worship of himself that had grown more pronounced since May 1967. In a personal letter to Zhou Enlai and the CCRG, Lin Biao on 16 June referred to recently staged performances during which not only the accustomed "[We] wish Chairman Mao eternal life" had been chanted but, with regard to Lin's frail health, as well: "[We] wish Vice-Chairman Lin eternal health." Lin claimed that to "establish the absolute authority of Chairman Mao" was entirely correct, but that his own person should be kept out of the public worship in order to "conform to objective reality."[25] Lin called upon the support of the CCRG and State Council in seeing to it that similar phrasings would not be tolerated in public documents or plays. He further requested to draft an official document to relay his opinion down to the county level. Lin's request was unusual, as he, being vice-chairman of the CCP and minister of defense, could have easily ordered the General Political Department to draft a similar directive.[26] Zhou and the CCRG members did not grant him the favor, probably because they were aware of the fact that the public worship of Lin was an asset that at a later point could be turned against him. Thus Lin Biao in December 1967 again wrote a letter, this time resembling an official document but issued in his name. In the letter, which he personally handed out to conference

---

[24] Zhonggong wenxian yanjiushi (ed.), *Mao wengao* 12, 376, n. 2.

[25] Lin Biao, "Gei Zhou zongli he zhongyang wenge xiaozu de yi feng xin" [A Letter to Premier Zhou and the CCRG], 16 June 1967, in CRDB.

[26] Schoenhals, *Doing Things with Words*, 41f.

participants, Lin specifically interdicted the compilation of quotation volumes, plays, memoirs, and selected writings in his name, as well as the slogan to "establish the eminent authority of Vice-Chairman Lin."[27] These early attempts to curb the cult did not result in the termination of all construction activities or the end of slogans related to Lin Biao. The only tangible result was the implementation of a bureaucratic routine to grant official permission for planned statues.[28] Fostering the prestige of powerful patrons within the CCP leadership retained its value, not necessarily by gaining support from above for conducting public worship this time but rather by relying on the patron's image to legitimize oneself vis-à-vis the masses. If Mao or Lin voiced their discontent with their respective cults, these utterances could easily be interpreted as an expression of modesty on behalf of the leaders.

In a long discussion, conducted in the middle of night by CCRG members Qi Benyu and Chen Boda with representatives from various Tianjin mass organizations on 8 September 1967, the question was brought up of whether the center approved of the construction of statues or would possibly even assist by providing raw materials. Qi answered by quoting the recent central document, but he was interrupted and asked whether he personally supported the building of statues. Qi replied that his personal attitude had nothing to do with this. "If you ask me, I am only satisfied if I see Mao statues everywhere; but the Chairman does not approve of it. [We] should act according to the sayings of the Chairman. One sentence of Chairman Mao surpasses ten thousand [of our] sentences, we should always act according to the supreme instructions."[29]

The question of statues had only been a minor aspect of the discussions among the many competitors for political power in Tianjin. According to numerous letters sent directly to the CCRG, the situation in the city had become anarchic. Frequent robberies and open sexual assaults had been reported to the authorities without resulting in any kind of consequence. During the often harsh discussion, the instrumental value of employing the sayings and image of Mao and other CCP leaders became a subject of

---

[27] Lin Biao, "Guanyu xuanchuan gongzuo de yi feng xin" [A Letter Concerning Propaganda Work], 13 December 1967, in CRDB.

[28] A number of statues thus were interdicted due to the lack of artistic quality; one example was the statue planned for the Beijing Aviation Institute. See "Zhou Enlai jiejian guofang kewei daibiao shi de jianghua" [Zhou Enlai's Speech at the Reception for Representatives from the National Defense Science Commission], 20 April 1968, in CRDB.

[29] "Zhongyang shouzhang di liu ci jiejian Tianjin fu Jing daibiaotuan tanhua jiyao" [Summary of CCP Leaders' Speeches at the Sixth Meeting with Representatives from Tianjin Visiting the Capital], 8 September 1967, in CRDB.

contention. Chen Boda harshly criticized a Tianjin representative for violating the original meaning of one of his own speeches. At other times, representatives would interrupt the CCRG members' speeches and read from the *Quotations* to prove the correctness of their standpoint. Chen Boda was particularly annoyed by attempts by different groups to establish "brand names" (*mingpai*) for their organizations in order to render them true Leftists in public perception, irrespective of the matter at hand. "'Brand names' are just like trademarks. Has the proletarian revolutionary faction been turned into a trademark?"[30] Seldom was the likeness of establishing political reputation and commodity branding perceived as sharply as in the case of Mao's old secretary.

The difficulties of securing the CCP Center's authority over the reproduction of its most crucial symbolic devices – namely, Mao's image and sayings – grew more pronounced during the following months and by no means ended with the issuing of Central Document *Zhongfa* [67] 219 and its renewal in September.[31] The informal networks established by rebel organizations had by mid-1967 spread far enough to have assembled large amounts of unpublished speeches and works of Mao Zedong that continued to be distributed in separate volumes to bolster Mao's "absolute authority" (*juedui quanwei*) and concomitantly strengthened the position of the rebel organizations. In some cases, local reprints of Mao's works would even carry slogans such as "strike down the revolutionary committee" or bear accusations against specific factions ("'27 January' stinks repugnantly") on the title page.[32] Until the end of the year, the CCP Center alone issued another two circulars to restrict the reprint of materials and photographic representations not approved of by the party. In Shanghai, a "clique of profiteers"[33] was ousted that had published for pecuniary reasons some two hundred restricted Mao speeches in editions entitled *Important Documents*. In other units, "everyday

---

[30] Ibid.

[31] "Zhongfa [67] 298, Zhonggong zhongyang guanyu renzhen guanche zhongyang '7.13' zhishi de tongzhi" [CCP Center Notice on Conscientiously Implementing the Center's "13 July" Instruction], 13 September 1967, in CRDB.

[32] See the examples from Ningxia autonomous region mentioned in "Zhongfa [67] 222, Zhonggong zhongyang guanyu yinshua Mao zhuxi zhuzuo bixu yansu de tongzhi" [CCP Center Notice: The Printing of Chairman Mao's Works Must Be Serious], 18 July 1967, in CRDB.

[33] "Zhongfa [67] 321, Zhonggong zhongyang guanyu Shanghai shi geweihui chahuo yi ge feifa bianyin, fanmei Mao zhuxi zhuzuo de touji-daoba jituan de tongzhi" [CCP Center Notice Concerning the Seizure of a Speculation and Profiteering Gang That Illegally Printed and Sold Chairman Mao's Works by the Shanghai Revolutionary Committee], 20 October 1967, in CRDB.

ILLUSTRATION 3. "Everyday life" pictures, showing Mao with "scientific and technological workers" on 6 April 1958 in Wuhan. (Author's personal copy.)

life pictures"[34] of Mao had been printed that were apt to contradict the
set-in-stone public image as omniscient helmsman portrayed in the media
(see Illustration 3). The symbols of the cult thus had acquired ideological,
political, and pecuniary value. To illustrate the ways in which the cult
symbols were employed in local conflicts, an example shall be provided
from the southwestern province of Guizhou.

THE DAFANG INCIDENT

The mountainous province of Guizhou had been one of the first to establish a provincial revolutionary committee. On 13 February 1967, power
had been assumed under the leadership of Li Zaihan, a former vice-
political commissar of the Guizhou Military Region and member of the
Guizhou Cultural Revolution Leadership Small Group. Li had behind the
back of the provincial leadership established links with the CCRG and Lin
Biao and received Mao's open support as new leader of the Guizhou
Revolutionary Committee, established on 17 December 1967. Mao's support presented Li with enormous revolutionary credit and he did his best to
instrumentalize what Pierre Bourdieu has termed "symbolic capital."[35] He
missed no occasion to display the utter devotion of the revolutionary
committee to Mao Zedong. In the congratulatory telegram sent to the
CCP Center the day after the revolutionary committee had been established, he added no less than four superlatives when addressing the "most,
most, most, most beloved great teacher, great leader, great commander,
and great helmsman Chairman Mao."[36] But while Li proved to be adept in
displaying his faithfulness to Mao, he fostered a veritable sub-cult himself.
By mid-1967, Li had his own quotations studied alongside the quotes of
Mao Zedong and Lin Biao. At times, he even negated the validity of Mao's
quotes – a crime for which he was later charged – if they could be

---

[34] "Zhongfa [67] 357, Zhonggong zhongyang yu zhongyang wenge guanyu yan jin zi fanyin
wei gongkai fabiaoguo de Mao zhuxi zhaopian de tongzhi" [Notice of the CCP Center and
the CCRG on Strictly Forbidding the Unauthorized Reprinting of Unpublished Photos of
Chairman Mao], 27 November 1967, in CRDB.

[35] Pierre Bourdieu, "The Social Space and the Genesis of Groups," in *Theory and Society*
14.6 (November 1985), 724.

[36] Guizhou sheng geming weiyuanhui chengli shishi dahui, "Gei Mao zhuxi de zhijing
dian" [A Congratulatory Telegram to Chairman Mao], 14 February 1967, in *Geming weiyuanhui
hao* [Revolutionary Committees Are Good], Xi'an: Shaanxi renmin chubanshe, 1968, 49.

interpreted as weakening his position.[37] Popular saying has it that meetings in Guizhou were commonly started with an additional, "We wish Comrade Li Zaihan relative health" (*bijiao jiankang*), after the common, "We wish Chairman Mao eternal life," and, "We wish Vice-Chairman Lin eternal health." Li Zaihan was therefore criticized throughout the period by local opponents for establishing his own position at the expense of the central leader cult.[38]

Immediately after the establishment of the revolutionary committee, Li Zaihan was accused of suppressing factions that did not conform to his policies. Aided by the provincial government, a united Red Guard Congress had been established on 10 April 1967 without distinguishing between "conservatives" and "rebels." As a consequence, a number of rebel organizations attacked the meeting and during a large protest march the following day established the so-called April 11th Combat Team.[39] Tensions between the April 11th Combat Team and the Support Red faction, which emerged as its major counterpart, quickly manifested themselves in a series of fights and insults. The Guizhou government clearly supported the latter faction. The April 11th Combat Team lodged its complaints of being suppressed by the provincial government by sending twenty of its members to Beijing to obtain support from the CCRG. The failure even to schedule a meeting with the busy party leaders not only led to further vilifications from the government-supported organizations[40] but also to public advice from an anonymous "Warrior of the Geo-Chemical Institute." In a letter from 15 May 1967, posted ten days later by the government in the Red Guard Committee's mouthpiece *Hongweibing*, he advised the rebels to "discard their juvenile thoughts and prepare for struggle."[41] By comparing the situation in Guizhou with that in Sichuan province, where similar tendencies of employing "white terror" on the side

---

[37] A list of his "crimes" may be found in "Chedi pipan Li Zaihan de cuowu yanxing. Yibai ershi li" [Thoroughly Criticize the Erroneous Words of Li Zaihan: 120 Examples], n.p., 1969.

[38] "Guizhou sheng geweihui yi feng gongkai xin" [An Open Letter to the Guizhou Revolutionary Committee], in *Shancheng chunlei* 27 (1968), 9.

[39] Zhonggong Guizhou shengwei dangshi yanjiushi (ed.), *Zhongguo gongchandang Guizhou sheng lishi dashiji* [Major Historical Events in the Guizhou CCP], Guiyang: Guizhou renmin chubanshe, 2001, 410.

[40] See "'4.11' zhong chongji gong'anting de toumian renwu juxin he zai?" ["What Are the Intentions of April 11th Combat Team Leaders Who Attacked the Public Security Office?], in *Hongweibing* (Guizhou), 24 May 1967, 4, reprinted in RGM 6, 2936.

[41] "Fujian: 'Dihuasuo yi bing' de fangeming xinjian" [The Counterrevolutionary Letter of the "Geo-Chemical Institute Warrior], in *Hongweibing* (Guizhou), 24 May 1967, 3f, reprinted in RGM 6, 2935.

of the state had been observed, the anonymous writer insightfully sketched out ways to gain the CCP Center's attention. As long as no major incidents were reported from Guizhou, the leadership would not consider the situation a problem and thus busy itself with solving urgent conflicts in other provinces. A significant change in the Center's perception of the local situation could be brought about only by uniting the rebel forces, concentrating on a few major issues that would force the provincial government to display its real nature, and establishing special propaganda forces to display the rebels' organizational power in order to gain public support. Although the patronizing attitude of the author did not find overwhelming approval, his sketched-out means were quickly adopted. The provincial government unintendedly multiplied the letter's impact by publishing it as an example of counterrevolutionary conviction.

Between late May and August 1967, the factions became interlocked in a series of fierce battles during which they employed the Mao cult for contradictory objectives. In early July, the first wave of hostile activities culminated in a widely reported incident that took place in the small town of Dafang, located roughly 150 kilometers northwest of the provincial capital, Guiyang (see Map 3). Despite the official banning of free travel to exchange experiences, thirty-eight members of Guiyang Teachers' University April 11th faction on 30 June 1967 set out on the pretext of celebrating the anniversary of the party's founding date with a partner organization in the city of Bijie. The revolutionary committee under Li Zaihan's leadership did not perceive the endeavor to be aimed at simple propagation of Mao Zedong Thought. The committee feared a spread of violence and factionalism in rural areas and thus relied on three of Mao's "supreme instructions" (*zuigao zhishi*): "grasp revolution, promote production,"[42] "return to study to conduct revolution," and "end the exchange of experiences" to expose the plan's evil nature.[43]

The government informed the local party organs about the rebel group's arrival. As the bus approached Dafang city, a crowd organized by the local party leadership intercepted it. According to members of the April 11th Combat Team, they were forced to a halt by a hostile mob that surrounded the bus, threw stones, and, after a worker had bruised his hand

---

[42] "'Si yi yi' chongji sheng geming weiyuanhui jingzuo shiwei de zhenxiang" [True Account of the April 11th Combat Team's Attack against the Revolutionary Committee and the Sit-In Protest], in *Liu liu zhanbao*, 9 July 1967, 3, reprinted in RGM 10, 4783.

[43] "'4.11' xuyi zhizao 'Dafang shijian' de zhenxiang" [True Account of the "Dafang Incident" Deliberately Created by the April 11th Combat Team], in *Liu liu zhanbao*, 9 July 1967, 4, reprinted in RGM 10, 4784.

MAP 3. Guizhou province and the site of the 'Dafang Incident'

while smashing the glass of the driver's window, started harassing them. The depiction of the incident in tabloids assembled by organizations supportive of the government side varied considerably. The bus accordingly had not been stopped deliberately but forced to a halt because it had "failed to comply with local traffic regulations."[44] As the driver failed to stop at the local parking lot, the heavily damaged bus was pulled off the main street crossing of Dafang by a tractor.

During the ensuing five-day siege of the wrecked bus on the street crossing, both factions staged propaganda activities to justify the correctness of their claims by reading sections from the *Quotations*. The April 11th propaganda troupe invoked Mao's dictum that "the basic truth of Marxism all goes back to one meaning: To rebel is justified."[45] Instead of attending the festivities of the party's founding anniversary in Bijie, they performed songs and rhymes in praise of the Chairman in the vehicle but were infuriated by the theft of a picture of "the reddest, reddest red sun in our hearts, Chairman Mao," and several "glistening" *Quotations*

---

[44] Ibid., 4784.
[45] See "Dafang shijian de zhenxiang (di er bufen)" [True Account of the Dafang Incident (Part Two)], in *411 zhanbao*, 26 July 1967, 4, reprinted in RGM 12, 5721.

volumes; "one of the hoodlums even destroyed a copy."[46] The leadership of the surrounding crowd placed a propaganda car on the opposite side of the road and blasted Mao's supreme directive, "Return to study to make revolution," against their adversaries and advised them not to meddle with the business of local peasants.[47] Besides the rhetorical warfare waged between the factions, a few peasants, who had flocked into the city to join the spectacle every night after work and according to the rebels "had no clue about the real situation,"[48] did their best to render the stay of the April 11th Combat Team members in Dafang uncomfortable. They would blast instruments to keep the rebels from falling asleep, open the top windows to let in the pouring rain or even urinate into the bus, and sexually harass the female team members through public surveillance when using the restrooms. As both factions could mount sufficient authoritative instructions, the situation turned into a stalemate until after four days the local groups won a decisive edge. On 3 July at noon, a peasant discovered that the Mao image on one of the April 11th Combat Team flags had been printed in black and faced the stick,[49] while the organization's name had been printed in bright red. To display the image of the Chairman in the color of revisionism was interpreted as a heinous crime that revealed the true conviction of the rebels. In an attempt to hide the flag, the students placed the flag "under their bottoms," which according to the official statement, was the final straw to unleash the anger of the masses, resulting in physical confrontation.

As the situation was becoming tense on the spot, news about the siege reached Guiyang, where immediately rescue forces were mustered. On 3 July, four hundred to five hundred April 11th Combat Team members captured twelve public buses with the assistance of a few workers, only to face a fate similar to that of the group in Dafang, this time in the township of Huangnitang.[50] A third rescue squad, consisting of only seven rebels plus two dozen peasants, whom the rebels had lured onto the bus by offering them free transportation, capsized while crossing the Yachi River on 10 July, resulting in twenty-two deaths.[51]

---

[46] Ibid., 5721
[47] "'411' xuyi zhizao," 4.
[48] Ibid., 4.
[49] Ibid., 4.
[50] "Dafang shijian de zhenxiang (di yi bufen)" [True Account of the Dafang Incident (Part One)], in *411 zhanbao*, 26 July 1967, reprinted in RGM 12, 5720.
[51] "Qianxi xian gong'anju lai dianhua tan 'guanyu Yachi he fanche qingkuang'" [Telephone Report of the Qianxi County Public Security Bureau on the "Situation on the Yachi River and the Capsized Bus"], in *Liu liu zhanbao*, 13 July 1967, 2, reprinted in RGM 10, 4786.

In the provincial capital Guiyang, in the meantime, students from the April 11th Combat Team's stronghold at Guiyang Normal University staged their protests in front of the provincial revolutionary committee's seat and read aloud an ultimatum to solve the Dafang Incident; otherwise, "revolutionary activities on an even greater scale"[52] would be taken into consideration. After being unable to schedule a reception with the leaders, the April 11th Combat Team members broke into the government court-yard, despite the efforts of the PLA guards who read quotations to try to keep the rebels from smashing the doors open,[53] and started to conduct a silent hunger strike. It was continued the following day on the main traffic crossing of Guiyang. During the seventy-eight–hour "sit-in," students from the capital and other sympathizers, totaling up to five thousand persons, joined the local rebels. Ordinary citizens presented the protesters with "several hundred volumes of Mao's *Selected Works* and *Quotations*"[54] to express their support. The strike finally ended on 10 July, after the provincial government had dispatched staff to investigate the Dafang affair and guaranteed a safe return. The violence, however, did not cease and similar incidents continued without cessation.

Between July and September 1967, the situation in China was indeed beyond control, as Mao Zedong himself was later to profess. The PLA, the only force that commanded sufficient personnel to contain the anarchic situation, had been reprimanded for unduly favoring the "conservative" faction and thus was not to interfere with the movement unless ordered to do so from above. As the Wuhan Incident in mid-July revealed, when two CCRG members were captured by a "conservative" mass organization sup-ported by local military commander Chen Zaidao, even control over the PLA was beginning to fade. Mao Zedong even pondered "arming the Left."[55] Mass organizations considered to be trustworthy, such as the Beijing Aviation Institute Red Flag, were therefore presented with rifles by the Beijing Garrison.

Just like the overall situation, control over the image and works of Mao Zedong had by and large been lost by the CCP Center, resulting in cult anarchy, as the Guizhou example reveals. All of the contending factions

---

See further "Kan ni hexin dao jishi" [Look at Where Your Focus Truly Lies], in *Hongweibing* (Guiyang), 27 August 1967, 2, reprinted in RGM 6, 2938.

[52] "Zhaohui" [Recall], in *411 zhanbao*, 26 July 1967, 2, reprinted in RGM 12, 5719.

[53] "'Si yi yi' chongji," 3.

[54] "Guizhou geming shi shang de kongqian zhuangju" [An Unprecedented Situation in Guizhou Revolutionary History], in *411 zhanbao*, 26 July 1967, 2, reprinted in RGM 12, 5719.

[55] Michael Schoenhals, "'Why Don't We Arm the Left?' Mao's Culpability for the Cultural Revolution's 'Great Chaos' of 1967," in *China Quarterly* 182 (2005), 289f.

championed different quotations from Mao's works, which because of the separation from their original contexts could be invoked in contradictory ways. CCRG member Wang Li, who was one of those captured by the Wuhan "million heroes" and was to be purged shortly thereafter as a scapegoat for the increasing attacks on the PLA, in a talk with representatives from Sichuan sharply denounced rumors that the movement should be conducted without the leadership of the CCP Center. He considered the establishment of the "absolute authority of Chairman Mao" to be the movement's primary task, which was to be accomplished by purging everyone who had contradicted Mao at any time. But establishing the universal rule of Mao Zedong Thought had become increasingly difficult due to the different connotations associated with it. Wang Li explicitly criticized the contradictory usage of Mao's quotations:

> Recently a bad habit has arisen. Studying Chairman Mao's works has been turned into a war of quotations with the aim of cursing people. Chairman Mao has repeatedly emphasized that the propagation of Marxism-Leninism and Mao Zedong Thought should be conducted by grasping its content and intellectual essence. When we apply Mao Zedong Thought to solve problems, the field of vision should be broad and not narrowed down to the tiny problems immediately at hand.[56]

The fragmented political situation had to be resolved in one way or the other, but solving the factional disputes continued as long as the question of who would turn out to be the main beneficiary of Mao's policies remained unclear. Different factions among the top leadership therefore vied for Mao's support and political gains. Although supplied with nearly absolute power, Mao even during the high tide of the Cultural Revolution did not resort to rule by fiat. He would watch a situation unfold and, after having come to a decision, would make use of the high-level power struggles to implement his policies, carefully trying to preserve a precarious balance among the factions. Given the anarchic situation, measures to regain control over both the political situation and the party's symbols of power presented no easy task. If Mao were to rely on brute force by ordering the PLA to restore order, the whole undertaking of the Cultural Revolution, which he had linked with his own fate in the most thorough fashion, would be rendered a farce. On the other hand, letting the masses educate themselves through constant struggle had not resulted in the formation of a commonly

---

[56] "Wang Li tongzhi qi yue wu ri jiejian '8.26' daibiao shi de jianghua" [Comrade Wang Li's Speech at the Reception for "26 August" Representatives on 5 July], in *Liu liu zhanbao*, 13 July 1967, 4, reprinted in RGM 10, 4788.

accepted new form of rule and thus endangered the governability of China. To learn from local experiences and get an overview of the situation himself, Mao Zedong conducted a three-month inspection tour through central and southern China between July and September 1967 to find a way of finally rendering the Cultural Revolution a success.

Traveling to different localities had been a frequently employed measure of the CCP leadership prior to the outbreak of the Cultural Revolution. The trips, during which Politburo comrades visited local communes and spoke to the populace, ideally were to provide the CCP leadership with an impression of the situation on the spot and to strengthen the ties between the center and localities. Naturally, local leaders would choose only favorable spots, but Mao was well known for his impulsive alterations of the scheduled plans. Impromptu visits had become much more difficult during the Cultural Revolution than before. Mao on a number of occasions explicitly resented the caution with which Zhou Enlai would try to keep him out of trouble, especially during the Wuhan Incident, when Mao stayed in the city at the time without the knowledge of the local leaders. The official assessment presented after Mao's tour described the situation as "excellent, not simply good."[57] It further described Mao's plan to make the situation even better in a few months time by invoking the legacy of the Yan'an-style Rectification campaign. Students, cadres, and leaders of mass organizations were to be organized in study classes to educate them to give up their erroneous, self-centered activities. Through continuous political education, the participants were to grasp the essence of Mao's dictum that no antagonistic contradictions existed among the people and to finally achieve the great alliance of all revolutionary forces. The measures that had proven effective in the past thus were to be resumed. But this time, it was not simply the population of a small town like Yan'an or the members of a hierarchical organization like the PLA that were to receive guidance from Mao's works but the whole populace. Exegetical bonding under military supervision thus came to be conducted on a gigantic scale and brought ritual modes of study to the fore.

From October 1967 onward, editorials called for the establishment of Mao Zedong Thought Study Classes at all levels of society.[58] Leaders of

[57] "Zhongfa [67] 313, Zhonggong zhongyang guanyu Mao zhuxi shicha ge di jianghua de tongzhi" [CCP Center Notice Concerning Chairman Mao's Speeches while Inspecting the Provinces], 7 October 1967, in CRDB.

[58] "Quanguo dou lai ban Mao Zedong sixiang xuexiban" [The Whole Nation Establishes Mao Zedong Thought Study Classes], in *Renmin ribao*, 12 October 1967, 1.

provincial factions that up to this point had failed to achieve the formation of revolutionary committees were assembled in the capital in so-called central study classes. The character of the study classes clearly revealed the disciplinary impetus behind them. Prior to that date, representatives of mass organizations or military regions had been accommodated in star-rated hotels and received free transportation. Sometimes they had even ordered saloon cars, as Kang Sheng angrily remarked in a discussion with representatives from Ningxia autonomous region on the need for establishing a frugal lifestyle.[59]

The central study classes were held in military compounds, often in the Beijing vicinity, to increase the pressure on the delegates to come up with tangible results. The daily routine for central study class participants was strict. Group study of Mao texts was followed by reappraisals of the provincial situation guided by Mao's supreme instructions. The central study classes were concluded only upon sealing an agreement between the respective factions.[60] A major incentive for the delegates, however, was the prospect of being received by the Chairman in person during a reception in the Great Hall of the People, an equivalent of the symbolical power bestowed on the Red Guards during the mass receptions of late 1966.

The star of the Red Guard organizations slowly began to dwindle after Mao's return from his inspection tour. Simultaneously, the public security apparatus under Xie Fuzhi, head of the Beijing Revolutionary Committee, started to crack down on independent news reporting to resume central control of the public sphere. Although it was to take about another year before this task was finally accomplished, accompanied by the rustication of most Red Guards, the change in public discourse became abundantly clear. The *Wenhui bao* on 30 September 1967 declared that all orders from the CCP Center had to be followed, irrespective of whether the exact content was understood at the present moment or not. It thus quoted from a speech Lin Biao had delivered at the Politburo meeting at the outset of the Cultural Revolution on 13 August 1966, a speech that came to be one of the most frequently

---

[59] "Kang Sheng, Li Tianhuan dui Ningxia junqu ji Ningxia zong zhihuibu daibiao de tanhua" [Speeches by Kang Sheng and Li Tianhuan to the Representatives of the Ningxia Military Region and the Ningxia General Command], 6 September 1967, in CRDB.

[60] The Guizhou central study class was, for example, established only in the process of purging Li Zaihan between 25 November 1969 and 17 April 1970. See Zhonggong Guizhou (ed.), *Guizhou lishi dashiji*, 426.

employed justifications of military supervision. In his talk, Lin Biao had dealt with the problem of understanding Mao's aims in unfolding the Cultural Revolution and conceded that even he did not always fully comprehend the new turns of the movement. "[W]e have to persist in following the Chairman's instructions. We shall carry out those we understand, as well as those we do not understand."[61] Although Lin's sentence was slightly modified by adding the adverb "temporarily" before "do not understand," there could be no mistake that unquestioning obedience and loyalty to the directives of the CCP Center came to be the main focus of party discourse.

[61] Lin Biao, "Zai zhongyang gongzuo huiyi shang de jianghua" [Speech at the Central Committee Working Meeting], 13 August 1966, in CRDB.

8

The Language of Loyalty

By the time Mao returned to Beijing in late September 1967 to announce his seemingly optimistic appraisal of the situation, revolutionary committees had been established in only seven of China's twenty-nine provinces and municipalities. Despite Mao's promising rhetoric, the situation was bleak. Physical confrontations between contending factions continued well into 1968 and took on ever more extreme forms. It was to take another year, until 5 September 1968, that the last revolutionary committees assumed power in the autonomous regions of Tibet and Xinjiang and only with the convention of the Ninth Party Congress in April 1969 was a new CCP leadership officially sanctioned. The ritual worship of Mao Zedong culminated during this phase of uncertainty about who was to emerge victorious from the rubble of the factional disputes. Fostering the cult came to assume a crucial role in trying to maximize individual gains in the struggle for power at different levels of society. But for most Chinese, taking part in public worship became a crucial element of surviving within a completely volatile situation dominated by witch hunts against supposed counterrevolutionaries during the campaign to "cleanse the class ranks" (*qingli jieji duiwu*). The rhetorical and ritual demonstrations of loyalty to Chairman Mao that came to dominate everyday life cannot be understood without taking into account this frenzied atmosphere within which people were sentenced to death because they had unintendedly misspelled a Mao quotation or burned a newspaper carrying his image.[1] This

---

[1] A peasant in Ankang County (Shaanxi province) was executed on 29 June 1970 for having claimed not to have had space in his small hut to put up a Mao poster and for having doubted the fact that Mao was to live for literally ten thousand years. See Ankang shi difangzhi bianzuan weiyuanhui (ed.), *Ankang xian zhi* [Ankang County Gazetteer], Xi'an: Shaanxi renmin chubanshe, 1989, 908.

chapter analyzes cult rhetoric in the continuing process of reestablishing political and symbolical power by looking at the cult's employment in everyday life. After a discussion of the role of the omnipresent Mao Zedong Thought Activist Congresses, the rhetoric of the most exuberant campaign of worshipping Mao Zedong, the "Three Loyalties" (*san zhongyu*) or "Three Loyalties, Four Boundlesses" (*san zhongyu, si wuxian*) campaign,[2] shall be examined. Special emphasis will be given to the characteristics and functions of the ensuing loyalty discourse that resulted in extravagant flattery and the propagation of ever-new miracles performed by applying Mao Zedong Thought.

MAO ZEDONG THOUGHT ACTIVIST CONGRESSES

The establishment of Mao Zedong Thought Study Classes provided the fundament for overcoming the omnipresent cult anarchy and proved to be instrumental in embedding the cult within everyday life. Study meetings or rallies to "remember hardship and think of sweetness" (*yiku sitian*), a variant of the PLA's "two remembrances" movement, came to fill most of the people's vacant time. Assemblies were held literally every night and everyone was forced through collective pressure to contribute actively by reviewing their own deeds in light of Mao Zedong Thought. The daily routine of the omnipresent group study of Mao quotations has continued to be one of the most widely shared remembrances of the Cultural Revolution. The vivid commemoration has to be explained by the incredible extent to which the study classes that were established in the fall and winter of 1967 came to interfere with everyday life. The study classes were to unify different perceptions of the Cultural Revolution by means of exegetical bonding. The military "three supports" offices took the lead in organizing and guiding study progress. Open attacks on the PLA, however, had weakened the army's standing in popular perception. To overcome these consequences, different parts of the army resumed the tradition of the "four good–five good" campaigns to emulate outstanding individuals or units, an instrument that had by and large been disrupted after the outbreak of the Cultural Revolution.

---

[2] The "Three Loyalties" refer to loyalty to Chairman Mao, loyalty to Mao Zedong Thought, and loyalty to Chairman Mao's proletarian revolutionary line. The "Four Boundlesses" indicate boundless worship, boundless hot love, boundless belief, and boundless loyalty.

In late 1966, a number of military regions had continued to choose model soldiers under the name of "Study the Works of Chairman Mao Activist Congresses" (*xuexi Mao zhuxi zhuzuo jijifenzi daibiao dahui*), and an all-military study activist congress had been planned for the second half of 1967. The assembly never took place, though, because the PLA General Political Department came under heavy attack for having propounded revisionist views,[3] and its tasks were incorporated into the antecedents of the Military Affairs Commission (*junshi banshizu*), which by March 1968 effectively replaced the Central Military Commission as the PLA's highest governing body.[4] From November 1967 onward, the number of activist congresses, now commonly termed "Lively Study and Apply Chairman Mao's Works Activist Congresses" (*huoxue huoyong Mao zhuxi zhuzuo jijifenzi daibiao dahui*), came to multiply. The purposes for invoking this tradition were manifold. On the one hand, the development of activists had proven to be an exceptionally valuable tool to exert control within the units, to offer models of identification, and to foster a stratum of like-minded successors. The constant need to propagate new models in the party media and especially the function of the activists as sowers of official ideology in study classes or during invited talks further contributed to the resumption of the congresses. The compilation of model talks and the circulation of experiences provided common ground for discussions on how to apply the newest directives of the CCP Center correctly.

The activist congresses would have remained a minor phenomenon had not Mao Zedong made use of them to demonstrate the conclusion of the phase of destroying the old superstructure and building up new power structures instead. Just like back in 1966, when he had publicly bestowed his authority on the Red Guards by reviewing them on top of Tiananmen, Mao Zedong chose to display his change of attitude by publicly meeting with the delegates of the Beijing Garrison Activist Congress during a reception on 13 November 1967 and with representatives from other study classes the next day. Mao's support for the disciplinary measures provided the revolutionary committees and preparatory small groups with additional public legitimacy. Lin Biao added further attention by presenting the four thousand delegates of the First Navy Study Congress on

---

[3] Yu Nan and Wang Haiguang, "Lin Biao jituan he Lin Biao shijian" [The Lin Biao Clique and the Lin Biao Incident], in Guo, Weng, and Han (eds.), *Shinian fengyu*, 397.

[4] The group had been formed on Zhou Enlai's initiative in June 1967 because of the absence of the acting chief-of-staff ,Yang Chengwu, who accompanied Mao on his inspection tour; see Jin, *Culture of Power*, 110.

29 November with a personal inscription.[5] Although the measure turned out to be effective in spreading the impact of the congresses, the requests for personal inscriptions grew exorbitantly and even led to violent struggles. As a consequence, Mao expressed in mid-December his discontent with the habit of writing inscriptions, and thereafter similar requests were generally turned down. However, Mao further encouraged the convention of activist congresses by continuing his meetings with study activists, which were mostly held in different rooms of the Great Hall of the People, where Mao had come to spend most of his time.

The congresses followed a standard pattern, starting out with the selection of trustworthy individuals or groups at the unit level, based on a catalogue of criteria drawn up by the local preparatory committees. A typical case is the criteria established by the Support the Left Office (*zhizuo bangongshi*) in Tumote, Inner Mongolia. Upon choosing the delegates for its first Lively Study and Apply Chairman Mao's Works Activist Congress in January 1968, the local revolutionary committee presented the target number of one thousand delegates for the seven-day congress and added a detailed allocation formula for determining how many activists each region or government department was to select. The guidelines further presented ten criteria upon which the local committees were to choose local models, among them a clear historical background, the swift adoption and application of Chairman Mao's directives, and complete reliance on the masses.[6] Based on these criteria, the selection started within each unit. After having been approved of by the local revolutionary committee, the activists were invited to the local government's guesthouse to commence their studies, taking along Chairman Mao's works, luggage, and food ration tickets.

The contemporary importance of the activist congresses is testified by the sheer amount of sources collected in local archives that deal with the preparation and organization of these congresses. The first measure in Tumote and other localities upon hearing about the necessity to convene

[5] Liu Zhenyang, "Dahai hangxing kao hangshou, gan geming kao Mao Zedong sixiang" [Sailing the Seas Depends on the Helmsman, Enacting Revolution Depends on Mao Zedong Thought], in *Renmin ribao*, 1 December 1967, 2.

[6] Tumote zuo/you qi renmin wuzhuangbu/Tumote qi zhujun zhizuo bangongshi, "Guanyu renzhen guanche zhixing Nei Meng, Wumeng geming weiyuanhui 'guanyu jin chun zhaokai quan qu xuexi Mao zhuxi zhuzuo xianjin jiti he jijifenzi daibiao huiyi de jueding' de tongzhi" [Notice on Conscientiously Implementing the Wumeng (Inner Mongolia) Revolutionary Committee Decision "On Holding an All-District Study Chairman Mao's Works Advanced Collectives and Activists Representatives Assembly This Spring"], 18 January 1968, 3f.

an activist congress was to review the recent performance of pre–Cultural Revolution activists and model heroes and to check whether they could be reactivated in the process of forming revolutionary committees. Therefore, the political background of hundreds of possible candidates had to be monitored; in many cases, such monitoring constituted the first formal action of the revolutionary committees. The activist congresses usually lasted about two weeks, during which local experiences were reviewed in the light of recent directives. Although in the early stages form and content of the congresses still varied, the proceedings became increasingly standardized. They included the setting up of an organizing secretariat comprised of different small groups in charge of organization, reports, newspaper work, and the drafting of documents for both internal and public use. The delegates were informed about the current proceedings and the focus of propagation through short conference bulletins with a Mao quotation, printed in red, as the headline, usually edited several times a day, depending on the number of small groups. The model reports and publicly accessible documents were compiled by a separate group and contained only the speeches themselves. The meetings usually started with an opening ceremony, followed by the study of documents and model speeches that were to be discussed and transformed into a concluding report on how to apply the insights in day-to-day work. Finally, the written experiences were circulated and accompanied by a proposal (*changyi shu*) listing the most remarkable successes and suggestions of the assembly.

While in the beginning meetings were held every night, the later congresses resumed a much more relaxed approach, with only eight hours of study, plus additional group excursions on the weekends.[7] The congresses came to provide the study classes with both competent training personnel and model reports that could be studied from the central study classes down to the household level. Besides the synchronization of public perception, the activist congresses came to assume a highly performative function, as local patron–client relationships resulted from the fostering of various sub-cults.

The activist congresses, especially those convened by institutions of national importance, provided a platform for the participants to display their preparedness to take on responsible positions in the new power structures. As formal rules of ascent were amiss, the search for possible

---

[7] Haijun di er ci huoxue huoyong Mao Zedong sixiang jijifenzi, di sanci sihao liandui wuhao zhanshi daibiao dahui mishuchu, *Dahui xuzhi* [Essential Knowledge for the Assembly], January 1970.

patrons enabling individual promotion led to a vast increase of cult rhetoric. Mao Zedong clearly remained the ultimate arbiter of the cult discourse, but below his meta-cult, several sub-cults emerged in praise of important figures either within the top leadership or at the local level. The trend of employing the cult as a vehicle to establish patron–client relationships was made extraordinarily clear in a number of speeches by high-ranking military cadres that were aimed primarily at showcasing Lin Biao and at outperforming potential rivals within the respective units. Soon a number of nonofficially approved publications that had thus far been reserved for Mao started to appear, including Lin Biao biographies and quotation volumes. By 1970, even an exhibition commemorating Lin's revolutionary successes at the Anti-Japanese Military and Political University in Yan'an was planned by supporters within the PLA.

The political structures based on loyalty instead of codified rights were highly conducive to the rapid development of these communication patterns characteristic of the personality cult. The dawning of the Ninth Congress sharply revealed the weaknesses of the Chinese body politic amid the institutional havoc brought about by the Cultural Revolution. Irrespective of the personal role of Lin Biao, his image as Mao's closest comrade-in-arms and successor made him a primary target of adulation by those weighing their chances and positioning themselves for high political offices after Mao's death. Yet Lin's public elevation presented an obvious danger for him. Under no conditions was his own cult to signal a growing ambition to replace Mao Zedong prematurely. That Mao remained suspicious about the ways his "authority" was invoked for various purposes was revealed by the publication of a *People's Daily* article that appeared on 3 November 1967 in the name of the acting chief-of-staff, Yang Chengwu, on "establishing the absolute authority of Chairman Mao in a big way."[8] The specific formulation had originated from the diary of a revolutionary martyr and had subsequently been employed by Red Guards and various CCP and PLA leaders alike. As long as the phrase was instrumentalized in ways congruent with Mao's views, Mao did not take offense or immediate action. But as the official party press took up the phrase, he rejected it as

---

[8] Yang Chengwu, "Dashu teshu weida tongshuai Mao zhuxi de juedui quanwei, dashu teshu weida de Mao Zedong sixiang de juedui quanwei. Chedi qingsuan Luo Ruiqing fandui Mao zhuxi, fandui Mao Zedong sixiang de taotian zuixing" [Establish the Absolute Authority of the Great Commander Chairman Mao in a Big Way, Establish the Absolute Authority of the Great Mao Zedong Thought in a Big Way: Thoroughly Settle the Heinous Crimes of Luo Ruiqing's Opposition to Chairman Mao and Mao Zedong Thought], in *Renmin ribao*, 3 November 1967, 22.

not being part of the "scientific language of Marxism."[9] Mao's reaction to Yang's article followed the same pattern he usually chose when dealing with disliked drafts that were submitted to him beforehand: he ignored it by writing, "I won't read it," on its back, a clear indicator of major discontent.

On 17 December 1967, Mao received a report from the Hunan Revolutionary Committee Preparatory Group. The report asked whether Mao would send an inscription for a newly constructed Mao statue that was to be unveiled during a celebration of Mao's seventy-fourth birthday in his native village of Shaoshan, which had just been connected to the national railway network. Mao took the opportunity to add a few thoughts on propaganda work. He reminded the local comrades about the decision of the CCP rejecting the celebration of birthdays, as well as refusing to write further inscriptions. His main gist, however, was directed against specific phrases:

(1) The formulation "absolute authority" [*juedui quanwei*] is not suitable. There never has been a single and absolute authority. All authority is relative. Everything absolute only exists within the relative. Likewise, the absolute truth is the summation of innumerable relative truths, and therefore the absolute truth similarly exists only among relative truths.

(2) The saying "establishing in a big way" [*dashu teshu*] is not suitable either. Authority and prestige can only be established in a natural way through the practice of struggle and cannot simply be fabricated. Prestige established in this fashion is necessarily doomed to fail.[10]

The passage reveals Mao's constant awareness about the power of formulations once they had been officially sanctioned and come into heavy rotation in public discourse. The enormous attention paid to single words by the CCP leadership hints at the close interrelation of language and power. Allowing for the usage of phrases like "persons in power taking the capitalist road" or even simply "establishing the absolute authority of Mao Zedong in a big way" presented much more than interchangeable semantic phrases. By defining the angle of how to approach and judge reality, party discourse turned words into tangible objects that governed people's everyday lives and determined the fate of those marginalized by revolutionary rhetoric.

Mao's criticism of the phrasings published under Yang Chengwu's name rendered Yang vulnerable and enabled a coalition of inner-army opponents to take advantage of the situation. Yang was purged in March

---

[9] See further Zhou Enlai on the same subject in "Zhou Enlai jiejian guofang kewei," in CRDB.
[10] Zhonggong wenxian yanjiushi (ed.), *Mao wengao* 12, 455.

1968, because he had failed to display sufficient loyalty to Mao Zedong, as Lin Biao claimed.[11] Lin thus placed even more emphasis on the necessity to display loyalty in every word and deed to avoid criticism and harassment. The frequent policy changes since the outset of the Cultural Revolution and the lack of transparency about the official sanctioning of certain phrases had come to endanger the governability of China as a whole. Along with the reestablishment of political power through study classes, congresses, and revolutionary committees, control had to be regained in the semantic realm as well. The year 1968 therefore witnessed the peak of language formalization and the near-merging of public and private speech.

THE LANGUAGE OF FLATTERY

Rana Mitter recently remarked that the Cultural Revolution probably was the period in twentieth-century history during which "language was most separated from meaning."[12] Although the formulation itself seems like an attempt to revive representational notions of an identity between denominating term and object, Mitter pointed at the strategic employment of the infinite capacities to reinterpret single characters in different contexts. Ji Fengyuan has referred to this phenomenon as "linguistic engineering"[13] in analogy to Karl Popper's notion of utopian social engineering. The term implies the conscious employment of language to transform traditional worldviews by altering content down to the level of single words or characters, for example, by placing them in unaccustomed contexts. Because of the changing of the semantic chain of references, commonsense meanings were to be substituted with revolutionary contents and thus to subvert the impact of traditional value systems. Due to the denigration of traditional moral concepts and the simultaneous use of single key words as reasons for defining political standpoints, the possibilities to attack others on grounds of revolutionary impurity were widened ad libitum. The

---

[11] Lin Biao, "Zai jundui ganbu dahui shang de jianghua" [Speech at an Assembly of Military Cadres], 24 March 1968, in CRDB. Other factors behind Yang's purge included conflicts with other military leaders, partly over family issues (see Jin, *Culture of Power*, 111ff.) and possibly his championing of the cults of both Lin Biao and Jiang Qing below the supreme Mao cult, very much to Lin's dissatisfaction; see Wang Nianyi, *Da dongluan de niandai* [A Decade of Great Upheaval], Zhengzhou: Henan renmin chubanshe, 1988, 288ff.

[12] Rana Mitter, *A Bitter Revolution: China's Struggle with the Modern World*, Oxford: Oxford University Press, 2004, 209.

[13] Ji Fengyuan, *Linguistic Engineering: Language and Politics in Mao's China*, Honolulu: University of Hawaii Press, 2004, esp. Chapter 1.

undermining of formal meanings and hidden allusions by way of using homophonous characters, metaphors, or allegories had a long tradition in Chinese history, but usually these means had been employed as strategies of resistance by critical individuals against the state and not vice versa. Rather than denoting definite objects, certain phrases employed during the Cultural Revolution have to be interpreted as "performatives,"[14] in John Austin's parlance – that is, as communicative action that in saying something actually establishes an action, such as displaying loyalty to Mao Zedong.

Even a superficial analysis of Cultural Revolutionary media reveals the frequent employment of terms in unaccustomed semantic contexts, highlighted by the contemporary placement of the characters in quotations marks. "Application," "selfishness," or "loyalty" had to be set apart in order to alert the readership about their special denomination. Another characteristic feature of the Cultural Revolutionary language was the excessive verbalization suggesting action by adding the suffix -*hua* behind the most unlikely combination of words.[15] Frequent examples are "proletarization" (*wuchanjiejihua*), "loyalty-fication" (*zhongzihua*), or even "Mao Zedong Thought-ification" (*Mao Zedong sixianghua*). A striking contrast to the formal pretension of movement and change is presented by a closer content analysis of public discourse during the period of reestablishing order. Whether one looks at the minutes of the thousands of study classes, the speeches delivered at activist congresses, or the daily editorials and comments published in the party media, the necessity to frame the content within the overarching concepts of class struggle and Mao worship exerted formal restrictions that heavily influenced the content of the media items.

As a consequence of the cult anarchy of 1967, the reestablishment of symbolical order went hand in hand with a drastic reduction in the number of printed articles and the variety of issues covered. Until the last revolutionary committees had been established in September 1968, the increased emphasis on loyalty to Chairman Mao led to the superimposition of a near-static cult discourse into all spheres of private and public life. Its implementation was secured through hundreds of thousands of PLA

---

[14] John L. Austin, *How to Do Things with Words: The William James Lectures Delivered at Harvard University in 1955*, 2nd edition, edited by J. O. Urmson and Marina Sbisà, Cambridge: Harvard University Press, 1975, 6.

[15] Similar observations have been made about the language of the Third Reich; see Victor Klemperer, *LTI. Notizbuch eines Philologen* [Lingua tertii imperii: A Philologists' Notebook], Leipzig: Reclam, 1975 [1957], 162ff.

soldiers conducting the "three supports, two militaries"; local members of the revolutionary committees; or simply fellow citizens watching for concordance of their neighbors utterances with Mao Zedong Thought.

Cult discourse has from the beginning been defined as a specific variant of the People's Republic's directed public sphere. Both variations were based on imposing a theoretical framework with an ultimate truth claim: Marxism-Leninism as defined by the collective leadership of the party in the one case and the absolutization of Mao Zedong Thought in the latter case. The difference between the patterns of communication before, during, and after the Cultural Revolution was thus a question of the degree of formalization rather than of fundamental difference. The ultimate arbiter of Cultural Revolutionary rhetoric was the notion of class struggle (*jieji douzheng*), characterized through sharp distinctions between friend and foe: the always-correct Mao Zedong Thought one the one hand, and the vicious "Chinese Khrushchev" as representative of the evils of revisionism and capitalism on the other hand. Although the aspect of class struggle provided the main point of reference throughout the Cultural Revolution, the relative importance attached to either Mao worship or attacks against his supposed enemies changed according to circumstances. Previous scholarly attention has mostly been devoted to Cultural Revolutionary "hate speech."[16] The focus here, however, is on the rhetoric of worship, the characteristics and functions of which are discussed in the remainder of this chapter.

The cult discourse in 1968 basically revolved around two major clusters of content: first, expressions of loyalty to Mao; and second, reports about practical implementation of Mao Zedong Thought. Like the Invocatio in medieval documents, most texts and speeches delivered during the period of reestablishing order start out with formally wishing the Chairman (and Vice-Chairman Lin) eternal life and eternal health. In many cases, the invocations of loyalty take on a lyrical component, resulting in either the reprint of poems and songs or emotional prose full of superlatives and expressions of utter devotion. Yet, as the examples of elevating Lin Biao during other activist congresses revealed, there is more to employing the rhetoric of worship than simple adoration. The strategic employment of the cult as way of establishing patron–client relationships played an

---

[16] See, for example, Elizabeth Perry and Li Xun, "Revolutionary Rudeness: The Language of Red Guards and Rebel Workers in China's Cultural Revolution," in *Indiana East-Asian Working Paper Series on Language and Politics in Modern China* 2 (1993), 1–18. On the notion of "hate speech," see Butler, *Excitable Speech*, Chapter 1.

important role in many of the most extravagant eulogies. Primary examples for the latter case are the opening speeches and closing addresses or telegrams given at the activist congresses. The type of language employed thus depended to a large extent on the occasion and medium. The following excerpt is taken from the congratulatory telegram sent by the first Lively Study and Apply Mao Zedong Thought Activist Congress of the Beijing Garrison in August 1967:

> Chairman Mao, oh Chairman Mao. You are the greatest leader of the whole party, the whole army, and all of our people. You are the most preeminent teacher of the international proletariat. You are the reddest, reddest red sun in our hearts! Chairman Mao, oh Chairman Mao, your loving compassion is deeper than the ocean and we are filled with boundless hot love toward you! Thousand songs, ten thousand melodies cannot express our boundless hot love for you. Thousand words, ten thousand characters do not even closely unbosom our boundless worship of you. The unrestrained sea and the empty sky are not enough to contain our boundless belief in you. A shaking earth and tumbling mountains are unable to shake the boundless loyalty of every red heart to you![17]

Although instrumental reasons and the specific occasion played an important role in producing such statements, the standards of worship set by prominent examples such as the Beijing Garrison Activist Congress increased the pressure for other congress conveners to live up to the cult rhetoric employed. A cursory reading of the preceding quoted sentences may give the impression of uniquely expressed emotions, but a thorough exposure to the stacks of similar material kept in archives or sold at flea markets reveals a high degree of uniformity down to the level of single phrases. Not to conform to the most recent expressions of worship bore the danger of being accused of not having created a sufficiently "dense political climate," or, even worse, of having proven to be "disloyal" to Mao Zedong. Thus especially the few remaining prominent personalities in the realm of culture such as the president of the Chinese Academy of Sciences, Guo Moruo, had to excel in the praise of Mao Zedong Thought in order to be spared the fate of being sent to do manual labor and undergo thought reform. Guo, in his greeting address to the academy's First Activist Congress, employed a variety of metaphors to characterize the insuperable impact of Mao Zedong Thought that still retained a slightly individual touch:

---

[17] "Beijing weishuqu gei Mao zhuxi de zhijing xin" [A Congratulatory Letter to Chairman Mao from the Beijing Garrison], in *Beijing ribao*, 14 August 1967.

Mao Zedong Thought is rain and dew, is air and sunshine. Only with the moisture and nourishment of Mao Zedong Thought [can we] look upon thousands of doubling waves of rice and beans. Mao Zedong Thought is the soul, is wisdom, and is strength. Only [if we are] armed with Mao Zedong Thought will there be heroes arising without cessation. This is the new heaven and new earth of the Mao Zedong period, new people and new things, our whole academy, all of China is like this, and in the future the whole world is going to be like this too.[18]

Paragraphs such as this have usually been denied attention by scholarship because of their lack of content. Yet their function never was to transmit any kind of raw and unprocessed information. Neither was quasireligious worship its main function. Such speeches were aimed at demonstrating personal loyalty by relying on the indefinite capacity of language to produce statements that are "linguistically flawless but semantically empty."[19] The massive flattery employed during the Mao cult is an extreme example of language serving a ritual instead of a transmissive function. It is the demonstration of a social skill rather than the relaying of messages. In his *Phenomenology of the Spirit*, Hegel devoted a short section to what he called the "language of flattery," which he characterized in the following way: "It has for its content the form itself, the form which language itself is, and is authoritative as *language*. It is the power of speech, as that which performs what has to be performed."[20] Long before John Austin was to become famous for his characterization of certain speech acts as "performatives" – of utterances that in saying something actually constituted an act of doing something – Hegel here hinted at the importance of a certain type of speech, flattery, that performed a different function than the transmission of content.

The demonstration of loyalty as the ultimate end of the language of flattery has seldom been as explicit as during the Three Loyalties campaign during 1968, when references to loyalty reached an all time high in Chinese party media. As Figure 3 indicates, in 1968, nearly every fifth article

---

[18] See Guo Moruo, "Ba Mao Zedong sixiang weida hongqi chashang kexue jishu zui gaofeng" [Hoist the Red Flag of Mao Zedong Thought at the Highest Peak of Science and Technology], 14 March 1968, in *Zhongguo Kexueyuan (Jing qu) shou jie huoxue huoyong Mao Zedong sixiang jijifenzi daibiao dahui* [First Lively Study and Apply Mao Zedong Thought Activist Congress at the Chinese Academy of Sciences (Capital District)], April 1968, 5.

[19] Butler, *Excitable Speech*, 157.

[20] Georg W. F. Hegel, *Phenomenology of the Spirit*, Oxford: Oxford University Press, 1977 [1807], 308.

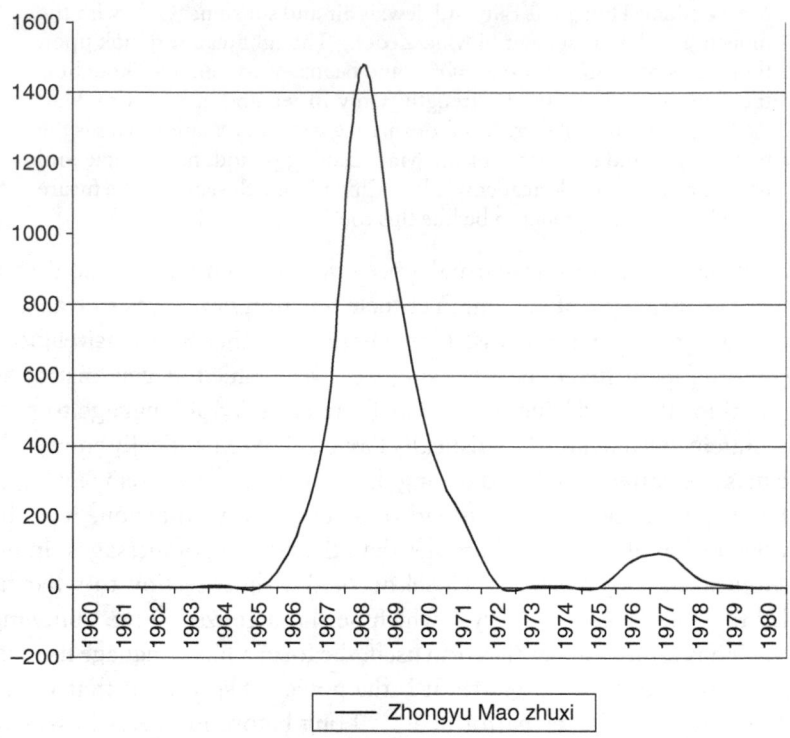

FIGURE 3. Appearances of the phrase "Loyal to Chairman Mao" in the *People's Daily*, 1960–80

published in the *People's Daily* made explicit reference to the phrase "loyal to Chairman Mao" (*zhongyu Mao zhuxi*).

The phrase, which since the beginning of the Cultural Revolution had come to be used occasionally, had gained enormous prominence through a minor campaign of emulating a certain Li Wenzhong and members of his platoon, who had sacrificed their lives to save a number of Red Guards from drowning.[21] The phrase was taken up by the Second PLA Air Force Study Congress in March 1968 and the press coverage of the congress set the tone for the Three Loyalties campaign that in the following months spread all over China. Editorials such as "Determining Loyalty by Looking at Action" (*zhong bu zhong, kan xingdong*) were published by all major Chinese newspapers in the first days of March 1968. Loyalty to the CCP

---

[21] "Wuxian zhongyu Mao zhuxi shi zui da de gong" [Boundlessly Loyal to Chairman Mao Is the Greatest Common Good], in *Jiefangjun bao*, 8 December 1967.

Chairman was to be proven through visible actions and not rhetorical invocations alone. To fulfill this task, the local military districts and revolutionary committees had to be given examples of how to apply the rhetorical worship in daily life.

MIRACLES OF MAO ZEDONG THOUGHT

The second big cluster of the cult discourse consists primarily of examples of how to apply Mao Zedong Thought in different situations. The wide range of topics held together by the notion of "application" (*yong*) can be broken down to three subheadings: role models; methods of studying and applying Mao Zedong Thought; and, finally, practical results, inventions, or "miracles" of Mao Zedong Thought. Interestingly, the antonym of loyalty in most cases was not directly defined as "disloyalty" but through the use of the character *si*, meaning "self" or "selfishness."[22] Loyalty to Mao Zedong thus came to merge with the character *gong*, indicating the public or common good, and indeed both phrases were interchangeably used during this period: "If one embodies the character 'selfishness' and does not fight it, that means being disloyal to Chairman Mao. The determination to fight selfishness is the watershed between the real and the bogus revolutionaries."[23]

The experiences of model heroes were usually first presented at local activist congresses. Stories with possible nationwide appeal were forwarded to the Military Affairs Commission or the CCP Center, which after evaluation would decide upon their possible instrumentality. The most prominent figurehead of the Three Loyalties campaign in 1968 was doubtlessly Comrade Men He, a deputy political instructor from Qinghai province, who had died while shielding fellow citizens from the explosion of a malfunctioning rocket. Men He thus was another example of the Lei Feng tradition of utter selflessness and devotion to Mao Zedong Thought.

On 23 April 1968, a central document was issued jointly by the CCP Center, the Central Military Commission, and the CCRG in the form of a command to confer posthumously the title "A good cadre boundlessly

---

[22] *Jiefangjun bao*, 17 February 1968.
[23] "Wuchanjieji zhuanzheng xia jixu jinxing geming de wuchanjieji xianjinfenzi de tuchu daibiao Li Wenzhong" [Li Wenzhong: A Prominent Exponent of the Advanced Proletarian Elements Continuing to Carry Out Revolution under the Dictatorship of the Proletariat], in *Renmin ribao*, 31 December 1967, 1.

loyal to Chairman Mao's revolutionary line" upon the deceased.[24] Men
He was the first individual cadre to be conferred a similar honor and thus
raised the prestige of this social group that had been a primary target of
Cultural Revolutionary violence. Along with the conferral of the title, the
CCP Center provided all recipients with background information on Men
He's life in order to facilitate a unified portrayal. In the following five
weeks, all revolutionary committees reacted by announcing specific study
campaigns to emulate Men He. In concerted fashion, the state media from
29 May 1968 onward started a major publicity campaign that included
multipage articles in all newspapers, reports on television, and radio
broadcasts, as well as small booklets, artistic performances, and an exhibition displaying the relics of Men He's frugal lifestyle. By differentiating
between different types of media and audiences, or "cross-platform marketing" in modern parlance, the CCP tried to achieve the maximum outcome for its measures.

For Men He's hometown and work unit, the bestowal of honor through
the CCP Center meant a mighty increase of attention. Men He's wife and
parents came to be sought-after guest speakers at activist congresses. The
Qinghai Revolutionary Committee along with the Qinghai Military
District leadership organized a "sympathy and solicitude delegation"
(*weiwen tuan*) including high-ranking cadres to visit Men He's birthplace
in Hebei province, to "report about the miracles of Men He, and to stage
cultural performances in praise of Men He."[25] The delegation was given
high political priority, and most of the provincial leadership either welcomed the cadres at the station or took part in activities during their visit.

The campaign to emulate Men He is a good example as well for the
actual application of Mao Zedong Thought – mainly articles and reports
describing ways of implementing the exhibited qualities of selflessness,
public service, and boundless loyalty to Mao Zedong. The character of
the depicted experiences varies greatly, depending on the source type.
Reports published in the state media reveal little about the remarkable

[24] "Zhongfa [68] 65, Zhonggong zhongyang, Zhongyang junwei, Zhongyang wenge xiaozu
    zhui shou Men He tongzhi 'wuxian zhongyu Mao zhuxi geming luxian de hao ganbu'
    chenghao de mingling" [Order of the CCP Center, the Central Military Commission, and
    the CCRG on Posthumously Awarding Comrade Men He the Title "A Good Cadre
    Boundlessly Loyal to Chairman Mao's Revolutionary Line"], 23 April 1968, in CRDB.
[25] "Hebei shengwei zhengzhibu guanyu jiedai Qinghai sheng weiwen Men He tongzhi
    jiaxiang weiwentuan de yijian" [Opinions of the Hebei Provincial Committee Political
    Department on Receiving the Sympathy and Solicitude Delegation from Comrade Men
    He's Hometown in Qinghai Province], 12 June 1968, HPA 919-1-21.

efforts to relate the study campaign to problems encountered in everyday life. In Shijiazhuang, capital of Hebei province, different kinds of study groups had been formed as a result of the campaign to study Men He in order to solve actual problems. A report of a visiting delegation from the Nanjing Financial Department Revolutionary Rebel United Committee that had traveled to Shijiazhuang to learn how to conduct the Three Loyalties campaign describes the discussions and methods employed in detail. Several study classes had been established to solve specific problems. One of the study groups, made up of both peasants and merchants, had come to focus on the issue of selling groceries. In fact, it had been the idea of the rebels in the grocery store that by way of sharing their views with the peasants tried to work out the defects that had resulted from "having received the poisonous influence of the counterrevolutionary revisionist line of the Chinese Khrushchev."[26]

According to the report, the meetings started out with rapprochements from the peasants, who took the study campaign as just another attempt by the merchants to exploit their good faith and had agreed to participate only after the meetings were to take place at the work brigade. This way, the PLA had to repair the local meeting room as a precondition. The merchants had decorated the newly renovated room with Mao pictures and quotations, but even that had engendered the suspicion of some peasants: "We should not pay too much attention to what they say at the moment, for in the end it will be us who will have to pay for it."[27]

To investigate the reasons for this deep-rooted suspicion, the meetings fostered the debate of a number of controversial issues. The peasants had been greatly enraged by the "Chinese Khrushchev's policies of 'seizing the peasants by the throat,'"[28] which had found expression in, for example, the establishment of norms and standards for grocery articles. Criteria of size, color, and form had been defined and products not meeting these demands were considered to be of lower value or had not even been accepted at all by the merchants. Attempts to straighten crooked cucumbers with paper wrappings had failed and furthermore resulted in unwelcome side effects. Under the wrapping, the cucumbers had turned yellow

---

[26] Jiangsu Nanjing caimao xitong geming zaofan lianhe weiyuanhui, *Guanyu xuexi Shijiazhuang shi kaizhan "san zhongyu" huodong qingkuang de huibao (xuanchuan gao)* [Report on Learning from the Development of "Three Loyalty" Activities in Shijiazhuang Municipality (Propagation Draft)], 1 June 1968, distributed on 28 June 1968, 8.

[27] Ibid., 9.

[28] Ibid., 9.

due to the lack of sunlight. Criticism of local representatives of the revisionist line and the abolishment of the former rules according to the report established a harmonious working relationship between peasants and merchants again. No longer were arbitrary factors such as cucumber size or the amount of money earned to play the most important part. Instead, mutual understanding was to be developed and fair prices were to be decided upon.

If the abstract discourse of class struggle and proletarian class feelings could be related to specific situations, such as the prizes for crooked cucumbers, the campaign to champion Men He and the Three Loyalties gained enormous appeal. Gifted speakers and model soldiers like Wang Guoxiang (see Illustration 4) were showered with expressions of admiration, often by way of presenting them with Mao badges. In most cases, however, the study groups and meetings had difficulties in filling the abstract moral guidelines with suitable examples. At the Beijing General Foodstuff Factory, the story of Men He's life record and deeds had been disseminated at several meetings, after which the workers of the different branches had "transmitted the news to workers on the night shift; everyone started writing big character posters and statements of resolution, determined to learn from Comrade Men He."[29] Yet besides propagating the experiences to other shifts, the food factory workers did not come up with major innovations except for the compilation of "inspirational phrases" (*haoyan zhuangyu*) in the spirit of Men He. The short phrases usually took the form of rhyming couplets or alliterations such as: "closely follow Chairman Mao, perpetually carry out revolution; closely follow Chairman Mao, turn the world into a red [ocean]."[30] In the Beijing Second Cotton Mill, the local Mao Zedong Thought study class even compiled a thirteen-page set of congratulations (*zhuci*) to the Chairman, which could be recited in prayer-like fashion.[31]

Besides the recitations as a choir, the phrases could also be practiced in memorized dialogues (*duikouzi*), a form that had been employed to spread the teachings of the Chairman since the very beginning of the Cultural Revolution. Each partner thus had to complete the sentence of the questioner by adding the fitting quotation. By propagating the concordance of every action with Mao Zedong, these couplets came to be employed in everyday

[29] Beijing shipin zongchang geming weiyuanhui zhengzhi bangongshi, *Beijing shipin zongchang huoxue huoyong Mao Zedong sixiang 5* [Beijing General Foodstuff Factory Lively Studies and Applies Mao Zedong Thought 5], 13 June 1968, 2.

[30] Ibid., 1–7.

[31] Jing mian er chang Mao Zedong sixiang xuexiban (ed.), *Zhuci* [Congratulations], 23 April 1968, 1ff.

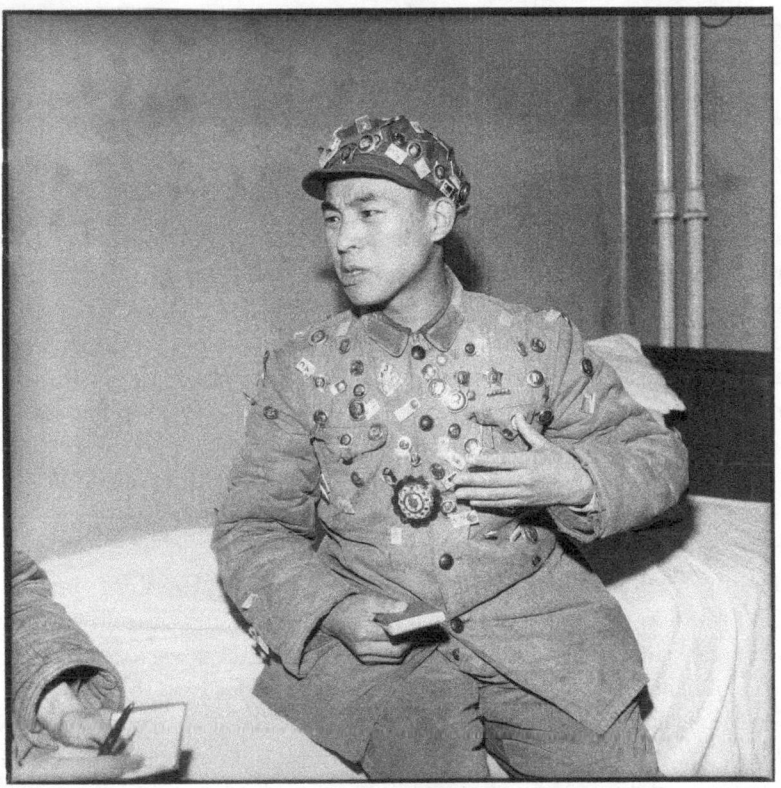

ILLUSTRATION 4. Wang Guoxiang, a model People's Liberation Army soldier shares his experiences of "learning and applying Mao's Thought" at a meeting in the Xinfa commune just outside Harbin, where the audience pinned some 170 Mao badges on his cap and uniform to express their admiration; Heilongjiang province, 16 April 1968. Li Zhensheng. (Contact Press Images.)

speech as well. The emphasis on "loyalty-ficating" every sentence reached its extreme by employing short quotations of Mao, Lin Biao, or revolutionary martyrs such as Men He as code words at the most different occasions. When selling goods, changing shifts, or even answering the phone, semantic performances of loyalty came to formalize even the most basic speech acts. The following excerpt from the local gazetteer of Mei County in Shaanxi province describes the common practices in a work office:

1. The first time using the phone, wish Chairman Mao eternal life!
2. From the second time onward, the first sentence when making a phone call is "serve the people"; the recipient answers, "comprehensively," "thoroughly."

3. When answering the phone before leaving work, the first sentence is "serve the people"; the recipient replies, "we should fight selfishness and repudiate revisionism."
4. When receiving guests, first ask Chairman Mao for instructions; then proceed with the study of the Supreme Instructions according to the content of the questions; before leaving, report back to Mao Zedong.[32]

Using ritualized formulae to demonstrate loyalty can be observed as a way of exerting power under many authoritarian and dictatorial regimes; one need only consider the use of "Heil Hitler!" in Nazi Germany. But no other twentieth-century leader cult took the matter to similar extremes as the Mao cult, when quotations of the leader came to replace even the most mundane speech acts during a period ranging roughly from March 1968 to April 1969, although the extent of implementation varied greatly. Nearly every Chinese local gazetteer with a slightly more detailed section on the Cultural Revolution mentions the phenomenon, although seldom by providing exact dates or examples.

Finally, attention shall be paid to the genre of texts describing "miracles of Chairman Mao." Most of these reports deal with specific innovations in the natural sciences, especially developments in modern weaponry and the sectors of health and hygiene. The emphasis on health work had developed from Mao's harsh criticism of the policies of the Ministry of Health in 1965.[33] Mao had accused the ministry of unduly favoring small elites of old cadres and the wealthy strata while rural medical care deteriorated. He advocated that students and doctors should temporarily be sent to the countryside instead; these became known as the "barefoot doctors" (*chijiao yisheng*). Although the medical training of many students ranged from three to six months and they were equipped with only some basic medicaments and later a little red book on healthcare, acupuncture, and moxibustion, they still knew how to cure basic ailments and could thus immediately engage in work on the spot. By proving their knowledge through immediate success, the barefoot doctors ideally could foster the prestige of the party by way of offering help in everyday problems and the health sector.

---

[32] Mei xian difangzhi bianzuan weiyuanhui (ed.), *Mei xian zhi* [Mei County Gazetteer], Xi'an: Shaanxi renmin chubanshe, 2000, 583. See as well the list of couplets reprinted in MacFarquhar and Schoenhals, *Mao's Last Revolution*, 266.

[33] Mao Zedong, "Guanyu weisheng gongzuo san ci tanhua" [Three Talks on Hygiene Work], 26 June 1965, in CRDB.

During the Cultural Revolution, especially between mid-1968 and the Ninth Congress, medical discourse came to serve as one of the primary examples of how Mao Zedong Thought advanced scientific knowledge and skills. The basic layout of all stories remained identical: an incurable ailment such as cancer or deafness was declared to have been overcome through the creative application of Mao Zedong Thought and the denigration of the policies of the Chinese Khrushchev. Although similar successes were claimed in other scientific disciplines during the Cultural Revolution as well, especially in weaponry and construction work, they did not develop into a lively genre comparable to medical discourse. The story that received most media coverage in 1968 but has been completely forgotten today is the story of Zhang Qiuju.[34] Zhang, a thirty-seven-year-old woman of lower-middle-class peasant descent, had been brought to the military health department of unit 4800 in Beijing by her husband in a pedicab with a womb swollen like a balloon. After listening to the odyssey of the couple and the failure of well-known specialists to treat her illness, PLA surgeons on 23 March proceeded with the operation. "In the operating room, today all four walls were covered with Chairman Mao posters and Chairman Mao quotations, thus destroying the old regulations of the capitalist medical health work line, and making the room appear especially bright."[35] Muttering Mao quotations, Zhang entered the room, weighing 214 pounds at a height of 1.57 meters. After a ten-hour operation, the surgeons removed a ninety pound tumor from her belly. This victory of Mao Zedong Thought was turned into a major publicity campaign, as Zhang had not only survived the operation but also recovered remarkably well. The PLA unit was awarded the title "wholeheartedly serving the people advanced health department" by the Military Affairs Commission.[36] The newspapers covered the story nationwide and even a special exhibition, which mainly consisted of the preserved tumor itself, toured the country.[37] In the following months,

---

[34] A collection of miraculous stories from the Cultural Revolution, including the story of Zhang Qiuju and the healing of deaf-mutes, can be found in George R. Urban, *The Miracles of Chairman Mao: A Compendium of Devotional Literature, 1966–1970*, London: Tom Stacey Limited, 1971.

[35] 4800 budui moubu weishengke dangzhibu, *Wuxian zhongyu Mao zhuxi geming luxian jiushi shengli* [Being Boundlessly Loyal to Chairman Mao's Revolutionary Line Means Victory], Beijing: Beijing junqu zhengzhibu/houjinbu, 1968, 26.

[36] *Dubao shouce (neibu cankao)* [Newspaper Readers' Handbook (Internal Reference)], Nanjing: Nanjing nongxueyuan geming weiyuanhui zhenggongzu/Nanjing wuxiandian gongyexiao geming weiyuanhui zhenggongzu, 1969, 525.

[37] One of the earliest accounts of Zhang's fate, along with a picture of her tumor, is to be found in *Xin Guizhou bao*, 26 May 1968, 3. See further *Yunnan ribao*, 10 December 1968.

several other miracles were reported, including coverage of how deaf-mute children had come to understand and recite certain Mao quotes through a special acupuncture method developed by a PLA unit.[38]

While the successes attributed to Mao Zedong Thought became ever more spurious, Mao was increasingly angered by the all-pervasive "empty verbiage" (*konghua*).[39] From late 1967 onward, Mao in internal party documents frequently crossed out excessive eulogies, but not even the CCP Chairman could single-handedly curb the cult discourse, which after all was based on structural deficits in the political system he had exploited himself to start the Cultural Revolution. Although Mao succeeded in banning certain phrases from official usage, the cult discourse remained stable until the establishment of the last revolutionary committees and visibly decreased in the public media only after the Ninth Party Congress. The tense political situation led to further manifestations of political loyalty by way of championing the cult and its symbols in a ritualized fashion. The Mao cult therefore witnessed a marked trend toward ritualization and commodification in the months leading up to the Ninth Party Congress.

---

[38] See the report in *Sichuan ribao*, 16 December 1968.

[39] "Zhonggong zhongyang bangongting yinfa Mao Zedong guanyu dui wai xuanchuan gongzuo de pishi (1967.3–1971.3.)" [CCP Center General Office Reprints Mao Zedong's Comments on External Propaganda Work (March 1967–March 1971)], 12 July 1971, in CRDB.

9

Rituals and Commodities

It was in late 1967 that ritual forms of worshipping Mao Zedong gained widespread currency in China. The best known of these rituals, "asking for instructions in the morning and reporting back in the evening" (*zao qingshi, wan huibao*), had first been mentioned in June 1967 as part of the military training experiences conducted at Shijingshan Middle School in the suburbs of Beijing. The contemporary report listed the usual means of persuasion such as study classes and comparisons between past and present, but was especially outspoken about ritualistic ways of employing the Mao cult. By criticizing the evil misdeeds of Liu Shaoqi, the students were to project their "insurmountable hatred" on the real enemies and to understand the pettiness of their quarrels. The constant building up of class hatred was to be combined with public expressions of true "proletarian class feelings" toward the correct leadership of Mao Zedong. To guarantee that the students did not deviate from the teachings of Mao Zedong, the students accordingly "invented" a system of comparing their own thoughts and deeds with Mao's sayings: "[I]n the morning, they take the problems accruing from the struggle of two lines and consult Chairman Mao's works for instructions. In the evening, they compare the thoughts and problems encountered during the day with the teachings of Chairman Mao and carry out a self-criticism."[1]

---

[1] "Shijingshan zhongxue shi zenyang zai jiefangjun bangzhu xia fuke nao geming de. Zai geming de da pipan zhong shixian geming de dalianhe" [How Shijingshan Middle School with the Help of the PLA Returned to Study to Carry Out Revolution: Realize the Great Revolutionary Alliance amid the Great Revolutionary Criticism], in *Renmin ribao*, 15 June 1967, 2.

The establishment of similar "asking for instructions and reporting back systems" (*qingshi huibao zhidu*) had been a common measure of the CCP leadership since the days of the civil war. It had been a way of assuming control in areas where the situation had become especially precarious. The local leadership thus was to report back on the situation before implementing policy initiatives of its own. Similar precautions had also been taken during the Gao-Rao affair in 1953 and were again to be initiated by most revolutionary committees during the anarchic years of 1967 and 1968.[2] Although the institutional system had been aimed at controlling policy outcomes and political power, the transfer of the system onto individual behavior was clearly aimed at unifying the perception of the present situation and at securing compliance to achieve the formation of revolutionary committees.

The experiences at Shijingshan received only a little media attention. Of much greater impact proved to be a report of a team from the Central Bureau of Guards, the CCP Center's security detail. Mao had increasingly come to distrust channels of information other than members of his staff or the division-strength Central Guards, also known as PLA unit 8341, which he deployed to act as his eyes and ears. The Central Bureau of Guards stood outside the military line of command and reported directly to Mao's security chief, Wang Dongxing. Mao's trusted bodyguards provided the Chairman with information about the situation in different localities – for example, about the Beijing General Knitting Mill, founded in 1952, which over the years had become a showcase of socialist nylon stockings production.

Mao decided to dispatch a team to the factory to forge an alliance between the two contending mass organizations. It was the first time that the Central Guards had become involved in the army's efforts to "support the Left," and Mao personally instructed the roughly eighty team members under the leadership of Deputy Political Commissar Sun Yi and Long March veteran Gu Yuanxin about their mission. They were to conduct political education work in a "profound, meticulous, and arduous"[3] fashion. After considering the specific situation at the Knitting Mill, Mao advised the team members to dispatch mainly female comrades in order

---

[2] For the implementation in Hebei, see Hebei sheng geming weiyuanhui, "Guanyu jianli qingshi baogao zhidu de qingshi" [Instruction on Establishing an Asking for and Reporting Back System], 22 June 1968, 1.

[3] Zhonggong wenxian yanjiushi (ed.), *Mao wengao* 12, 366.

to gain the trust of the workers by providing medical care and offering help in problems of everyday life.

Despite Mao's comprehensive reasoning, uniting the two factions turned out to be tremendously difficult. Among the factory's 2,183 workers, some 800 had joined the East Is Red Revolutionary Committee and about 1,200 the Red Rebel Command. The omnipresent employment of Mao's image and teachings to justify parochial claims led the workers to distrust the announcement of the team leaders that they had been sent by the CCP Chairman personally. Mao, however, had also deployed his physician, Li Zhisui, to the Knitting Mill.[4] Only after they had trailed Li's carriage back to Zhongnanhai were the workers convinced about the team's political credibility. After having proven their special background, the Central Guards team immediately started with a thorough propagation of Mao Zedong Thought. The approach owed much to the previous experiences of other military units, especially in Shijingshan Middle School, as the concluding report revealed:

> We attached the greatest influence to studying. We established study organizations and a healthy system of studies; furthermore, we decorated the study surroundings. We made use of different forms like asking the Chairman for instructions when going to work and reporting back to the Chairman after finishing work (by collectively studying quotations). We organized Mao Zedong Thought propaganda teams and established study groups, as well as sharing experience in application meetings [*jiang-yonghui*] in order to propagate Mao Zedong Thought comprehensively among the workers and their relatives. Thus within a short period of time we aroused a high tide of studying and applying Chairman Mao's works in a living way.[5]

Never before had an official CCP Center document endorsed the stimulation of ritualistic or, in contemporary parlance, formalistic worship. Thus in December 1966, the CCP Center had explicitly prohibited the Red Ocean (*hongse haiyang*) campaign initiated by the Beijing Aviation

---

[4] Li and Thurston, *Private Life*, 482–7. Most of the remembered dates and numbers, however, do not correlate with contemporary documents.

[5] "Zhongfa [67] 350, Zhonggong zhongyang zhuanfa 'Beijing zhenzhi zongchang geming weiyuanhui xian Mao zhuxi bao xi' de xin he 'Zhongguo renmin jiefangjun 8341 budui guanyu Beijing shi zhenzhi zongchang zhigong de qingkuang de baogao'" [The CCP Center Transmits a Letter of the "Beijing General Knitting Mill Revolutionary Committee to Chairman Mao Bearing Good News" and the "Report of PLA Unit 8341 on the Situation of Industry-Supporting Efforts at the Beijing General Knitting Mill"], 17 November 1967, in CRDB.

Institute Red Flag.[6] The campaign had been aimed at the revolutionization of the cityscape in honor of the CCP Chairman's birthday by painting walls and houses in bright red. Mao, however, had not been pleased by these extravagancies. On 30 December 1966, the CCP Center had passed a directive forbidding similar activities, since mere aestheticization was deemed politically pointless and, furthermore, a number of enemies had tried "on purpose to employ this method to prevent the populace from sticking up big character posters owing to lack of space."[7] One year later, however, priorities had shifted. Although "formalistic" activities were still not encouraged by the CCP leadership, by 1967 they were tolerated as long as they helped to foster unity.

The Knitting Mill report relied on the experiences of numerous previous trial units but elevated them to a completely new level. This was not an isolated newspaper article about certain experiences with limited relevance but an official CCP central document, *Zhongfa* [67] 350, which came to be distributed in twenty thousand copies to all military and civilian units down to the county level. It was the only document issued in the name of the CCP Center during the Cultural Revolution that effectively propagated a ritualistic worship of "Chairman Mao" and thus attained enormous attention. The system of "asking for instructions in the morning" was further extended by a series of habitual actions that were to secure the concordance of every action with Mao Zedong Thought (see Illustration 5):

> Before work we ask the Chairman for instructions in order to see and think clearly and gain a sense of direction;
>   After work we report back to Chairman Mao and review our work and thoughts;
>   During production we look at the mirror in front of the workshops (the *Quotation* tablets) to derive a mighty increase in work enthusiasm;
>   When trading shifts, we exchange quotations as a way of showing concern and offering help.[8]

The omnipresence of Mao icons and the replacement of ordinary speech with the reverential exchange of quotations (*song yulu*) were to leave

---

[6] Yan Fan, *Da chuanlian. Yi chang shiwuqianlie de zhengzhi lüyou* [The Great Exchange of Revolutionary Experience: An Unprecedented Occasion for Political Travel], Beijing: Jingguan jiaoyu chubanshe, 1993, 156f.

[7] "Zhongfa [66] 629, Zhonggong zhongyang, guowuyuan guanyu zhizhi da gao suowei "hongse haiyang" de tongzhi" [CCP Center and State Council Notice Forbidding the Large-Scale Conducting of the So-Called "Red Ocean"], 30 December 1966, in CRDB.

[8] Ibid.

ILLUSTRATION 5. Military hospital patients make their morning pledge of loyalty to Mao's picture, Harbin, Heilongjiang province, 5 September 1968. Li Zhensheng. (Contact Press Images.)

no room for alternative exegesis. Deviations from the prescribed routines were regarded as disloyal behavior and thus potentially engendered drastic consequences. Despite the metaphors of elated or even ecstatic states of mind, which the participants experienced upon establishing a revolutionary committee in their factory after months of massive confrontations, the functional and clearly disciplinary approach behind the installment of the system of rituals was beyond doubt. The main aim of the cult rituals was not to increase personal worship but to strengthen group cohesion by providing the masses with a sense of shared common ground. But since the focal point of attention was presented by an individual ascribed with superhuman qualities, the rise of quasireligious modes of worship was one foreseeable consequence. Mere performances of loyalty or "acting as if"[9] presented another option. Irrespective of whether partaking in the rituals was inspired by true belief or induced by political pressure, it served to make the masses "more docile,"[10] as Blaise Pascal speculated in his famous wager on God.

Unit 8341 relied on different strategies in the Knitting Mill depending on the different subjects who were to be reeducated: the cadres, the rebel leaders, and the masses. While the masses, according to Mao, did not want disorder and thus could easily be united by having to study certain key texts, the rebel leaders had to give up their egoistic views through extended study sessions. The main problem, however, rested with the cadres, who were still needed to organize and supervise production. Most cadres had become "angry, discouraged, and unconvinced"[11] because of the series of struggle sessions and refused to take part in the new system in an exalted, and thus conspicuous, position. The main task of the cadre study classes therefore was to reintegrate them into the movement by making them both accept the criticism of the masses and understand how grateful they should be to live in the age of Mao Zedong.

On 11 November 1967, finally, after a complicated process of choosing representatives, the Beijing General Knitting Mill revolutionary committee was established. The committee's representatives sent a congratulatory telegram to Mao the same day, exalting him in the most exuberant fashion. Mao replied by adding a comment: "I've read this. It is very good. Thank you, comrades!"[12] He then had the report and his comment distributed nationwide. The factory workers were delighted about this sign of attention from the highest command. The note was first posted on the factory blackboard, where everyone filed past it. Afterward, it was photographed and displayed above the factory's entrance. The Beijing General Knitting Mill became a nationally celebrated model unit and along with five other factories – the New China Printing Plant, the North Lumber Yard, the Second Chemical Plant, the Nankou Motor Vehicle Plant, and the 7 February Motor Vehicle Plant – received lavish attention in the media. The *People's Daily* alone published over one hundred articles between

---

[9] See Wedeen, *Ambiguities*, 67ff.

[10] "You want to find faith and you do not know the road. You want to be cured of unbelief and you ask for the remedy: learn from those who were once bound like you and who now wager all they have. [...] They behaved just as if they did believe, taking holy water, having masses said, and so on. That will make you believe quite naturally, and will make you more docile," Blaise Pascal, *Pensées*, Hammondsworth: Penguin, 1966 [1670], 152f.

[11] "Zhongfa [67] 350"; see the report in *Sichuan ribao*, 16 December 1968.

[12] "Zhongfa [67] 350."

1967 and 1971 on the experiences of the Knitting Mill. This enormous publicity was due to the installment in the factory of a special journalist corps from the capital's most important news agencies in late 1967. Just like physician Li Zhisui, the journalists were to join in the everyday life and work of the factory staff, reform their thinking, and in the meantime produce model reports in praise of the factory's successes.[13] The reports served to popularize Mao's abstract instructions by providing detailed examples of how local units were to proceed in order to end the anarchic warfare.

Because of the attention paid to the experiences of the factory, different members of the CCP top echelon, such as Lin Biao's wife Ye Qun, tried to gain influence over the now famous unit by deploying her own staff to influence the factory's direction and to claim a share of its glory. Mao Zedong himself took pride as well in the apparent success of his model units, which on various occasions would be referred to as his "spots" (*dian*) by other leaders, such as his wife, Jiang Qing, who would go to great lengths to come up with her own points of special attention.[14] After deploying Mao Zedong Thought Propaganda Teams to Qinghua and Beijing universities in late July 1968, largely staffed with workers from the six factories under the leadership of the Central Guards, the "six factories and two universities" (*liu chang, er xiao*) became a synonym for the successful reunification of the contending factions and continued to be propagated well into the mid-1970s.

The experiences of unit 8341 at the Beijing General Knitting Mill had an enormous impact on the Mao cult. The rituals of worship were taken up by other military units trying to cope with excessive factionalism. Various contemporary reports mention the rituals of "asking for instructions in the morning" or the compulsory "daily reading." The rituals were complemented by all kinds of confessional activities conducted before Mao's cult symbols. If some type of thought or action could be claimed to have violated Mao's supreme authority, Mao was to be asked for forgiveness and penalties were imposed through the local unit.

Although in the case of the Cultural Revolution's best-known ritual, the "asking for instructions in the morning," there can be little doubt about

---

[13] Fang Hanqi, Ning Shufan, and Chen Yeshao (eds.), *Zhongguo xinwen shiye tongshi* [General History of the Chinese News Industry], vol. 3, Beijing: Zhongguo renmin daxue chubanshe, 2000 [1999], 350–4.

[14] See Jeremy Brown, "Staging Xiaojinzhuang: The City in the Countryside, 1974–1976," in Joseph Esherick, Paul Pickowicz, and Andrew G. Walder (eds.), *The Cultural Revolution as History*, Stanford: Stanford University Press, 2006, 153–84.

the formative role played by the PLA in shaping its forms, other rituals appeared that did not attain official sanction but developed within the same political climate of turning even the most mundane action into performances of loyalty to Mao Zedong. These included the so-called "quotation gymnastics" (yulu cao).[15] Daily broadcasts of morning gymnastics had become part of Chinese everyday life since 1951. A mere week after the CCP Center had distributed the model experiences of unit 8341, a special edition of the Shanghai Sports Battle Line announced the creation of quotation gymnastics through the Shanghai Sports Headquarters Rising Corps "Chairman Mao Quotation Gymnastics" Creation Group. According to the report, the aim had been to develop the daily gymnastics into an occasion for praising Chairman Mao to "thoroughly eradicate the revisionist sports line and to establish a revolutionary Mao Zedong Thought sports line."[16]

The quotation gymnastics consisted of a series of nine exercises (see Illustration 6), arranged in six parts and offered a coherent storyline. It started with the attempt to display eternal loyalty by wishing the "reddest, reddest red sun in our hearts," Mao Zedong, eternal life and ascertaining the crucial role of the CCP. Part two consisted of a series of three exercises representing the "three constantly read articles" and aimed at the destruction of selfish feelings. Part three, modeled on the quotation "political power grows from the barrel of a gun," was to remind the practitioners about the necessity never to forget class struggle. The quotation was to be repeated six times, accompanied by symbolic moves representing the assassination of enemies in all directions. After the last repetition, the leader was to shout three more sentences: "Aim at U.S. imperialism," "Aim at Soviet revisionism," "Aim at all reactionary parties." Each time these shouts were followed by a collective shouting of "kill!" and the

---

[15] The earliest variant of the quotation gymnastics is said to have been developed by the Beijing Sports Academy's Worker-Peasant-Soldier Revolutionary Committee and was published in a special edition of a local Red Guard tabloid on 14 October 1967. The Beijing quotation gymnastics are said to have been strongly influenced by the PLA work in Shijingshan Middle School and to have consisted of sixteen exercises (oral information of participants). Unfortunately, I have not been able to retrieve the original document so far. The National Sports Committee finally was to publish a thirty-two–page instruction manual of several different quotation gymnastics in 1968. The manual celebrated the PLA as inventor of the gymnastics with reference to the Shijingshan Middle School report; see Guojia tiwei "Hongse xuanchuanyuan" (ed.), Mao zhuxi yulu cao huibian, n.p., 1968.

[16] Shanghai tiyu yundong weiyuanhui geming weiyuanhui and Shanghai tiyu zhanxian geming zaofan silingbu (eds.), "Tiyu geming de chunlei" [Spring Thunder of the Sports Revolution], in Tiyu zhanxian (Shanghai), 20 November 1967, 1.

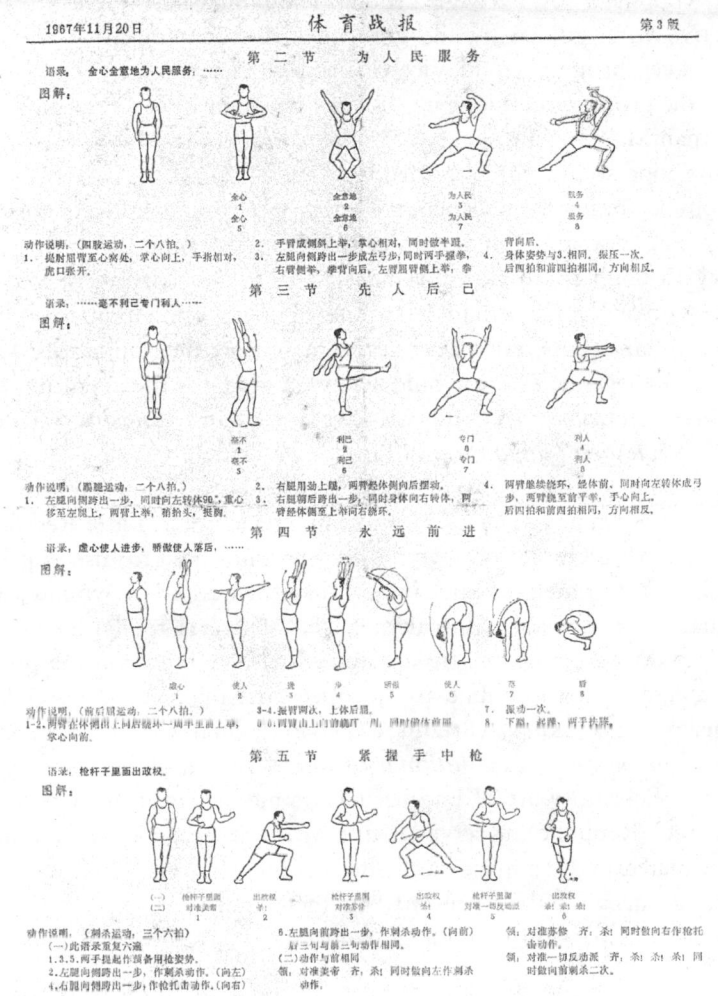

ILLUSTRATION 6. Part of the "Chairman Mao Quotation Gymnastics," *Shanghai Sports Battleline*, 1967. (Author's personal copy.)

mimicking of stabbing with bayonets. Part four quoted Mao's poem "A Reply to Comrade Guo Moruo, to the Tune of *Manjiang hong*," and was to represent the stormy tides and the unwavering will to fight the enemies of socialism. Part five was to display the determination to follow Chairman Mao's great strategic plan, and part six, finally, was to express the "boundless hot love, boundless worship, boundless reverence" of the whole world's populace toward Mao Zedong. The gymnastics were to end with a collective vow, guided by the group leader who would exclaim, "We should keep firmly in mind Vice-Chairman Lin's teaching," upon which the whole group would join in: "Read Chairman Mao's books, listen to Chairman Mao's sayings, act according to Chairman Mao's instructions, become good soldiers of Mao Zedong."[17]

From beginning to end, then, the quotation gymnastics were conceived of as what Chang-tai Hung has called the construction of a "narrative history through rhythmic movements."[18] The participants staged their heartfelt love for Chairman Mao and their determination to fight the revisionist and imperialist enemies with utmost determination. Half a year later, the same group would also gain fame for the invention of the "Wishing Chairman Mao Eternal Live Taijiquan" (*Jingzhu Mao zhuxi wanshou wujiang" taijiquan*).[19]

The gymnastics were quickly copied and adapted to different settings. At Beijing Normal University, for example, a special "Little Red Soldier Chairman Mao Quotation Gymnastics" was invented for use in primary schools.[20] Yet of much greater impact than the quotation gymnastics and taijiquan was to be the "loyalty dance." There is to date no specific founding document of this ritual dance. It clearly relied on the previous instrumentalization of public group dances in Yan'an days, especially the northern Chinese *yangge* variants, as David Holm has shown in his classic *Art and Ideology in Revolutionary China*.[21] The politicized *yangge* as "official celebratory art"[22] had been a common sight in the first years of the People's Republic and served to display the new regime's achievements. Yet the increasingly simplistic and officially prescribed moves failed to gain the dance urban public support. By the mid-1950s, therefore, public dancing as expression of political conviction played a marginal role in urban life.

The renewed emphasis on politicizing and rejuvenating traditional art forms, and especially the importance attached to the new "model operas"

[17] Ibid., 1.
[18] Chang-tai Hung, "The Dance of Revolution: Yangge in Beijing in the Early 1950s," in *China Quarterly* 181 (2005), 87.
[19] See *Tiyu zhanxian*, 26 April 1968.
[20] See Beijing shida tiyuxi geweihui "Mao zhuxi yulu hongxiaobing cao" chuangbianzu, "Mao zhuxi yulu hongxiaobing cao" [Little Red Soldier Chairman Mao Quotation Gymnastics], in *Jiaoyu geming*, 20 January 1968, 2.
[21] David Holm, *Art and Ideology in Revolutionary China*, Oxford: Clarendon Press, 1991.
[22] Hung, "Dance of Revolution," 84.

(*yangbanxi*)[23] after the outbreak of the Cultural Revolution, had resulted in the staging of various local plays and dances in honor of Mao Zedong by Red Guard troupes. Yet prior to 1967 there is no mentioning of the term "loyalty dance" in any contemporary source. By mid-1968, however, it spread like a prairie fire throughout China, even to regions where public dancing was not part of the common culture and thus led to considerable public embarrassment.[24] Just like the gymnastics, the loyalty dance was not a device implemented by the CCP Center but a grassroots invention aimed at a physical demonstration of loyalty. The dance, which could be performed alone or in groups, continued to flourish for roughly a year and consisted of various subforms, all of which included performances of expressing boundless hot love and absolute loyalty to the CCP Chairman by means of stretching the arms from the heart to the sun or to Mao's portrait. One form even attempted to transform the body artistically into the Chinese character "loyalty" (*zhong*) by using outstretched arms and kicking feet.

References to these types of activities in local annals or secondary literature are usually highly unspecific. They lump together all "strange words and deeds"[25] of the period and render them a kind of common craze. Contemporary reports are much more difficult to obtain and only seldom does a true founding document exist as in the case of the quotation gymnastics or the "eternal life" taijiquan. Mention of cult rituals usually takes the form of prohibitions to conduct certain types of worship. A typical example is the following report of the Tianjin Municipal Revolutionary Committee published in May 1969, which lists cult excesses conducted the previous year. According to the report, in a number of Tianjin factories members of the local revolutionary committee in mid-1968 had taken up the habit of dancing and had made a twice daily "loyalty dance break" a mandatory part of daily production work. Knowledge of the dance moves had in some places also been included as part of the criteria upon which the "four/five good activists" were selected. Students were reported to have skipped classes to practice their dancing skills, and in the case of one particular factory, seven instructors had been employed to teach the correct moves to workers with limited dancing

---

[23] On the content and propagation of the *yangbanxi*, see especially Clark, *Cultural Revolution*.

[24] Anita Chan, Richard Madsen, and Jonathan Unger, *Chen Village: The Recent History of a Peasant Community in Mao's China*, Berkeley: University of California Press, 1984, 169ff.

[25] Jin Chunming, Huang Yuchong, and Chang Huimin (eds.), *"Wenge" shiqi guaishi guaiyu* [Weird Things and Weird Words from the Period of the "Cultural Revolution"], Beijing: Qiushi chubanshe, 1989.

ILLUSTRATION 7. Kang Wenjie, a five-year-old prodigy, performs the "loyalty dance" for the representatives of the conference on "Learning and Applying Mao Zedong Thought" at Harbin's Red Guard Stadium, Heilongjiang province, 28 April 1968. Li Zhensheng. (Contact Press Images.)

abilities.[26] The dancing skills, however, were not the most important aspect, although child prodigies such as Kang Wenjie received great attention (see Illustration 7).[27] Rather, the demonstration of boundless loyalty was deemed to be of supreme importance. "To dance well or not is a problem of technique. But to dance or not to dance is a question of standpoint."[28]

As the report reveals, the correct enactment of the cult rituals was by no means trivial and can be understood only against the background of the parallel campaign to "cleanse the class ranks" that had started in late 1967 in Shanghai and was to gain full momentum in the summer of 1968. The campaign provided the newly established revolutionary committees with a rationale to dispose of "hidden enemies" or in many cases competitors for power.[29] The complete lack of reliable legal norms regarding what

[26] Tianjin shi geming weiyuanhui, "Jin'ge [69] 082, Guanyu dangqian xuanchuan gongzuo zhong cunzai de jige wenti he jinhou yijian" [On Certain Problems in Current Propaganda Work and Future Opinions], 9 May 1969, 3.
[27] See Li Zhensheng, *Red-Color News Soldier: A Chinese Photographer's Odyssey through the Cultural Revolution*, London: Phaidon, 2003, 216f.
[28] "Tianjin shi geming weiyuanhui, Jin'ge [69] 082," 3.
[29] MacFarquhar and Schoenhals, *Mao's Last Revolution*, 256.

effectively constituted counterrevolutionary behavior made the violation of Mao symbols or insufficient displays of loyalty a criterion that most people understood as constituting a major offense. Everyone who, intentionally or not, failed to partake in the cult rituals, misspelled Mao quotations, or vilified cult symbols faced being sentenced as an "active counterrevolutionary" (*xianxing fangeming*) by the PLA military control commissions that had come to assume legal power in most parts of China by 1968.

Examples of these types of punishment are to be found in basically every work on the Cultural Revolution, usually cited from memory. Contemporary historical evidence is more difficult to come by. Local gazetteers sometimes mention the number of persons persecuted during the campaign. In Baishui County, Shaanxi province, 517 persons were struggled against because of various deviations from the acceptable rules of speech and behavior. For example, a member of a local medical team was sentenced as an active counterrevolutionary for having written a big character poster on the back of an old newspaper without noticing that he had placed his criticism on the reverse side of a Mao picture. When holding the paper against the light, it could be proven that he had placed the character "bad" exactly at the same height as Mao's portrait, an act that constituted the major evidence of his supposed counterrevolutionary behavior.[30]

Other sources reveal similar absurd sentences. A confession report of a peasant surnamed Yang from Hebei province documents that he was sentenced for having confused the expressions "loyalty" and a homophonous Hebei dialect phrase meaning "okay," thus rendering the phrase "determining loyalty by looking at action" completely meaningless.[31] Yet his most heinous crime consisted of using an old newspaper carrying Mao's image as toilet paper, as watchful neighbors were to report to the local production team.[32] Little is known about the fate of many of these individuals who were incarcerated or even executed for these symbolic transgressions. Most cases were reviewed and often overturned only in the late 1970s as part of the attempt to legitimize the turning away from the politics of the Cultural Revolution.[33] Without doubt, fear and societal pressure to conform to the omnipresent flattery of Mao Zedong's genius played a crucial role in shaping the extent of this most extravagant phase of worship.

[30] Baishui xian xianzhi bianzuan weiyuanhui (ed.), *Baishui xian zhi* [Baishui County Gazetteer], Xi'an: Xi'an ditu chubanshe, 1989, 460.

[31] Yang XX, "Qingzui shu" [Letter of Apology], September 1968, 1.

[32] Ibid.

[33] See Daniel Leese, "Revising Political Verdicts in Post-Mao China: The Case of Beijing Fengtai District," unpublished paper.

The rituals of worship developed out of an intricate relationship among the CCP Center, midlevel revolutionary committees or PLA units, and the populace. The CCP leadership was by no means fond of "mass inventions" such as the loyalty dances that had developed without official recognition. With the exception of the General Knitting Mill report, the CCP leadership refrained from circulating similar experiences within official documents. Yet until after the Ninth Party Congress, no public criticism was voiced against the ritualistic worship. Anger about the unauthorized modes of veneration was vented at internal party meetings; for example, the following exchange occurred during a discussion of central leaders with military representatives in April 1968:

> Jiang Qing: Have you received authorization for conducting the quotation gymnastics? How can [such things] evolve if they have not been authorized? No formalism or vulgarization should be conducted. The Chairman's Thought should not be debased or distorted.
> Huang Yongsheng [Chief-of-Staff]: The Chairman's quotations are being shouted everywhere.
> Premier [Zhou Enlai]: Even the traffic police use the quotations as a baton, how should this work? [...]
> Revered Kang [Kang Sheng]: I heard that you even study the quotations before eating.
> Lin Biao: The CCP Center should investigate these problems and pass a resolution.[34]

The CCRG strongly resented these demonstrations of loyalty. Because everyone could partake in them and thus derive symbolic capital from the enactment, the opportunities for the CCRG to exercise top-down intervention were effectively decreased. Although the employment of competing Mao quotations had presented a major problem in the past, now the omnipresent performances of loyalty angered the party leadership. But given the continuing armed struggles among rival factions, the cult's cohesive force remained too precious to discard.

The general emphasis on loyalty made the active expounding of the cult and especially the Three Loyalties campaign a frequently employed measure of the newly established power structures. The midlevel bureaucracy in particular thus joined in the ritualistic worship. In provinces such as Hebei or Guangdong, where revolutionary committees had only recently been invested with political power, the campaign was especially strong because the provincial leadership was in need of proving its revolutionary standpoint and thus provided units with material subsidies to buy paint, lime, or

---

[34] Lin Biao, "Jiejian XX, XX jun shi de zhishi" [Instructions while Receiving the XX, XX Military Units], 6–9 April 1968, in CRDB.

cement.[35] Cities such as Shijiazhuang (as seen in Chapter 8) achieved specific prominence in the spring of 1968 and were visited by representatives from other revolutionary committees eager to learn from the most advanced techniques of worshipping Mao Zedong and consolidating power.[36] Local and provincial leadership organs thus tried to outshine each other in presenting their administrative units as models of Mao worship by merging the verbal, ritual, and decorative aspects of the Mao cult in attempts to achieve the "loyalty-fication"[37] or "Mao Zedong Thought-ification"[38] of the entire day. A resulting report presented by the Red Guard Headquarters at Beijing Middle School No. 64 consisted of the attempt to have Mao Zedong Thought take the lead "at any place, in every action, and at every time; to take the quotations to guide every word and deed: 'Just the way Chairman Mao said it, I am going to do it'" (*Mao zhuxi zenme shuo, wo jiu zenme zuo*).[39] From arriving at school armed with Mao's writings and badges, through the employment of various "asking for instructions" ceremonies and quote exchanges during the lessons, until "reporting back" to Mao's portrait at home in the evening, all daily routines were to be adjusted to the Mao cult. Contemporary benchmarks for evaluating successful implementation are listed at the end of the preliminary report compiled by the Red Guard Headquarters. They consisted of three items:

1. To master the quotation gymnastics and the formation of the quotation slogans.

---

[35] In Chongzuo County in the Guangxi Zhuang autonomous region, for example, the revolutionary committee allotted some 650 yuan to three primary schools in order to facilitate the "loyalty-fication" of the surroundings; see "Chongzuo xian geming weiyuanhui shengchanzu guanyu fenpei gao 'zhong'zihua huanjing buzhu jingfei de tongzhi" [Notice of the Chongzuo County Revolutionary Committee Production Group Concerning the Allocation of Subsidy Funds to Conduct the "Loyalty-fication" of the Environment], 25 September 1968.

[36] See as well MacFarquhar and Schoenhals, *Mao's Last Revolution*, 264–7.

[37] See "Rang 'zhong yu Mao zhuxi' wu ge jinguang shanshan da zi ranhong mei gen shenjing" [Let the Five Glistening Characters "Loyal to Chairman Mao" Set Every Nerve Aflame], in *Shijiazhuang ribao*, 15 March 1968, 1.

[38] "Yong Mao Zedong sixiang tongshuai shengming de mei yi miaozhong. Shijiazhuang guomian yichang zhigong 'yi ri huodong Mao Zedong sixianghua' pianduan" [Rely on Mao Zedong Thought to Command Every Minute of Life: Extracts from the Shijiazhuang First Cotton Fiber Factory Workers' "Mao Zedong Thought-ify the Whole Day's Action"], in *Shijiazhuang ribao*, 24 March 1968, 1.

[39] Beijing liushisi zhong hongweibing zongbu, "Kaizhan 'yi ri zhongzihua' huodong chubu yijian" [Preliminary Opinions on Launching a "Loyalty-ficate the Whole Day" Campaign], 13 April 1968, 1.

2. To stick "loyalty" characters on the quotation volumes and the school tables.
3. To learn by heart Chairman Mao quotations crucial for the present work and to exchange these. For example, if we conduct educational revolution this week, we should learn by heart quotations on educational revolution.[40]

The success of the campaign was thus measured in the achievement of certain tangible results, such as mastering the moves of the quotation gymnastics. Even the employment of certain quotations was clearly focused on their instrumental value to attain predetermined goals and not necessarily an equivalent to the recitation of religious gospel. Yet religious or quasireligious worship of "Chairman Mao" was one possible result of the campaign, especially in rural areas.

CULT COMMODITIES

Popular reaction to the volatile political situation took on many different forms. Since passive endurance was perceived as coterminous with harboring hidden resentment toward the CCP Chairman's policies, the active expounding of the cult became an omnipresent phenomenon. One possible consequence engendered by the dominant rhetoric and rituals of worship was Mao's inclusion into the local pantheon. The quasireligious confessions before Mao's portrait were thus turned into divine worship. Although similar phenomena had already been observed in the 1950s,[41] they now spread more widely in rural areas, where Mao came to replace other deities on the house altar,[42] a custom that continues to the present. But even in urban Shanghai citizens could be observed conducting the rituals of the "Three Loyalties" in private.[43] Many brigade headquarters established "loyalty chambers" (*zhongzi shi*) or "loyalty halls" (*zhongzi tang*), which were clearly modeled on ancestral temples. The halls were decorated with pictures of the "red sun" Mao Zedong and large-scale quotation boards. Fresh flowers would be placed before Mao's image and his works were put on display on "precious red book shrines" (*hong*

---

[40] Ibid., 1.
[41] Schoenhals, *Saltationist Socialism*, 203f., n. 63.
[42] Stefan R. Landsberger, "The Deification of Mao: Religious Imagery and Practices during the Cultural Revolution and Beyond," in Woei Lien Chong (ed.), *China's Great Proletarian Cultural Revolution: Master Narratives and Post-Mao Counternarratives*, Lanham, MD: Rowman & Littlefield, 2002, 139–84.
[43] White, *Policies of Chaos*, 303.

baoshu tai). Similarly, down to the production-team level, "instruction shrines" (*qingshi tai*) were established, usually on the village square or in front of the most representative local building. These monuments usually resembled traditional memorial sites or archways. They were inscribed with Mao quotations and engraved with sunflowers and loyalty symbols. Although today only few of these monuments remain, they were fairly common phenomena in rural China during the late 1960s. According to a survey conducted in Taibai County in Shaanxi province, no fewer than 1,242 instruction shrines and 3,149 precious red book shrines had been established by January 1969 in this county alone.[44]

The manifestations of loyalty, however, were not confined to religious architecture in the countryside. Quite to the contrary; the near talismanic quality that the character *zhong* assumed also became visible in the emergence of thousands of different cult commodities. While up to the Three Loyalties campaign the dominant cult products had been the Little Red Book and Mao images, now a massive drive toward commodification resulted in a huge variety of more or less standardized cult products (see Illustration 8). A present-day stroll through Chinese antique markets still reveals the incredible variety. Although many of the items on display no longer stem from the Cultural Revolution itself, they mirror the multitude of objects once crafted to display boundless loyalty. The products ranged from traditional handicrafts, such as embroidery works of PLA soldiers ("every pinprick is an expression of our heartfelt love for the Chairman"), to porcelain and enamelware. Kitsch products such as red plastic hearts imprinted with the Chairman's portrait and the "loyalty" sign flourished in the same fashion as porcelain luster with a red "loyalty" inlay. Fancy red plastic bound briefcases were available for the study of Mao texts and quotation cards could be collected in red plastic folders. Even traditional silk bags, previously used for Buddhist sutras and now imprinted with the character "loyalty," were handmade to contain the Little Red Book. For a short time, the habit of carrying large, framed Mao pictures around the neck came to be regarded as the ultimate expression of loyalty[45] – as

---

[44] Taibai xian difangzhi bianzuan weiyuanhui (ed.), *Taibai xian zhi* [Taibai County Gazetteer], Xi'an: Sanqin chubanshe, 1995, 426.

[45] "Recently, another fad has occurred: [Mao] pictures are carried in plastic or glass frames before the chest." See Tianjin shi geming weiyuanhui, "Jin'ge [69] 054, Guanyu zhizhi zai qing 'jiu da', ying guoqing deng huodong zhong chuxian de fukua langfei xianxiang de jueding" [Decision on Forbidding All Phenomena Related to Exaggeration and Waste that Appeared during Activities to Welcome the Ninth Congress and to Celebrate National Day], 24 March 1969, 2.

ILLUSTRATION 8. Workers in the Harbin Arts and Crafts Factory make Mao plaques, Heilongjiang province, 18 July 1968. Li Zhensheng. (Contact Press Images.)

shown on the cover of this book – especially in peripheral regions with a strong Buddhist tradition such as Tibet and Inner Mongolia.

Mao quotes virtually came to be printed on every type of object, as a directive on current problems in propaganda work published by the Tianjin Municipal Revolutionary Committee in May 1969 reveals. It is among the most detailed contemporary accounts edited by an official state organ to describe the scope of the "loyalty-fication" movement and therefore shall be quoted in more detail:

> Many units conducted the so-called "loyalty-ficate the surroundings" [*zhongzihua huanjing*] in a big way, attaching Chairman Mao portraits, quotations, and poems on the inside and outside of the houses. In terms of politics, it was insufficiently solemn and in terms of economic behavior it resulted in thriftlessness. Even on cotton cloth, graphic reproductions of

the "three constantly read articles" were printed; carpets and blankets were embroidered with Chairman Mao portraits and quotations came to be printed on the packaging of sales products. Towels, pillows, wooden furniture, wine bottles, medicine wrappings, wallets, toys, and candy-paper, all were imprinted with quotations. This was thought to be "placing politics at the fore" and thus to be an expression of "loyalty to the Chairman." "Red hearts" and "loyalty" characters completely void of any class meaning were pasted onto everything. Many shops arranged so-called "loyalty cabinets" [*zhongzi ge*], seemingly all shop windows were turned into "loyalty windows" [*zhongzi chuang*]. Even in the service sector, including foodstuff and grocery stores, barbershops, let alone public baths, everyone established "loyalty cabinets" and "loyalty windows," thinking that this was how to build a "glistening red great school of Mao Zedong Thought" instead of focusing on how to conduct the lively study and application of Mao Zedong Thought. The populace raised many objections [against these measures].[46]

Mao and the character *zhong* were applied to every possible item as brand symbols of revolutionary conviction (see Illustration 9). Here an interesting difference to the crafting of cult commodities in Nazi Germany is noteworthy. During the Third Reich, various firms tried to gain official permission to utilize the Führer's prominence as a brand symbol for different types of products, including "Hitler-cakes" and "Hitler-shoes," and thus to increase the sale of their specific commodities.[47] In China, to the contrary, most cult products of 1968 were not originally crafted with pecuniary motives. Most items were sold at a price below manufacturing costs or even distributed as gifts to others in order not to give the impression of harboring the ulterior motive of making money. When trying to purchase a Mao object in shops, one even replaced the profane phrase "to buy" (*mai*) with the polite expression "*qing*," previously used to acquire sacrificial objects. The Maoist "worship of truth" thus ultimately became imbued with all types of traditional notions of religious worship that contradicted the original intentions of the CCP leadership in fostering the cult.

Mao badges played a special role among the cult commodities. Badges were the only cult items besides Mao's works and pictures that were manufactured by the state itself.[48] Mao badges had come to be increasingly common after July 1966, when many state factories or private

[46] Tianjin shi geming weiyuanhui, "Jin'ge [69] 082," 3f.

[47] See Beatrice Heiber and Helmut Heiber (eds.), *Die Rückseite des Hakenkreuzes. Absonderliches aus den Akten des Dritten Reiches* [The Swastika's Backside: Strange Tales from Files of the Third Reich], Munich: DTV, 1993, 119, 123ff.

[48] The history of the Mao badges has probably become the best-researched subtopic of the Mao cult. For further readings in English, see, for example, Melissa Schrift, *Biography of a*

ILLUSTRATION 9. Hundreds of thousands gather in front of the North Plaza Hotel carrying homemade portraits of Mao in a show of loyalty and support, Harbin, Heilongjiang province, 21 June 1968. Li Zhensheng. (Contact Press Images.)

organizations issued badges in commemoration of specific events or as proof of having visited a certain revolutionary site. In the PLA, the wearing of two badges became mandatory from May 1967 onward after the General Political Department had come to issue to all soldiers a five-star Mao badge along with a rectangular badge carrying the slogan "serve the people."[49] By August 1967, according to the minutes of a meeting on the situation of distributing Mao badges in Hebei province convened by the Second Light Industry Department and the Trade Department, "basically every urban worker, student, soldier wears Chairman Mao badges."[50] By the end of the year, in Hebei province alone, 10 million badges had been manufactured by the state and an influx of at least 9 million badges from other provinces had been reported. Thus on average roughly half of the 44 million inhabitants had been provided with Mao badges.[51] These numbers, however, were tiny compared to the production of badges in Beijing or Shanghai. Between May 1966 and December 1967, the fifteen official units entrusted with the production of badges in the capital had manufactured a total of 207 million badges of over 200 different kinds, private producers not included.[52] Every badge-producing unit was required to send five specimens to the Museum of the Chinese Revolution in Beijing – the museum was to pay for the postage – as examples of revolutionary art, and as part of a repository for future international exhibitions.[53] The variety of badges was to signal the creativeness of the masses and the eternal victory of Mao Zedong Thought.

Today, the overall estimates for the Cultural Revolution period range well over 2.5 billion badges produced. Yet they were not distributed evenly. According to the results of the Hebei investigation teams, most urban citizens owned up to a dozen or more Mao badges while in the countryside only the youth who had been exchanging experiences were in possession of Mao badges. In the countryside, the efforts to distribute

[49] Xu Ren, Xu Miao, and Xu Ying, *Mao Zedong xiangzhang wushi nian* [Fifty Years of Mao Zedong Badges], Xi'an: Shaanxi lüyou chubanshe, 1993, 12. The best overview regarding the production of Mao badges in the PLA is Ma Jingjun, *Jundui Mao Zedong xiangzhang de shouzang yu jianshang* [The Collection and Appreciation of PLA Mao Zedong Badges], Beijing: Beijing shouzangjia xiehui, 2008.

[50] "Mao zhuxi xiangzhang shengchan, faxing bufen diqu zuotanhui xiaojie" [Short Summary of a Discussion on the Production and Distribution of Chairman Mao Badges in Some Regions], 11 August 1967, HPA 957-6-5.

[51] Hebei sheng shangyeting/Hebei sheng erqingting, "Guanyu Mao zhuxi xiangzhang lianhe diaocha baogao" [Combined Investigation Report on Chairman Mao Badges], 31 December 1967, HPA 957-5-23.

[52] "Dangdai Zhongguo de Beijing" bianjibu (ed.), *Dangdai Beijing dashiji* [Record of Major Events in Contemporary Beijing], Beijing: Dangdai Zhongguo chubanshe, 2003, 237.

[53] Zhonghua renmin gongheguo di er qing gongyebu wenjian, "Guanyu wo bu yu Zhongguo geming bowuguan zhengji quanguo Mao zhuxi xiangzhang zuowei chuguo zhanlan, geming wenwu de tongzhi"[Instruction Regarding the Collection of Chairman Mao Badges from all over the Country through the Second Light Industry Department and the Museum of the Chinese Revolution for the Purpose of International Exhibitions and Collection as Revolutionary Artefacts], 8 September 1967, HPA 957-5-23.

badges and Mao works through mobile sales personnel or PLA soldiers were accordingly stepped up. By early 1968, to wear or not wear a badge had become a question of loyalty as well. Many cities thus had to establish specific offices for dealing with the requests of local factories to manufacture sufficient badges.[54] As a larger size of the badges came to be associated with greater loyalty to the CCP Chairman, aluminum, plastic, and porcelain badges with a diameter of 30 centimeters and greater came to be produced. Smaller badges in some cases were even retracted and used to produce larger ones.

The enormous demand led to a substantial reallocation of resources, mainly aluminum, into the production of badges. Zhou Enlai in March 1969 would heavily criticize this waste of resources.[55] The question of how to carry the badges to prove one's loyalty was another topic of frequent discussion. The common pattern was to wear the badges on the left side, slightly above the heart. But a number of rural residents took pride in displaying their loyalty to the Chairman by attaching the badges directly to their skin.[56] The cult products and their specific utilizations thus became part of an entangled web of symbols aimed at demonstrating revolutionary conviction.

In addition to the manufacturing of cult commodities, the construction of monuments to honor the CCP Chairman, to celebrate the successes of the Cultural Revolution, and to strengthen the power of the revolutionary committees resumed on an infinitely larger scale in 1968.[57] While in the countryside shrines had been the dominant monuments, in many of China's cities, the second half of 1968 was filled with plans about constructing "Long Live the Victory of Mao Zedong Thought Halls" (*Mao Zedong sixiang shengli wansui guan*). The idea had sparked from an exhibition of more than two hundred huge photos showing Mao during different stages of the communist revolution that had been on display in

---

[54] The Beijing Municipal Revolutionary Committee on 3 April 1968 established a special office in charge of the manufacturing of badges; see "Beijing gongyezhi" bianji weihui (ed.), *Beijing gongye zhi. Yinshua zhi* [Beijing Industry Gazetteer: Printing Gazetteer], Beijing: Zhongguo kexue jishu chubanshe, 2001, 25.

[55] Zhonggong wenxian yanjiushi (ed.), *Zhou Enlai nianpu* 3, 287f.

[56] Baishui xian (ed.), *Baishui xian zhi*, 459.

[57] The form of the monuments varied according to local customs. In Hami, a city in the autonomous region of Xinjiang located on the Silk Road, a Chairman Mao pagoda was erected, 14 by 14 meters in diameter and 19.75 meters high with colored Mao portraits on all sides. See Zhang Rengan, Yusufu Yunusi, and Lu Huaying (eds.), *Zhongguo gongchandang Hami shi (xian) lishi dashiji, 1949.10–1998.12* [Major Historical Events in the Hami City (County) CCP, October 1949–December 1998], Wulumuqi: Xinjiang renmin chubanshe, 1999, 278f.

the capital on National Day in 1967 with the consent of the CCP Center. Plans to copy the exhibition in different localities had already been harbored by many provincial governments in September 1967,[58] but only during the process of consolidating power in the autumn and winter of 1968 and 1969 did the construction plans become reality.[59]

The city of Handan in southern Hebei may serve as an example here. The construction of the exhibition hall started in mid-July 1968 after the Hebei Revolutionary Committee had announced that permanent exhibitions were to be established in the five largest cities of the province. The whole building area, which included the "Long Live Hall" itself, two minor exhibition halls, a huge square, and a Mao statue, was finished after only five months' work, on Mao's birthday in December 1968. The plans and layout for the new hall were impressive and incorporated a whole array of symbolic devices. The Long Live Hall itself was shaped so as to resemble the character "loyalty." It was the largest building in town by far and, along with the square, covered an area of 67,746 square meters.[60] The main entrance faced east, toward the rising sun. The Mao statue was based on the model of the Beijing Mining Institute and measured 12.26 meters high. All structures had been made of the best materials available. Under the premise of preserving the victory of Mao Zedong Thought for eternity, the hall had been built earthquake-proof and contained the highest standard of technical equipment. According to an estimate of the CCP Handan District Committee in 1982, the project – which one has to remember did not take place in the nation's capital but in a minor provincial city – cost the local government the enormous sum of 2.55 million yuan.[61] The invested amount of money and the actual worth of the building in terms of labor force and raw materials, however, according to the CCP report, differed greatly: "The actual costs for the building of the hall range between 4.2–4.3 million yuan. Yet, a large amount of manpower, resources, and technical expertise has been offered without compensation from the whole district ..., the government departments, the

---

[58] See Lin Li, "Suiyue de jianzheng. Sichuan sheng zhanlanguan ji Mao zhuxi suxiang xiujian shimo" [Witness of the Times: The Story of Building Sichuan Province Exhibition Center and the Chairman Mao Statue], in *Sichuan dang'an* 3 (2004), 25.

[59] The name derived from Lin Biao's inscription and led to the changing of earlier variants such as "Wishing Chairman Mao eternal life exhibition hall" in the case of Sichuan. See ibid., 25.

[60] Wu Guangtian, "'Wansui guan.' Yi zuo jianzhu yunhan de lishi" ["Long Live Hall": History Contained in a Piece of Architecture], in *Wenshi jinghua* 173.10 (2004), 34.

[61] Ibid., 36.

military, factories, universities, street committees, and rural production teams."[62]

The construction work could not have proceeded so quickly if it had not been supervised by the responsible departments. Yet most work units mobilized workers who would participate in the ongoing work for a few days without pay. Others simply joined on their own initiative. In Handan, an estimated 260,000 people took part in the construction work over a period of five months, not all of them helping out with construction work, though. Similar to when statues were being constructed on university campuses in mid-1967, propaganda troops would perform plays and songs to strengthen the work spirit, whereas others would look after the material well-being of the workers as a different expression of "offering loyalty" (*xian/biao zhong*).[63] Peasants joined with their horse-carts and transported "loyalty stones" (*zhongzi shi*) or "loyalty wood" (*zhongzi mu*) to the construction site. The building of the Long Live Halls was to result in nothing less than a physical "crystallization" of loyalty, as a report from Nanchang, the capital city of Jiangxi province, put it:

> At this place, every brick and every tile, every blade of grass and every tree, every picture and every landscape all radiate the glowing shine of loyalty; every window and every door, every room and every chamber, every step and every ledge are crystallizations of loyalty. To achieve this, the heart has to think of loyalty, the energy has to be employed for loyalty, the sweat has to flow for loyalty, the blood has to surge for loyalty, [while] striding the path of loyalty, creating deeds of loyalty, and climbing the high peak of loyalty. The people gather under the sign of loyalty, they fight under the sign of loyalty, and march forward under the sign of loyalty.[64]

In the end, none of the Long Live Halls was supplied with complimentary sets of the photo exhibition, as Mao had personally come to intervene against its distribution. Most exhibition halls thus had to put on display in the huge building spaces replicas and presents "offered" by different groups for celebrations of the establishment of the Long Live Halls.

This second wave of materializing the gains of the Cultural Revolution through creating monuments of victory differed in several important

---

[62] Ibid., 36.

[63] "Mao Zedong shengli wansui" guan Jiangxi sheng choujian weiyuanhui bangongshi (ed.), *Huoxue huoyong Mao Zedong sixiang jingyan jiaoliuhui dianxiang cailiao* [Exemplary Materials of the Lively Study and Application of Mao Zedong Thought Experience Exchange Meeting], 5 November 1968.

[64] "Zhongyu Mao zhuxi hongxin de jiepin" [The Crystallization of a Red Heart Loyal to Chairman Mao], in *Xin Nanchang bao*, 30 September 1968, 1.

aspects from the Red Guard phase of building Mao statues. The Red Guards had not been able to command similar resources as the revolutionary committees. Mao Zedong statues had so far by and large been confined to university campuses. In late 1968, in nearly every locality, at least one Mao statue was built after careful examination of different models. The Chengdu Long Live Hall Preparatory Group visited no less than twenty-two statues and exhibitions[65] before it decided on plans for its specific statue in front of the Long Live Hall. According to still incomplete statistics from the Tianjin Municipal Departments of Finance, Industry, and Culture, by early 1969 a total of 970 huge Mao statues had been built in the Tianjin area alone, some of them despite previous orders to prevent "phenomena of thriftlessness."[66] A branch of the Tianjin Steel Plant had even demolished six of its production sites to make room for its statue. Other units without sufficient practical knowledge of how to build a statue had resorted to "inviting guests and offering presents, [securing] advantages through illegal measures, and [relying] on personal connections."[67] The exchange of cult commodities and symbols was part of a complex web of power relations, as was exemplified by the most bizarre instance of Cultural Revolutionary worship, the veneration of mangos in late 1968.

MANGO WORSHIP

Despite the promises of achieving unity by relying on revolutionary committees, the struggles between different factions had not subsided by mid-1968. The fights were especially violent in Guangxi[68] and the northwestern provinces, including Shaanxi. This prompted the CCP Center to issue two central documents in July 1968 that criticized the present state in unusually sharp words and called for an immediate end to all armed hostilities. In the capital, meanwhile, Mao Zedong experimented with the formation of "Worker Peasant [Soldier] Mao Zedong Thought Propaganda Teams" (*gong nong [bing] Mao Zedong sixiang xuanchuan dui*), made up primarily of workers and activists from model factories such as the Beijing General Knitting Mill. These teams were to enter those units

---

[65] Lin Li, "Suiyue de jianzheng. Sichuan sheng zhanlanguan ji Mao zhuxi suxiang xiujian shimo (xu)" [Witness of the Times: The Story of Building Sichuan Province Exhibition Center and the Chairman Mao Statue (Continued)], in *Sichuan dang'an* 4 (2004), 44.

[66] Tianjin shi geming weiyuanhui, "Jin'ge [69] 082," 2.

[67] Ibid., 2.

[68] See Zheng Yi, *Hongse jinian bei* [Scarlet Memorial], Taibei: Huashi wenhua gongsi, 1993.

that were still conducting armed struggle. The first of Mao's trial spots was Qinghua University, where members of the Jinggangshan Regiment and the "April 14th" factions had been fighting without cessation for roughly three months. The propaganda team, made up of some thirty thousand members who had been assembled the night before in the Beijing New China Printing Factory, entered the campus of Qinghua University on 27 July rather poorly prepared, carrying Mao pictures and ordering a ceasefire.[69] Only after heavy resistance of the Jinggangshan Regiment under Kuai Dafu, who was unaware of the fact that Mao had given the order himself, did the propaganda team win over the campus. At the end of the day, five team members had been killed and 731 had been wounded by grenades, bottles, and stones that had been hurled at them by the remaining Red Guards.[70] The following night, Mao received the five main student leaders in the Great Hall of the People and declared that he himself had been the "black hand"[71] behind the dispatching of the propaganda team and thus ended the already waning importance of the Red Guards, most of whom would be sent down to the countryside by the end of the year.

Mao's endorsement of the propaganda team's actions was further substantiated symbolically by presenting its members with a couple of mangos that had been a gift of the Pakistani foreign minister, Mian Arshad Hussain. Mao had given the roughly four dozen mangos to his security chief Wang Dongxing, who with Mao's consent had sent the fruit to Qinghua University as a sign of Mao's appreciation for the propaganda team's efforts. For the team members and students, the mangos were the first tangible objects they had received from Mao. Many of them had seen Chairman Mao in person either during the 1966 mass receptions or during one of the activist meetings, but very few had received items actually presented by Mao, which thus endowed the gifts with a completely different aura.

The mangos were first draped on a table covered with red cloth at Qinghua University. According to a *People's Daily* report, workers were quoted uttering near-biblical rhetoric upon actually seeing the fruit: "These are not simple mangos, they are rain and dew; they are the

---

[69] Mao's personal physician, Li Zhisui, was part of the team as well. For his tragicomic account, see Li and Thurston, *Private Life*, 499–503.

[70] Tang, *Yi ye zhi qiu*, 31.

[71] Mao Zedong, "Zhaojiang shoudu hongdaihui 'wu da lingxiu' shi de tanhua" [Conversation upon Calling the "Five Great Leaders" of the Capital Red Guard Congress], 28 July 1968, in CRDB.

sunshine."[72] The fruit was shared among the institutions that had been part of the propaganda team and was carried in processions to the respective work units, where great ceremonies were held to greet the arrival of the "precious gift" (*zhengui lipin*), the mangos. Li Zhisui reports the difficulty in preserving the mango at Beijing General Knitting Mill. It was covered in wax to keep it from decomposing and placed on a shrine in the factory auditorium, where everyone could pay his or her respects. Later, however, the mango started to rot and had to be replaced by a facsimile.[73]

The demand for the mangos as tokens of Mao's appreciation grew exorbitantly. Requests for receiving one of the mangos were sent along with congratulatory notes to the propaganda team units and the Beijing Municipal Revolutionary Committee. Provincial organizations with good connections to counterparts in the capital possessing more than one mango were lucky to receive an original. But quickly replicas produced in the name of the Beijing Municipal Revolutionary Committee came to replace the rotting fruits and provided a reservoir for those provinces that otherwise would have received none. After manufacturing a series of official replicas in glass caskets, the mangos were sent to the different provinces starting in mid-September (see Illustration 10). On 19 September 1968, a half-million people greeted the arrival of the mango replicas in Chengdu[74]; two days later, a replica reached Nanchang in Jiangxi province[75]; and on 22 September, the first plastic mangos reached Chongqing municipality. The same day at 12:31 P.M., a special train delivered a mango to Guiyang, the provincial capital of Guizhou province. On 28 September, finally, the *Yunnan Daily* reported on a welcoming crowd of one hundred thousand to celebrate the arrival of a mango replica in the provincial capital of Kunming. The symbolic power provided by the possession of the mango was exemplified by the attendance of high-level officials of the revolutionary committees while welcoming the gift from Beijing. In Guiyang, Li Zaihan, head of the Guizhou Revolutionary Committee, took charge of

---

"Keke mangguo enqing shen – Xinxin xiangzhi hongtaiyang. Mao zhuxi zengsong zhengui liwu de teda xixun zhuankai yihou" [Every Mango Is Full of Deep Kindness – Every Heart Longs for the Red Sun: The Time after the Incredibly Happy News Had Spread that Chairman Mao Offered a Precious Gift], in *Renmin ribao*, 8 August 1968, 3.

[73] Li and Thurston, *Private Life*, 503.

[74] Sichuan shengwei xuanchuanbu (ed.), *Sichuan xuanchuan gongzuo dashiji* [Records of Major Events in Sichuan Propaganda Work], Chengdu: Sichuan renmin chubanshe, 2003, 64. See further the pictures of the arrival of the mangos reprinted in *Sichuan ribao*, 20 September 1968, 4.

[75] *Xin Nanchang ribao*, 21 September 1968.

ILLUSTRATION 10. Returning from the National Day celebration in Beijing, Heilongjiang's revolutionary committee delegation is greeted at Harbin's railway station with gifts of wax mangos, Harbin, Heilongjiang province, 14 October 1968. Li Zhensheng. (Contact Press Images.)

the mango himself. Standing in the back of a pickup truck, he championed the mango casket the whole way from the train station to the revolutionary committee's headquarters. Since the streets were crowded by some two hundred thousand people, the drive lasted for several hours.[76]

By bestowing the Qinghua propaganda team with the mangos as a token of his appreciation, Mao Zedong provided them with considerable symbolic capital. This capital did not cease upon the redistribution of the fruit to various local-level units or upon the replication of the originals with plastic mangos. Even until early 1969, participants of Mao Zedong Thought study classes in the capital would return with mass-reproduced mango facsimiles and still gain media attention in the provinces.[77] Greeting this immediate symbol of appreciation from Mao Zedong with utmost reverence provided local units or revolutionary committees with a fairly uncontestable instance

[76] "Shoudu gongren jieji ba Mao zhuxi zeng de zhengui liwu zhuan songgei wo sheng gongren jieji he quan sheng geming renmin" [The Capital Working Class Has Offered the Precious Gift Presented by Chairman Mao Especially for the Working Class of Our Province and All Revolutionary People in the Whole Province], in *Xin Guizhou bao*, 24 September 1968, 1.

[77] See *Sichuan ribao*, 1 February 1969.

of displaying loyalty, since cherishing the CCP Chairman's mangos did not entail burdensome political choices. By partaking in the aura of this "precious gift," lower-level officials tried to maximize their own profit by presenting themselves as the staunchest defenders of Mao Zedong Thought and beneficiaries of the CCP Chairman's trust. Probably most astonished about the episode of mango worship was the Pakistani government, which had presented Mao with the gift and interpreted the incredible importance attached to the fruit as an outstanding foreign policy success. To build on the unique opportunity presented by the mango appreciation, Pakistan on 31 August 1968 endowed the Chinese government with a varied selection of one hundred different kinds of mangos and one hundred mango seedlings. Yet without the CCP Chairman's immediate intervention and redeployment of the gift for domestic politics, the media echo regarding this token of Chinese–Pakistan friendship remained marginal.[78]

The episode of worshipping mangos represents the most bewildering example of reevaluating symbols of power during the Cultural Revolution. The mangos served multiple functions in a complex web based on personal favors, obligations, and loyalties.[79] The fact that commodities such as badges or mango replicas could take on lives of their own and function in ways never intended by the CCP leadership was due to a fundamental erosion of the communist political system. Formal bureaucratic routines had been bypassed and superseded through charismatic relationships between the CCP Center and the provinces. Although these developments had already been inherent in the Leninist party system prior to the Cultural Revolution, now the consequences of this utmost political and personal insecurity came to the fore. Not only were the policies, or, in case of the mangos, the symbols of certain patrons championed by the lower ranks to display allegiance and loyalty, all types of local units sent gifts to Beijing as well. The CCP Center had had to cope with these phenomena before, especially during the Great Leap Forward, and had called for a cancellation of such practices. The CCRG had renewed these restrictions in late 1967,[80] but the guidelines proved to be insufficient to curb the massive

---

[78] "Ba zhengfu xiang wo guo zhengfu zengsong mangguo he mangguo shumiao" [The Government of Pakistan Has Presented Our Government with Mangos and Mango Seedlings], in *Renmin ribao*, 8 September 1968, 6.

[79] See as well Michael Dutton, "Mango Mao: Infections of the Sacred," in *Public Culture* 16.2 (2004), 161–87.

[80] For example, "Zhongfa [67] 360, Zhongyang wenhua geming xiaozu guanyu bu yao gei zhongyang wenhua geming xiaozu song li de tongzhi" [CCRG Notice on Not Sending Presents to the CCRG], 28 November 1967, in CRDB.

inflow of gifts on National Day in 1968. In most cases, the presents consisted of homegrown fruit or other agricultural products, but there were also several new "inventions," and Guizhou province under the leadership of Li Zaihan turned out to be especially creative. The Guizhou Revolutionary Committee opted for presenting Mao with a highly expensive object, a tiny X-ray machine presented in a silver box with the inscription "always loyal to Chairman Mao."[81] Peasants from Guizhou, on the other hand, were reported to send "loyalty pigs" – that is, pigs with a shaven "loyalty" character on the forehead – to the CCP Center.[82]

These excesses of public veneration underscored Mao's perception that the cult no longer served the intended function of providing him with an immediate and nonbureaucratic link to the revolutionary masses. Popular reaction had turned into a bewildering array of quasireligious worship, loyalty performances, and cult-symbol exchanges that resisted top-down control. Although the rituals and cult commodities had been the consequence of or reactions to the disciplinary measures enacted through PLA military supervision and study classes, they had come to serve a plethora of functions independent of the aims of the CCP Center. After the successful formation of the last revolutionary committees on 5 September, the rhetoric of worship in the *People's Daily* was drastically reduced. Certain phrases such as "boundless worship" or "supreme instructions" vanished completely from official discourse, while general references to the "lively study and application" continued until Lin Biao's fall in 1971.

The diminution of rhetorical veneration had been made possible after Mao Zedong at the Central Caucus on 25 September had approved of dropping a slogan in praise of the CCRG during the preparations of National Day celebrations.[83] Previously, Mao had deleted a number of flattering references from draft articles but not on matters of equal importance. Zhou Enlai, well versed in interpreting Mao's general mood, during a central propaganda conference carefully advised leading media personnel to tone down the cult. A member of the military command in charge of the Xinhua News Agency remarked to Zhou that Xinhua, in a nonspecified newspaper report, had failed to mention the sending of a congratulatory telegram to Mao Zedong; he felt that this might have unintentionally offended the Chairman, being

---

[81] See the photographs in *Xin Guizhou bao*, 27 September 1968.
[82] Corresponding local newspaper reports are mentioned in Cheng Shi, Wang Xiaoling, and Kai Zheng, *Wenge xiaoliaoji* [Cultural Revolutionary Laughing Matters], Chengdu: Xi'nan caijing daxue chubanshe, 1988, 18. I have, however, been unable to trace these reports in contemporary newspapers.
[83] Zhonggong wenxian yanjiushi (ed.), *Zhou Enlai nianpu* 3, 260.

misinterpreted as insufficiently expressing the boundless love of the masses. Zhou responded: "At present, congratulatory telegrams are sent to the Chairman for all kinds of important and unimportant issues. This unhealthy tendency should be terminated."[84] Zhou further advised the media staff to pay more attention to content rather than form. He even praised a few reporters from capitalist news media, who, against the general capitalist trend of "making a living from selling rumors," tried to stick to the facts. Zhou therefore advised the editors: "Our communist newspapers should proceed accordingly."[85] Although the popular cult thus continued unabated into 1969 and well beyond, the tide began to turn at the apex of the CCP, and Lin Biao, as the most prominent public supporter of the cult, was soon heading for trouble.

[84] Ibid., 261.
[85] Ibid., 260.

10

Curbing the Cult

Criticism of the inventions and miracles of the cult had occasionally been voiced prior to the convention of the Ninth Party Congress in April 1969, as seen in the case of criticizing the quotation gymnastics or certain phrases. Yet the task of toning down the cult remained highly sensitive. The official image of the CCP Chairman was not to be tarnished, nor was criticism of the cult to reflect negatively on the previous course of the Cultural Revolution. According to the CCP constitution, national party congresses were to be held every five years. The convention of the CCP's Ninth Congress in 1969 was thus eight years overdue. The congress took place in utmost secrecy. The delegates were flown in on special air force planes to the military part of Beijing airport in the city's western suburbs and were secluded from the public in three of the capital's hotels without permission to contact the outside world.[1] There had been no prior announcement and the public was informed about the congress only after the opening ceremony on 1 April 1969. Although the portraits of the founding fathers of Marxism-Leninism were prominently on display in the hall's lobby, a monumental picture of Mao Zedong dominated the venue and it was Mao's physical presence that excited many of the newly chosen delegates. Mao's short opening speech was interrupted by cheers after every sentence. Lin Biao presented the political report as wished for by Mao but he had not taken part in Zhang Chunqiao's preparation of the final draft. Jiang Qing was therefore later to criticize Lin for the poor presentation of the report and the stuttering pronunciation, both of

---

[1] See Chi Zehou, "Zhonggong 'Jiu da' neimu suoyi" [Random Memories of the Background to the "Ninth Party Congress"], in *Yanhuang chunqiu* 3 (2003), 42.

which were largely due to the text being completely unfamiliar to him.[2] The congress passed a new party constitution that included Lin Biao's status as Mao's successor and chose a new Central Committee.

The cult was not a subject of official discussions but nevertheless omnipresent. In many small groups, Mao Zedong Thought activists retold their experiences of praising the CCP Chairman. While casting votes on 24 April, a young delegate took advantage of the situation, jumped on the podium, and shook hands with Mao, Zhou, and Lin. Others quickly followed, taking the once-in-a-lifetime opportunity of actually touching Chairman Mao. Only after bodyguards had emerged from behind the curtains and formed a human *cordon sanitaire* in front of the podium could the formal voting procedure be continued.[3] A safer option of getting in touch with cult objects was the collection of Mao or Lin memorabilia. As the organizing committee had emphasized the frugal character of the congress and had not supplied the delegates with any badges or other presents, as soon as the congress was declared to be over and the party leadership had withdrawn from the stage, all items movable from the congress presidium, including cups, pencils, and draft papers, were quickly snatched as trophies.

A week before the congress, Zhou Enlai had heavily criticized the spending of enormous amounts of money and the waste of precious resources to produce badges.[4] He had advocated that city dwellers should share their own collections with the rural populace. Indeed, a kind of charity campaign to donate badges and extra copies of the *Selected Works of Mao Tse-tung* to poor peasants in barren mountain regions was conducted soon afterward.[5] Although Zhou was mainly concerned about the economic losses engendered by the rampant worship, the CCRG core members were much more unsettled by the unauthorized usage of the cult's symbolic power. In an enlarged meeting of the Ninth Congress Presidium on 16 April at 1 A.M., Central Caucus members discussed the organization of cultural activities for the delegates in the evenings. After pointing out various inappropriate films and operas, Kang Sheng brought up the topic of recent forms of worship. This time it was not the quotation gymnastics, which had enraged Jiang Qing the year before, but the omnipresent loyalty dance that came to be intensely criticized. The unusual

---

[2] Jin, *Culture of Power*, 118.

[3] Chi, "Jiu da," 46.

[4] Zhonggong wenxian yanjiushi (ed.), *Zhou Enlai nianpu* 3, 287.

[5] See, for example, Tianjin shi geming weiyuanhui, "Jin'ge [69] 073, Guanyu xiang shanqu pin xiazhong nong xianzeng Mao zhuxi yulu he xiangzhang de tongzhi" [Notice Concerning the Offering of Chairman Mao Quotations and Badges for Poor and Lower-Middle Peasants in Mountainous Regions], April 1969, 1.

frankness and detail of the document merit an extended translation of the original:

> **Revered Kang:** At present, the loyalty dance is being danced everywhere. It is something completely normal. They say it is loyal to Chairman Mao but in reality it is opposing Chairman Mao. In the streets of Beijing the loyalty dance is also being danced. They say it is loyal to Jiang Qing; in reality, it is opposing Jiang Qing. It is even said that there are instructors who teach it. Comrades, consider for a while what kind of problem this is. Is this loyal to Chairman Mao? This is opposing Chairman Mao! Some comrades who have witnessed such phenomena did not dare to bring up the topic, afraid of being accused of opposing Chairman Mao.
>
> **Premier:** In some places, private homes have been demolished to build exhibition halls.
>
> **Revered Kang:** At present, everywhere private homes are demolished to construct some kind of exhibition hall and to construct Mao statues. The Center has repeatedly issued instructions but they don't listen. This equals opposition to the Center. This is aimed at amassing personal political capital. What does it have to do with reverence or love for Chairman Mao? It is completely aimed at amassing personal political capital. The loyalty dance vulgarizes politics. It is opposing Marxism-Leninism. Loyal to whom? It is loyal to Liu Shaoqi. Loyal to whom? A few comrades place the character "selfishness" at the fore. Not to pay attention to it made them fear that people would say they are opposing Chairman Mao but this is simply disloyalty. If the Center calls not to do it and you still do it, isn't that opposing Chairman Mao?
>
> **Jiang Qing:** Thirty years ago, the Chairman strictly opposed the celebration of birthdays, the sending of gifts, to name [things after him], and strictly opposed that some artworks [should be] written [in his honor]. I have always adhered to Chairman Mao. The present loyalty dance has been completely stripped of class content. It is loyal to whom?
>
> **Revered Kang:** There further exists loyalize this, loyalize that; wasting the nation's wealth. This is loyal to oneself, giving oneself political capital.
>
> **Yao Wenyuan:** The masses say: Determining loyalty by looking at action.
>
> **Revered Kang:** Let the masses get to know the Center's directives and the masses will definitely agree.
>
> **Jiang Qing:** Some demolished a large number of private homes; doesn't that mean they placed the blame on the Chairman?
>
> **Revered Kang:** We daily propagate that we oppose multiple centers but these kinds of things are not being reported.
>
> **[Zhang] Chunqiao:** In the past, Liu and Deng used the restriction on printing Chairman Mao's works to oppose Chairman Mao. Now one uses these kinds of methods to oppose Chairman Mao.
>
> **Revered Kang:** I heard that some delegates danced the loyalty dance beside the Chairman: Doesn't that mean throwing mud in our faces? It is a kind of protest against the Center!

Premier: Please all of you investigate these things, including the comrades from Beijing. Where it has already been conducted, restrict it. Clarify these things yourselves first and then report to the Center. A few performances solely display enthusiasm and fanatically boast [Mao Zedong Thought] but completely lack rhythm.[6]

The document is among the most fascinating evidence on the non–centrally directed nature of many forms of the Mao cult during its high tide in 1967–68. The rituals of worship that had primarily been shaped by the PLA experiences of emotional bonding had secured the primacy of form over content. The securing of "political" or rather symbolic capital by staging performances of loyalty to Mao Zedong enraged some of the seasoned party veterans since it rendered their accustomed monopoly of interpreting Mao Zedong Thought defunct. The straightforward arrogance of power matter-of-factly expressed by Kang Sheng represents the reality of how leading party officials understood the workings of the "mass line."

The main reasons that the cult could be cooled down after the Ninth Congress were twofold: it had served its mobilizing function and after having installed new power structures, the necessary bureaucratic means existed to replace the cohesive powers that had been a crucial device to legitimize the presence of the military "three supports" personnel. The new members of the Central Committee and the revolutionary committees alike had been chosen on the grounds of their political reliability and loyalty to Mao. Given the formation of new political bodies at all levels of society based on personal loyalty, the extraconstitutional mobilization of certain strata against the former party establishment through instigating personal worship was no longer necessary. Furthermore, the already overstretched integrative powers of the cult had clearly resulted in adverse trends. The impact of the quotation wars and the sometimes quasireligious outward displays of worship had heavily tarnished the claims of Mao Zedong Thought to represent a scientific theory and not a faith-based dogma. Two months after the convention of the Ninth Congress, the CCP Center issued a central document that was to curb the most rampant forms of worship. The document was not directed against the cult as such; it aimed rather at interdicting "formalistic" activities and at regaining the interpretative monopoly of defining the content of Mao's image in public. The short document listed seven topics, without adding further explanations:

[6] "Mao zhuxi zai Zhongguo gongchandang di jiuci quanguo daibiao dahui shang de zhongyao zhishi" [Important Instruction of Chairman Mao at the Ninth CCP Congress], n.p.: 1969, 28. Thanks to Michael Schoenhals for sharing this source.

1. Leading personnel at all levels should positively guide the masses in the study of Mao Zedong Thought, to successfully proceed with thought-revolutionization, to achieve actual results, and not to pursue formal aspects only.
2. Repeating the Center's "Directive on the problem of constructing Chairman Mao statues" of 13 July 1967: From today on, modeling images of the Chairman has to be conducted strictly in accordance with this directive.
3. Unless authorized by the Center, there should be no more manufacturing of Mao badges.
4. Newspapers should no longer place Chairman Mao's image regularly in their headlines.
5. Chairman Mao's image should not be printed on every kind of commodity and wrapping; the usage of Chairman Mao's quotations should be handled accordingly. It is forbidden to print Mao's image on porcelain wares.
6. "Loyalty" has a class character and should not be attached indiscriminatingly to anything. There should be no "loyalty-fication" campaigns and no feudalistic style architecture should be erected. Where such things have been done in the past, they should be dealt with in appropriate fashion.
7. There should be no formalistic activities like "asking for instructions in the morning and reporting back in the evening," readings of quotations before having lunch, or salutes toward the Chairman's portrait.[7]

The circular presents the most detailed criticism of the ritualistic cult forms the CCP was to produce. Both the commodification and sacralization of Mao Zedong, although the latter term was not explicitly mentioned, were interdicted. Instead, the CCP Center tried to regain political control over its most important brand symbol.

Unlike back in 1956, the document completely failed to provide reasons for the development of the cult, let alone investigate possible consequences in terms of policy lines or constitutional amendments. Mao's changed stand on the public displays of worship had consequences on the party's internal communication as well. The issuing of the directive on curbing the formalistic cult was a first step in enabling the building of cases against those who had "distorted" the true meanings of Mao Zedong Thought for personal motives. A year later, the Second Plenum of the Ninth Congress

---

[7] Zhonggong wenxian yanjiushi (ed.), *Mao wengao* 13, 50.

was convened on Mount Lushan. Here the question of how Mao's "genius" was to be referred to or possibly instrumentalized culminated in a sequence of events that were to have drastic consequences for both the goals of the Cultural Revolution and the credibility of the cult.

GENIUS LOCI: THE SECOND LUSHAN PLENUM

The Second Plenum in August and September 1970 is one of the most controversial episodes of the Cultural Revolution. It has incited great scholarly and public attention as it is commonly interpreted as the first clearly discernible sign of a rupture between Mao and Lin Biao. The plenum was to discuss a revised state constitution to be adopted by the Fourth National People's Congress later that year. It was the issue of whether or not to abolish the office of state chairman (*guojia zhuxi*), who was to act as formal state representative and symbolic figurehead, as Liu Shaoqi had done since 1959, that provoked a major confrontation between the PLA and the CCRG members. The military had massively enlarged its influence by staffing the majority of the local and provincial revolutionary committees. The leading personnel of all major army branches had furthermore been selected according to their immediate loyalty to Lin Biao. The influence of the radical theoreticians around Jiang Qing had been waning after the CCRG had by and large been disbanded on 12 September 1969.[8] Nevertheless, the remaining core of Jiang Qing, Zhang Chunqiao, and Yao Wenyuan retained extraconstitutional power through their backing by Mao. The fragile working relationship between both groups had been strained by a number of personal grievances and diverse family feuds.[9]

The first sign of Mao's growing discomfort with the military's dominance had been the issuing of the "Vice-Chairman Lin's First Directive" through Chief-of-Staff Huang Yongsheng on 17 October 1969. The expounding of the leader cult had by late 1969 been clearly superseded by the spreading of war scares and the imminent threat posed by a Soviet attack. Mao was enraged by the passing of a directive that basically set the whole Chinese military apparatus on alert without his prior consent, although Huang probably acted upon the assumption that Mao had been informed. The feeling of having been left out of the loop of information did

[8] See MacFarquhar and Schoenhals, *Mao's Last Revolution*, 297.
[9] On the role of families in Chinese elite politics during the Cultural Revolution, see especially Jin, *Culture of Power*, Chapter 6.

not rest lightly with Mao. The de facto power wielded by Lin Biao and his loyal followers probably strengthened the perceived necessity to counterbalance the military stronghold through a reestablishment of the civilian party organization and the elevation of military cadres on whose loyalty he could count.

The issue of whether or not to abolish the position of state chairman had been placed on the agenda when Mao's security chief, Wang Dongxing, on 8 March 1970 relayed Mao's views on the subject to the reestablished Politburo. As head of the CCP General Office in charge of the CCP's paper flow, Wang was usually extraordinarily well informed about Mao's present mood. Mao, who was resting in Wuhan at the time, had reacted upon a written request of Zhou Enlai on how to proceed with the section on the office of the state chairman during the revision of the state constitution. According to Wang Dongxing's memoirs and the conventional CCP evaluation of the events, Wang informed the Politburo about Mao's objections to establishing the office and especially to assuming the office himself.[10] Wang's report is crucial for the unfolding of the following events, given Mao's unwillingness to discuss the matter further and the fact that Lin's later insistence that Mao should assume the office would have been a fundamental alteration of Lin's previously displayed behavior of remaining closely in step with all of the CCP Chairman's directives. The episode has been explained by the CCP as being part of a plot of Lin Biao to strengthen his position against possible contenders after Mao's death. In the past decade, however, a number of accounts have contested this version of the events and explained Lin's situation as a culmination of the political culture fostered by Lin's habit of trying to flatter the Chairman within an increasingly unpredictable environment: "Lin Biao's essential tragedy was that he found himself at the center of a totalizing political system at its most extreme, where pervasive politics allowed no honorable exit."[11]

The reasons that Lin would press the issue that Mao should assume the position of state chairman are not satisfyingly explained unless one takes into account the possibility that, as often occurs in Chinese memoirs, observers have distorted historical events not by forgery but through strategic omissions. There seems to be no dissent that Mao's denial to

---

[10] Wang Dongxing, *Mao Zedong yu Lin Biao fangeming jituan de douzheng* [The Struggle between Mao Zedong and the Counterrevolutionary Lin Biao Clique], Beijing: Dangdai Zhongguo chubanshe, 2004 [1997], 19f.

[11] Teiwes and Sun, *Tragedy of Lin Biao*, 167.

assume the office was channeled through Wang Dongxing, but according to the memoirs of air force head Wu Faxian, that was only half of the message. Wu claims that the second part of the message consisted of an offer that Lin Biao should assume the vacant position, which Wang not only relayed to the Politburo but also repeated again during a meeting held the same evening with Lin Biao's entourage.[12] If Wu's version of the events is to be trusted, then Lin's insistence that Mao should assume the office and not Lin himself, who hated representative functions more than anything else, becomes understandable. Yet it brings into question Mao's motives in advancing the issue. The account of Wu's daughter Jin Qiu mentions that in late April 1970 Mao's secretary, Xu Yefu, called Lin's office and proposed that Dong Biwu, the last remaining founding member of the CCP besides Mao, should assume the office along with several younger vice-chairmen who would of course be potential successors and thus a threat to Lin's authority. Being highly dissatisfied with the Lin family's nepotism and especially the airs put on by Lin's son Lin Liguo and a small group of supporters in the air force, Mao advised Lin to name a successor as well and dropped the name Zhang Chunqiao. Roderick MacFarquhar and Michael Schoenhals have therefore advanced the interpretation that Mao probably tried to entrap Lin by showing his ambition to take on the position and thus to topple the military's dominance.[13] Lin's constant denial to accept the offered title himself, however, forced Mao to look for a different opportunity to discredit his "closest comrade-in-arms."

The issue of establishing the office of state chairman was not resolved until the convention of the Second Plenum. In the discussions of the small group entrusted with the preparation of the revised constitution, comprising Kang Sheng, Zhang Chunqiao, Chen Boda, Wu Faxian, navy chief Li Zuopeng, and alternate Politburo member Ji Dengkui, the only agreement on the issue of the state chairmanship was that no agreement could be reached. The question of whether Mao Zedong Thought should be written into the constitution as the country's guiding principle incited even more conflict. Given the omnipresent Mao cult of the preceding years, with its campaigns against anyone who had opposed Mao or his thought, as well as the example of the Eighth Congress during which the two references to Mao Zedong Thought in the party constitution had been deleted, the army generals and Chen Boda insisted on continuing to employ the phrase. Zhang Chunqiao and Kang Sheng, on the other

[12] Manuscript quoted in Jin, *Culture of Power*, 121.
[13] MacFarquhar and Schoenhals, *Mao's Last Revolution*, 326f.

hand, had noticed Mao's growing repugnance with the rhetoric of worship. During the Ninth Congress, Mao had dropped from the CCP constitution the "three adverbs" ("comprehensively," "creatively," and "with genius") commonly used in reference to his thought.

The cause for the clash at Lushan was provided by a remark of Zhang Chunqiao to Wu Faxian during a small group meeting on 13 August 1970. Zhang reportedly stated: "Some people mention Marxism and Mao Zedong Thought all the time but it does not mean that they are real Marxists. Someone claimed that [Mao] 'creatively' developed Marxism but even Khrushchev had 'creatively' developed Marxism."[14] Wu strongly objected to Zhang's views and later received Lin's backing as the criticism no doubt was directed against Lin Biao himself, who while not having invented the phrase had come to be regarded as the main exponent of this view due to the inclusion of the adverb in the foreword to the *Quotations*. Sparked by Zhang's remark, the question of how to describe Mao's genius therefore came to be a battleground for strengthening charismatic relationships with the respective leaders.

Ten days later, on 23 August 1970, the plenum officially opened. A few hours before the convention, the Politburo Standing Committee members met with Mao. Lin Biao used the opportunity to take up the issue of the quarrel between Zhang and Wu, probably both to gain Mao's support for the continued usage of the cult rhetoric and at the same time to shield his supporter Wu Faxian against criticism, thus fulfilling his part in the patron–client relationship. In his unprepared speech, Lin avoided the issue of state chairmanship by calling Mao "principal of the proletarian dictatorship" (*wuchanjieji yuanshou*)[15] instead, but defended the use of the adverbs "creatively, comprehensively, and with genius," as well as the mentioning of Mao Zedong Thought in the constitution, as he had always done in the preceding decade.

Encouraged by the high-level backing and the repeated listening to a recording of Lin's speech the following day, the different small groups, arranged according to administrative regions, took on the issue of Mao's "genius," which became a hotly debated topic. The criticism became especially lively, as it was recognized that the real target was Zhang

---

[14] Jin, *Culture of Power*, 122

[15] Lin Biao, "Zai Zhongguo gongchandang di jiu jie er zhong quanhui di yi ci quanti hui shang de jianghua (jielu)" [Speech at the First Full Assembly of the Second Plenum of the Ninth CCP Congress (Extract)], 23 August 1970, in CRDB. The authenticity of the source is not completely clear as most other works refer to the phrase "national principal" (*guojia zhi yuanshou*); compare MacFarquhar and Schoenhals, *Mao's Last Revolution*, 330.

Chunqiao, whom many cadres perceived as being co-responsible for the Cultural Revolution's violent excesses. Chen Boda and Wu Faxian, in their speeches before the North China Group and Southwestern Group, heavily quoted from Lin's foreword to the *Quotations* and drew on historical examples from the writings of the Marxist-Leninist canon mentioning the existence of "genius." Certain people were said to have taken advantage of Mao's modesty to "debase Mao Zedong Thought"[16] and to negate the existence of genius altogether. Even Wang Dongxing, the CCP Chairman's security chief, jumped the train and emphasized the support that the request to choose Mao as new head of state and Lin Biao as his deputy had enjoyed among the prestigious PLA unit 8341.[17]

The views of the North China Group found great support among the delegates, so Mao was faced with the choice of either accepting the office of state chairman, thus allowing for a potentially drastic wave of criticism against the former CCRG members, or negating the concept of genius and the whole personality cult on which Lin Biao's public reputation was founded. For the first time, Mao Zedong was faced with making a crucial decision on how to further handle his public cult and with it the acclaimed successes of the Cultural Revolution. Mao chose the second option. The loss of the former CCRG would have greatly diminished his extraconstitutional powers of favoring different factions to achieve his desired results. Yet a straightforward criticism of Lin Biao would have been impossible in 1970 given the public prestige the latter commanded. Instead, Mao chose Chen Boda, the weakest link in the Lin Biao entourage, as the target against whom he vented his anger. On 31 August, Mao circulated a personal letter entitled "Some Opinions of Mine" in which the "genius theoretician"[18] Chen Boda was attacked on highly vague grounds and with complete disregard for the long-standing services and the important role Mao's former secretary had played in the process of writing many essays that came to constitute the basis of Mao Zedong Thought.[19] Chen Boda's fall from grace and the following campaign to criticize him led to a further estrangement between Mao and Lin, who would withdraw from public life

---

[16] "Chen Boda zai Zhongguo gongchandang jiu jie er zhong quanhui Huabeizu de fayan" [Chen Boda's Speech at the Second Plenum of the Ninth CCP Congress North China Group Meeting], 24 August 1970, in CRDB.

[17] Wang, *Mao yu Lin*, 46f.

[18] Mao Zedong, "Wo de yi dian yijian" [Some Opinions of Mine], 31 August 1970, in CRDB.

[19] On historical relations between Mao and Chen, see Wylie, *Emergence of Maoism*, Chapters 3 and 4.

nearly completely in the following months, rejecting even to meet Edgar Snow during his visit in December 1970, when Mao Zedong publicly ridiculed the cult and its rhetoric for the first time, as mentioned in this book's introduction.

It was to take another year until Mao, during an inspection tour aimed at reestablishing his charismatic relationships with important local cadres in the civilian and military realm, hinted at a larger scheme behind the Lushan controversy. By claiming that Lin and his clique had engaged in an organized "surprise attack and underground activities"[20] aimed at splitting the party and usurping power, Mao attacked Lin Biao himself. Mao further ridiculed the cult rhetoric again:

> I have discussed the issue with Comrade Lin Biao that some of his formulations are not quite appropriate. ... [Phrases] like "peak" or "one sentence surpasses ten thousand sentences" have been used to excess. One sentence is just one sentence, how should it surpass ten thousand sentences! ... I have told them six times I would not serve as state chairman. One time probably equals one sentence that would make sixty thousand sentences. They still did not listen. It did not even surpass half a sentence, [its impact was] tantamount to zero.[21]

The growing disenchantment and Mao's announcement that upon his return Lin would have to shoulder some responsibility probably led a small group around Lin's son, Lin Liguo, to panic and consider assassinating Mao. None of the debated assassination plans was carried out, though. Instead, in a hectic escape, Lin Biao, probably against his will, along with his wife, son, and a few loyal attendants, boarded a plane in Beidaihe, where Lin had been curing his ailments. The plane crashed in the early morning hours of 13 September 1971 in the Mongolian steppe near Undur Khan, killing all nine passengers. The reasons for the crash have never been completely clarified, but technical problems and fuel shortage remain the most plausible explanations.[22]

For the credibility of the Cultural Revolution's agenda, the death of Mao's chosen successor was a fatal blow. The images of Mao and Lin Biao had become so closely intertwined that attempts to expose the alleged betrayal and coup attempt of Lin proved to be nearly inexplicable within the confines of the Cultural Revolutionary discourse. After all, every

---

[20] Mao Zedong, "Zai waidi xunshi qijian tong yantu gedi fuzeren tanhua jiyao" [Summary of Conversations with Local Leaders in Various Places along the Way during an Inspection Tour through the Provinces], August/September 1971, in CRDB.

[21] Ibid.

[22] Compare Jin, *Culture of Power*, 194f.

official publication since the outbreak of the Cultural Revolution and even the new party constitution had confirmed Lin Biao's status as the best student of Mao Zedong Thought and Mao's chosen successor. It took two years until Lin was openly criticized in the media. Up to that point, he was referred to as a "political swindler of the Liu Shaoqi–kind," thus setting him on the track to replace Mao's former public bête noire. Simultaneously, the CCP Center from 18 September 1971 onward issued a flood of internal documents to an ever-widening readership exposing the crimes committed by the "Lin-Chen anti-party clique." The fear of possible disturbances even led to the cancellation of National Day festivities in 1971 and the following years, an act without precedent in the history of the People's Republic. The documents compiled by a newly established Special Case Examination Group including Zhou Enlai, Kang Sheng, and eight other members of the CCP Center mainly focused on the alleged crimes committed during the Second Plenum and on Project 571, the alleged plan to assassinate Mao Zedong and stage a counterrevolutionary coup.[23] Only after the convention of the Tenth Party Congress in August 1973, during which Lin was publicly criticized, did the somewhat esoteric campaign to criticize Lin Biao and Confucius in early 1974 provide an attempt to explain the fall of Mao's former heir.

LINGERING POISON: CRITICIZING LIN BIAO AND CONFUCIUS

By the time of Lin Biao's fall, a functioning state and party bureaucracy had by and large been restored. The task of supervising the media now rested with the Central Propaganda Group, including Jiang Qing, Zhang Chunqiao, and Yao Wenyuan, which had been established shortly after the Second Plenum of the Ninth Congress. Although the radicals had been the victors in the destruction of Lin Biao's power base in the army, the task of criticizing Lin bore a considerable danger for them as well. If Lin was to be held accountable for the excesses of the Cultural Revolution, it would have to be interpreted as an "ultra-left" error in line and thus engender simultaneous criticism of the radicals as well. Thus a description of Lin's deviation as "left in form but right in essence"[24] was deemed to be the best circumscription. Zhou Enlai, as representative of the state apparatus, on

---

[23] See the translation in Michael Y. M. Kau (ed.), *The Lin Piao Affair: Power Politics and Military Coup*, White Plains, NY: International Arts and Science Press, 1975, 78–95.

[24] See MacFarquhar and Schoenhals, *Mao's Last Revolution*, 354f.

the other hand had an interest in labeling the excesses "ultra-left" to secure a refocusing on economic issues and the rehabilitation of old cadres. The designations used to circumscribe the line of the "political swindler" Lin therefore came to cause considerable confusion in the regulated party discourse until Mao settled the issue by defining the deviations to be "ultra-rightist."[25]

Given the personal stakes involved, the Central Propaganda Group in many respects proceeded along the traditional lines of the former Central Propaganda Department in dealing with the inexplicable betrayal of high-level party members, which can be summarized by three steps: first, carefully deleting references to the personae non gratae in the public media; second, clearing the material remains hinting at a prior existence of factionalism; and third, defining a new master-narrative to be expounded upon through heavy-rotation press campaigns and small group discussions, at the end of which open criticism in the media became possible again within a fundamentally changed discourse.

Lin Biao's name and pictures vanished from the official media in September 1971 and reappeared only with the convention of the Tenth Party Congress in late August 1973, which deleted his name from the party constitution, where it still had been prominently on display even two years after his death. Eradicating the material imprints of Lin Biao and his specific work style turned out to be more difficult than adopting new regulations for official speech. New morning gymnastics had been propagated by the State Council and the Central Military Commission on 31 August 1971, even before Lin's death. The "four good–five good" campaigns, the activist congresses, and the sharing of experience in application meetings were obviously forbidden by a central document in November 1971.[26] At the same time, copies of the party constitution and other collections of the Ninth Congress were to be "turned in to the central authorities for disposal."[27] Works about Lin Biao, epitaphs, and portraits had to be returned to the local authorities. The attempt to eradicate all visual references to Lin Biao was a major logistical undertaking. Few books published after 1966 did not at some point refer to Vice-Chairman Lin or carry his quotations and picture. Lin's inscriptions had been chiseled

---

[25] On the complex reversal and especially the relationship between Mao and Zhou, see Teiwes and Sun, *End of the Maoist Era*, 42–66.

[26] The only reference to the central document so far is to be found in Kau (ed.), *The Lin Piao Affair*, 76f. The designation as Zhongfa [1971] 64, however, is wrong, as this document refers to the establishment of the Special Case Examination Group against Lin.

[27] Kau (ed.), *The Lin Piao Affair*, 76.

into most Cultural Revolutionary monuments, exhibition halls, and the sockets of Mao statues alike. Art works or commodities carrying Lin's image ranged in the dozens of millions. The approach adopted by the authorities therefore aimed at minimizing economic losses by implanting a wide array of techniques, including "crossing out, washing, scraping off, plating, ripping out, cutting out, dyeing, gluing, exchanging, and painting."[28] Millions of Chinese thus set out to scrupulously wipe out the "Lin poison" (*Lin du*) from all written and visual documents. Whole books were crosschecked for references to Lin, meticulously blackening all characters hinting at his prior existence. Pictures showing Lin Biao alone could simply be ripped out, but those showing Mao and his former successor together could only be handled by marking a cross in the face of Lin Biao.

Given the enormous amount of commodities to be handled, some provinces still had items with Lin Biao's image for sale the following years or at least had them stockpiled in warehouses. According to statistics provided by the Liu'an County Department Store in Anhui province, it was discovered during an inventory in July 1973 that there were still 117 types of products bearing Lin Biao's handwriting, quotations, or picture, totaling 292,000 pieces.[29] Among them, 184,900 pieces could be "technically amended" (*jishu chuli*) and thus be resold, whereas the rest would have to be "dealt with accordingly." Similar successes were reported from Shanghai municipality, where naturally the variety of products imprinted with traces of the "hypocrite Lin" surpassed its provincial counterparts. The First Trade Department of Shanghai thus singled out 211 product types worth 7.08 million yuan that were in some way related to the former CCP vice-chairman.[30] The clearance, however, had not been conducted in all units so far:

> In a number of units there still exists insufficient knowledge about the importance of clearing the "Lin poison"; ... until today, there has been no cleansing [work] or it has been conducted in a very incomprehensive

[28] "Shangyebu zhuanfa Anhui sheng shangyeju 'guanyu chedi qingcha chuli you Lin Biao yihuo shouji, wenzi, tuhua de shangpin de tongzhi'" [Department of Commerce Transmits a Notice of the Anhui Provincial Commerce Department "On Thoroughly Cleansing and Handling Commodities Carrying Calligraphies, Characters, or Images of the Lin Biao Gang"], 10 July 1973, in Shangyebu caihuiju (ed.), *Shangye caiwu huiji wenjian huibian* [Collection of Commercial and Financial Documents], vol. 2, 1981, 1416.

[29] Ibid., 1415.

[30] "Guanyu Shanghai, Baoding deng di chuli you Lin Biao yihuo tici, shouji shangpin de qingkuang jianbao" [News Brief on the Situation of Handling Commodities Carrying Calligraphies and Writings of the Lin Biao Gang in Shanghai, Baoding, and other Places], in ibid., 1418.

fashion. Some units even take paper used to award prices with Lin Biao's
handwriting, enamel mugs, and other products for open sale; others
distribute picture frames carrying Lin's image ..., resulting in extremely
bad political influence among the masses.[31]

By August 1973, the removal of the linguistic and material remains of the
Lin-style Mao cult was perceived as having been conducted thoroughly
enough to allow for the reappearance of Lin's name in public discourse,
this time within a changed semantic context by replacing Liu Shaoqi as the
Cultural Revolution's primary object of negative integration.

The difficulties posed by categorizing Lin Biao as either "ultra-leftist" or
"ultra-rightist" had been overcome through Mao's favoring of the latter.
Yet there was little credible evidence to substantiate the claim itself besides
the fact of Lin's death, the discussion surrounding the genius and head-of-
state issues, and the nepotism fostered in the Lin family. The personality
cult presented the most formidable object of criticism, but Mao's open
involvement in and the former CCRG's reliance on similar strategies
complicated its instrumentalization. Mao's letter to Jiang Qing had been
among the main items circulated internally to demonstrate Mao's opposition to the cult, but the criticism focused less on the Mao cult as such than
on the elevation of Lin through proposing a "genius theory" with ulterior
motives. A number of newspaper articles in 1972 had tackled the issue of
the role of heroes by referring back to Plekhanov, according to whom
heroes appeared necessarily during any mass movement, but as products
and not as creators of history.[32] The veneration of leaders was thus
justified along the very same lines as it had been argued during the criticism of the secret speech. The credibility of the argument, however, had
been weakened considerably through historical experience. Thus the CCP
leadership was in need of further proof to demonstrate Lin's attempt to
exercise a "landlord-comprador-bourgeois fascist dictatorship based on
the landlords, rich peasants, counterrevolutionaries, bad elements, and
Rightists."[33]

---

[31] Ibid., 1416.
[32] Yun Gang, "'Yingxiong' shiguan de yige xin bianzhong" [A New Expression of a
"Heroic" View of History], in *Renmin ribao*, 11 June 1972, 2.
[33] "Zhongfa [72] 24, Zhonggong zhongyang guanyu zuzhi chuanda he taolun 'fensui Lin
Biao fandang jituan fangeming zhengbian de douzheng (cailiao zhi san)' de tongzhi ji
cailiao" [CCP Center Notice and Materials on Organizing the Propagation and Discussion
of "The Struggle to Destroy the Counterrevolutionary Coup d'État of the Lin Biao Anti-
Party Clique (Materials Part 3)"], 2 July 1972, in CRDB.

According to the remembrances of his physician Li Zhisui, Mao Zedong had been physically shaken by the death Lin Biao and the resulting loss of credibility,[34] but he had not been too much involved in the details of the criticism campaign as he was busy with other issues, including opening up to the United States in foreign relations, deciding who would replace Lin Biao as successor, and determining how to secure the successes of the Cultural Revolution after Lin's fall. When discussing the agenda of the Tenth Congress in 1973, Mao refocused the direction of revolution in the superstructure by singling out Confucius and Confucianist thought as representatives of a slaveholder society and called for a reappraisal of the first Chinese emperor Qin Shihuangdi and the school of legalism instead. Mao explicitly brought up the topic again during a discussion with his short-time heir apparent Wang Hongwen and Zhang Chunqiao on 4 July 1973, and mentioned that Confucius had been worshipped by both the Guomindang and Lin Biao, thus for the first time linking the unlikely pair.[35] The foundation of the accusation had been a number of items including calligraphy scrolls and the infamous flash cards with excerpts from classical works that had been found during searches of Lin Biao's residence in Maojiawan.

The criticism of Lin Biao and Confucius served multiple purposes. Although on the surface it was to debunk traditional notions of virtue and propriety and to link Lin Biao with feudalist superstitions, the campaign combined a plethora of diverging objectives. It, first of all, entailed a thinly veiled criticism of Premier Zhou Enlai by criticizing his namesake, the Duke of Zhou, whom Confucius had characterized as an ideal statesman. Jiang Qing in particular tried to instrumentalize the allegorical meanings of the campaign and to shift the emphasis from criticizing Lin Biao to singling out "present-day Confucians." The campaign furthermore served as a means to return the PLA under "unambiguous civilian control."[36] In several provinces, the military influence on the revolutionary committees came to be heavily criticized, leading to a reshuffling of leadership positions.[37]

---

[34] Li and Thurston, *Private Life*, 542.

[35] Mao Zedong, "Tong Wang Hongwen, Zhang Chunqiao de tanhua jiyao" [Summary of Talks with Wang Hongwen and Zhang Chunqiao], 4 July 1973, in CRDB.

[36] Teiwes and Sun, *End of the Maoist Era*, 164.

[37] On the situation in Zhejiang province, see Keith Forster, "The Politics of Destabilization and Confrontation: The Campaign against Lin Biao and Confucius in Zhejiang Province, 1974," in *China Quarterly* 107 (September 1986), 433–62.

Yet aside from sparking elite power struggles, the campaign also provided ample materials that could be interpreted as being directed against the ritualistic Mao cult for which Lin was held accountable. The main document criticizing Lin Biao and Confucius, *Zhongfa* [74] 1,[38] resembled the collections of word crimes in the early Cultural Revolution, with the difference that Lin's utterances were not contrasted with "correct" citations from Mao but rather were arranged to match the content of selected quotations from the Confucian classics. The genius issue was linked to Confucius' category of being "born knowledgeable,"[39] which was said to have provided the intellectual fundament for the expounding of the genius cult. The most important topic, however, was a sentence taken from the Yanyuan chapter of the *Confucian Analects* commonly translated as "to subdue one's self and return to propriety" (*ke ji fu li*).[40] In the original semantic context, the character *li* most certainly referred to ways of personal conduct as laid down in the classical rites codices. The meaning of the phrase, said to have been displayed in two hanging scrolls over Lin's bed, probably too was a reminder for careful personal behavior at Mao's court, very much along the same lines as a number of short entries from his wife's work diary in 1961 quoted in the collection, most prominently three personal do's and don'ts: "Don't interfere ..., don't criticize, don't report bad news." Instead, one should "respond, praise, and report good news."[41] Indeed, this had been the bottom line of Lin's actions after 1959.

The character *li* in the context of *Zhongfa* [74] 1, however, referred to more than questions of propriety. According to the official guidance material offering interpretive help on how to explain the classical text passages to an often semiliterate audience, *li* was explained as "ceremonial rites" aimed at stabilizing gentry rule.[42] Although the material did not further elaborate on the issue except for referring to Lin's sinister aim of restoring capitalism and establishing his clan as new gentry, the question of

---

[38] "Zhongfa [74] 1, Zhonggong zhongyang zhuanfa 'Lin Biao yu Kong Meng zhi dao (cailiao zhi yi)' de tongzhi ji fujian" [CCP Center Transmits the Notice "Lin Biao and the Way of Kong and Meng (Materials Part 1)" and Appendices], 18 January 1974, in CRDB.

[39] See James Legge, *The Chinese Classics*, vol. 1. *Confucian Analects, the Great Learning, the Doctrine of the Mean*, Hong Kong: Hong Kong University Press, 1960 [1861], 313.

[40] See ibid., 250.

[41] Among the short entries were the following: "Who doesn't speak falsely will be purged. Who doesn't speak falsely won't accomplish great deeds," or, "Close the eyes and nourish the spirit – act according to [the instructions from] above." See "Zhongfa [74] 1," in CRDB.

[42] "Guanyu 'Lin Biao yu Kong Meng zhi dao' fudao cailiao" [Tutorial Materials on "Lin Biao and the Way of Kong and Meng"], February 1974, 3.

how to interpret *li* could well be understood as a reference to the rites and mode of communication characteristic of the Mao cult. Lin Biao and Confucius were thus characterized as exponents of a slave society held together through ceremonial rites or, rather, a strict system of formalized speech acts and deeds serving to strengthen the authority of the ruler and privileged classes.

The thin line between exposing Lin's crimes while maintaining the Mao cult laid the intellectual groundwork for a fundamental criticism of the present system of rule that was not lost among the audience. The most erudite answer was published in form of several big character posters that were made public in Guangzhou in late 1974 by three former Red Guards writing under the pseudonym Li-Yi-Zhe.[43] In their well-known poster *On Socialist Legality and Democracy*, they singled out the erosion of legal principles and democracy to have been the most devastating consequence of what they referred to as the "Lin Biao system" (*Lin Biao tixi*).[44] This system was said to be grounded in the absolutization of Mao Zedong Thought, threatening to knock down everyone with different, not even necessarily opposing, views. By taking up the phrase of "rule through rites" (*lizhi*), they immediately related the system to the lively study and application campaigns and activist congresses, which they described as being "imbued with religious sentiments":[45]

> We have not forgotten the replacement of everything else through (empty-headed) politics, rewarding the diligent and good, and punishing the lazy and bad; the holy script–like "daily reading," the increasingly hypocritical "sharing experience in application" talks, the ever more absurd "conducting of revolution in the deepest recesses of the mind," the "demonstrations of loyalty" favoring political opportunists, the nondescript "loyalty dances," the tedious formalities of the rites of loyalty and piety, pestering beyond endurance – morning prayers, atoning for one's crimes in the evening, during assemblies and brigade meetings, at the start, end, and exchange of shifts, when buying or selling goods, writing letters, picking up the phone, even before having lunch, etc., every occasion was covered and smeared with an intense climate of religious flavor. Generally speaking, to have loyalty-fication account for one hundred percent of the time, and one hundred percent of the space, or some kind of "this good"

---

[43] On the background and fate of the Li-Yi-Zhe group, see Anita Chan, Stanley Rosen, and Jonathan Unger (eds.), *On Socialist Democracy and the Chinese Legal System: The Li Yizhe Debates*, Armonk, NY: M. E. Sharpe, 1985, 1–28.

[44] Li-Yi-Zhe, "Guanyu shehui zhuyi de minzhu yu fazhi" [On the Democracy and Legal System of Socialism], 7 November 1974, in CRDB.

[45] Ibid.

or "that good" movement, all this has been a competition of "Left! Left! Left!," a rivalry of being the " … most … most … most," enacted during countless "activist congresses" which in reality were fairs of falsehood, vice, and ugliness, gambling halls with "little investment and huge profits."[46]

What made the arguments of the authors a threat for the present ruling elite was their combination with the call to establish a basic legal framework to abolish once and for all the emergence of a privileged party stratum and the roots of the "social-fascist dictatorship of feudal character."[47] Without explicitly mentioning a possible death of the by now eighty-year-old CCP Chairman, the authors warned of the rise of future leaders claiming to impersonate the revolutionary line of Mao Zedong Thought, who again would be deemed above popular criticism.

The three authors were detained for their views, but the possible consequences in case of Mao's death had been pointed out only too well. The endless changes in line, which the ruthless CCP Chairman had sanctioned to prevent any faction from becoming strong enough to present a threat to his power, lingered over the last years of his rule. The cult had been toned down by replacing overt worship with indirect praise of his "line," but fundamentally, Mao-centered politics remained stable. What prevailed among the populace was an ever-growing cynicism and open acts of symbolic defiance, especially during the spontaneous expressions of veneration and esteem expressed in poems, letters, and big character posters on Tiananmen Square after the death of the long-ailing Zhou Enlai in early 1976.[48] Although Mao's death on 9 September 1976 was followed by elaborate ceremonies of mourning, there were no comparable spontaneous expressions of grief. The Mao cult, however, was not over with the demise of Mao's physical body but was resumed after the death of the dictator.

PRESERVATION AND TRANSFORMATION

Up to the very end, it had been Mao's presence that kept the CCP central leadership together. Although the basic party institutions at the different levels had been reestablished in the early 1970s, fundamental political

---

[46] Li-Yi-Zhe, "Xiangei Mao zhuxi he si jie renda" [For Chairman Mao and the Fourth National People's Congress], 7 November 1974, in CRDB.

[47] Li-Yi-Zhe, "Shehui zhuyi," in CRDB.

[48] Compare Sebastian Heilmann, *Sozialer Protest in der VR China. Die Bewegung vom 5. April 1976 und die Gegen-Kulturrevolution der Siebziger Jahre* [Social Protest in the People's Republic of China: The 5 April Movement of 1976 and the Countercultural Revolution of the 1970s], Hamburg: Institut für Asienkunde, 1994, 140ff.

cleavages had been roiling beneath the surface. The only questions the Politburo agreed upon in the immediate aftermath of Mao's death were decisions aimed at offering a last tribute to Mao Zedong and demonstrating personal loyalty even beyond death. The remaining Leftists in the Politburo, Jiang Qing, Zhang Chunqiao, Yao Wenyuan, and Wang Hongwen,[49] could not count on sufficient institutional backing except for the Shanghai Municipal Revolutionary Committee. They had no sympathizers among the old elites, and thus without doubt held the weakest hand. A mere month after Mao's death, the "Gang of Four," as they had been mockingly termed by Mao Zedong, were arrested in a military coup carried out by members of PLA unit 8341 on the orders of acting premier Hua Guofeng, Wang Dongxing, and Ye Jianying. Only sparse information was released to the provincial committees to prevent uprisings. Instead, important leaders of former CCRG strongholds such as Shanghai were requested to travel to Beijing in person but were not arrested, on the condition of guaranteeing the stability of the new order.[50] Only two days after the imprisonment of the Gang of Four on 6 October, the construction of a memorial hall for the deceased was declared, despite Mao's wish not to be put on display like Stalin. Concomitantly, the publication of the fifth volume of Mao's *Selected Works* was announced; it had been ready for print since 1968, but due to Mao's reluctance, the volume had not yet been published. Both projects were to be conducted under the leadership of Hua Guofeng.

Within the fluid situation after Mao's death, it was Hua who nominally emerged as his successor. Hua had previously been Hunan party secretary and had proven his loyalty since the days of the Great Leap Forward. By 1973, he had become full member of the Politburo, and after Zhou Enlai's death, Hua had been appointed acting premier in January 1976 due to Mao's growing dissatisfaction with the intellectual capabilities of Wang Hongwen and the political choices of Deng Xiaoping, who had recently been rehabilitated. Mao had died without having accomplished the most basic task he had set for himself when embarking on the crusade against revisionism: the choosing of a capable successor to avoid the fate of Stalin both personally and in terms of policy line.

---

[49] As Frederick Teiwes and Warren Sun have recently shown in great detail, the Gang of Four was no clear "faction" with unanimously shared goals, neither was there a coherent faction of beneficiaries or Cultural Revolutionary victims. Loyalties and affiliations within the party elite were highly complex and often crossed traditionally established boundaries. See Teiwes and Sun, *End of the Maoist Era*, Chapter 8.

[50] Elizabeth Perry and Li Xun, *Proletarian Power: Shanghai in the Cultural Revolution*, Boulder, CO: Westview Press, 1997, 184ff.

Hua was publicly announced as Mao's successor during a rally at Tiananmen Square on 24 October 1976, after which he took over the offices of CCP chairman and head of the Central Military Commission. He thus combined the institutional powers of the offices of the state executive, the party, and the military leadership. Not even Mao had been vested with equal formal powers. Yet after Mao's demise, Hua remained unsure about the consequences to be drawn from his predecessor's political legacy. He had risen through the ranks by displaying loyalty to Mao and the policies of the Cultural Revolution, and he continued to do so after becoming party chairman. The language of loyalty was once more reinvigorated on a massive scale. Although Hua did not adopt Lin Biao's aggressive stand toward displaying his status as best student of Mao Zedong Thought, he fostered his image as loyal servant to the ideals of Mao and developed a nascent cult as "wise leader Chairman Hua" (*yingming lingxiu Hua zhuxi*), even physically trying to enhance his resemblance to his predecessor by adopting Mao's hairstyle.[51]

Hua's policies remained loyal to the policies of Mao Zedong and he even announced the reemergence of movements similar to the Cultural Revolution in the future. Hua underestimated the resistance that the latter announcement engendered among the pre–Cultural Revolutionary elites. Despite Mao's efforts to reshuffle the leadership bodies, the highest prestige and the largest personal networks were still commanded by the generation of Long Marchers, many of whom had suffered and survived the turmoil. Although Hua's status and image were bolstered through both institutional titles and the media, his power was increasingly counterbalanced by the third rise of Deng Xiaoping, boosted by his backing within party circles and the military alike. By July 1977, Deng was effectively restored to his offices and although formally outranked by Hua, he came to be the gray eminence of Chinese politics, revealing again that "officials counted for more than institutions in China."[52] Hua continued to hold his offices until he was finally sent into semiretirement in 1981 as Deng Xiaoping emerged victorious. The manipulation of symbols and images as well as political offices had proven to be insufficient to secure Hua's political fate. By announcing the reenactment of the Cultural Revolution, he had estranged many high-ranking party members for whom factionalism and the attack by non-party persons had become a nightmare to be prevented at all costs. As Mao had predicted, the establishment of "fake

---

[51] Martin, *Kult und Kanon*, 50f.
[52] MacFarquhar and Schoenhals, *Mao's Last Revolution*, 452.

authority" not backed by charismatic relationships spun over decades did not automatically result in political authority but ultimately had to fail.

Deng Xiaoping was much more cautious in dealing with Mao's legacy. He had been deeply involved in refuting Khrushchev's secret speech and had been a witness to the consequences brought forth by the attack on Stalin's legacy. While criticizing the excesses of Mao's rule, Deng admitted having been an accomplice in the early stages of the Mao cult, as without top-level backing it would never have been able to evolve on such a large scale. Yet he remained vague about the extent to which the effects of the Mao cult on the public sphere should be curbed. He firmly supported the replacement of the omnipresent reliance on Mao's words, because the gap between original context and later usages had given rise to manipulations.[53] Deng's actions were not solely based on philosophical stringency but as well on strategic observations: he would not have stood a chance, given the number of less than flattering remarks Mao had made about Deng, if legitimacy were to be accounted for in terms of being championed by Mao quotations.

CCP discussions slowly shifted toward attacking the Gang of Four's vulgarization of Mao Zedong Thought, a point Deng Xiaoping had emphasized since 1960. Most authors of critical articles that appeared in the party media were associated with the Central Party School under Hu Yaobang. By early 1978, attacks on formalism and the rituals of the cult featured prominently in numerous articles and front-page editorials. Lin Biao and the Gang of Four were accused of having employed the cult to foster their agendas and of having forced them onto an unwilling populace:

> The masses were seriously opposed to this type of asking for instructions in the morning and reporting back in the evening, loyalty dances, and quotation gymnastics enacted by Lin Biao. It therefore was rather easy to destroy it. The "Gang of Four" developed a much more intelligent method than Lin Biao, never to forget "politics," "lines," "theory." .... By conducting these activities, they made it easy first of all to deceive the populace and, second, to scare people. Whoever dared to have slightly opposing views was immediately labeled counterrevolutionary.[54]

From mid-November 1978 onward, a few big character posters appeared at what became known as the Democracy Wall on Xidan Street in Beijing; the posters dealt in various ways with the issue of the personality cult.

[53] Deng Xiaoping, *Deng Xiaoping wenxuan* [Selected Works of Deng Xiaoping], vol. 2, Beijing: Renmin chubanshe, 1994 [1983], 38.

[54] Jie Si, "Fandui xingshi zhuyi" [Oppose Formalism], in *Renmin ribao*, 31 January 1978, 3.

Simultaneously, a large number of petitioners flocked into the capital to have their unjust cases from the Cultural Revolution reevaluated. As the CCP had not yet announced an official verdict on how to judge Mao Zedong's involvement in the Cultural Revolution, the first public criticisms were daring actions. Yet it soon became obvious that highly different evaluations of Mao existed among the populace, only few of which were as explicit as Wei Jingsheng, a former Red Guard, who declared Mao to be a feudal despot. With his call for democratization, Wei attacked the continuing prescription of correct standpoints from the CCP-dominated public sphere as resembling a "religious cult."[55] These arguments were to be one of the reasons for sentencing Wei to fifteen years in prison.

The mounting tide of criticism that mostly contained backing for Deng's policies but in a few cases developed into calls for an abolishment of the party dictatorship necessitated both an official evaluation of the CCP Chairman's legacy and a consideration of its effects on the stability of party rule. The restoration of order and the pre-1957 modus of CCP governance were the priorities of the new leadership body and an all-out attack on the personality cult would invariably have led to criticism of the concept of the vanguard party. While renouncing the infallibility of individuals, Deng reverted to his standpoint expressed at the Eighth Party Congress in 1956 and distinguished between exaggerated praise for the individual and heartfelt veneration for the collective leadership of the CCP, as well as between Mao Zedong Thought, defined as the collective wisdom of applying Marxism-Leninism within the context of the Chinese Revolution, and its distortions:

> Without Chairman Mao there would be no New China; this is no exaggeration to the slightest degree. ... If there would be no Mao Zedong Thought there would not be the CCP of today; this [too] is no exaggeration at all. Mao Zedong Thought will forever be a spiritual treasure trove for our whole party, the military, and all Chinese ethnicities. We should comprehensively and correctly understand and grasp the scientific basics of Mao Zedong Thought, and further develop them under new historical conditions. Of course, Comrade Mao Zedong was not without shortcomings and faults. Requesting that revolutionary leaders should be without faults and shortcomings is not Marxism-Leninism. We should guide and educate all party members, all political instructors in the military, and all members of the different nationalities to apprehend scientifically and historically the great contributions of Comrade Mao Zedong.[56]

---

[55] Compare Merle Goldman, *Sowing the Seeds of Democracy in China: Political Reform in the Deng Xiaoping Era*, Cambridge: Harvard University Press, 1994, 44.

[56] Deng, *Deng weuxuan* 2, 149. See further ibid., 171.

Mao's historical contributions to the communist cause in China and the lack of a Chinese Lenin to balance Mao's relative importance made it impossible to claim political legitimacy for CCP rule without cherishing his memory. As Frederick Teiwes and Warren Sun have observed, for dedicated Chinese revolutionaries, it "would have amounted to rejecting their own life's endeavors, as much as their leader"[57] if they had indulged in an all-embracing de-Maofication. The consequences of a Khrushchev-type secret speech on the legitimacy of CCP rule thus had to be circumvented by carefully emphasizing Mao's role in the Chinese Revolution and by blaming the outgrowths of the personality cult on the Lin Biao and Jiang Qing "anti-party cliques."

In a huge Nuremberg-style trial, held between November 1980 and January 1981 that was to demonstrate the success of implementing legal structures, the incarcerated radicals and the remaining circle of Lin Biao's followers were sentenced for several crimes, most importantly the scheming to usurp power and the persecution of loyal party members. The cult featured prominently in the coverage of the process and listed the individual fates of various victims who had come to be labeled "active counter-revolutionaries" for having opposed Lin Biao or the CCRG. The role of Lin Biao and the Gang of Four with respect to the cult was defined as having "turned the feelings of the masses toward certain leaders into tributary services of a modern superstition."[58] The cult thus came to be explained along the old lines of feudal remnants and its instrumentalization through the Lin Biao and Jiang Qing antiparty cliques, who were said to have attempted establishing a "feudal-fascist dictatorship" built on the traditions of patriarchy and "one-word rule."[59] Mao's subtle distinctions between the correct phrasings *geren chonghai* and *geren mixin* were replaced by an indiscriminate usage, sometimes complemented by references to "modern superstition" (*xiandai mixin*) or "god-building activities" (*zaoshen yundong*).

After further discussions at the Fourth Plenum of the Eleventh Congress in September 1979 and a year-long preparation of various drafts, the Sixth Plenum on 27 June 1981 finally passed a resolution that was to present the CCP's official assessment of Mao's legacy. The Cultural Revolution was defined as the most severe setback for the People's Republic since the

---

57 Teiwes and Sun, *End of the Maoist Era*, 626f.
58 Mu Qing, Guo Chaoren, and Lu Fowei, "Lishi de shenpan" [Trial of History], in *Renmin ribao*, 27 January 1981, 3.
59 "Fengjian zhuyi sixiang yidu yinggai suqing" [All Feudalist Thinking Should Be Removed], in *Renmin ribao*, 18 July 1980, 5.

founding in 1949 and the main responsibility rested with the former CCP Chairman, who "confused right and wrong and the people with the enemy":[60]

> Comrade Mao Zedong's prestige reached a peak and he began to get arrogant at the very time when the party was confronted with the new task of shifting the focus of its work to socialist construction. ... The result was a steady weakening and even undermining of the principle of collective leadership and democratic centralism in the political life of the party and the country. This state of affairs took place only gradually, and the Central Committee of the party should be held partly responsible.[61]

Mao, according to the _Resolution_, had been a tragic hero, who steadfastly held on to his ideas even if they turned out to be false as in his later years. The year 1957 came to be the watershed in defining right from wrong in terms of policy line, as Deng Xiaoping added to the draft of the resolution that had been prepared by veteran Hu Qiaomu under the auspices of Hu Yaobang.[62] Just like twenty-five years earlier in the discussions about the impact of the secret speech, the novelty of the communist movement was taken as an excuse for allowing certain errors and deviations to appear. The prominent role of leaders was emphasized yet again, while singling out the consequences of feudalism and centuries of "feudal autocracy" that had been instrumentalized by Lin Biao and the Gang of Four. Inner-party democracy and collective leadership were to prevent similar failures in the future. The aim of preserving Mao and Mao Zedong Thought for the stability of party rule had remained the most important task, as Deng Xiaoping had added in one of his corrections to the draft resolution: "The most crucial point of the resolution, the most basic problem still is that we hold on to and develop Mao Zedong Thought. Within and outside the party, domestically and internationally, we have to add emphasis, description, and explanation to this problem."[63] For this reason, the most prominent examples of the cult, such as Mao's portrait on Tiananmen, were to remain in place forever, as Deng told his Italian interviewer Oriana Fallaci in August 1980.[64] Even the mausoleum, although it had not been appropriate to build it in the first place, should not be torn down in order not to give rise to rumors. Dealing with the physical remains of the Mao cult therefore proceeded in a much more secretive fashion than the huge show trial or the removal of the Lin cult items.

[60] Schoenhals (ed.), _China's Cultural Revolution_, 299.
[61] Ibid., 303.
[62] Deng, _Deng wenxuan_ 2, 294f.
[63] Ibid., 296.
[64] Ibid., 344.

In a series of instructions issued between 1978 and 1980, the elevated levels of publishing Mao quotes were ended and the stocks were cleared of "loyalty" commodities that still bore witness to the high tide of the cult in 1968.[65] Instructions were passed to the media to decrease the adulation of individual leaders,[66] outdated slogans were cleared, and the reverence accorded even to the stockpiled *Quotation* volumes in Beijing was diminished by allowing for their disposal in case of damage.[67] The huge Cultural Revolutionary monuments presented the CCP with difficulties. Most of the former Long Live Halls were simply renamed, just like many city squares, and were turned into provincial or city museums due to their superior material quality.[68] The Mao statues were addressed in a separate central document on 6 November 1980. In accordance with the party's policy of retaining a positive image of Mao, it was decided against a renewed wave of iconoclasm: "There is absolutely no need to destroy them all in concert. On the contrary, it would be a disservice to the people of China if not a few statues of Comrade Mao Zedong ... were not left standing."[69] In all places where public discussions about whether or not to remove the statues occurred, they were to be retained in order not to harm revolutionary feelings. Still, over the following decade, most of the statues vanished from most university campuses and work units on the pretext of conducting renovations. In some places, such as Guiyang, the statues remained on the central city square but underwent renovation. Thus Mao's green army uniform was replaced with the grayish blue civil dress known as a Sun Yat-sen suit.[70]

By mid-1981, the CCP leadership could congratulate itself on its attempt to depersonalize Mao Zedong Thought securely and to avoid the destabilizing consequences of denouncing the most prominent leader and symbol of the Chinese Revolution. A split within the CCP had been

---

[65] A translation of the directives can be found in Geremie R. Barmé, *Shades of Mao: The Posthumous Cult of the Great Leader*, Armonk, NY; London: M. E. Sharpe, 1996, 128ff. See further Michael Schoenhals, "Selections from Propaganda Trends, Organ of the CCP Central Propaganda Department," in *Chinese Law and Government* 24.4 (1992), 5–93.

[66] See DXG 2, 706. The directive was relayed to the public by Yu Jinan, "Zijue de zunshou 'shao xuanchuan geren' de fangzhen" [Self-Consciously Follow the Guideline of "Reduce the Propagation of Individuals"], in *Renmin ribao*, 4 September 1980, 5.

[67] Barmé, *Shades of Mao*, 9f.

[68] For the case of Sichuan, see Lin, "Suiyue de jianzheng 2," 45.

[69] Translated in Barmé, *Shades of Mao*, 133.

[70] Liu Yongxiang, "Guiyang renmin guangchang Mao zhuxi suxiang diaosu qianhou" [The Times of the Chairman Mao Statue at Guiyang People's Square], in *Wenshi tiandi* 7 (2002), 42.

circumvented and the adverse effects on national stability and party rule by conducting a radical de-Maoization had been avoided. The party had succeeded in cooling down the official Mao cult but had not abolished it. Thus the rise in public requests for Mao pictures led to the reprint of portraits of several prominent communist leaders, most importantly Mao Zedong, from 1983 onward.[71] Yet by preserving one-party rule based on the dissemination of a controlled stream of censored information, the party had merely suppressed, and not answered, the question of what constituted a personality cult and how to curb its effects. Instead of instrumentalizing the cult as a means of charismatic mobilization to out-maneuver the party bureaucracy, as Mao Zedong had done, his successors, during continuous periods of relaxing and strengthening control over the public sphere, came to rely on their own moderate versions of personality cults as a means of fostering unity within the party and the nation. The common study of leader speeches and the spiritual guidance to be drawn from an ever-expanding legacy of Marxism-Leninism down to the theory of the "Scientific Development View" advocated in the name of CCP General Secretary Hu Jintao in 2007 have perpetuated these paternalistic policies. Far from being an arcane remnant of emperor worship, the instrumental value of personality cults still bears its imprints on present-day CCP politics.

---

[71] Barmé, *Shades of Mao*, 8.

Conclusion

It is a remarkable characteristic of modern personality cults that they are declared to be alien to the fundamental laws and principles of every political system by their own representatives. Democratic politicians tend to relegate the phenomenon to totalitarian or at least authoritarian forms of government. Many dictators on the other hand claim the popular nature of their respective cults. Saparmurat Niyasov, better known as Turkmenbashi, who cultivated one of the most excessive leader cults in recent years, once said: "I'm personally against seeing my pictures and statues in the streets – but it's what the people want."[1] Most communist leaders invoked feudal relics in the superstructure to explain the appearance of personality cults in their own party-states, which were purportedly built on a scientific and rational worldview. Even the architects of the massive leader cults in Nazi Germany or Benito Mussolini's fascist dictatorship in Italy tried to quell the impression of having deliberately relied on the emotional appeal of personalized politics and symbols. Instead, they tried to emphasize the scientific nature of their ideologies. Adolf Hitler thus in a talk with two leading apologists of his personality cult, Alfred Rosenberg and Heinrich Himmler, explicitly warned against transforming national socialism, which he described as "a cool and highly-reasoned approach to reality based on the greatest of scientific knowledge,"[2] into a mystic cult movement.

The divergence between the propagation of a scientific and rational worldview and the emotional symbolism of personality cults pervaded the discussions on the Mao cult from the very outset. In the early 1940s,

---

[1] Mary Jayne McKay, "Turkmenbashi Everywhere: If You Think Saddam Was Fond of Himself, Visit Turkmenistan," *CBS Broadcasting*, 4 January 2004 (http://www.cbsnews.com/stories/2003/12/31/60minutes/main590913.shtml).

[2] Quoted from Michael Burleigh, "National Socialism as a Political Religion," in *Totalitarian Movements and Political Religions* 1.2 (2000), 11.

Mao and his coterie first employed the cult as a means of securing loyalties and establishing Mao as the primus inter pares of CCP politics. The expediency of employing the cult as a branding strategy served the dual goal of providing the party with an integrating symbol that could simultaneously be used to counter the propagation of the Chiang cult. After succeeding in ending the feuds within the party and having successfully established the communist party-state, the public cult was steadily toned down, paralleling the increase of bureaucratic routines.

Mao's supremacy within the Politburo remained unchallenged even after Khrushchev's attack on the Stalin cult and its consequences in February 1956. Yet the secret speech sparked the only period until Mao's death that witnessed critical discussions about personality cults. The reverberations of the secret speech in Eastern Europe alarmed the CCP leadership as they raised possible implications of shattering the founding myths and most prominent symbols of the movement. But Mao did not heed the admonitions of his colleagues and adopted a strategy of inviting public criticism and opening up the public sphere, based on the probably correct estimate that CCP rule was more popular than the dictatorship of communist parties in Eastern Europe. The failure of the Hundred Flowers campaign, due to its incompatibility with the top-down party bureaucracy, tarnished Mao's image as omniscient helmsman, and renewed proof of Mao's leadership abilities was required. With the Soviet model having been shunned, and with no other external models to rely upon, Mao legitimized a "correct" personality cult as a dialectical means to achieve emancipation from the Soviet model. Only with the disastrous impact of the Great Leap Forward, which shattered belief in Mao's infallibility, did it become necessary to wage huge media campaigns to reinterpret experienced history based on a claim of the absolute truth of Mao Zedong Thought. Especially in the PLA, a nondialectical, "incorrect" personality cult as worship of the CCP Chairman and his thought came to be propagated.

Up to the Great Leap Forward, Mao's role within the CCP was clearly exceptional but still restrained by the formal party institutions and bureaucracy. Starting with the appointment of Lin Biao as minister of defense, Mao came to place in key positions individuals who knew that their tenure was built on personal rather than institutional loyalties. They therefore championed the cult as demonstrations of their continuing commitment, even if the correctness of Mao's views was contradicted by policy failures. At the same time, Mao came to realize that the party bureaucracy was no longer a tool that would yield to all of his wishes. His frequent complaints about the fostering of "independent kingdoms" in various bureaucratic units reveal less his sense of an imminent threat to his leadership position than his growing dissatisfaction with the bureaucratic party-state. The staging of anti-Soviet polemics through the Anti-Revisionist Writing Group, which solely depended on Mao's requests, thus was indicative of his increasing reliance on charismatic relationships. By relying on trustworthy individuals and extraconstitutional bodies that directly responded and acted upon Mao's behest, he tried to prevent the rise of "revisionism."

The outbreak of the Cultural Revolution and the careful purges of those party members holding crucial posts at the CCP Center brought about a charismatic form of leadership. A similar form of leadership, in the case of the Nazi dictatorship, has been called the "dual state,"[3] divided between the "normative state" (*Normenstaat*) in charge of running day-to-day administration and the "special-measures state" (*Maßnahmenstaat*) acting on the immediate wishes of the leader. While the remaining state organs continued to fulfill their tasks and effectively ensured that the Cultural Revolution did not completely drown in anarchy, the rise of extraconstitutional bodies such as the CCRG, which due to the lack of clear areas of competence constantly rivaled for power with the state and the military, increased Mao's agency considerably. He could assume the role of both "referee and coordinator"[4] and favor the political faction he deemed most expedient in the present situation. Representatives of all factions, on the other hand, would try to flatter Mao Zedong in order to increase their influence.

The Cultural Revolution witnessed the replacement of bureaucratic routines by charismatic relationships and it is in this respect that the Chinese case offers interesting parallels with other dictatorships. The applicability of Max Weber's ideal type of charismatic leadership has often been invoked to explain the rise of personality cults, but attributing these cults to personal charisma has often led to unsatisfactory results. Neither Mao nor Stalin was endowed with extraordinary rhetorical skills that would have set them apart from the masses. Yet they were able to forge charismatic relationships based on loyalty, conviction, or simply intimidation. These relationships, however, were not static, and catastrophes such as the Great Leap increased the necessity to strengthen personal bonds throughout the hierarchies; for example, Mao traveled frequently

---

[3] Ernst Fraenkel, *The Dual State: A Contribution to the Theory of Dictatorship*, New York: Oxford University Press, 1941.
[4] Lepsius, "Charismatic Leadership," 187.

to renew the loyalty of local party secretaries and military commanders. By personally seeing to the promotion of loyal followers, Mao continued to weave his net of charismatic relationships that sometimes might still have been based on belief in his extraordinary abilities but probably more often represented a well-understood principle of political ascent.

The systematic weaknesses of the communist party-state, by failing to specify an institutionalized ladder of political careers, provided the crucial framework that allowed for the staging and sustaining of personality cults. As long as distinctive policy directives were issued from the CCP Center, loyalty could be proven through the claimed overfulfillment of targets or the advocacy of certain measures associated with a Politburo patron at the expense of others. During the Cultural Revolution, the goals of which remained a complete mystery to most, rhetorical veneration came to be the most common way of expressing loyalty once Lin Biao had raised the stakes by declaring Mao Zedong Thought to be sacrosanct. By endorsing Lin Biao's Politburo report and the purge of leading CCP comrades, Mao ensured that his thought became the sole source of the regime's legitimacy. The words of Mao as the living fountain of truth assumed performative qualities; thus party members constantly relied on his sayings in order to avoid the fate of being exposed as counterrevolutionary. Based on such asymmetric relationships that always made the client dependent on his patron, a similarly asymmetric type of communication evolved that brought forth ever-new blossoms of the language of loyalty.

By using his incredible media reputation as symbolic capital, Mao could incite enormous mobilization efforts by receiving Red Guards or representatives of mass organizations. He saw to it that the meetings were covered widely in newspapers and the national broadcasting networks. Footage of Mao's meetings with the Red Guards or his benevolent greetings to the masses was constantly provided by special film teams that covered his actions for a greater audience. Mao thus made strategic use of mass media techniques to have images of the charismatic situation in Beijing spread nationwide. But aside from being linked to the "red sun," "revolution," and the "correct line," the specific content of what Mao actually stood for remained vague. Mao's directions for the movement, commonly expressed in short quotations, were not self-explanatory and thus had to undergo exegesis through one of his "perception managers,"[5] which

---

[5] Michael Schoenhals, "The Global War on Terrorism as Meta-Narrative: An Alternative Reading of Recent Chinese History," in *Sungkyun Journal of East Asian Studies* 8.2 (2008), 188.

because of internal competition would occasionally give the news and interpretation an individual spin.

Charismatic mobilization was instrumental in creating the massive impact of the Cultural Revolution, yet the near-complete lack of positive aims of the movement, as well as the decreasing number of steering capacities, led to a championing of the symbols of worship through all emerging groups and factions. Mao's aloofness resulted in the open-textured nature of the movement. The lack of a master plan for the Cultural Revolution was based on the very idea of mobilizing the masses to guide themselves and followed the logic of self-development, which Lenin had laid out in his treatise on dialectics. Wang Shaoguang, in his insightful study of the Cultural Revolution in Wuhan, points out that the cult served to mobilize and energize the masses but failed to control them: "[T]he cult of personality per se could not help to realize Mao's will, however faithful millions of people might claim themselves to be, because Mao destroyed the social control mechanisms that were necessary for him to dictate and co-ordinate the popular forces."[6]

Wang's observation implies a certain imperative on Mao's side, a clear direction in which to move the masses. Up to mid-1967, however, there is basically no indication of Mao being unsatisfied with the course of the movement. Revolution was to be enacted by enacting revolution and the goals and actors would be defined in the process itself. In this respect, the unleashing of the Cultural Revolution was more radical in its theoretical and practical consequences than any other twentieth-century communist experiment. Mao perceived the reproduction of class inequalities through specialization and bureaucratization to be the reason for the developments in the Soviet Union and Eastern Europe after Stalin's death. By destroying the very foundations of the party-state itself and replacing it with lean power structures based completely on personal loyalties, Mao tried to circumvent the fate of the slow death of revolution and simultaneously the routinization of charismatic relationships.

By mid-1967, cult anarchy and "quotation wars" had greatly diminished the expediency of charismatic mobilization The attacks on the second remaining source of power besides the cult, the PLA, increased Mao's awareness of the necessity to retain a basic degree of control. The renewal of exegetical bonding among the Red Guards revealed the limited cohesion provided by the group study of simplified quotations alone, which

[6] Wang, *Failure of Charisma*, 87.

evaporated as soon as the restrictive framework of short-term military training was removed. The physical backing of state authority through the PLA changed the anarchic usage of the cult into an ever more elaborate system of performances aimed at displaying loyalty through rhetorical or physical acts. The cult therefore came to assume a disciplinary quality as a credible demonstration of state authority and secured the formation of new political structures based solely on personal devotion to Mao Zedong. The forging of charismatic relationships thus went hand in hand with the renewed attempt to control Mao's image and sayings as indistinct symbols of integration that had to be paid ritual respect. And yet the rituals of worship resisted central control and developed in directions unplanned for by the party leadership.

Although Mao badges and posters had been in existence prior to the Cultural Revolution and supplied by the regime itself, statues and other monuments appeared only beginning in 1967. Despite and sometimes even against the CCP Center's explicit orders, the monuments were employed as demonstrations of symbolic capital in factional struggles. To exert at least some control over the construction works, the CCP Center established an authorization procedure to guarantee the aesthetic and political correctness of the statues. The CCP Center thus was only marginally involved in the creation of these cult monuments and the rise of ritual modes of worship. And yet Mao's approval of the report from the PLA unit 8341 about establishing a revolutionary committee in the Beijing General Knitting Mill was of paramount importance for spreading the impact of rituals that had first evolved locally and then had spread through the exchanging of experiences and media coverage. The most famous ritual, the "asking for instructions in the morning," was an adaptation of the common mode of centralizing decision-making processes in times of war, when the prior approval of the CCP Center was required before reaching important decisions and reporting back on its successes later. The military background explains the ritual's emergence during the military training conducted at the Shijingshan Middle School. By approving of the report's circulation, Mao bestowed his blessing on the ritual activities of worship that swept China with a vengeance after November 1967. The advantage of the physical demonstrations of loyalty was their nondistinct character. By going through the moves of the cult, subjects demonstrated submission to state authority and simultaneously reduced the danger of being accused of counterrevolutionary deeds. Ascribing symbolic value to even the smallest aspects of everyday life led to both a commodification and sacralization of Mao Zedong's image.

The dimension of public worship and performances – the rituals, prayers, and monuments of belief – are among the most vexing subjects to deal with analytically when studying personality cults. On the one hand, the role of religious faith and belief should not simply be negated, as, for example, Steve Smith has shown for the early People's Republic.[7] Religious narratives clearly played a role in the Mao cult, especially in rural areas and in early Red Guard discourse. Not every instance of the personality cult thus can be explained with the instruments of rational choice theory. On the other hand, these instances should not lead to attributing a religious dimension to all expressions of the cult. The Cultural Revolutionary Mao cult was a primarily political and clearly modern phenomenon. To focus solely on the religious aspects would be to confuse form with substance.

The rise of rituals of worship such as the "asking for instructions" leads one to wonder how far the concept of political religion, which has been applied with varying rigidity to the fascist dictatorships of Hitler and Mussolini as well as to communist rule, provides insights for the analysis of leader cults. Emilio Gentile, who has been the most prominent proponent of reviving the concept in the past three decades, has defined political religions as "a type of religion which sacralizes an ideology, a movement or a political regime through the deification of a secular entity transfigured into myth, considering it the primary and indisputable source of the meaning and the ultimate aim of human existence on earth."[8] In his most recent book, entitled *Politics as Religion*, Gentile has widened the spectrum and described the process of determining the aims of human existence on earth in the modern world no longer through traditional religions but through politics, resulting in what he termed the "sacralization of politics."[9] He draws a clear distinction between civil religions, as in case of the United States, and political religions that come in various variants, including "totalitarian religions."[10] Gentile goes to great lengths to refute arguments claiming metaphorical usage only for transferring the concept of religion to the sphere of politics and sets out to prove that the

---

[7] Steve Smith, "Local Cadres Confront the Supernatural: The Politics of Holy Water (*Shenshui*) in the PRC, 1949–1966," in *China Quarterly* 188 (2006), 999–1022.

[8] Emilio Gentile, "Fascism, Totalitarianism and Political Religion: Definitions and Critical Reflections on Criticism of an Interpretation," in *Totalitarian Movements and Political Religions* 5.3 (2004), 328.

[9] The phrase had been used by Gentile first as a description of Italian fascism only but has become the key concept of his generalized approach as well. See Emilio Gentile, *Politics as Religion*, Princeton, NJ: Princeton University Press, 2006, xiv.

[10] Ibid., 15.

system of beliefs, symbols, and rituals created by political entities since the late-eighteenth century was more than simply a tool to manipulate the masses.

The understanding of personality cults as advanced in this book is in many ways congruent with the aims proposed by Gentile. The cult of Chairman Mao was to replace all previous loyalties and belief systems, and there can be no doubt that both Mao's revolutionary credentials and media campaigns resulted in a thorough sacralization of Mao in public discourse. Yet the crucial point of whether the concept of political religion should be transferred to the realm of politics, as Gentile himself concedes, lies with the definition of religion itself. If employing a non-transcendental, anthropological approach along the lines suggested by Clifford Geertz[11] or a functionalist understanding of religion as proposed by Emile Durkheim,[12] the application seems to be justified.

The inherent dangers of employing the term, however, are presented by an oversimplistic usage. The concept of political religion bears the risk, though not with Gentile, to claim simple analogies between traditional and modern phenomena of worship without taking changing political circumstances or the instrumental employment of symbols and rituals into account. If we emphasize patriarchic cultural traditions alone, the specific power relations and negotiations are all too easily dismissed. Although surely continuities between the worship of Mao and folk deities existed on the reception side – as Stefan Landsberger and others have shown[13] – religious explanations alone are insufficient to explain the actual shaping and sustaining of the cult phenomenon. For this reason, this book has avoided the usage of the concept of political religion and has instead focused on the historical reconstruction of fundamental modes of asymmetric communication and the employment of integrating symbols that may be found in politics, religion, or the business world alike. Analyzing personality cults as an outgrowth of authoritarian political communication, charismatic relationships, and the instrumentalization of political icons to secure symbolic capital offers a wider range of possible comparisons with phenomena relying on similar strategies in completely different settings that are not necessarily aimed at inciting belief but at generating compliance, as Lisa Wedeen has succinctly shown in the case of the cynical cult of Hafez al-Assad.[14]

---

[11] Clifford Geertz, "Religion as a Cultural System," in Michael Banton (ed.), *Anthropological Approaches to the Study of Religion*, London: Tavistock, 1966, 1–46.
[12] Emile Durkheim, *Elementary Forms of Religious Life*, New York: Free Press, 1995 [1912].
[13] Landsberger, "Deification of Mao."
[14] Wedeen, *Ambiguities*, 156f.

The emergence of rituals of worshipping Mao Zedong was a consequence of the cult's disciplinary function and the accompanying repressive political climate and should not be interpreted as expression of religious worship in the first place. The quasireligious aura that the cult accrued, especially in 1968, was an awkward phenomenon for the remaining party leadership as it provided alternative sources of symbolic or, in the words of Kang Sheng, "political capital." The cult rhetoric was thus drastically diminished as soon as revolutionary committees had been installed in all provinces and autonomous regions. The cult rituals, finally, were formally interdicted after the Ninth Party Congress in 1969. Historical contextualization reveals the changing character of the Mao cult from a charismatic source of extrabureaucratic mobilization to an instrument of fostering compliance, and therefore offers comparisons with other leader cults beyond religious interpretations.

This, however, does not rule out the possibility of interpreting communism as such as a political religion.[15] Yet in this case, we have to look for "European-derived religious models"[16] rather than pre-modern Chinese examples, as Rana Mitter has recently argued. Revolutionary romanticism, the championing of violence as transformative experience, and iconoclasm were not part of traditional Chinese religion or the emperor cult but shaped by modern European experience and mediated through the Chinese New Culture movement in the 1910s and 1920s. The concept of political religion thus might be fruitfully employed in comparing modern personality cults, as long as it follows a succinct definition and does not belittle the detailed analysis of political contexts and power relations as antiquated positivism.

The existence of personal worship, fetishism, and cults in dictatorships based on scientific truth claims should sharpen attention about the insufficient cohesive powers commanded by systems of rationally functioning bureaucracies and the integrating function provided by cults. Hartmut Böhme has therefore reversed Max Weber's famous dictum and spoken of a trend toward "re-enchantment" in modern societies and claimed that politics, even in democracies, cannot function without some form of cult,

---

[15] On this point, see, as well, Mark Gamsa, "The Religious Dimension of Politics in Maoist China," in *Religion Compass* 3.3 (2009), 459–70.

[16] Rana Mitter, "Maoism in the Cultural Revolution: A Political Religion?" in Roger Griffin, Robert Mallett, and John Tortorice (eds.), *The Sacred in Twentieth-Century Politics: Essays in Honour of Professor Stanley G. Payne*, Houndmills: Palgrave Macmillan, 2009, 143.

while on the contrary cults can function "without democracy."[17] Kang Youwei's future state in the Age of Great Equality would therefore have probably been doomed to failure due to its sterility. The CCP, on the other hand, has tried to circumvent this dilemma by retaining the cohesive powers of a diminished political leader cult until the present, though clearly framed by collective leadership, as well as allowing for various non-political star cults to blossom within what are officially referred to as "culture industries."

The question of whether the populace actually believes in the claims of the leader cult is of secondary importance given the CCP's monopoly of power. Up to the Cultural Revolution, Mao had always been able to negate publicly his responsibility for policy failures, thus damaging the image of the party but not his own.[18] The cult anarchy during the Cultural Revolution and the alleged treachery of the cult's most prominent supporter, Lin Biao, however, resulted in a profound erosion of trust in the infallibility of the CCP Chairman. Still it did not change the fundamental patterns of communication. Instead of inspiring public belief, the cult was turned from a popular into a cynical device of rule. After 1978, most loyalties were shifted and eased Deng Xiaoping's radical transformation of China toward a market economy. The constant twists in line had evaporated prior existing faith in the eternal correctness of Mao's teachings. It therefore was to take another decade of disillusionment and the violent crackdown on the protests at Tiananmen Square before Mao's image made its reappearance, imbued with all kinds of nostalgic, religious, and commercial sentiments, and thus contradicted the long-standing efforts of the CCP to petrify Mao's image and safely relegate it along with Marxism-Leninism to the realm of the party historians.

The multifaceted posthumous cult of Mao Zedong could draw on a variety factors, including disillusionment, nostalgia, renewed national pride, the incorporation of religious traditions, and commercial interests, all of which worked together in turning the former CCP Chairman into what Geremie Barmé has termed "EveryMao,"[19] an empty signifier freely attachable to varying trends. The deep immersion of Mao's image within CCP history as well as Cultural Revolutionary cleavages within the party have perpetuated the necessity to control the public image of Mao and have so far

---

[17] Hartmut Böhme, *Fetischismus und Kultur* [Fetishism and Culture], Reinbek bei Hamburg: Rowohlt, 2006, 23.

[18] Similar cases are reported from the Soviet Union and Nazi Germany, where "Wenn das der Führer wüßte ..." ("If only the Führer knew that ...") became a common proverb.

[19] Barmé, *Shades of Mao*, 19.

kept the party leadership from following Khrushchev's example. Instead of reassessing Mao's legacy, the Cultural Revolution was declared taboo for critical research. Yet until the party finally allows for an independent assessment of Mao and opens its archives, the shadow of Mao will continue to haunt his successors.

Bibliography

Archival Sources

The following stacks have been accessed at the Hebei Provincial Archives (Shijiazhuang) within the limits of the official restrictions. The exact titles and numbers of the respective documents are given in the footnotes.

Stack Number	Stack Title	Period
855	Hebei Provincial Party Committee	1949–82
864	Propaganda Department of the Hebei Provincial Party Committee	1949–76
896	Hebei Provincial Party Committee of the Communist Youth League of China	1949–76
907	Hebei Provincial People's Government	1949–85
919	Hebei Provincial Revolutionary Committee	1968–82
957	Hebei Provincial United Handicrafts Cooperative	1949–83
996	Hebei Provincial Industrial and Commercial Administrative Control Bureau	1951–76
1030	Hebei Provincial Culture Office	1949–77
1032	Hebei Provincial Broadcasting and Television Office	1949–76
1053	Hebei Provincial Publishing and Distribution Bureau	1949–76

Sources and Literature

The following list includes both quasi-archival sources and published literature in Chinese and Western languages. Documents or leader speeches quoted from collections such as the Chinese Cultural Revolution Database CD-ROM or the Red Guard tabloids appear in the footnotes with full details and are not listed separately again in the bibliography.

4800 budui moubu weishengke dangzhibu, *Wuxian zhongyu Mao zhuxi geming luxian jiushi shengli* [Being Boundlessly Loyal to Chairman Mao's Revolutionary Line Means Victory], Beijing: Beijing junqu zhengzhibu/houjinbu, 1968.

A'erbaniya "Renmin zhi sheng bao" bianjibu, "Chedi jielu Heluxiaofu jituan guanyu suowei fandui 'geren mixin' de weixian yinmou" [Thoroughly

Expose the Dangerous Intrigue of the Khrushchev Clique Concerning the So-Called Opposing "Personality Cults"], Beijing: Renmin chubanshe, 1964.

Aijmer, Göran, "Political Ritual: Aspects of the Mao Cult during the Cultural Revolution," in *China Information* 11.2/3 (1996), 215–31.

Andreas, Joel, "Battling over Political and Cultural Power during the Chinese Cultural Revolution," in *Theory and Society* 31 (2002), 463–519.

"The Structure of Charismatic Mobilization: A Case Study of Rebellion during the Cultural Revolution," in *American Sociological Review* 72 (2007), 434–58.

Ankang shi difangzhi bianzuan weiyuanhui (ed.), *Ankang xian zhi* [Ankang County Gazetteer], Xi'an: Shaanxi renmin chubanshe, 1989.

Apor, Balázs, Jan C. Behrends, Polly Jones, and E. A. Rees (eds.), *The Leader Cult in Communist Dictatorships: Stalin and the Eastern Bloc*, Houndmills: Palgrave Macmillan, 2004.

Apter, David E. and Tony Saich, *Revolutionary Discourse in Mao's Republic*, Cambridge, MA: Harvard University Press, 1994.

Austin, John L., *How to Do Things with Words: The William James Lectures Delivered at Harvard University in 1955*, 2nd edition edited by J. O. Urmson and Marina Sbisà, Cambridge, MA: Harvard University Press, 1975.

"Ba zhengfu xiang wo guo zhengfu zengsong mangguo he mangguo shumiao" [The Government of Pakistan Has Presented Our Government with Mangos and Mango Seedlings], in *Renmin ribao*, 8 September 1968.

Baishui xian xianzhi bianzuan weiyuanhui (ed.), *Baishui xian zhi* [Baishui County Gazetteer], Xi'an: Xi'an ditu chubanshe, 1989.

Barmé, Geremie R., *Shades of Mao: The Posthumous Cult of the Great Leader*, Armonk, NY: M. E. Sharpe, 1996.

Bauer, Wolfgang, *China and the Search for Happiness: Recurring Themes in Four Thousand Years of Chinese Cultural History*, translated by Michael Shaw, New York: Seabury Press, 1976.

Bei Guancheng, "I Saw Chairman Mao!!!" in Schoenhals (ed.), *China's Cultural Revolution*, 148–49.

"Beijing gongyezhi" bianji weihui (ed.), *Beijing gongye zhi. Yinshua zhi* [Beijing Industry Gazetteer. Printing Gazetteer], Beijing: Zhongguo kexue jishu chubanshe, 2001.

Beijing liushisi zhong hongweibing zongbu, "Kaizhan 'yi ri zhongzihua' huodong chubu yijian" [Preliminary Opinions on Launching a "Loyalty-ficate the Whole Day" Campaign], 13 April 1968.

Beijing ribao bangongshi (ed.), *Kan Jiefangjun bao xiangdao de jige wenti* [Look How the *Liberation Army News* Thought of a Few Questions], 28 May 1965.

Beijing shi Fengtaiqu difangzhi bianzuan weiyuanhui (ed.), *Beijing shi Fengtaiqu zhi* [Beijing City Fengtai District Gazetteer], Beijing: Beijing chubanshe, 2001.

Beijing shi gong'anju Chongwen fenju (ed.), *Beijing Chongwen gong'an shiliao* [Beijing Chongwen Public Security Historical Materials], 3 vols., Beijing: Neibu kanwu, 2000.

Beijing shida tiyuxi geweihui, "Mao zhuxi yulu hongxiaobing cao" chuangbianzu, "Mao zhuxi yulu hongxiaobing cao" [Little Red Soldier Chairman Mao Quotation Gymnastics], in *Jiaoyu geming*, 20 January 1968.

Beijing shipin zongchang geming weiyuanhui zhengzhi bangongshi, *Beijing shipin zongchang huoxue huoyong Mao Zedong sixiang 5* [Beijing General Foodstuff Factory Lively Studies and Applies Mao Zedong Thought 5], 13 June 1968.

"Beijing weishuqu gei Mao zhuxi de zhijing xin" [A Congratulatory Letter to Chairman Mao from the Beijing Garrison], in *Beijing ribao*, 14 August 1967.

Bergère, Marie-Claire, *Sun Yat-sen*, translated by Janet Lloyd, Stanford: Stanford University Press, 1998 [1994].

Bernstein, Eduard, *Ferdinand Lassalle as a Social Reformer*, London: Swan Sonnenschein, 1893.

Böhme, Hartmut, *Fetischismus und Kultur* [Fetishism and Culture], Reinbek bei Hamburg: Rowohlt, 2006.

Bourdieu, Pierre, "The Social Space and the Genesis of Groups," in *Theory and Society* 14.6 (November 1985), 723–44.

Language and Symbolic Power, Cambridge: Polity Press, 1991.

Brown, Jeremy, "Staging Xiaojinzhuang: The City in the Countryside, 1974–1976," in Esherick, Pickowicz, and Walder (eds.), *The Cultural Revolution as History*, 153–84.

Bu Weihua, "Pipan 'zichanjieji fandong luxian'" [Criticizing the "Reactionary Capitalist Line"], in Guo, Wang, and Han (eds.), *Shinian fengyu*, 90–118.

Burleigh, Michael, "National Socialism as a Political Religion," in *Totalitarian Movements and Political Religions* 1.2 (2000), 1–26.

Butler, Judith, *Excitable Speech: A Politics of the Performative*, New York, London: Routledge, 1997.

Chan, Anita, Richard Madsen, and Jonathan Unger, *Chen Village: The Recent History of a Peasant Community in Mao's China*, Berkeley: University of California Press, 1984.

Chan, Anita, Stanley Rosen, and Jonathan Unger (eds.), *On Socialist Democracy and the Chinese Legal System: The Li Yizhe Debates*, Armonk, NY: M. E. Sharpe, 1985.

Chang Jung and Jon Halliday, *Mao: The Unknown Story*, New York: Alfred A. Knopf, 2005.

"Chedi pipan Li Zaihan de cuowu yanxing. Yibai ershi li" [Thoroughly Criticize the Erroneous Words of Li Zaihan: 120 Examples], n.p.: 1969.

Cheek, Timothy, "Introduction: The Making and Breaking of the Party-State in China," in Cheek and Saich (eds.), *New Perspectives*, 3–19.

Propaganda and Culture in Mao's China: Deng Tuo and the Intelligentsia, Oxford: Clarendon Press, 1998.

Cheek, Timothy (ed.), *A Critical Introduction to Mao*, Cambridge: Cambridge University Press, 2010.

Cheek, Timothy and Tony Saich (eds.), *New Perspectives on State Socialism in China*, Armonk, NY: M. E. Sharpe, 1997.

Chen Donglin, *Neiluan yu kangzheng."Wenhua da geming" de shi nian (1966–1971)* [Civil Disorder and Resistance: The Ten Years of the "Cultural Revolution" (1966–1976)], Changchun: Jilin renmin chubanshe, 1994.

"Chen Mingshu gongran wumie Mao zhuxi. Minge zhongyang xiaozu yizhi tong-chi Chen Mingshu kuangwang wuzhi" [Chen Mingshu Openly Slanders Chairman Mao: The Central Leadership Group of the Revolutionary Committee of the Chinese Guomindang Unanimously Denounces Chen Mingshu's Arrogance and Shamelessness], in *Renmin ribao*, 15 July 1957.

Chen Tsung-Hsi, Wang An-Tsiang and Wang I-Ting, *General Chiang Kai-Shek: Builder of New China*, Shanghai: Commercial Press, 1929.

Chen Xiaoya, "Mao Zedong gei Jiang Qing de xin zhenwei bian" [Is Mao Zedong's Letter to Jiang Qing Authentic or Fake?], in Ding Kaiwen (ed.), *Chongshen Lin Biao zui'an* [Reassessing the Criminal Case of Lin Biao], New York: Mingjing chubanshe, 2004, 614–20.

Chen Yunqian, *Chongbai yu jiyi. Sun Zhongshan zhuhao de jiangou yu chuanbo* [Worship and Memory: The Construction and Propagation of the Political Symbol Sun Zhongshan], Nanjing: Nanjing daxue chubanshe, 2009.

Cheng, J. Chester (ed.), *The Politics of the Chinese Red Army: A Translation of the Bulletin of Activities of the People's Liberation Army*, Stanford, CA: Hoover Institution on War, Revolution, and Peace, 1966.

Cheng Shi, Wang Xiaoling, and Kai Zheng, *Wenge xiaoliaoji* [Cultural Revolutionary Laughing Matters], Chengdu: Xi'nan caijing daxue chubanshe, 1988.

Chi Zehou, "Zhonggong 'Jiu da' neimu suoyi" [Random Memories of the Background to the "Ninth Party Congress"], in *Yanhuang chunqiu* 3 (2003), 42–9.

Chiang, Kai-shek, *China's Destiny*, New York: Macmillan, 1947.

"Chongzuo xian geming weiyuanhui shengchanzu guanyu fenpei gao 'zhong'zihua huanjing buzhu jingfei de tongzhi" [Notice of the Chongwen County Revolutionary Committee Production Group Concerning the Allocation of Subsidy Funds to Conduct the "Loyalty-fication" of the Environment], 25 September 1968.

Clark, Paul, *The Chinese Cultural Revolution: A History*, Cambridge: Cambridge University Press, 2008.

Clifton, Rita and John Simmons, *Brands and Branding*, Princeton, NJ: Bloomberg Press, 2004.

Cong Jin, *Quzhe fazhan de suiyue* [Years of Tortuous Development], Zhengzhou: Henan renmin chubanshe, 1989.

Corner, Paul (ed.), *Popular Opinion in Totalitarian Regimes: Fascism, Nazism, Communism*, Oxford: Oxford University Press, 2009.

Da pipan ziliao xuanbian. Lu Dingyi fangeming xiuzhengzhuyi jiaoyu yanlun zhaibian [Selection of Criticism Materials: Extracts from Lu Dingyi's Counterrevolutionary Reactionary Utterances on Education], Shanghai: "Neikan" fanxiubing, May 1967.

Dallin, Alexander, Jonathan Harris, and Grey Hodnett (eds.), *Diversity in International Communism: A Documentary Record, 1961–1963*, New York: Columbia University Press, 1963.

"Dangdai Zhongguo de Beijing" bianjibu (ed.), *Dangdai Beijing dashiji* [Records of Major Events in Contemporary Beijing], Beijing: Dangdai Zhongguo chubanshe, 2003.

Deng Lifeng, "'San zhi liang jun' shulun" [Treatise on the "Three Supports, Two Militaries"], in *Dangdai Zhongguoshi yanjiu* 8.6 (2001), 39–52.

"Renmin jiefangjun de 'san zhi liang jun'" [The PLA's "Three Supports, Two Militaries"], in Guo, Wang, and Han (eds.), *Shinian fengyu*, 176–208.

Deng Xiaoping, *Deng Xiaoping wenxuan* [Selected Works of Deng Xiaoping], 3 vols., Beijing: Renmin chubanshe, 1994 [1983].

Dikötter, Frank, *Mao's Great Famine: The History of China's Most Devastating Catastrophe, 1958–62*, London: Bloomsbury, 2010.

Ding Xiaoping, "Fulu: 'Mao Zedong yinxiang' jiuban tushu kaozheng suoyin" [Appendix: Verified Index to Old Editions of 'Accounts of Mao Zedong'], in Ding Xiaoping and Fang Jiankang (eds.), *Mao Zedong yinxiang* [Accounts of Mao Zedong], Beijing: Zhongyang wenxian chubanshe, 2003, 298–303.

Dongfang hong zhanxiao (ed.), *Xuexi jiefangjun zhengzhi gongzuo jingyan* [Studying the Experiences of PLA Political Work], n.p., December 1966.

Dubao shouce (neibu cankao) [Newspaper Readers' Handbook (Internal Reference)], Nanjing: Nanjing nongxueyuan geming weiyuanhui zheng-gongzu and Nanjing wuxiandian gongyexiao geming weiyuanhui zheng-gongzu, 1969.

Durkheim, Emile, *Elementary Forms of Religious Life*, New York: Free Press, 1995 [1912].

Dutton, Michael, "Mango Mao: Infections of the Sacred," in *Public Culture* 16.2 (2004), 161–87.

Editorial Department of the *People's Daily*, *More on the Historical Experience of the Dictatorship of the Proletariat*, Beijing: Foreign Languages Press, 1959.

On the Historical Experience of the Dictatorship of the Proletariat, Beijing: Foreign Languages Press, 1959.

Eighth National Congress of the Communist Party of China: Documents, Beijing: Foreign Languages Press, 1981.

"Enwei'er Huocha tongzhi de jianghua (zhi yi)" [Comrade Enver Hoxha's Speech (Part 1)], in *Renmin ribao*, 17 November 1961.

Esherick, Joseph, "Founding a Republic, Electing a President: How Sun Yat-sen Became *Guofu*," in Shinkichi and Schiffrin (eds.), *China's Republican Revolution*, 129–52.

Esherick, Joseph, Paul Pickowicz, and Andrew G. Walder (eds.), *The Cultural Revolution as History*, Stanford, CA: Stanford University Press, 2006.

Esherick, Joseph W. and Jeffrey N. Wasserstrom, "Acting Out Democracy: Political Theater in Modern China," in *Journal of Asian Studies* 49.4 (November 1990), 835–65.

Fang Hanqi, Ning Shufan, and Chen Yeshao (eds.), *Zhongguo xinwen shiye tongshi* [General History of the Chinese News Industry], vol. 3, Beijing: Zhongguo renmin daxue chubanshe, 2000 [1999].

Fang Qiu, "Bu neng huibi yaohai wenti. Ping Wu Han tongzhi 'guanyu "Hai Rui ba guan" de ziwo piping'" [One Cannot Avoid the Crucial Questions: Critique of Comrade Wu Han's "Self-Criticism Concerning 'Hai Rui Dismissed from Office'"], in *Renmin ribao*, 7 April 1966.

Feng Jianhui, *Zouchu geren chongbai* [Doing Away with Personality Cults], Zhengzhou: Henan renmin chubanshe, 2001.

"Fengjian zhuyi sixiang yidu yinggai suqing" [All Feudalist Thinking Should Be Removed], in *Renmin ribao*, 18 July 1980.

Forster, Keith, "The Politics of Destabilization and Confrontation: The Campaign against Lin Biao and Confucius in Zhejiang Province, 1974," in *China Quarterly* 107 (September 1986), 433–62.

Fraenkel, Ernst, *The Dual State: A Contribution to the Theory of Dictatorship*, New York: Oxford University Press, 1941.

Gamsa, Mark, "The Religious Dimension of Politics in Maoist China," in *Religion Compass* 3.3 (2009), 459–70.

Gao Hua, *Hong taiyang shi zenyang sheng qilai de. Yan'an zhengfeng yundong de lailong qumai* [How the Red Sun Rose: A History of the Yan'an Rectification Movement], Hong Kong: Chinese University Press, 2000.

Gao Wenqian, *Wannian Zhou Enlai* [Zhou Enlai's Later Years], New York: Mingjing chubanshe, 2003.

Geertz, Clifford, "Religion as a Cultural System," in Michael Banton (ed.), *Anthropological Approaches to the Study of Religion*, London: Tavistock Publications, 1966, 1–46.

Gentile, Emilio, "Fascism, Totalitarianism and Political Religion: Definitions and Critical Reflections on Criticism of an Interpretation," in *Totalitarian Movements and Political Religions* 5.3 (2004), 326–75.

Politics as Religion, Princeton, NJ: Princeton University Press, 2006.

Gill, Graeme, "The Soviet Leader Cult: Reflections on the Structure of Leadership in the Soviet Union," in *British Journal of Political Science* 10 (1980), 167–86.

Gittings, John, *Survey of the Sino–Soviet Dispute: A Commentary and Extracts from the Recent Polemics 1963–1967*, London: Oxford University Press, 1968.

Goldman, Merle, *Sowing the Seeds of Democracy in China: Political Reform in the Deng Xiaoping Era*, Cambridge, MA: Harvard University Press, 1994.

"Guanyu 'Lin Biao yu Kong Meng zhi dao' fudao cailiao" [Tutorial Materials on "Lin Biao and the Way of Kong and Meng"], February 1974.

Guizhou sheng geming weiyuanhui chengli shishi dahui, "Gei Mao zhuxi de zhijing dian" [A Congratulatory Telegram to Chairman Mao], 14 February 1967, in *Geming weiyuanhui hao* [Revolutionary Committees Are Good], Xi'an: Shaanxi renmin chubanshe, 1968, 49–52.

"Guizhou sheng geweihui yi feng gongkai xin" [An Open Letter to the Guizhou Revolutionary Committee], in *Shancheng chunlei* 27 (1968), 8–16.

Guo Dehong, Wang Haiguang, and Han Gang (eds.), *Quzhe tansuo (1956–1966)* [Complicated Explorations (1956–1966)], Chengdu: Sichuan renmin chubanshe, 2004.

(eds.), *Shinian fengyu (1966–1976)* [Ten Years of Troubled Times (1966–1976)], Chengdu: Sichuan renmin chubanshe, 2004.

Guo Moruo, "Ba Mao Zedong sixiang weida hongqi chashang kexue jishu zui gaofeng" [Hoist the Red Flag of Mao Zedong Thought at the Highest Peak of Science and Technology], 14 March 1968, in *Zhongguo kexueyuan (Jing qu) shou jie huoxue huoyong Mao Zedong sixiang jijifenzi daibiao dahui* [First Lively Study and Apply Mao Zedong Thought Activist Congress at the Chinese Academy of Sciences (Capital District)], April 1968.

Guojia tiwei "Hongse xuanchuanyuan" (ed.), *Mao zhuxi yulu cao huibian* [Collection of Chairman Mao Quotation Gymnastics], n.p., 1968.

Haijun di er ci huoxue huoyong Mao Zedong sixiang jijifenzi and Di sanci sihao liandui wuhao zhanshi daibiao dahui mishuchu (eds.), *Dahui xuzhi* [Essential Knowledge for the Assembly], January 1970.

Han Gang, "Zhengfeng yundong he fanyoupai douzheng" [Rectification Movement and Struggle the against Rightists], in Guo, Wang, and Han (eds.), *Quzhe tansuo*, 119–87.

Harrison, Henrietta, *The Making of the Republican Citizen: Political Ceremonies and Symbols in China 1911–1929*, Oxford: Oxford University Press, 2000.

Hebei sheng geming weiyuanhui, "Guanyu jianli qingshi baogao zhidu de qingshi" [Instruction on Establishing an Asking for and Reporting Back System], 22 June 1968.

Hebei sheng Xinhua shudian (ed.), *Hebei tushu faxing zhi* [Hebei Book Distribution Gazetteer], 2 vols., unrevised manuscript, 1990.

Hebei sheng xuanchuanbu (ed.), *1958–1965 dashiji* [Major Events in the Years 1958–1965], unpublished manuscript, 21 February 1966.

Hegel, Georg W.F., *Phenomenology of the Spirit*, Oxford: Oxford University Press, 1977 [1807].

Heiber, Beatrice and Helmut Heiber (eds.), *Die Rückseite des Hakenkreuzes. Absonderliches aus den Akten des Dritten Reiches* [The Swastika's Backside: Strange Tales from the Files of the Third Reich], Munich: DTV, 1993.

Heilmann, Sebastian, *Sozialer Protest in der VR China. Die Bewegung vom 5. April 1976 und die Gegen-Kulturrevolution der Siebziger Jahre* [Social Protest in the People's Republic of China: The 5 April Movement of 1976 and the Counter-Cultural Revolution of the 1970s], Hamburg: Institut für Asienkunde, 1994.

Heller, Klaus and Jan Plamper (eds.), *Personenkulte im Stalinismus* [Personality Cults in Stalinism], Göttingen: V&R unipress, 2005.

Heller, Steven, *Iron Fists: Branding the 20th-Century Totalitarian State*, London: Phaidon Press, 2008.

Holm, David, *Art and Ideology in Revolutionary China*, Oxford: Clarendon Press, 1991

Holmes, Michael, *Communication Theory: Media, Technology, Society*, London: Sage, 2005.

Hongdaihui zhengfa gongshe wenge jianxun bianjibu (ed.), "Liandong dongtai" [United Action Platform], in *Wenge jianxun zengkan* 62, 6 May 1967, 4.

Hu Ping and Zhang Shengyou, "Lishi chensi lu. Jinggangshan hongweibing da chuanlian ershi zhounian cha" [Historical Reflections in Memory of the Twentieth Anniversary of the Red Guards' Great Exchange of Experiences Trips to the Jinggang Mountains], in Zhou Ming (ed.), *Lishi zai zheli chensi. 1966–1976 nian jishi* [Here History Is Lost in Thought: True Record of the Years 1966 to 1976], vol. 5, Taiyuan: Beiyue wenyi chubanshe, 1989, 1–68.

Huang Yao, *Luo Ronghuan nianpu* [Chronicle of the Life of Luo Ronghuan], Beijing: Renmin chubanshe, 2002.

Huang Yongqiang, "Geming weiyuanhui jigou qingkuang (Shenyang junqu canmou Huang Yongqiang tongzhi jieshao)" [The Situation of the Revolutionary

Committee Institutions (Explained by Shenyang Military District Staff Officer, Comrade Huang Yongqiang], in Shandong sheng weisheng fangyizhan hongqi gongshe xuanchuanzu (ed.), *Dou pi gai canzheng ziliao* [Materials on Participating in Struggle-Criticism-Reform], n.p., 1968.

Hung, Chang-tai, "The Dance of Revolution: Yangge in Beijing in the Early 1950s," in *China Quarterly* 181 (2005), 82–99.

"Mao's Parades: State Spectacles in China in the 1950s," in *China Quarterly* 190 (2007), 411–31.

Ishimaru, F. T., *Chiang Kaishek ist Gross* [Chiang Kaishek Is Great], Hankow: Chengchung Verlag, 1938.

Ji Fengyuan, *Linguistic Engineering: Language and Politics in Mao's China*, Honolulu: University of Hawaii Press, 2004.

Jiangsu Nanjing caimao xitong geming zaofan lianhe weiyuanhui, *Guanyu xuexi Shijiazhuang shi kaizhan "san zhongyu" huodong qingkuang de huibao (xuanchuan gao)* [Report on Learning from the Development of "Three Loyalty" Activities in Shijiazhuang Municipality (Propagation Draft)], 1 June 1968.

"Jiazhang liandui sixiang gongzuo de yi ba yaoshi. Ji Lanzhou budui de yiku yundong" [A Key to Strengthening Ideological Work in the Companies: On the Remembering Bitterness Campaign in the Lanzhou Armed Forces], in *Jiefangjun bao*, 28 September 1960.

Jie Si, "Fandui xingshi zhuyi" [Oppose Formalism], in *Renmin ribao*, 31 January 1978.

Jin Chunming, Huang Yuchong, and Chang Huimin (eds.), *"Wenge" shiqi guaishi guaiyu* [Weird Things and Weird Words from the Period of the Cultural Revolution], Beijing: Qiushi chubanshe, 1989.

Jin Dalu, "Shanghai jiedai waisheng hongweibing de wu ge jieduan" [The Five Phases of Receiving Red Guards from Other Provinces in Shanghai], in *Qingnian yanjiu* 9 (2005), 42–9.

Jin Qiu, *The Culture of Power: The Lin Biao Incident in the Cultural Revolution*, Stanford, CA: Stanford University Press, 1999.

Jing mian er chang Mao Zedong sixiang xuexiban (ed.), *Zhuci* [Congratulations], 23 April 1968.

Jones, Polly, "From Stalinism to Post-Stalinism: De-Mythologising Stalin, 1953–56," in *Totalitarian Movements and Political Religions* 4.1 (2004), 127–48.

Junshi kexueyuan junshi lishi yanjiubu (ed.), *Zhongguo renmin jiefangjun liushi nian dashiji (1927–1987)* [Major Events in Sixty Years of the PLA (1927–1987)], Beijing: Junshi kexue chubanshe, 1988.

Junzheng daxue pi Lin pi Kong bangongshi (ed.), *Chedi pipan Lin Biao yi huo paozhi "Lin Biao yulu," "Lin Biao jinianguan" zuixing dahui pipan fayan huiji* [Collection of Criticism Speeches from the Thoroughly Criticize the Crimes of the Lin Biao Gang Concocting "Quotations from Lin Biao" and a "Lin Biao Memorial Hall" Assembly], n.p., 1–5.

Kau, Michael Y. M. (ed.), *The Lin Piao Affair: Power Politics and Military Coup*, White Plains, NY: International Arts and Science Press, 1975.

"Keke mangguo enqing shen – Xinxin xiangzhi hongtaiyang. Mao zhuxi zengsong zhengui liwu de teda xixun zhuankai yihou" [Every Mango Is Full of Deep

Kindness – Every Heart Longs for the Red Sun: The Time after the Incredibly Happy News Had Spread that Chairman Mao Offered a Precious Gift], in *Renmin ribao*, 8 August 1968.

Kershaw, Ian, "'Working towards the Führer': Reflections on the Nature of the Hitler Dictatorship," in Ian Kershaw and Moshe Lewin (eds.), *Stalinism and Nazism: Dictatorships in Comparison*, Cambridge: Cambridge University Press, 1997, 88–106.

Khrushchev, Sergei, *Nikita Khrushchev and the Creation of a Superpower*, University Park: Pennsylvania State University Press, 2000.

King, Richard (ed.), *Art in Turmoil: The Chinese Cultural Revolution 1966–76*, Vancouver: UBC Press, 2010.

Klein, Naomi, "America Is Not a Hamburger: President Bush's Attempts to Rebrand the United States Are Doomed," in *The Guardian*, 14 March 2002.

Klemperer, Viktor, *LTI. Notizbuch eines Philologen* [Lingua Tertii Imperii: A Philologists' Notebook], Leipzig: Reclam, 1975 [1957].

Landsberger, Stefan R., "The Deification of Mao: Religious Imagery and Practices during the Cultural Revolution and Beyond," in Woei Lien Chong (ed.), *China's Great Proletarian Cultural Revolution: Master Narratives and Post-Mao Counternarratives*, Lanham, MD: Rowman & Littlefield, 2002, 139–84.

Leese, Daniel, "The Mao Cult as Communicative Space," in *Totalitarian Movements and Political Religions* 8.3/4 (September 2007), 623–39.

"Mao the Man and Mao the Icon," in Timothy Cheek (ed.), *A Critical Introduction to Mao*, Cambridge: Cambridge University Press, 2010, 219–40.

"Revising Political Verdicts in Post-Mao China: The Case of Beijing Fengtai District," unpublished paper.

Legge, James, *The Chinese Classics, vol. 1: Confucian Analects, the Great Learning, the Doctrine of the Mean*, Hong Kong: Hong Kong University Press, 1960 [1861].

Lenin, Vladimir I., "On the Question of Dialectics (1915)," in *Collected Works*, vol. 38, Moscow: Progress, 1972, 355–64.

Lepsius, M. Rainer, "The Model of Charismatic Leadership and Its Applicability to the Rule of Adolf Hitler," in *Totalitarian Movements and Political Religions* 7.2 (2006), 175–90.

Li Gongzhong, *Zhongshan ling. Yi ge xiandai zhengzhi zhuhao de dansheng* [The Sun Yat-sen Mausoleum: The Making of a Political Symbol in Modern China], Beijing: Shehui kexue wenxian chubanshe, 2009.

Li Ke and Hao Shengzhang, *"Wenhua da geming" zhong de renmin jiefangjun* [The PLA during the "Great Cultural Revolution"], Beijing: Zhonggong dangshi ziliao chubanshe, 1989.

Li Leiming, *Lishi de jiyi. Mao Zedong xiangzhang shangxi* [Historical Recollections: Appreciating Mao Zedong Badges], Beijing: Zhongyang wenxian chubanshe, 2006.

Li Xuekun and Zhang Peihang, "Dangnei geren chongbai de lishi kaocha. Jian bo Kang Sheng de zaoshen miulun" [Historical Exploration of Inner-Party Personal Worship: Refuting Kang Sheng's Absurd God-Building Theory], in *Dangshi yanjiu* 2 (1981), 22–7.

Li Zhensheng, *Red-Color News Soldier: A Chinese Photographer's Odyssey through the Cultural Revolution*, London: Phaidon, 2003.

Li Zhisui and Anne F. Thurston, *The Private Life of Chairman Mao: The Memoirs of Mao's Personal Physician Dr. Li Zhisui*, New York: Random House, 1994.

"Liandong de qianshen. 'Xicheng jiuchadui' de zui'e shi" [A Precursor of United Action: A History of Crimes of the "Western District Picket Corps"], in Hongweibing Shanghai silingbu (ed.), *Polan "liandong,"* Shanghai: Neibu kanwu, May 1967.

Lin Biao, "Foreword to the Second Edition of Quotations from Chairman Mao Tse-tung," in *Quotations from Chairman Mao Tse-tung*, 1966.

Lin Li, "Suiyue de jianzheng. Sichuan sheng zhanlanguan ji Mao zhuxi suxiang xiujian shimo" [Witness of the Times: The Story of Building the Sichuan Province Exhibition Center and the Chairman Mao Statue], in *Sichuan dang'an* 3 (2004), 24–5.

"Suiyue de jianzheng. Sichuan sheng zhanlanguan ji Mao zhuxi suxiang xiujian shimo (xu)" [Witness of the Times: The Story of Building the Sichuan Province Exhibition Center and the Chairman Mao Statue (Continued)], in *Sichuan dang'an* 4 (2004), 44–5.

Lin Ling, "Cong 'an lao fenpei, an xu fenpei' de zhengyi xiangqi de" [Thinking about the Correct Translation of "Each According to His Ability, Each According to His Needs"], in *Renmin ribao*, 25 December 1958.

Lin Yunhui, "Ershi shiji liushi niandai geren chongbai de qiyuan" [The Origins of the Personality Cult in the 1960s], in *Dangshi bolan* 11 (2005), 35–8.

Linebarger, Paul Myron Anthony (ed.), *Gospel of Sun Chung Shan, According to Paul Linebarger*, Paris: Editions-Mid-Nations, 1932.

Linebarger, Paul Myron Wentworth, *Sun Yat-sen and the Chinese Republic*, New York: AMS Press, 1969 [1925].

Liu Gao and Shi Feng (eds.), *Xin Zhongguo chuban wushi nian jishi* [Recollections about Fifty Years of Publishing in New China], Beijing: Xinhua chubanshe, 1999.

Liu Yongxiang, "Guiyang renmin guangchang Mao zhuxi suxiang diaosu qian-hou" [The Times of the Chairman Mao Statue at Guiyang People's Square], in *Wenshi tiandi* 7 (2002), 36–42.

Liu Zhenyang, "Dahai hangxing kao hangshou, gan geming kao Mao Zedong sixiang" [Sailing the Seas Depends on the Helmsman, Enacting Revolution Depends on Mao Zedong Thought], in *Renmin ribao*, 1 December 1967.

Lu Xing, *Rhetoric of the Chinese Cultural Revolution: The Impact on Chinese Thought, Culture, and Communication*, Columbia: University of South Carolina Press, 2004.

Lu Xun, "Tan suowei 'Danei dang'an'" [Discussing the So-Called "Palace Archives"], in *Yusi* 4.7 (28 January 1928), 1–8.

Lü Hong, "Wo ren hongweibing jiedai congzhan zhanzhang de rizi" [My Days as Head of the General Red Guard Reception Station], in *Yanhuang chunqiu* 12 (1998), 44–8.

Lüthi, Lorenz M., *The Sino–Soviet Split: Cold War in the Communist World*, Princeton, NJ: Princeton University Press, 2008.

Ma Jingjun, *Jundui Mao Zedong xiangzhang de shouzang yu jianshang* [The Collection and Appreciation of PLA Mao Zedong Badges], Beijing: Beijing shouzangjia xiehui, 2008.

MacFarquhar, Roderick, *The Hundred Flowers Campaign and the Chinese Intellectuals*, New York: Praeger, 1960.

Origins of the Cultural Revolution, 1: Contradictions among the People, 1956–1957, London: Oxford University Press, 1974.

Origins of the Cultural Revolution, 2: The Great Leap Forward, 1958–1960, New York: Columbia University Press, 1983.

Origins of the Cultural Revolution, 3: The Coming of the Cataclysm, 1961–1966, Oxford: Oxford University Press and Columbia University Press, 1997.

MacFarquhar, Roderick, Timothy Cheek, and Eugene Wu (eds.), *The Secret Speeches of Chairman Mao: From the Hundred Flowers to the Great Leap Forward*, Cambridge, MA: Council on East Asian Studies/Harvard University, 1989.

MacFarquhar, Roderick and Michael Schoenhals, *Mao's Last Revolution*, Cambridge, MA: Belknap Press of Harvard University Press, 2006.

"Mao Tse-tung's Speeches at the CCP Chengtu Conference (Part 1)," in *Issues and Studies* 11 (1973), 95–8.

"Mao Tse-tung's Speeches at the CCP Chengtu Conference (Part 2)," in *Issues and Studies* 12 (1973), 103–12.

Mao Zedong, *Quotations from Chairman Mao Tse-tung*, Beijing: Foreign Languages Press, 1966.

Mao Tsetung Poems (Chinese-English), Beijing: Shangwu yinshuguan chuban, 1976.

Selected Works of Mao Tse-tung, 4 vols., Beijing: Foreign Languages Press, 1967.

"Mao Zedong shengli wansui" guan Jiangxi sheng choujian weiyuanhui bangong-shi (ed.), *Huoxue huoyong Mao Zedong sixiang jingyan jiaoliuhui dianxiang cailiao* [Exemplary Materials of the Lively Study and Application of Mao Zedong Thought Experience Exchange Meeting], 5 November 1968.

Mao Zedong sixiang wansui [Long Live Mao Zedong Thought], n.p., 1969.

"Mao zhuxi guanyu wuchanjieji wenhua da geming de weida zhanlüe bushu de zhishi" [Chairman Mao's Instruction Regarding the Great Strategic Plan for the Great Proletarian Cultural Revolution], in *Renmin ribao*, 8 March 1968.

"Mao zhuxi he Lin Biao, Zhou Enlai deng tongzhi jiejian le xuesheng daibiao bing jianyue le wenhua da geming dajun de youxing" [Chairman Mao, Lin Biao, Zhou Enlai, and Other Comrades Receive Student Representatives and Inspect the Cultural Revolutionary Mass Parade], in *Renmin ribao*, 19 August 1966.

"Mao zhuxi yongyuan liushuai women qianjin. Ji Mao zhuxi quanshen juxing suxiang de luocheng" [Chairman Mao Forever Commands Us Forward: Remembering the Completion of the Large Full-Length Statue of Chairman Mao], in *Jinggangshan*, 6 May 1967.

"Mao zhuxi zai Zhongguo gongchandang di jiu ci quanguo daibiao dahui shang de zhongyao zhishi" [Important Instruction of Chairman Mao at the Ninth CCP Congress], n.p., 1969.

Marcuse, Jacques, *The Peking Papers: Leaves from the Notebook of a China Correspondent*, New York: Dutton, 1967.

Martin, Helmut, *Kult und Kanon. Entstehung und Entwicklung des Staatsmaoismus 1935–1978* [Cult and Canon: The Origins and Development of State Maoism, 1935–1978], Hamburg: Institut für Asienkunde, 1978.

 Cult and Canon: The Origins and Development of State Maoism, Armonk, NY: M. E. Sharpe, 1982.

McKay, Mary Jayne, "Turkmenbashi Everywhere: If You Think Saddam Was Fond of Himself, Visit Turkmenistan," CBS Broadcasting, 4 January 2004 (http://www.cbsnews.com/stories/2003/12/31/60minutes/main590913.shtml).

Mei xian difangzhi bianzuan weiyuanhui (ed.), *Mei xian zhi* [Mei County Gazetteer], Xi'an: Shaanxi renmin chubanshe, 2000.

Meisner, Maurice, *Marxism, Maoism, and Utopianism: Eight Essays*, Madison: University of Wisconsin Press, 1982.

Mitter, Rana, *A Bitter Revolution: China's Struggle with the Modern World*, Oxford: Oxford University Press, 2004.

 "Maoism in the Cultural Revolution: A Political Religion?" in Roger Griffin, Robert Mallett, and John Tortorice (eds.), *The Sacred in Twentieth-Century Politics: Essays in Honour of Professor Stanley G. Payne*, Houndmills: Palgrave Macmillan, 2009, 143–65.

Mu Qing, Guo Chaoren, and Lu Fowei, "Lishi de shenpan" [Trial of History], in *Renmin ribao*, 27 January 1981.

"Muqian quanguo youpai fenzi de gaizao qingkuang" [Current National Situation of Rightists Undergoing Reform], in Zhongyang gong'anbu (ed.), *Gong'an gongzuo jianbao* [Public Security Work Bulletin], **67**, 20 September 1959, 2.

Myers, James T., *The Apotheosis of Chairman Mao: Dynamics of the Hero Cult in the Chinese System 1949–1967*, Ph.D. dissertation, George Washington University, 1969.

Pang Xianzhi and Jin Chongji, *Mao Zedong zhuan (1949–1976)* [Biography of Mao Zedong, 1949–1976], 2 vols., Beijing: Zhongyang wenxian chubanshe, 2003.

Pascal, Blaise, *Pensées*, Hammondsworth: Penguin, 1966 [1670].

Perry, Elizabeth, "Shanghai's Strike Wave of 1957," in Cheek and Saich (eds.), *New Perspectives*, 234–61.

Perry, Elizabeth and Li Xun, "Revolutionary Rudeness: The Language of Red Guards and Rebel Workers in China's Cultural Revolution," in *Indiana East-Asian Working Paper Series on Language and Politics in Modern China* 2 (1993), 1–18.

 Proletarian Power: Shanghai in the Cultural Revolution, Boulder, CO: Westview Press, 1997.

Plamper, Jan, "Introduction: Modern Personality Cults," in Heller and Plamper (eds.), *Personality Cults in Stalinism*, 13–44.

Plekhanov, Georgi, *Lun geren zai lishi shang de zuoyong* [On the Role of the Individual in History], Moscow: Waiguowen shuji chubanju, 1950.

 Polemic on the General Line of the International Communist Movement, Beijing: Foreign Languages Press, 1965.

Popper, Karl R., *The Open Society and Its Enemies*, 2 vols., Princeton, NJ: Princeton University Press, 1963 [1945].

"Quanguo dou lai ban Mao Zedong sixiang xuexiban" [The Whole Nation Establishes Mao Zedong Thought Study Classes], in *Renmin ribao*, 12 October 1967.

Radchenko, Sergey, *Two Suns in the Heavens: The Sino–Soviet Struggle for Supremacy, 1962–1967*, Washington: Woodrow Wilson Center Press, 2009.

"Rang 'zhong yu Mao zhuxi' wu ge jinguang shanshan da zi ranhong mei gen shenjing" [Let the Five Glistening Characters "Loyal to Chairman Mao" Set Every Nerve Aflame], in *Shijiazhuang ribao*, 15 March 1968.

Rigby, Thomas (ed.), *The Stalin Dictatorship: Khrushchev's "Secret Speech" and Other Documents*, Sydney: Sydney University Press, 1968.

Rinden, Robert W., *The Cult of Mao Tse-Tung*, Ph.D. dissertation, University of Colorado, 1969.

Ruo Shui, "Lun 'ge gong song de' he 'fandui xianzhuang'" [On "Singing the Praises of" and "Opposing the Status Quo"], in *Renmin ribao*, 11 July 1957.

San Mu, "Guanyu 'wenge' qianhou Mao Zedong zhuzuo de chuban shimo" [The Story of Publishing Mao Zedong's Works in the Cultural Revolution Period], in *Shehui kexue luntan* 1 (2004), 83–91.

Schiffrin, Harold Z., *Sun Yat-sen and the Origins of the Chinese Revolution*, Berkeley: University of California Press, 1968.

Schoenhals, Michael, "Mao Zedong: Speeches at the 'Moscow Conference,'" in *Journal of Communist Studies* 2.2 (1986), 109–28.

Saltationist Socialism, Ph.D. dissertation, Stockholm, 1987.

Doing Things with Words in Chinese Politics: Five Studies, Berkeley: Center for Chinese Studies/ University of California, Berkeley, 1992.

"Selections from Propaganda Trends, Organ of the CCP Central Propaganda Department," in *Chinese Law and Government* 24.4 (1992), 5–93.

(ed.), *China's Cultural Revolution 1966–1969: Not a Dinner Party*, Armonk, NY: M. E. Sharpe, 1996.

"'Why Don't We Arm the Left?' Mao's Culpability for the Cultural Revolution's 'Great Chaos' of 1967," in *China Quarterly* 182 (2005), 277–300.

"The Global War on Terrorism as Meta-Narrative: An Alternative Reading of Recent Chinese History," in *Sungkyun Journal of East Asian Studies* 8.2 (2008), 179–201.

Schrift, Melissa, *Biography of a Chairman Mao Badge: The Creation and Mass Consumption of a Personality Cult*, New Brunswick, NJ: Rutgers University Press, 2001.

Shambaugh, David, "Building the Party-State in China, 1949–1965: Bringing the Soldier Back In," in Cheek and Saich (eds.), *New Perspectives*, 125–50.

Shanghai shi gong'anju geming zaofan lianhe zhihuibu and Zhengzhibu zaofandui (eds.), *Chedi jielu shi gong'anju jiu dangzu yuyong gongju. Jiu wenge bangongshi de taotian zuixing* 2 [Thoroughly Expose the Hired Tools of the Old City Public Security Bureau Party Organization: The Heinous Crimes of the Old Cultural Revolution Management Office, Part Two], September 1967.

Shanghai shi jiedai gedi geming xuesheng bangongshi (ed.), "'Waidi xuesheng lai Hu qingkuang fanying' jianbao" [Bulletin on the "Situation of Students from

Other Parts of the Country Coming to Shanghai"], Shanghai, August–December 1966.

Shanghai tiyu yundong weiyuanhui geming weiyuanhui and Shanghai tiyu zhanxian geming zaofan silingbu (eds.), "Tiyu geming de chunlei" [Spring Thunder of Sports Revolution], in *Tiyu zhanxian* (Shanghai), 20 November 1967, 1–4.

Shangyebu caihuiju (ed.), *Shangye caiwu huiji wenjian huibian* [Collection of Commercial and Financial Documents], 4 vols., n.p., 1981.

Sharman, Lyon, *Sun Yat-sen: His Life and Its Meaning*, Stanford, CA: Stanford University Press, 1968 [1934].

"Shi bu shi lichang wenti?" [Is It a Question of Standpoint?], in *Renmin ribao*, 14 June 1957.

Shi Zhe and Li Haiwen, *ZhongSu guanxi jianzheng lu. Shi Zhe koushu* [Witness to Sino–Soviet Relations: Recollections of Shi Zhe], Beijing: Dangdai Zhongguo chubanshe, 2005.

"Shijingshan zhongxue shi zenyang zai jiefangjun bangzhu xia fuke nao geming de. Zai geming de da pipan zhong shixian geming de dalianhe" [How Shijingshan Middle School with the Help of the PLA Returned to Study to Conduct Revolution: Realize the Great Revolutionary Alliance amid the Great Revolutionary Criticism], in *Renmin ribao*, 15 June 1967.

Shinkichi, Eto and Harold Z. Schiffrin (eds.), *China's Republican Revolution*, Tokyo: University of Tokyo Press, 1994.

Shoudu dazhuan yuanxiao hongdaihui and Cuihui fan geming zuzhi "Liandong" zhanlanhui (eds.), *Cuihui fan geming zuzhi "Liandong" zhanlanhui. Neirong jieshao* [Destroy the Counterrevolutionary Organization "United Action" Exhibition: Explanation of Contents], August 1967.

"Shoudu gongren jieji ba Mao zhuxi zeng de zhengui liwu zhuan songgei wo sheng gongren jieji he quansheng geming renmin" [The Capital Working Class Has Offered the Precious Gift Presented by Chairman Mao Especially for the Working Class of Our Province and All Revolutionary People in the Whole Province], in *Xin Guizhou bao*, 24 September 1968.

Shoudu hongweibing chedi cuihui "liandong" geming lianluo weiyuanhui and Beijing gangyuan fuzhong kanglianjun (eds.), *Liandong fan Mao Zedong sixiang zuixing 50 lie* [Fifty Examples of United Action Crimes of Opposing Mao Zedong Thought], May 1967.

Sichuan shengwei xuanchuanbu (ed.), *Sichuan xuanchuan gongzuo dashiji* [Major Events in Sichuan Propaganda Work], Chengdu: Sichuan renmin chubanshe, 2003.

Smith, Steve A., "Local Cadres Confront the Supernatural: The Politics of Holy Water (*Shenshui*) in the PRC, 1949–1966," in *China Quarterly* 188 (2006), 999–1022.

Snow, Edgar, *Red Star over China*, London: Victor Gollancz, 1937.

The Long Revolution, New York: Random House, 1972.

Song Yongyi, *Chinese Cultural Revolution Database* (CD-ROM), Hong Kong: Chinese University Press/Universities Service Centre, 2006.

(ed.), *Xinbian hongweibing ziliao: A New Collection of Red Guard Publications*, Oakton, VA: Center for Chinese Research Materials, 2001.

Sun Changxian, *Fandui geren chongbai* [Oppose Personality Cults], Beijing: Renmin chubanshe, 1956.

Sun Yat-sen, *Kidnapped in London. Being the Story of My Capture by, Detention at, and Release from the Chinese Legation, London*, Bristol: Arrowsmith, 1897.

Taibai xian difangzhi bianzuan weiyuanhui (ed.), *Taibai xian zhi* [Taibai County Gazetteer], Xi'an: Sanqin chubanshe, 1995.

Tang Shaojie, *Yi ye zhi qiu. Qinghua daxue 1968 nian "bairi da wudou"* [One Leaf Knows the Autumn: The "One Hundred–Day Great Armed Struggle" at Qinghua University], Hong Kong: Zhongwen daxue chubanshe, 2003.

Taubman, William, *Khrushchev: The Man and His Era*, New York: Norton, 2003.

Taylor, Jeremy E., "The Production of the Chiang Kai-shek Personality Cult, 1929–1975," in *China Quarterly* 185 (2006), 96–110.

Teiwes, Frederick C., *Politics and Purges in China: Rectification and the Decline of Party Norms, 1950–1965*, Armonk, NY: M. E. Sharpe, 1979.

Leadership, Legitimacy, and Conflict in China: From a Charismatic Mao to the Politics of Succession, Armonk, NY: M. E. Sharpe, 1984.

Politics at Mao's Court: Gao Gang and Party Factionalism in the Early 1950s, Armonk, NY: M. E. Sharpe, 1990.

Teiwes, Frederick C. and Warren Sun, *The Tragedy of Lin Biao: Riding the Tiger during the Cultural Revolution, 1966–1971*, Honolulu: University of Hawaii Press, 1996.

The End of the Maoist Era: Chinese Politics during the Twilight of the Cultural Revolution 1972–1976, Armonk, NY: M. E. Sharpe, 2007.

Tianjin shi geming weiyuanhui, "Jin'ge [69] 054, Guanyu zhizhi zai qing 'jiu da,' ying guoqing deng huodong zhong chuxian de fukua langfei xianxiang de jueding" [Decision on Forbidding All Phenomena Related to Exaggeration and Waste That Appeared during Activities to Welcome the Ninth Congress and to Celebrate National Day], 24 March 1969.

"Jin'ge [69] 073, Guanyu xiang shanqu pin xiazhong nong xianzeng Mao zhuxi yulu he xiangzhang de tongzhi" [Notice Concerning the Offering of Chairman Mao Quotations and Badges for Poor and Lower-Middle Peasants in Mountainous Regions], April 1969.

"Jin'ge [69] 082, Guanyu dangqian xuanchuan gongzuo zhong cunzai de ji ge wenti he jinhou yijian" [On Certain Problems in Current Propaganda Work and Future Opinions], 9 May 1969.

Toranska, Teresa, *"Them": Stalin's Polish Puppets*, New York: Harper & Row, 1987.

Tumote zuo/you qi renmin wuzhuangbu and Tumote qi zhujun zhizuo bangongshi, "Guanyu renzhen guanche zhixing Nei Meng, Wumeng geming weiyuanhui 'guanyu jin chun zhaokai quan qu xuexi Mao zhuxi zhuzuo xianjin jiti he jijifenzi daibiao huiyi de jueding' de tongzhi" [Notice on Conscientiously Implementing the Wumeng (Inner Mongolia) Revolutionary Committee Decision "On Holding an All-District Study Chairman Mao's Works Advanced Collectives and Activists Representatives Assembly This Spring"], 18 January 1968.

Unger, Jonathan, "The Cultural Revolution at the Grass Roots," in *China Journal* 57 (January 2007), 109–37.

Urban, George R., *The Miracles of Chairman Mao: A Compendium of Devotional Literature, 1966–1970*, London: Tom Stacey Limited, 1971.

Wagemann, Mildred Lina, *The Changing Image of Mao Tse-Tung: Leadership Image and Social Structure*, Ph.D. dissertation, Cornell University, 1974.

Wagner, Vivian, *Erinnerungsverwaltung in China. Staatsarchive und Politik in der Volksrepublik* [Administrating Memory in China: State Archives and Politics in the People's Republic], Cologne: Böhlau, 2006.

Walder, Andrew G., *Fractured Rebellion: The Beijing Red Guard Movement*, Cambridge, MA: Harvard University Press, 2009.

Wang Dongxing, *Mao Zedong yu Lin Biao fangeming jituan de douzheng* [The Struggle between Mao Zedong and the Counterrevolutionary Lin Biao Clique], Beijing: Dangdai Zhongguo chubanshe, 2004 [1997].

Wang, Helen, *Chairman Mao Badges: Symbols and Slogans of the Cultural Revolution*, London: British Museum Press, 2008.

Wang Jining, "Zhanshu dongzuo yao huojiao huoxue huoyong" [Tactical Movements Should Be Lively Taught, Lively Studied, and Lively Applied], in *Jiefangjun bao*, 11 July 1958.

Wang Li, *Xianchang lishi. Wenhua da geming jishi* [On the Scene of History: Chronicle of the Great Cultural Revolution], Hong Kong: Oxford University Press, 1993.

Wang Nianyi, *Da dongluan de niandai* [A Decade of Great Upheaval], Zhengzhou: Henan renmin chubanshe, 1988.

Wang Shaoguang, *Failure of Charisma: The Cultural Revolution in Wuhan*, Oxford, New York: Oxford University Press, 1995.

Wedeen, Lisa, *Ambiguities of Domination: Politics, Rhetoric, and Symbols in Contemporary Syria*, Chicago: University of Chicago Press, 1999.

Wei Meiya, "'Mao zhuxi yulu' bianfa quancheng xunzong" [Complete Account of the Compilation of *Quotations from Chairman Mao*], in *Yanhuang chunqiu* 17.8 (1993), 10–24.

"'Mao zhuxi yulu' chuban jiemi" [Solving the Mystery of Publishing the *Quotations from Chairman Mao*], in *Dangshi bolan* 7 (2004), 4–10.

"Weishenme geren chongbai shi weifan Makesi Liening zhuyi jingshen de" [Why Personality Cults Violate the Spirit of Marxism-Leninism], in *Renmin ribao*, 30 March 1956.

White, Lynn T. III, *Policies of Chaos: The Organizational Causes of Violence in China's Cultural Revolution*, Princeton, NJ: Princeton University Press, 1989.

Whyte, Martin King, *Small Groups and Political Rituals in China*, Berkeley: University of California Press, 1974.

Wilbur, C. Martin, "Environment, Character, Chance, and Choice: Their Interplay in Making a Revolutionary," in Shinkichi and Schiffrin (eds.), *China's Republican Revolution*, 111–28.

Wong, John Y., *The Origins of an Heroic Image: Sun Yat-sen in London, 1896–1897*, Hong Kong: Oxford University Press, 1986.

Wu Guangtian, "'Wansui guan'. Yi zuo jianzhu yunhan de lishi" [Long Live Hall: History Contained in a Piece of Architecture], in *Wenshi jinghua* 173.10 (2004), 32–9.

Wu Hung, *Remaking Beijing: Tiananmen Square and the Creation of a Political Space*, London: Reaktion, 2005.

Wu Lengxi, *Yi Mao zhuxi. Wo qinshen jingli de ruogan zhongda lishi shijian pian-duan* [Remembering Chairman Mao: Fragments of Certain Major Historical Events which I Personally Experienced], Beijing: Xinhua chubanshe, 1995.

"Tong Jiaying gongshi de rizi" [Days of Working Together with Comrade Jiaying], in Dong Bian, Zhang Deshan, and Zeng Zi (eds.), *Mao Zedong he ta de mishu Tian Jiaying* [Mao Zedong and His Secretary Tian Jiaying], Beijing: Zhongyang wenxian chubanshe, 1996, 113–59.

Shinian lunzhan – 1956–1966. ZhongSu guanxi huiyilu [A Decade of Polemics, 1956–1966: A Memoir of Sino–Soviet-Relations], 2 vols., Beijing: Zhongyang wenxian chubanshe, 2000 [1999].

Wu Qisi and Li Bin, "Heiban bao. Huo sixiang jiaoyu de zhendi" [Blackboard Newspapers: The Front of Lively Thought Education], in *Jiefangjun bao*, 16 January 1965.

"Wuchan jieji wenhua da geming de ganglingxing wenjian" [A Programmatic Document of the Great Proletarian Cultural Revolution], in *Hongqi* 10, 9 August 1966.

"Wuchan jieji zhuanzheng xia jixu jinxing geming de wuchan jieji xianjinfenzi de tuchu daibiao Li Wenzhong" [Li Wenzhong: A Prominent Exponent of the Advanced Proletarian Elements Continuing to Carry Out Revolution under the Dictatorship of the Proletariat], in *Renmin ribao*, 31 December 1967.

"Wuxian zhongyu Mao zhuxi shi zui da de gong" [Boundlessly Loyal to Chairman Mao Is the Greatest Common Good], in *Jiefangjun bao*, 8 December 1967.

Wylie, Raymond F., "Mao Tse-tung, Ch'en Po-ta and the 'Sinification of Marxism,' 1936–38," in *China Quarterly* 79 (1979), 447–80.

The Emergence of Maoism: Mao Tse-tung, Ch'en Po-ta, and the Search for Chinese Theory 1935–1945, Stanford, CA: Stanford University Press, 1980.

Xu Jianhua, "Mao Zedong tongzhi you fandui geren chongbai dao jieshou geren chongbai de guocheng" [Comrade Mao Zedong and the Process from Opposing Personality Cults to Accepting Personality Cults], in *Dangshi yanjiu* 5 (1984), 72–8.

Xu Ren, Xu Miao, and Xu Ying, *Mao Zedong xiangzhang wushi nian* [Fifty Years of Mao Zedong Badges], Xi'an: Shaanxi lüyou chubanshe, 1993.

Xu Youyu, *Xingxing sese de zaofan. Hongweibing jingshen suzhi de xingcheng ji yanbian* [Rebels of All Stripes: A Study of Red Guard Mentalities], Hong Kong: Zhongwen daxue chubanshe, 1999.

Xuan Zhu, "Tan duli sikao" [On Independent Thinking], in *Renmin Ribao*, 3 July 1956.

Xuanjiao dongtai [Trends in Propaganda and Education], Beijing, 1956.

Xuexi ziliao [Study Materials], Beijing: Neibu kanwu, 1969.

Yan Fan, *Da chuanlian. Yi chang shiwuqianlie de zhengzhi lüyou* [The Great Exchange of Revolutionary Experience: An Unprecedented Occasion for Political Travel], Beijing: Jingguan jiaoyu chubanshe, 1993.

Yan Jiaqi and Gao Gao, *Turbulent Decade: A History of the Cultural Revolution*, Honolulu: University of Hawaii Press, 1995.

Yang Chengwu, "Dashu teshu weida tongshuai Mao zhuxi de juedui quanwei, dashu teshu weida de Mao Zedong sixiang de juedui quanwei. Chedi qingsuan Luo Ruiqing fandui Mao zhuxi, fandui Mao Zedong sixiang de taotian zuixing" [Establish the Absolute Authority of the Great Commander Chairman Mao in a Big Way, Establish the Absolute Authority of the Great Mao Zedong Thought: Thoroughly Settle the Heinous Crimes of Luo Ruiqing's Opposition to Chairman Mao and Mao Zedong Thought], in *Renmin ribao*, 3 November 1967.

Yang XX, "Qingzui shu" [Letter of Apology], September 1968.

Yao Wenyuan, "Ping xin bian lishiju 'Hai Rui ba guan'" [Critique of the New Historical Play *Hai Rui Dismissed from Office*], in *Wenhui bao*, 10 November 1965.

Yi Lin futongshuai wei guanghui bangyang wuxian zhongyu weida lingxiu Mao zhuxi [With Vice-Commander Lin as Glorious Example Boundlessly Loyal toward the Great Leader Chairman Mao], 2 vols., Beijing: n.d.

"Yong Mao Zedong sixiang tongshuai shengming de mei yi miaozhong. Shijiazhuang guomian yichang zhigong 'yi ri huodong Mao Zedong sixianghua' pianduan" [Rely on Mao Zedong Thought to Command Every Minute of Life: Extracts from the Shijiazhuang First Cotton Fiber Factory Workers' "Mao Zedong Thought-ify the Whole Day's Action"], in *Shijiazhuang ribao*, 24 March 1968.

Yu Houdao, *Gongheguo lingxiu, yuanshuai, jiangjun jiaowang shilu* [Records of the Interactions among PRC Leaders, Marshals, and Generals], Chengdu: Sichuan renmin chubanshe, 2001.

Yu Jinan, "Zijue de zunshou 'shao xuanchuan geren' de fangzhen" [Self-Consciously Follow the Guideline to "Reduce the Propagation of Individuals"], in *Renmin ribao*, 4 September 1980.

Yu Nan and Wang Haiguang, "Lin Biao jituan he Lin Biao shijian" [The Lin Biao Clique and the Lin Biao Incident], in Guo, Wang, and Han. (eds.), *Shinian fengyu*, 385–417.

Yuan zhonggong Beijing shiwei waidi geming shisheng jiedai weiyuanhui (ed.), *Beijing shi jiedai lai Jing chuanlian de geming shisheng he hongweibing gongzuo zongjie* [Summary of the Beijing City Reception of Revolutionary Teachers and Students from Other Places Traveling to the Capital and of Red Guard Work], September 1967.

Yun Gang, "'Yingxiong' shiguan de yi ge xin bianzhong" [A New Expression of a "Heroic" View of History], in *Renmin ribao*, 11 June 1972.

Zagoria, Donald S., *The Sino–Soviet Conflict, 1956–1961*, New York: Atheneum, 1964.

"Zai lun lichang wenti" [Discussing the Question of Standpoint Again], in *Renmin ribao*, 29 June 1957.

Zhang Huicang and Ye Jiefu, "Wo suo qinli de Mao zhuxi ba ci jiejian hongwei-bing" [My Personal Experiences of Chairman Mao's Eight Red Guard Receptions], in *Dangshi bocai* 2 (2006), 32–6.

Zhang Rengan, Yusufu Yunusi, and Lu Huaying (eds.), *Zhongguo gongchandang Hami shi (xian) lishi dashiji, 1949.10–1998.12* [Major Historical Events in the Hami City (County) CCP, October 1949–December 1998], Wulumuqi: Xinjiang renmin chubanshe, 1999.

Zhao Feng, *"Zhong"zi xia de yinying. Wenhua da geming zhong de guai xianxiang* [Shadows under the "Loyalty" Sign: Weird Phenomena during the Cultural Revolution], Beijing: Chaohua chubanshe, 1993.

Zheng Qian, "Dui xinbian lishiju 'Hai Rui ba guan' de pipan" [The Criticism of the New Historical Play *Hai Rui Dismissed from Office*], in Guo, Wang, and Han (eds.), *Shinian fengyu*, 1–22.

Zheng Yi, *Hongse jinian bei* [Scarlet Memorial], Taibei: Huashi wenhua gongsi, 1993.

Zhonggong Guizhou shengwei dangshi yanjiushi (ed.), *Zhongguo gongchandang Guizhou sheng lishi dashiji* [Major Historical Events in the Guizhou CCP], Guiyang: Guizhou renmin chubanshe, 2001.

Zhonggong zhongyang wenxian yanjiushi (ed.), *Jianguo yilai Mao Zedong wengao* [Mao Zedong's Post-1949 Manuscripts], 13 vols., Beijing: Zhongyang wenxian chubanshe, 1987–98.

(ed.), *Zhou Enlai nianpu, 1949–1976* [Chronicle of the Life of Zhou Enlai, 1949–76], 3 vols., Beijing: Zhongyang wenxian chubanshe, 1997.

Zhonggong zhongyang xuanchuanbu bangongting and Zhongyang dang'anguan bianyanbu (eds.), *Zhonggong gongchandang xuanchuan gongzuo wenxian xuanbian* [Selection of Documents on CCP Propaganda Work], 4 vols., Beijing: Xuexi chubanshe, 1996.

Zhongguo renmin jiefangjun guofang daxue dangshi dangjian zhenggong jiaoyanshi (ed.), *Zhonggong dangshi jiaoxue cankao ziliao* [Reference Materials for the Teaching of Party History], Beijing: Guofang daxue chubanshe, 1980.

"Zhongguo renmin jiefangjun tongjian" bianji weiyuanhui (ed.), *1927–1996. Zhongguo renmin jiefangjun tongjian* [1927–96: People's Liberation Army Comprehensive Handbook], 3 vols., Lanzhou: Gansu renmin chubanshe, 1997.

Zhongyang xuanchuanbu bangongting (ed.), *Dang de xuanchuan gongzuo wenjian xuanbian* [Selection of Documents on Party Propaganda Work], 4 vols., Beijing: Zhonggong zhongyang dangxiao chubanshe, 1994.

"Zhongyu Mao zhuxi hongxin de jiepin" [The Crystallization of a Red Heart Loyal to Chairman Mao], in *Xin Nanchang bao*, 30 September 1968.

Zhou Yuan (ed.), *Hongweibing ziliao: A New Collection of Red Guard Publications. Part I: Newspapers*, Oakton, VA: Center for Chinese Research Materials, 1999.

Glossary

A few entries relating to specific campaigns have been annotated in order to avoid confusion.

八千麻袋事件 : Baqian madai shijian
表忠 : Biao zhong
比较健康 : Bijiao jiankang
参考消息 : Cankao xiaoxi
倡议书 : Changyi shu
吃忆苦饭 : Chi yiku fan
赤脚医生 : Chijiao yisheng
代食品简报 : Dai shipin jianbao
大树特树 : Dashu teshu
打着红旗反红旗 : Dazhe hongqi fan hongqi
点 : Dian
顶峰 : Dingfeng
东北王 : Dongbei wang
东方红 : Dongfang hong
独尊 : Du zun
对口字 : Duikouzi
独立王国 : Duli wangguo
多中心论 : Duo zhongxin lun
反对所谓个人迷信 : Fandui suowei geren mixin
高举 : Gaoju
革命圣地 : Geming shengdi
个人崇拜 : Geren chongbai
个人迷信 : Geren mixin
个人膜拜 : Geren mobai
共 : Gong
工农兵毛泽东思想宣传队 : Gong nong bing Mao Zedong sixiang
  xuanchuandui

国父 : Guofu

国家之元首 : Guojia zhi yuanshou

国家主席 : Guojia zhuxi

豪言壮语 : Haoyan zhuangyu

红宝书 : Hong baoshu

红宝书台 : Hong baoshu tai

红色海洋 : Hongse haiyang

环境革命化 : Huanjing geminghua

活学活用 : Huoxue huoyong

讲用会 : Jiangyonghui

解放思想, 破除迷信 : Jiefang sixiang, pochu mixin

阶级斗争 : Jieji douzheng

积极分子 : Jijifenzi

紧跟 : Jin'gen

精神原子弹 : Jingshen yuanzidan

敬祝毛主席万寿无疆太极拳 : Jingzhu Mao zhuxi wanshou wujiang taijiquan

技术处理 : Jishu chuli

九评 : Jiu ping

绝对权威 : Juedui quanwei

军事办事组 : Junshi banshizu

抗大 : Kangda

克己复礼 : Ke ji fu li

空话 : Konghua

垃圾学 : Lajixue

老三篇 : Lao san pian ("Three constantly read articles," referring to the following of Mao's writings: *The Foolish Old Man Who Removed the Mountains*, *In Memory of Norman Bethune*, and *Serve the People*)

礼 : Li

联动 : Liandong

两忆, 三查 : Liang yi, san cha ("Two remembrances, three examinations," PLA campaign in the wake of the Great Leap Forward, referring to: remembering class hardship and national hardship; examining standpoint, fighting morale, and work attitude)

林彪体系 : Lin Biao tixi

林毒 : Lin du

六厂, 二校 : Liu chang, er xiao ("Six factories, two schools," CCP slogan referring to model experiences of the following institutions: Beijing General Knitting Mill, Beijing Xinhua Printing Plant, Beijing No. 3

Chemicals Plant, Beijing Northern Suburb Timber Mill, Beijing 7
February Locomotive and Rolling Stock Plant, Nankou Locomotive
and Rolling Stock Plant, Qinghua University, and Peking
University)

礼治 : Lizhi

毛泽东思想胜利万岁馆 : Mao Zedong sixiang shengli wansui guan

毛泽东思想学习班 : Mao Zedong sixiang xuexiban

毛泽东思想化 : Mao Zedong sixianghua

毛主席语录碑 : Mao zhuxi yulubei

名牌 : Mingpai

南京路上好八连 : Nanjinglu shang hao ba lian

内部参考 : Neibu cankao

清理阶级队伍 : Qingli jieji duiwu

请示汇报制度 : Qingshi huibao zhidu

请示台 : Qingshi tai

旗袍 : Qipao

三八作风 : San ba zuofeng ("Three-Eight working style," PLA slogan
referring to three Mao quotes: "Firm and correct political
orientation," "Persevering and simple style of work," "Flexible
tactics and strategy," as well as four adverbs made up of two
characters each: "united," "alert," "earnest," and "lively")

三支, 两军 : San zhi, liang jun ("Three supports, two militaries," PLA
campaign referring to: support of the Left, the workers, and the
peasants, as well as military training and military supervision)

三忠于 : San zhongyu ("Three Loyalties," Cultural Revolutionary
campaign referring to: loyalty to Chairman Mao, loyalty to Mao
Zedong Thought, and loyalty to Chairman Mao's revolutionary
line)

身教 : Shenjiao

双轨 : Shuang gui

私 : Si

四个第一 : Si ge di yi ("Four firsts," PLA campaign referring to: placing the
human factor, political work, ideological work, and living thought
above military weapons, nonpolitical and nonideological work, and
dogmatism)

四好, 五好 : Si hao, wu hao ("Four good–five good," twin campaign within
the PLA since the early 1960s; the content of the designations
changed over time. During the Cultural Revolution, it referred to
the following. Four good (company-level): political work and
unbookish ideas, a good work style, military training, and a good

lifestyle. Five good (individual soldiers): good in politics, military training, style of work, fulfilment of tasks, and physical education)

四无限 : Si wuxian ("Four boundlesses," Cultural Revolution campaign referring to: boundless worship, boundless hot love, boundless belief, and boundless loyalty to Mao Zedong)

送语录 : Song yulu

天天读 : Tiantian du

晚节不忠, 不足为训 : Wan jie bu zhong, bu zu wei xun

万寿无疆 : Wanshou wujiang

万岁 : Wansui

伟大战略部署 : Weida zhanlüe bushu

慰问团 : Weiwen tuan

无产阶级元首 : Wuchanjieji yuanshou

无产阶级化 : Wuchanjiejihua

献忠 : Xian zhong

现代迷信 : Xiandai mixin

县委书记 : Xianwei shuji

现行反革命 : Xianxing fangeming

形式主义 : Xingshi zhuyi

秀才 : Xiucai

宣教动态 : Xuanjiao dongtai

学习毛主席著作积 极分子代表大会 : Xuexi Mao zhuxi zhuzuo jijifenzi daibiao dahui

样板戏 : Yangbanxi

秧歌 : Yangge

言教 : Yanjiao

忆苦思甜 : Yiku sitian

英明领袖华主席 : Yingming lingxiu Hua zhuxi

用 : Yong

愚公移山 : Yugong yi shan

语录操 : Yulu cao

早请示, 晚汇报 : Zao qingshi, wanhui bao

造神运动 : Zaoshen yundong

珍贵礼品 : Zhengui lipin

致敬电 : Zhijing dian

支左办公室 : Zhizuo bangongshi

忠 : Zhong

忠不忠, 看行动 : Zhong bu zhong, kan xingdong

中发 : Zhongfa

中央碰头会议 : Zhongyang pengtou huiyi

忠字阁 : Zhongzi ge
忠字木 : Zhongzi mu
忠字石 : Zhongzi shi
忠字室 : Zhongzi shi
忠字堂 : Zhongzi tang
忠字舞 : Zhongzi wu
忠字猪 : Zhongzi zhu
忠字化 : Zhongzihua
祝词 : Zhuci
主任 : Zhuren
主席 : Zhuxi
最高指示 : Zuigao zhishi

Index

9 780521 152228